FAMILY EVALUATION IN CHILD CUSTODY LITIGATION

FAMILY EVALUATION IN CHILD CUSTODY LITIGATION

RICHARD A. GARDNER, M.D.

Associate Clinical Professor of Child Psychiatry
Columbia University, College of Physicians and Surgeons

Visiting Professor of Child Psychiatry
University of Louvain, Belgium

Creative Therapeutics
P.O. Box R, Cresskill, New Jersey 07626

PRINTED IN THE UNITED STATES OF AMERICA

10   9   8   7   6   5   4   3   2

Library of Congress Cataloging in Publication Data

GARDNER, RICHARD A.
  Family evaluation in child custody litigation.

  Bibliography: p. 343
  Includes index.
    1. Custody of children—United States. 2. Forensic
Psychiatry.   I. Title. [DNLM: 1. Family. 2. Divorce.
3. Parent—Child relations. 4. Child welfare. WA 320
G228f]

KF547.G37	346.7301'7	81–22144
ISBN 0–933812–08–6	347.30617	AACR2

To my wife Lee
 and
 our three children
 Andrew, Nancy, and Julie

 May all of you
 find this book useful,
 each in your own special way

Then said the king: 'The one saith: This *is* my son that liveth, and thy son *is* the dead; and the other saith: Nay; but thy son *is* the dead, and my son *is* the living.' And the king said: 'Fetch me a sword.' And they brought a sword before the king. And the king said: 'Divide the living child in two, and give half to the one, and half to the other.'

Then spoke the woman whose the living child *was* unto the king, for her heart yearned upon her son, and she said: 'O my lord, give her the living child, and in no wise slay it.' But the other said: 'Let it be neither mine nor thine, *but* divide *it*.' Then the king answered and said: 'Give her the living child, and in no wise slay it: she *is* the mother thereof.'

And all Israel heard of the judgment which the king had judged: and they feared the king: for they saw that the wisdom of God *was* in him, to do judgment.

I Kings 3:23–27

In all that is decent. . .in all that is just, the framers of our
Constitution could never have intended that the "enjoyment of
life" meant that if divorce came, it was to be attended by
throwing the two unfortunates and their children into a judicial
arena, with lawyers as their seconds, and have them tear and
verbally slash at each other in a trial by emotional conflict that
may go on in perpetuity. We have been humane enough to
outlaw cock-fights, dogfights and bullfights; and yet, we do
nothing about the barbarism of divorce fighting, and trying to
find ways to end it. We concern ourselves with cruelty to
animals, and rightfully so, but we are unconcerned about the
forced and intentionally perpetrated cruelty inflicted upon the
emotionally distressed involved in divorce. We abhor police
beating confessions out of alleged criminals, and yet we cheer
and encourage lawyers to emotionally beat up and abuse two
innocent people and their children, because their marriage has
floundered. Somewhere along the line, our sense of values,
decency, humanism and justice went off the track.

*From a Petition for a Writ of Certiorari
submitted to the Supreme Court of the
United States of America by Cleveland,
Ohio, attorney Sanford J. Berger on
behalf of a divorced client's request
for protection from cruel and unusual
punishment (associated with penalities
suffered in divorce litigation) as
guaranteed by the Eighth Amendment
of the United States Constitution.*

 Contents

⚖ Acknowledgments

I am deeply indebted to the litigating parents from whom I have learned most of what is contained in this book. My hope is that what I have learned from all of these parents will prove useful, through this book, in helping reduce the grief that other parents are and will be experiencing.

To attorneys and judges, as well, I have a debt. Some of their lessons have been bitter ones—both for myself and their clients—and others more constructively taught. In both cases, lessons were learned which have been incorporated into this book—lessons that I hope will prove useful to others.

As ever, my faithful secretary, Linda Gould, patiently dedicated herself to the typing of the manuscript in its various renditions. Her unswerving loyalty is deeply appreciated. In the later stages of the work I was fortunate in having the assistance of Carol Gibbon, who cheerfully contributed to the typing task.

Frances Dubner, who faithfully edited so many of my previous works, again proved her dedication with sensitive and most useful suggestions. And Barbara Christenberry not only edited the manuscript, but carried the book forward from its earliest stages of production to its final form. Her interest, reliability, and commitment are deeply appreciated.

Other Books by Richard A. Gardner

The Child's Book About Brain Injury

The Boys and Girls Book About Divorce

Therapeutic Communication with Children:
      The Mutual Storytelling Technique

Dr. Gardner's Stories About the Real World, Volume I

Dr. Gardner's Stories About the Real World, Volume II

Dr. Gardner's Fairy Tales for Today's Children

Understanding Children—A Parents Guide to Child Rearing

MBD: The Family Book About Minimal Brain Dysfunction

Psychotherapeutic Approaches to the Resistant Child

Psychotherapy with Children of Divorce

Dr. Gardner's Modern Fairy Tales

The Parents Book About Divorce

The Boys and Girls Book About One-Parent Families

The Objective Diagnosis of Minimal Brain Dysfunction

Dorothy and the Lizard of Oz

The Boys and Girls Book About Stepfamilies

Dr. Gardner's Fables for Our Times

FAMILY EVALUATION IN CHILD CUSTODY LITIGATION

⚖ Introduction

Determining whether or not a person accused of committing a criminal act is guilty or innocent is a problem that has confounded mankind since the dawn of civilization. Finding successful methods of determination was crucial for the survival of civilized societies. Many methods have been devised to assist those involved in making such important determinations. One of these involves both the accuser and the accused each presenting to a presumably impartial third party (or group) the arguments that support his or her position. Each side is allowed to withhold, to a reasonable degree, information that would weaken its position if divulged and is encouraged to present in full detail that information which supports its contention. Out of this conflict of presentations the impartial party(ies) is allegedly in the best position to determine who is telling the "truth." This system is called the adversary system. No one claims that it is perfect; but its proponents hold that it is the best we have and that the likelihood of the accused being treated fairly is greater with the adversary system than with any other system yet devised.

Until recently (the 1960s and 1970s, in the United States), the adversary system was the main one utilized in divorce cases. This was consistent with the concept that the kinds of indignities complained of in divorce conflicts were minor crimes called *torts* (*Latin:* wrongs). Once viewed as crimes, divorce conflicts were justifiably considered in the context of adversary proceedings. Divorce laws in most states were predicated on concepts of guilt and innocence, that is, within the context of punishment and restitution. The divorce was granted only when the complainant or petitioner proved that he or she had been wronged or injured by the defendant or respondent. In most states the acceptable grounds for divorce were very narrowly defined and, depending upon the state, included such behavior as mental cruelty, adultery, abandonment, habitual drunkenness, nonsupport, and drug addiction. The law would punish the offending party by granting the divorce to the successful complainant.

If the court found that both the husband and the wife were guilty of marital wrongs, a divorce was not granted. If *both* parties, for instance, had involved themselves in adulterous behavior, they could not get a divorce. Therefore, in such situations, the parties often agreed to alter the truth in a way that would result in their obtaining a divorce. Often this would require one party to take public blame—court records in such cases are usually public. Frequently one party would agree to be the adultress or the adulterer, or the one who had inflicted mental cruelty on the other. "Witnesses" were brought in (usually friends who were willing to lie in court) to testify in support of the various allegations, and everyone agreed to go through the little theatrical performance. Even the judge knew that the play was necessary to perform if he was to have grounds to grant the divorce. All appreciated the cooperation of the witnesses, and there was practically no danger of their being prosecuted for their perjury. Although such proceedings rarely made headlines in the newspapers, they were available for public scrutiny and distribution. The knowledge of this possibility became an additional burden to the person who, because of the greater desire for the divorce, was willing to be considered guilty, while allowing the spouse to be considered innocent. In addition, there were possible untoward psychological sequelae resulting from the acceptance of the blame, and this could contribute to residual problems following the divorce.

In recent years there has been greater appreciation by state legislatures of the fact that the traditional grounds for divorce are not simply wrongs perpetrated by one party against the other, but that both parties have usually contributed to the marital breakdown. In addition, the kinds of behavior complained of by the petitioner came to be viewed less as crimes and more as personality differences, aberrations, and/or psychopathology.

With such realizations came the appreciation that adversary proceedings were not well suited to deal with such conflicts. Accordingly, an ever-growing number of states have changed their laws regarding the grounds for divorce and the ways in which people can dissolve their marriages. These new statutes are generally referred to as *no fault divorce laws*. They provide much more liberal criteria for the granting of a divorce. For example, if both parties agree to the divorce their living apart for a prescribed period may be all that is necessary. (And the period may be shorter if no children are involved.) One does not have the problem of designating a guilty and an innocent party. Some states will grant a divorce on the basis of "incompatibility." The term may not be defined any further, and it may be quite easy for the couple to demonstrate that they are incompatible. The latest phase of such liberalization enables some individuals to divorce entirely without legal assistance. In California, a state that has often been at the forefront of such liberalization, a couple can now obtain a divorce via mail and the payment of a small fee, if they have no children and there is no conflict over property.

The passage of no-fault divorce laws has been, without question, a significant step forward. By removing it from adversary proceedings, divorce is more readily, less traumatically, and usually less expensively obtained. However, many no-fault divorce laws require the agreement of *both* parties to satisfy the new liberal criteria. Divorce can rarely be obtained unilaterally. If one party does not agree, then adversary proceedings are necessary if the person desiring the divorce is to have any hope of getting it. In addition, the new laws have not altered the necessity of resorting to adversary proceedings when there is conflict over such issues as visitation, support, alimony, and custody. Although no-fault divorce laws have reduced considerably the frequency of courtroom conflicts over divorce, litigation over custody is not only very much with us, but for reasons to be described soon, is on the increase. And the adversary system—a system designed to determine whether an accused individual has committed a criminal act—is being used to determine which of two parents would better serve as custodian for their children.

A short description of the criteria used in Western society in the past to determine custody will enable the reader to place in proper perspective our present situation regarding custody determination. In the days of the Roman Empire, fathers were automatically given custody of their children at the time of divorce. (Divorce was quite common, incidentally, when the Empire was at its peak.) Mothers had no education or reasonably marketable skills, and so they were not considered as fit to care for their children alone. Such was the power of fathers that they could, at their whim, sell their children into slavery and (after proper release from councils convened for the purpose) could literally kill their children. The power of fathers to kill their children extended up to the fourteenth century, but the power to sell children into servitude was retained for another 100–200 years (Derdeyn, 1976a).

It is not until the nineteenth century that we see the beginnings of change. In 1817, in a well-publicized case, Percy Shelley, the poet, lost custody of his children because of his "atheism" and "immorality" (specifically, marital infidelity). It is reasonable to assume that it was not the adultery alone that caused him to lose his children—if that were the case there would have been few fathers retaining custody. It was the *combination* of adultery *and* atheism that "did him in." In addition, it is reasonable to assume that there were many other adulterous atheists who were still retaining custody, but that Shelley, as a well-known figure, served well as an example to others.

But Shelley's was an isolated case. Not until the middle of the nineteenth century do we see the first indications of what came to be called the "tender years presumption." The courts began to work under the presumption that there were certain psychological benefits that the child could gain from its mother that were not to be so readily obtained from its father. The notion of wresting a suckling infant from its mother's breast came to be viewed as somehow "wrong." Accordingly, mothers began to be given custody of their infant children. But when the children reached the ages of 3 to 4 (the upper limit of the "tender years" period), they were considered to have gained all that they needed from their mothers and they were transferred to their fathers, their "rightful and just" parents anyway.

In the late nineteenth century we see the birth of the Women's Liberation movement. Women began to wrest entrance into educational institutions and gained training in various skills (to a very limited degree, however, in the nineteenth century). By the end of the nineteenth century, little headway was made regarding custody of children. This was primarily related to the notion (supported by the courts) that to give a mother custody of the children while requiring the father to contribute significantly, if not entirely, to their financial support was unjust to the father. That which we accept today as perfectly reasonable was beyond the comprehension of the nineteenth-century father. Until this change in attitude came about, mothers could not reasonably hope to gain custody. The only women who could hope for custody were those who had the wherewithal to support their children independently.

The change in attitude came about by what was possibly an unanticipated route—the Child Labor Laws, passed in the early part of this century (Ramos, 1978). Prior to the twentieth century, children were an important economic asset. Before the appearance of the Child Labor Laws, children as young as 5 to 6 years of age worked in such places as factories and mines and contributed to the family's support. In agricultural communities they were used as farm hands as well. Fathers, therefore, had the power to keep—and were very desirous of keeping—these important economic assets. With the passage of the Child Labor Laws, children became less of a financial asset and more of a liability. These laws made fathers more receptive to giving up their children to their ex-wives and were an important factor in the twentieth-century shift in attitude. Fathers no longer rallied around the flag of "injustice" when asked to support children in the home of their ex-wives.

In the 1920s the states gradually changed their laws, and custody was no longer automatically given to fathers. Rather, the sex of the parent was not to be considered as a factor in determining parental preference. Only criteria related to parental capacity—regardless of sex—were to be utilized. During the next fifty years these statutes were generally interpreted in favor of mothers. A father had to prove a mother grossly unfit (e.g., an alcoholic, drug addict, sexual "pervert") before he could even hope to gain custody. In the early 1970s, we began to see a male "backlash." Maternal preference was "sexist," cried some fathers. Courts were asked to look again at the laws under which they were working and were requested to apply more closely what was stated there.

Suddenly, fathers who had previously thought that they had no chance of gaining custody found out that they had. But love of the children and concern for their welfare was not the only motive for fathers who were now beginning to fight for custody. Less noble motives such as vengeance, guilt assuagement, and competition were now allowed expression and possibly even realization. Since the early to mid 1970s, then, children have become "open territory" in child custody conflicts. The frequency of such litigation is burgeoning, and there is no evidence for a decline in the near future. New interpretations (or, strictly speaking, reexamination) of the original statutes have increased the complexity of such litigation as well. As Derdeyn (1978) points out, courts now have to work much harder. Traditional formulas all fell along what would now be considered sexist lines. Using such formulas made the judge's work easier. The child automatically went either to the father or the mother—depending upon the particular period in history. Now a detailed inquiry into each parent's parental assets and liabilities is necessary before anything approaching a judicious decision can be made.

This is where we stand today in the early 1980s. At no time in the history of Western civilization has there been more litigation over custody and, unfortunately, the adversary system—a system designed to determine whether an accused party has committed a criminal act—is the method most commonly used to determine which is the preferable parent. In most cases, the people primarily involved in making such decisions—judges and attorneys—have little, if any, training in child development and psychology, Yet it is they who have traditionally been left with the decision as to which is the better parent for custodial purposes.

We in the mental health professions are in a unique position to assist courts in making custody decisions. Our training and experience enable us to be particularly sensitive to the kinds of child-rearing considerations that are scrutinized in custody litigation. Our understanding of psychopathological processes enables us to assess better than the courts the parental qualities being evaluated in such conflicts. We are fallible, of course, and our recommendations should not be given ultimate authority. Our contributions should be given serious consideration by the courts, but the client should still have the opportunity to resort to courtroom adversarial proceedings if he or she wishes to pursue that course. At the conclusion of this book, I will outline a program that would make it even less likely that parents involved in custody disputes would resort to adversarial courtroom proceedings. But even with such a program, I believe that they should have the ultimate right to utilize the adversarial method if they so wish.

There are some mental health professionals who believe that it is beyond the realm of their competence to make a specific recommendation to the court regarding which parent should be the preferred one. Others hold that, considering our present state of knowledge (or, possibly more correctly, ignorance), it is grandiose of us to be making such recommendations. Ostensibly, such modesty may appear praiseworthy. Those who take this position claim that psychiatry is in its infancy and that we do not have enough information at this point to be able to provide such recommendations with a high degree of certainty. I am in agreement that such is the state of our art/science, but I am not in agreement that we are at such a primitive level that we cannot make reasonable recommendations. The children cannot wait until our knowledge has advanced to the point where we can make predictions with an extremely high degree of accuracy. (Perhaps we never will.) We do have to act now and we have, I believe, enough information to help us make reasonably judicious recommendations in the vast majority of cases.

One reason why many mental health professionals do not feel qualified to make custody recommendations is that they allow themselves to be restricted with regard to their flexibility and the time available for data collection. Under such restrictive circumstances examiners may feel less qualified to come up with a final decision. However, if they were given full opportunity for data collection, they would, I believe, be in a position to gain greater conviction for their conclusions. Another reason why mental health professionals hesitate to involve themselves in custody litigation relates to their fear of going to court. The courtroom is strange and foreign territory. Even the most experienced testifiers may be fearful of cross-examination. It is one of the aims of this book to provide mental health professionals guidelines not only for conducting custody evaluations, but for providing courtroom testimony as well. Such knowledge and competence is the most predictable way to reduce these fears.

My main thesis in this book (and this will be repeated many times, in many different ways) is that mental health professionals serve best as impartials and that they should do everything possible to avoid serving the courts as advocates of either side. They should have free access to any information, from either party, that can assist them in making a recommendation to the court regarding which of the parents would better serve the needs of the children. It is the main purpose of this book to describe, in detail, exactly how the mental health professional should proceed in order to attain this goal. It will *not* describe how to serve as an advocate, because I consider such involvement to be a disservice to the courts, the parents, and the children (with rare exception). In addition, it is most often a disservice to both the legal and the mental health professions for a mental health professional to appear in this capacity.

Some mental health professionals believe that they should limit themselves to providing the court with further information from both sides in order to help the court make a judicious decision. The assumption here is that the court is in a better position to make the final decision than the mental health professional. I, personally, believe that our training and experience put us in a better position for making such recommendations than the court. This is especially the case because we have more time to conduct our evaluations than the courts generally do. Often, a judge may be asked to make fifteen or twenty custody decisions a day. Under such circumstances, it is unrealistic to expect the court to make judicious decisions. Even for the very wealthy, who can afford days or weeks in court, the amount of information that may be provided the judge may be so massive that it is mind boggling. Even then, a judicious decision may not be made. I am not claiming that we in the mental health professions will invariably make judicious recommendations; I am only saying that we are more likely to do so. Furthermore, the judge rarely has significant training as a mental health professional and is thereby compromised in his ability to make the decision regarding parental fitness. In the 1967 President's Commission on Law Enforcement and Administration of Justice, in a study of juvenile court justices, it was found that half had not received undergraduate degrees, a fifth had received no college education at all, and a fifth were not even members of the Bar.

Kirschner (1979), an attorney, holds that the mental health professional is far more qualified than the legal professional to make recommendations regarding custody. Watson (1969) deplores the practice of some judges who insist that the attorneys, between themselves and in consultation with their clients, come up with a custodial arrangement. He considers this an abandonment of the judge's responsibilities to serve the best needs of the children because he considers the attorneys not fully qualified to have such great power in making this decision. I am in agreement with him and believe that the mental health professional, serving as an impartial, is in a far better position to provide such recommendations. If the attorneys are used, one is likely to get a compromise, and not all compromises are necessarily in the children's best interests. This is especially the case if the compromise involves splitting of the children. On other occasions the compromise involves relinquishing of monetary demands. Here again the children are used as bargaining chips, and the attorneys are party to such utilization.

I fully appreciate that the evaluation described in this volume is generally very time consuming, expensive, and therefore only available to those with means or those willing to make significant financial sacrifices in order to avail themselves of such a thorough assessment. This should not, in my opinion, be a reason for criticizing it. When penicillin first came out in the late 1930s it was so rare a drug that crystals of it were extracted from patients' urines in order to be reused. It was also prohibitively expensive for the vast majority of the population. Because an expensive procedure is only available to a small percentage of the population is no reason to criticize it. Although we may deplore the fact that this is the case, we still do well to utilize the method when we can. Accordingly, to the degree to which the examiner can provide parents with the kind of exhaustive and intensive evaluation described herein, to that degree he or she will be providing them with what I consider to be the optimum kind of evaluation. To that degree, the family will be provided with the most meaningful and useful service with regard to the decision of which parent should have custody.

It is important for the therapist to appreciate that there may be no issue around which so much hostility grows as that of custody. Frustrations associated with conflicts over support, alimony, and visitation are small when compared with the pains that can potentially be suffered when one loses custody of one's children. Examiners evaluating parents in this situation must appreciate that they are dealing with an issue that may be the most highly charged they may ever be confronted with. The stakes are extremely high. One's children—one's most treasured possessions—hang in the balance. And there may be extreme viciousness involved. Accordingly, examiners who involve themselves in custody litigation must have "thick skins." They must be able to tolerate the hostility that the parents often exhibit toward one another and, unfortunately, may ultimately direct toward the evaluator. The examiner should appreciate, from the outset, that one (and sometimes both) of the parents will ultimately be extremely angry at the person who provided a recommendation that was instrumental in depriving the parent of the child(ren). The only situation in which the examiner can escape such venting of anger is the one in which the parent basically doesn't want custody anyway and is "going through the motions" of custody litigation in order to assuage guilt or present him- or herself as loving.

The two most common ways in which the disappointed parent may express retaliation is to 1) withhold payment of fees and 2) complain about the therapist to professional societies. As will be discussed subsequently, I have in recent years devised a payment program designed to protect myself from the first form of retaliation (a not uncommon occurrence, unfortunately). However, there is practically no defense against the second. At the time of this writing, I have been actively involved in the full-time practice of psychiatry for almost 25 years. In all that time there have been only two formal complaints registered against me to my professional societies. In both cases they were made by parents whose position I did not support in custody litigation. (Although in both cases the Ethics Committees found no wrongdoing or inappropriate behavior on my part, I found both experiences time consuming, irritating, and somewhat provoking.) My suspicion is that with the present burgeoning of custody litigation, Ethics Committees will be receiving more such complaints.

Just as attorneys are not well versed in the behavioral sciences because it is generally not part of their required legal education, mental health professionals usually receive little, if any, training in the law and legal procedures. This book is written, in part, in an attempt to correct this deficiency in the educational processes of both disciplines. It is written for attorneys to apprise them of the techniques used by mental health professionals in conducting custody evaluations. And it is written for mental health professionals in the hope that it will enhance my colleagues' expertise in conducting this important kind of evaluation.

The custody evaluation cannot be taken too seriously. The future course of the child's whole life is likely to be affected by the decision. It may be a heavy burden for the mental health professional to bear, but we are in the best position to provide advice in this area and thus it is our moral obligation to do so. Although conducting such an evaluation may be among the most difficult and draining challenges with which the mental health professional may be confronted, it can also be among the most rewarding. My hope is that this book will help my colleagues share with me the rewards and gratifications I have enjoyed from conducting such evaluations—the frustrations and travail involved notwithstanding.

1

The Adversary System vs. The Impartial Expert

My basic thesis in this chapter is that the adversary system—its ancient heritage and value in criminal proceedings notwithstanding—is ill suited to deal optimally with custody conflicts, causes psychopathology in parents who resort to it to settle custody conflicts, is psychologically detrimental to children, and is therefore antithetical to good psychiatric practice.

THE ATTORNEY VS. THE IMPARTIAL EXPERT

The attorney who is committed to the adversary system and the impartial expert may have great difficulty communicating with each other on the subject of custody litigation. I can best describe the problem with this vignette (a composite of many conversations that I have had over the last fifteen years):

I receive a telephone call from an attorney in which he begins with the following statement: "Doctor Gardner, my name is Mr. So-and-So. I'm an attorney and was referred to you by Dr. So-and-So." The introduction is innocuous enough. It is with the next sentence that the trouble begins. It is usually a run-on sentence, with the second half being stated much more rapidly than the first: "I would like to know whether I can engage your services in testifying on behalf of my client who is involved in a custody conflict with her husband" (the pace suddenly quickens here); "however, doctor, I want you to know that the best interests of the children are paramount."

To this I generally respond, "Suppose, after seeing your client, I conclude that I cannot support her position and I decide that it would be in the best interests of the children for them to live with their father. Would you still use my testimony in court?"

The attorney then often answers in a confused and irritated manner: "Doctor, you can't be serious, suggesting that I use your testimony to support my adversary's client. Are you suggesting that I put you on the stand to testify on behalf of the other side?"

In response I say: "But I understood you to have said before that the best interests of the children were paramount. If that were truly the case, I would think you would welcome my testimony in order to do what is best for them. What you're telling me now suggests that supporting your client is paramount!"

At this point the attorney may tell me (directly or indirectly) that it is clear that he has made a mistake in calling me and that the person who referred him to me wasn't aware of how ignorant I was of legal matters.

This attorney is essentially doing what he was taught in law school, namely, to support his client's position. He knows that psychiatrists are concerned with children's best interests and that the best way to ingratiate himself to me is to profess a similar commitment. However, the basic inconsistency in his comments quickly becomes apparent. One cannot support one's client's claim for custody and at the same time state that the children's interests are paramount. At times it is in the children's best interests to live with the client whom the attorney is representing; and at times it is not. When the latter is the case the attorney must make a choice. Almost invariably that choice will be to support the client's claim, not the children's needs.

In addition, the attorney who is deeply committed to the adversary system may see nothing inappropriate in asking me to testify on behalf of his client *before I have even seen her.* I cannot be too critical of him here, because there are mental health professionals who will promise to provide such support before anyone has been seen. Such "hired guns" in this examiner's opinion, are a disgrace to our profession. The attorney with whom I had the aforementioned conversation is a product of his system—a system based on respect for the adversarial process as a way of solving human problems. He is committed to a system in which "truth" comes from conflict. And I am a product of my system—a system based on the premise that free and open inquiry is the best way to gather data for settling human conflicts.

Some attorneys do not so quickly dismiss me and are receptive to discussing the matter further. If such is the case, I tell the attorney that, whenever possible, I do not serve as an *advocate* in custody litigation, but make every reasonable attempt to serve as an *impartial expert*. (The terms "whenever possible" and "every reasonable attempt" are inserted in order to leave open the possibility that I will serve as an advocate in selected cases. In the next chapter I will discuss such situations in detail.). I then again inquire whether he wishes to discuss the matter further with me. Many respond that they are looking for an advocate and would not consider, under any circumstances, involving themselves with an expert who might ultimately support their adversary's position. They are so deeply committed to the adversary system that they would consider themselves disloyal to their clients if they even entertained the notion of bringing in an impartial.

Others, and fortunately their numbers are increasing, will consider this alternative. In such cases, I send the attorney a reprint of a short article of mine describing the rationale for psychiatrists serving as impartial experts, rather than as advocates (Gardner, 1979a; see Appendix I). In addition, I enclose a copy of the procedures that must be followed to gain my involvement (Appendix II). These will be discussed in detail in the next chapter.

Another way in which the attorney's and the mental health professional's orientations differ is well demonstrated by the following vignette:

Two clients have appointments to see an attorney. The first is a man. He has never previously been married and is presently married to a woman who has been divorced and who has two children. She has custody of the two children. He comes to the attorney to ask his advice regarding the advisability of adopting his stepchildren. The attorney strongly discourages him from doing so, informing him that if this marriage were to end in a divorce, and if he were to have adopted the children, then he would have the obligation to provide for their support. However, if he does not adopt them, he would have no obligations for their support after a divorce. Accordingly, the attorney strongly dissuades his client from going ahead with the plans for adoption.

The next client to see the same attorney is a woman. She has been divorced, has two children, and is now married for the second time to a man who has never been married before. She has custody of the children. She has come to the attorney to ask his advice about her new husband adopting the children. He advises her to proceed as rapidly as possible with the adoption plans. He tells her that once her new husband has adopted the children, he will be obligated to support them, even if this marriage ends in divorce. Furthermore, he warns her that if her new husband were not to adopt the children, he would have no obligation at all to provide for their support if there were to be a divorce.

In each case the attorney is protecting his client's best interests. At no point in his advice to these clients is there any consideration for the welfare of the children. His primary consideration is the pocketbook of his clients. The decision as to whether or not to adopt should be based on a variety of considerations including the financial and the psychological effects on the parties concerned. Parenting is far more a psychological than a monetary phenomenon. The feelings and attitudes of the adoptive father, the reactions of the children (especially with regard to their feelings about being adopted and how this will affect their relationship with their natural father as well as their stepfather), and the reactions of the mother should all be taken into consideration. Again, my point is well demonstrated: the lawyer's primary obligation is to serve the client, the parent who has enlisted his or her services. At times, the parent's position may also be in the children's best interests; at times it may not. And the attorney cannot possibly know whether this is the case unless he or she has information from the other parent and has explored the many sides of the question. The adversary system does not permit the attorney him- or herself to do this. The impartial expert has a court mandate to do so.

Some attorneys will often strongly suspect that their client is indeed in the weaker position in custody litigation, but will in subtle ways encourage the client not to reveal such information because it may weaken his or her position. In short, they are encouraging their client to lie to them (lies of omission rather than lies of commission). They will not ask questions that may push the client into the position of revealing information that may be detrimental to his or her claim. Or the attorneys may overtly or covertly encourage the client not to disclose any information to them that might compromise the client's position—lest the lawyer be placed in an ethically conflictual situation. A kind of tacit agreement is made between the lawyer and the client that certain things will not be revealed. Such a conspiracy of silence may be necessary to the maintenance of the lawyer-client relationship. In this way the lawyer rationalizes that he or she is being ethical, avoids lying to the court, and cannot be considered to be encouraging perjury on the client's part or otherwise permitting a fraud to be perpetrated on the court. And not incidentally, such a conspiracy of silence may be necessary if the lawyer is to keep the client and the attendant fee.

The whole procedure of selective elicitation of information from a client is totally antithetical to the psychiatrist's approach to a problem. Psychiatrists work on the principle that they must be free to get as much information as possible from their patients and that nothing should restrain them from gaining any data that they may consider relevant. If a therapist suspects that the patient is withholding information, it behooves him or her to inquire into the matter and to help the patient appreciate that the therapist is ill equipped to help if he or she is being deprived of any information relevant to the patient's difficulties.

Most lawyers believe that they can be as successful in helping a client whose cause they may not be particularly in sympathy with as they can with one whose position they strongly identify with. From law school days they are deeply imbued with the notion that their obligation as a lawyer is to serve the client and to do the best job they can, even though they may not be in sympathy with the client's position and even though they might prefer to be on the opponent's side. This, in my opinion, is another weakness of the adversary system (its strengths notwithstanding). It assumes that an attorney can argue just as effectively when he has no commitment to his client's position as when he does.

In most law schools the students are required to involve themselves in "moot court" experiences in which they are assigned positions in a case. The assignment is generally made on a chance basis and has nothing to do with the student's own conviction on a particular matter. In fact, it is often considered preferable that the assignment be made in such a way that the student must argue in support of the position for which he or she has less conviction. On other occasions, the student may be asked to present arguments for both sides. I am in full agreement that such experiences can be educationally beneficial. We can all learn from and become more flexible by being required to view a situation from the opposite vantage point. However, I believe that those attorneys who hold that one can argue just as effectively without conviction as one can if one has the conviction are naive. Noncommitted attorneys are going to do a less effective job in most cases. Accordingly, their clients are coming into the courtroom in a weakened position. Most attorneys are not likely to turn away a client whose position they secretly do not support, and it would be very difficult for a parent to find one who is going to openly admit that he or she basically doesn't support the client's position. This is another reason for my recommending that parents, if they possibly can, avoid the adversary system in settling custody disputes.

Therapists, on the other hand, generally work in accordance with the principle that if they have no conviction for what they are doing with their patients, the chances of success in the treatment are likely to be reduced. So if, for example, the therapist's feelings for a patient are not strong, if he or she does not have basic sympathy for the patient's situation, if the relationship is not a good one, or if the therapist is not convinced that the patient's goals in therapy are valid, the likelihood of the patient's being helped is small. Without such conviction the therapy becomes boring and sterile—with little chance of anything constructive coming out of it.

I recently was in a situation where I had good reason to believe that an attorney was basically not supporting his client, and that such lack of conviction contributed to his poor performance in the courtroom. In this particular case I was supportive of the mother's position and, although an impartial, I was treated as an advocate in the courtroom (the usual situation). Early in the trial the *guardian ad litem* suggested that I, as the impartial, be invited into the courtroom to observe the testimony of a psychiatrist who had been brought in as an advocate for the father's side. The father's attorney agreed to this. I was a little surprised when I learned of this because I did not see what he had to gain by my having direct opportunity to observe his client's expert. I thought that there would be more to lose than gain for this attorney because it would be likely to provide me with more "ammunition" for the mother.

When the advocate expert testified, I took notes and, as was expected, observed the attorney to provide him with ample time to elaborate on his various points. (This is standard procedure when questioning an expert who supports one's position.) When I took the stand, I was first questioned by the mother's attorney, the attorney whose position I supported. He, in turn, gave me great flexibility with regard to my opportunities for answering his questions. Then, the father's attorney began to question me. To my amazement, he allowed me to elaborate on points on which I disagreed with him. He persistently gave me this opportunity and I, of course, took advantage of it.

During a break in the proceedings, the judge asked him, "Why are you letting Gardner talk so much?" I believe this was an inappropriate statement for the judge to make, but it confirms how atypical and seemingly inexplicable the father's attorney's examination of me was. The lawyer shrugged his shoulders, said nothing, and on my return to the stand continued to allow me great flexibility in my answers. I had every reason to believe that he was a bright man and "knew better." I had no doubt that he did not routinely proceed in this way. To me, this attorney's apparently inexplicable behavior was most likely motivated by the desire (either conscious or unconscious) that his own client, the father, lose custody because of his recognition that the mother was the preferable parent for these children at that time. He "went through the motions" of supporting his client, but did so in such a way that he basically helped the other side win the case.

Watson (1969), an attorney, encourages lawyers to refuse to support a client's attempt to gain custody when the attorney does not consider the client to be the preferable parent. The suggestion is made from the recognition that one doesn't do as well with the client whose position one does not have the conviction for, as well as from ethical considerations. This is a noble attitude on this attorney's part. Unfortunately, far too few lawyers will subscribe to this advice and most succumb to the more practical consideration that if they do not support their client's position they will lose him or her and the attendant fee (which in divorce cases may not be inconsequential).

The attorney and the therapist both deal with human problems, with disputes between people, and often with behavior that is undesirable and even antisocial. The orientation of the therapist, however, is generally that of trying to help the individual change the personality pattern and the symptomatic manifestations that contribute to the antisocial behavior. Although the attorney, at times, may be respectful of and sympathetic to these underlying processes, his or her orientation is much more toward the use of punishment as a way of deterring individuals from repeating undesirable and antisocial acts. I believe that punishment is effective in deterring some people from committing antisocial acts, but that psychotherapy, as well, can have a prophylactic effect on such behavior. I am not criticizing the punitive goal of the legal structure. I am pointing out only that practitioners of the two professions, because of their differing goals and orientations, view divorce litigants very differently and often have great difficulty communicating and cooperating with one another in this area.

THE ADVERSARY SYSTEM AS A CAUSE OF PSYCHOPATHOLOGY

People who are divorcing are fighting. And divorcing people who are fighting over their children are fighting even harder. The adversary system, which purports to help the parents resolve their differences is likely to prolong and intensify the hostilities. The litigants are provided with weapons to use against one another—"ammunition" that they may not have realized they possessed. Attorneys are engaged who usually contribute to the ever-increasing vicious cycle of vengeance. Disputes are unnecessarily prolonged and the hardship on both parties is often increased immeasurably. Often the divorce proceedings become a more cruel operation and cause greater psychological pain to the parties than the marriage which brought about the decision for divorce in the first place.

Louis Nizer, in his book *My Life in Court* (1968), states: "All litigations evoke intense feelings of animosity, revenge and retribution. Some of them may be fought ruthlessly. But none of them, even in their most aggravated form, can equal the sheer, unadulterated venom of a matrimonial contest." If I were writing this, I would add the following sentence: "And of all the forms of marital litigation, the most vicious and venomous by far is custody litigation!" Therapists who involve themselves in such proceedings must have thick skins. They must be willing to involve themselves in one of the most vicious and draining forms of litigation. The stakes are higher than in any other form of courtroom conflict in that here the parents' most treasured possessions—the children—are at stake. Conflicts over money and property pale in comparison to the ruthlessness with which parents will fight over the children.

Sopkin (1974) describes in dramatic terms how sordid and sadistic such litigation can be. He focuses particularly on the role of attorneys in intensifying and prolonging such conflicts. In his article "The Roughest Divorce Lawyers in Town" (although the "town" referred to by Sopkin is New York City, the legal techniques described are ubiquitous and by no means confined to that city), he describes a brand of attorney often referred to in the field as a "bomber."

Sopkin quotes one such bomber (Raoul Lionel Felder, a New York City divorce attorney) as saying: "If it comes to a fight, it is the lawyer's function using all ethical, legal and moral means to bring his adversary to his knees as fast as possible. Naturally, within this framework the lawyer must go for the 'soft spots.'" The kinds of antics that such lawyers utilize and promulgate are indeed hair-raising. One husband is advised to hire a gigolo to seduce his wife in a setting where a band of private detectives are engaged to serve as witnesses. Another husband is advised to get his English-born wife deported because she is not yet a citizen.

Elsewhere Sopkin states: "Getting a lawyer out of his office is expensive, but to crank up a bomber, pump him full of righteous indignation, and ship down to the matrimonial courts can be terribly expensive—running fifteen, twenty, or twenty-five thousand dollars." "Bombers are in business to accommodate hate." "But the incontrovertible fact remains that if there is big-time money at stake, or serious custody questions at stake, or you want to leave your husband/wife with nothing but a little scorched earth, get a bomber." Although Sopkin's examples are not typical, they are not rare either. In litigation "winning" is the name of the game. The lawyer with the reputation for being "a softie" is not going to have many clients. Although more human and less pugilistic attorneys certainly exist, once swept up in adversary proceedings their "fighting instincts" often come to the fore. Although the more sensitive may even then not be willing to stoop to the levels of the bombers, they still are likely to utilize all kinds of deceptive maneuvers to "win" for their clients.

Weiss (1975) states the problem well:

> It is possible for lawyers to negotiate too hard. In pursuit of the best possible agreement for their clients, some lawyers seem to worsen the post-marital relationship of their clients and the clients' spouses. They may for example, actively discourage a client from talking with his or her spouse for fear that the client will inadvertently weaken his or her negotiating position, or will in thoughtless generosity make concessions without obtaining anything in return. Or they may take positions more extreme than their client desires in order eventually to achieve an advantageous compromise, but by so doing anger the client's spouse and further alienate the spouse from the client. Some separated individuals reported that until negotiations were at an end, their relationship with their spouse became progressively worse.

Gettelman and Markowitz (1974) provide a good example of the problem:

> For many divorcing couples, their biggest headaches begin after they retain their respective attorneys. Recently we talked with the ex-wife of a famous and wealthy stage actor. It had taken her three years to obtain a divorce in California, which is one of the more progressive states! In her words, "Once the lawyers smelled money, they acted in cahoots to bleed us and draw out the proceedings." Although their separation had started out amicably, they grew to loath each other; she believed that both his lawyers and her own successfully manipulated her and her husband into feeling victimized by each other.

Elsewhere, Weiss (1975) quotes a divorcing parent:

> The lawyers got involved, and we had that situation where we were told not to talk to each other and there was a lot of mistrust. And it got to be impossible. Like I was afraid anything I said would be used against me. Our communication just stopped completely. I said "God, I just can't believe that it has come to this where we have known each other for ten years and we can't say anything at all to each other.... There was so much bitterness and so much anger and so much mistrust."

The criticisms of the adversary system as applied to divorce and custody proceedings come not only from mental health professionals, but from some lawyers and judges as well. Glieberman, an attorney, in his book *Confessions of a Divorce Lawyer* (1975) states:

> I made sure that each client I handled—whatever else he or she thought about me—came away feeling two things: One, I was thorough as hell. Two, I was out to win. Frankly the second was easy. I love to argue and win. . . .
>
> If a divorce was what someone wanted then my client and I became a team, did everything in our power, not just to win but to win big. . . .
>
> There's only one rule on divorce settlements: If you represent the wife, get as much as possible. If you represent the husband, give away as little as possible. . . .
>
> Now, as I walk through the outer door of my office heading for the courtroom, I know that I'm walking to a case where there will be no compromises, no conciliations, no good feelings to balance the bad. This will be an all-out confrontation, a real tooth and nail fight. I'll love it. . . .
>
> Now finally we're here. And it's a real circus. The other side has two accountants, a tax lawyer, three expert witnesses and a defendent; our side has one accountant, a comptroller, no tax lawyer because I've become an expert at that, and seven expert witnesses.

Forer (1975), a judge, criticizes the legal profession's own Code of Professional Responsibility, a criticism which is most relevant to divorce and custody litigation:

> A lawyer is licensed by the government and is under a sworn duty to uphold and defend the law and the constitution of the United States. Despite the license and the oath, the role of the lawyer is by definition and by law amoral. . . . He must press the position of his client even thought it is contrary to the public good, popular opinion and widely accepted standards of behavior. Canon 7 of the Code of Professional Responsibility promulgated by the American Bar Association declares in part, "The duty of a lawyer, both to his client and to the legal system is to represent his client zealously within the bounds of the law." In other words, the skilled judgment of the lawyer that his client's case is spurious or without merit is irrelevant. The lawyer must, therefore, be a hessian, a mercenary, available for hire to do the bidding of whoever pays him. . . . If the client wishes to sue or contest a claim, the lawyer must either zealously pursue his client's interest or withdraw from the case. If Lawyer A withdraws, Lawyer B will accept the case and the fee.

Lindsley (1980), a judge, is critical of the utilization of the adversary system in custody disputes. He states:

> The adversary process, historically effective in resolving disputes between litigants over contracts, torts, business matters, and criminal

charges, where objective evidentiary facts have probative significance, is not suited to the resolution of most relations problems. In family disputes, the evidence that we would find most meaningful is more likely to consist of subtle, subjective, human relations factors best identified and discerned by psychologists and behaviorists who do not approach the inquiry as antagonists. When you add the concept of "fault" as the necessary basis for deciding questions relating to the family, *I think it is fair to say that no other process is more likely to rip husband, wife, father, mother, and child apart so thoroughly and bitterly* (italics mine).

My main criticism of attorneys involved in custody conflicts is that via their commitment to the adversary system—as a first step in resolving custody conflicts—they are bringing about psychopathology when it doesn't exist and exacerbating and prolonging it when it does. There are many couples who, at the time of their divorce, make a serious attempt to avoid psychologically debilitating litigation. They have observed the deterioration of friends and relatives who have gone through protracted litigation and want to make every attempt to avoid such unnecessary and traumatic sequelae to their divorce. Unfortunately, many such well-meaning couples, in spite of every attempt to avoid it, gradually sink into the same kind of deteriorating and psychologically devastating experience. An important contributing element to such unfortunate deterioration is the legal profession's reflex commitment to the adversary system.

I recognize fully that it is important for each parent to be represented by an attorney who is committed to supporting the client's interests and protecting the party from agreeing to an arrangement that may ultimately be injudicious and injurious. However, the way in which most attorneys proceed in such cases is often calculated to prolong the litigation. They are often obstructionistic and uncommunicative. All four parties sitting down together and trying to hash out the problem is rarely done. Calculated stalling is also much more the rule than the exception. Time is often on the side of one party and the psychologically debilitating effects of such stalling are rarely given consideration. With the exception of the wealthy, such prolongation is also financially draining. This, in itself, contributes to the psychiatric trauma and deterioration. One, and sometimes both, parties are ever slaving to pay horrendous legal bills. Although attorneys will almost invariably deny it, one contributing element to the prolongation of the litigation is the fact that the longer the litigation, the more money the attorney will earn.

Another situation that contributes to the parents' and the children's deterioration in custody litigation is the slowness of the courts. Court calendars may often be backed up three and four years. Although attempts to quicken the pace in custody litigation is often professed, my experience has been that the average case in which I am involved lasts one to two years. Sometimes this results in the children's spending one to two more years in the less desirable home with the less qualified parent. By such time, however, the children may become so committed and adjusted to the less desirable situation that recommending a switch may be injudicious, the custodial parent's deficiencies notwithstanding. Often there is an attorney supporting and orchestrating the delay in order to ensure that his client "wins." He knows that merely prolonging the legal action can play a significant role in his achieving this goal. What is not taken into consideration is that the children in many such cases are the "losers."

The psychological wear and tear on parents and children involved in custody litigation has not been given the attention it deserves. Most therapists whose patients have been involved in such litigation have observed such deterioration. I, personally, have seen people embroiled in such conflicts develop neurotic and even psychotic symptomatology—symptoms that I considered to be directly the result of the stresses of their divorce litigation. I have seen suicidal attempts, alcohol and drug abuse, psychotic breaks, and heart attacks which I considered directly attributable to the psychological trauma of protracted divorce and/or custody litigation. And I have seen marked intensification of pre-existing psychogenic symptoms, exacerbations that would not have taken place had the patients been able to avoid prolonged adversarial proceedings.

Bazelon (1974), a highly respected judge who has concerned himself deeply with mental health issues, holds that the adversary system is not necessarily detrimental to clients. Its ultimate aim, he states, is to gain knowledge and resolve differences. It attempts to resolve differences through the opposition of opposing positions. Its ultimate aim is resolution and the cross-examination process is one of the important ways in which information is gained. I am in agreement with Bazelon regarding the methods and aims of the adversary system. I am not, however, in agreement with his statement regarding the risk of detriment to clients. His statement that the adversary system is "not necessarily" detrimental implies little risk for the development of psychopathology. My experience has been that in divorce, and especially custody, cases the risk for the development of psychopathology is extremely high. Bazelon's discussion is idealistic in that he does not make reference to the sly tricks, duplicity, courtroom antics, and sneaky maneuvers that lawyers will often utilize in order to win. He makes no mention of attorneys' attempts to unreasonably discredit the expert, cast aspersions on his character, and try to make him look silly or stupid.

Although Judge Bazelon's view is that of the majority of jurists, there are dissenters among the judiciary. One of the most outspoken critics of the use of the adversary system in solving custody disputes is Judge Byron F. Lindsley who states (1976):

> The adversary process, historically effective in resolving disputes between litigants where evidentiary facts have probative significance, is not properly suited to the resolution of most family relations problems.... Where there are children and the parties cannot or will not recognize the impact of the disintegration of the marriage upon the children, where they fail to perceive their primary responsibilities as parents—i.e., custody and visitation—we make it possible for parents to carry out that struggle by the old, adversary, fault-finding, condemnation approach.... This kind of battle is destructive to the welfare, best interests, and emotional health of their children.

I fully appreciate that many attorneys begin their involvement with divorcing litigants by attempting to calm them down and bring about some compromises in their demands. However, when such efforts fail, many get swept up in the conflict and join their clients in trying to win the battle and punish the spouse. (And taking the children away is one predictable way of implementing such punishment.) The training of lawyers primes them for such encounters. Therapists, because of their orientation toward understanding and reducing hostility, are less likely to rise so quickly to a patient's cry for battle and lust for vengeance. Accordingly, lawyers are often criticized for inflaming their clients, adding to their hostility, and thereby worsening divorcing spouses' difficulties. A common retort to this criticism is: "We're only doing what our clients ask us to do." Such lawyers claim that they are just the innocent tools of their clients and that their obligation is to respond to their clients' requests—even though they may appreciate that a client's course may be detrimental to him- or herself, the spouse, and the children.

I believe that this response is a rationalization. I believe that lawyers have greater freedom to disengage themselves from a client's destructive behavior than they profess. I believe that financial considerations often contribute to their going along with the client because of the fear that if they do not they will lose the client and the fee. (Unfortunately, there are physicians, as well, who recommend unnecessary medical treatment. For both professions the practice is unconscionable.) Many lawyers discourage litigation out of an awareness of its psychological destructiveness and the appreciation that they may reduce their income per hour if they go to court—because only the wealthiest clients can afford the formidable expense of protracted courtroom litigation. To the wealthy client, the latter consideration does not often serve as a deterrent for the lawyer and the psychological considerations are often then ignored.

THE ATTORNEY VS. THE "EXPERT" AS ADVOCATE

Mental health professionals who are foolish enough to testify on behalf of one parent without having seen the other (such as would be the case if the professional were to accept the kind of invitation extended to me during the telephone conversation discussed earlier in this chapter) may open themselves to serious criticism. This is especially the case when they have not even made attempts to evaluate the other parent. In such cases, I would recommend that the attorney, whose position the mental health professional is not supporting, conduct the type of cross-examination described below. After obtaining the professional's name, address, and other data providing his or her qualifications to testify, I suggest the following inquiry. (The reader should appreciate that if the rules of cross-examination are to be invoked strictly, the attorney can insist that the witness confine him- or herself to only three possible responses: "yes," "no," or "I cannot answer yes or no." In a situation where the witness is a mental health professional testifying on behalf of one parent, without having examined the other, I strongly suggest he or she rigidly enforce the right to insist upon one of these three responses only.)

> Attorney: Would you not agree, Doctor, that it is somewhat simplistic to categorize people as being either "good" or "bad" and that a more realistic view of people is to consider them to be mixtures of both assets and liabilities?

> Mental health professional (Mhp): Yes. (A mhp must say *yes* here. If he or she does not, the mhp's credibility is compromised because the statement is so patently true.)

> Attorney: Do you agree, then, Doctor, that parents are no exception to this principle and that they too are mixtures of both "good" and "bad" qualities?

> Mhp: Yes. (Again, the mhp has no choice but to answer *yes* or else his or her credibility will be compromised.)

> Attorney: Would you not agree, Doctor, that in ascertaining who is the *better* of two parents with regard to as-

suming custody, that we are not trying to find out who is the "good parent" and who is the "bad parent," but who is the *better* of the two parents?

Mhp: Yes. (Again, the mhp cannot but answer *yes*, even though he or she can now sense what is to follow.)

Attorney: Would you not agree also, Doctor, that in trying to determine who is the *better* of two parents it is *preferable* to see *both* if one is to determine most judiciously who is the *better* parent?

Mhp: Yes. (Here again, if the mhp says *no* he or she looks foolish.)

Attorney: Would you not go further and agree that an evaluation of parental preference is *seriously compromised* if both parents have not been seen?

Mhp: Yes. (Here again, it would be very difficult for the mhp to avoid a yes answer, even though he or she recognizes that such a response weakens significantly his or her position.)

Attorney: Doctor, have you conducted a psychiatric evaluation on Mrs. Jones?

Mhp: Yes.

Attorney: How many times have you seen Mrs. Jones?

Mhp: (The mhp states the number of interviews conducted with Mrs. Jones.)

Attorney: Can you tell us the exact dates of each of your interviews with her and the duration of each interview?

Mhp: (Mhp presents the dates of the interviews and the duration of each.)

Attorney: What was the total number of hours of interview time with Mrs. Jones?

Mhp: (Mhp states the total number of hours of interviewing.]

Attorney: Have you ever conducted an evaluation of Mr. Jones with regard to his parental capacity?

Mhp: No.

Attorney: To the best of your knowledge, is Mr. Jones in this courtroom today?

Mhp: Yes.

Attorney: Can you please point to the person whom you believe to be Mr. Jones?

Mhp: (Mhp points to the person whom he believes to be Mr. Jones.)

Attorney: Is it possible that that individual is not Mr. Jones?

Mhp: Yes.

Attorney: As I understand it, Doctor, you are here today to testify that Mrs. Jones is a better parent than Mr. Jones. Is that not correct, doctor?

Mhp: Yes.

Attorney: And is it also not correct, Doctor, that you not only have never conducted an evaluation of Mr. Jones, but are not even certain whether he is actually the person you claim him to be?

Mhp: Yes.

Attorney: In accordance with what you said before about a custody evaluation being seriously compromised if both parties are not seen, would you not have to conclude that your own evaluation in this matter must be similarly suspect?

Mhp: (If the mhp answers *no*, his testimony is compromised because he is being inconsistent and the attorney would do well to point this out. If he hedges, or responds that he cannot answer yes or no, his testimony is similarly compromised and invites the attorney to point out his inconsistency. If he answers *yes* [the more likely response], the attorney does well to respond this way:)

Attorney (turning to the judge): Your honor, because Dr. X has, by his [her] own admission, stated that his [her] testimony has been significantly compromised by the failure to evaluate Mr. Jones, I do not think anything useful can be obtained by further inquiry. Accordingly, I believe it would be a waste of the court's time to proceed further and I therefore have no further questions.

The attorney does well to stop here. The attorney's adversary will have already questioned the expert and so is not likely to have any more questions. At this point the judge, of course, may ask further questions. However, the judge may feel compromised by such an inquiry because of the admission made by the expert that his or her comments not be taken seriously. If the attorney wishes to proceed, however, in order to "rub salt into the expert's wounds," my recommendation is that he focus on all hearsay statements made by Mrs. Jones about her husband. The attorney's main emphasis should be on the doctor's accepting as valid the criticisms of her husband made by Mrs. Jones. Even if the professional has not accepted as completely valid Mrs. Jones's allegations, his conclusions are likely to be based on the supposition that at least some of them are true (otherwise he or she would not be providing testimony in support of her position). Stopping at the aforementioned point would be a more powerful denigration of the so-called expert's testimony than proceeding with a detailed inquiry into the report's content. I believe that if more mental health professionals were exposed to such cross-examination, fewer would be willing to serve as advocates and this would be a service to all parties concerned—the courts, the legal profession, the mental health professions, and the families themselves.

THE IMPARTIAL EXPERT

Impartial experts are in the best position to make a custody recommendation to the court. If they are to do their jobs properly, they must have the court's support (preferably via a signed court order) to interview the parents and children and to invite (they cannot require) others, such as stepparents, live-in parental surrogates, prospective stepparents, etc., who can provide them with meaningful information. The goal of these interviews is a statement regarding who is the *better* parent. Impartial experts do this by determining each parent's assets and liabilities *as a parent* and then weighing (as best they can) each parent's assets against his or her liabilities. A comparison is then made between the two parents with regard to the balance of assets against liabilities. For example, in the section of the report where the evaluator summarizes the recommendations, he or she might state: "Mr. R's liabilities as a parent far outweigh his assets; whereas Mrs. R's assets as a parent far outweigh her liabilities. Accordingly, I recommend that the court grant Mrs. R custody of the children." Or "Both Mr. and Mrs. S appear to be equally competent as parents. However, Mr. S's availability for parenting is compromised significantly by the fact that his work obligations allow him little flexibility with regard to taking care of the children after school, during school vacation periods, and at times of sickness. Mrs. S, as a homemaker, is much more available to the children. All of the other liabilities that each parent exhibits do not appear to be significant. Accordingly, I suggest that the court allow Mrs. S to continue to have custody of the children."

Until recently, courts more frequently relied on the testimony of advocates in custody conflicts. Fortunately, in recent years, the value of the impartial expert is being increasingly appreciated. Kubie (1964), was one of the earliest in the field of psychiatry to stress the importance of therapists serving as impartials, rather than as advocates. As far back as 1964 he stated that he would not testify in court in a custody conflict unless he was appointed by the judge as an impartial expert. Derdeyn (1975) described a custody case in which there was a parade of mental health professionals on either side and the effect of all of their testimony was to cancel each other out. He criticizes strongly the professionals in the case for having agreed at the outset to serve as advocates. He makes a strong plea for psychiatrists to serve only as impartial experts. James (1978) is also a strong proponent of psychiatrists serving only as impartial experts and describes a number of examples of misguided recommendations that resulted when a psychiatrist served only as an advocate.

Some impartial experts prefer to be viewed as advocates of the child or the children. This is consistent with the "best interests of the child" presumption which is the guideline under which courts are operating at the present time. I prefer to view myself as someone who does not simply represent the child, but attempts to make a recommendation that takes into consideration the best interests of all concerned—the child, the parents, and others who may be involved. This involves a balancing of the needs of the various parties. It may involve compromise. To focus specifically on the best interests of the child may be too narrow a view in some cases. Such restriction may not give proper consideration to the needs of parents and may result in parental deprivation and/or psychological trauma. The term I would prefer to use is the "best interests of the family."

Solow and Adams (1977) are strong advocates of the psychiatrist serving as an impartial expert, rather than as an adversary. However, they suggest that both parents agree beforehand that the psychiatrist's recommendations shall be binding. I am in full agreement that the psychiatrist should serve as an impartial, but I am not in agreement that his or her opinion should be binding. This places a heavy burden on the psychiatrist and assumes a degree of omniscience that we do not possess. The parents should still have the opportunity to appeal the impartial's decision, and have their attorneys cross-examine him or her in court. Solow and Adams go so far as to require the parents to sign a statement that they will consider the psychiatrist's recommendations binding. I would suspect that many judges in such cases might take issue with this proviso and even try to discourage the parents and attorneys from going along with it.

Criticizers of the impartial expert concept argue that the mental health professional who places him- or herself in such a position is "playing judge." I do not agree. I make it clear from the outset, to both parents and attorneys, that I fully appreciate that I am fallible and that my recommendation is subject to courtroom scrutiny. I emphasize the fact that it is the judge, and not I, who has the power to make the final decision and that my contribution is best viewed as valuable input.

Another criticism of the impartial expert is that he is "playing God." Such criticizers claim that there is a grandiosity in placing oneself in this position. I believe that the impartial expert is not "playing God" nearly so much as the judge. But both are playing God in the sense that they cannot but be affected by their own biases and prejudices—their attempts at objectivity notwithstanding. The best that we can hope to obtain from the impartial expert is the attempt to be impartial and neutral. We all have prejudices that stem from our childhood and subsequent experiences and it is unreasonable to expect that the impartial expert will be absolutely free from such contaminations to the inquiry. It is to be hoped that these biases will not play a significant role in the impartial's recommendation. The neutrality of the impartial is partially related to his or her hoped-for objectivity and partially to the fact that he or she has full access to both parties and has the opportunity to gain the relevant information from each. Each attorney gets a one-sided view. And the judge, because of the way in which material is presented to him in adversary proceedings, also gets filtered information. The Group for the Advancement of Psychiatry clearly recognizes the limitations of the filtered information supplied by each side to the judge. In their monograph on child custody (1980) they state:

> The judge is ordinarily limited to the record before him, and it is difficult for him to compensate for the inadequacies of trial counsel or witnesses. Courts differ in their willingness to order staff investigations and reports to supplement the record, and facilities for such services also vary from court to court. Furthermore, if a judge has strong convictions about child-rearing or a bias for or against a particular theory of child development, the facts available may be filtered through these preconceptions. Most judges strive to eliminate personal bias and to protect the best interests of children; nevertheless, in some instances, the judge's tacit convictions help shape the resulting decision.

The impartial expert has the greatest flexibility and the widest opportunity to gain the most extensive and accurate information. Even if we assume that the impartial is as likely to be as biased and prejudiced as the judge, the impartial is in a better position to make a recommendation because of his or her greater freedom to collect meaningful data from both sides. Impartial experts are in a unique position and this is what makes them so valuable to the court—the risk of prejudicial contamination notwithstanding.

The impartial expert's own system of values inevitably will play a role in his or her decision making. In this regard there is little difference between the impartial's role as a court expert and his or her role as a therapist. There are therapists who state that they strictly refrain from imposing their own values on their patients. I like to divide such therapists into two categories: 1) those who are lying and 2) those who really believe what they are saying. Therapists in the latter category are at best naive and at worst simple-minded. I cannot conceive of a therapeutic program that does not involve some attempt on the therapist's part to convert the patient to his or her own way of viewing the world. A mother brings her son to the therapist because, although of high intelligence, he is doing poorly in school. The therapist agrees that this is a psychological problem and tries to help the child "reach his potential." Such a therapist is tacitly agreeing with the mother that educational pursuits are valuable. There are many in this world, however, who take a different position. Some parents are perfectly satisfied if their children reach the point of minimal competence with the "3 Rs." Others do not even see the need for such a degree of education and are satisfied with their children growing up and living on welfare. The therapist who believes that his male patient should resolve his Oedipus complex subscribes to the view that incest is undesirable. Although I share the therapist's opinion here, there are many societies where this is not the case. The examples are legion. We hope that the values that therapists will be imposing on their patients will be ones that will serve the patients well. We hope that therapists will not impose maladaptive values on their patients and will be enough in touch with their own areas of distortion (more likely the case if they have been in analysis) that they can guard against such impositions. And this holds true whether the therapist is doing treatment or involving him- or herself in custody evaluations as an impartial expert.

There are certain situations in which the therapist is likely to be at "high risk" for the imposition of biases in the custody evaluation. The therapist who has been involved personally in a custody battle, for his or her own children, is not as likely to be as objective as the colleague who has not had the misfortune to be embroiled in such a conflict. The likelihood that such a therapist will identify irrationally or inappropriately with one of the parties is high. The likelihood that there will be similarities between the examiner's own experiences and that of one, or even both, of the clients is great. And such similarities are likely to evoke emotional responses that becloud objectivity.

Another situation that is likely to produce emotional reactions in some therapists is the one in which one or both of the parents has been involved in adulterous behavior. If the therapist views such individuals as immoral, depraved, sinners, perverts, etc., he or she is likely to lose objectivity and be biased against the parent who has been involved in the extra-marital sex. In recent years courts have become increasingly appreciative of the fact that one's personal-private, voluntary sexual life is not generally related to parental capacity. There was a time when the adulterous mother (but interestingly not as often the father) was automatically considered "unfit" to be a parent. This is no longer the situation in most courts in the United States. The therapist who still subscribes to this view will be introducing what I consider to be an irrelevant consideration in most cases. Such therapists are compromised significantly in conducting meaningful custody evaluations.

Some impartial experts refer to themselves as an *amicus curiae* (*Latin*: friend of the court). Strictly speaking, the impartial expert is not an amicus curiae. An amicus curiae is generally a group or organization, rather than an individual. The amicus curiae contributes information to the court to help the court make its decision. The impartial expert does so as well. However, the amicus curiae usually has a specific position to support and the court knows this position from the outset. The impartial expert starts clean, with no previous fixed notion regarding what recommendation he or she will make to the court. In custody litigation the impartial expert does not, from the outset, know which parent will be supported. A judge may invite a brief from an amicus curiae or the amicus curiae may ask the court if it wishes to receive a brief. The amicus curiae, then, will often play the role of an advocate; the impartial expert does not start as an advocate, but may end up being one.

An example of an amicus curiae would be the American Civil Liberties Union submitting a brief to a judge who is being asked to decide whether a neo-Nazi organization should be permitted to march in a demonstration. Other organizations might also wish to submit briefs, such as the Anti-Defamation League of the B'nai Brith. Another example might be a situation in which a psychiatrist is being brought up on charges of malpractice or criminal conduct for not having revealed a patient's homicidal tendencies to a person the patient was planning to murder. The family of the murdered party might bring such a psychiatrist up on charges. The American Psychiatric Association might submit an amicus curiae brief to the court in such a situation. In short, the impartial expert is an individual, whereas the amicus curiae is usually an organization. And the impartial expert begins as a neutral; the amicus curiae is often an advocate from the outset. Both, however, should be viewed as "friends of the court" in that both can be useful to the court in making its decision.

CHOOSING THE IMPARTIAL EXPERT

I believe that the ideal method of choosing the impartial expert is for the parents themselves to agree upon the person and then recommend that individual to the court for its approval. The parents might make inquiry among friends, attorneys, physicians, psychiatrists, etc., and then see which name or names appears most frequently. They do well to inquire into the particular qualifications and experiences of the individuals under consideration. When the parents themselves have selected the impartial, and both have agreed without coercion to the choice, they are less likely to feel imposed upon by his or her recommendations. Having confidence from the outset that the person has been a good choice, they are more likely to be receptive to his or her recommendations.

When the person is agreed upon, the parents do well to inform the attorneys of their choice and to gain their approval. If all four have agreed then the next step is to verbally invite the impartial to participate. The impartial expert must then decide if he or she wishes to be involved. I require that both parents sign a statement which describes in detail the provisos of my involvement. (This will be discussed in the next chapter.) When these provisos are satisfied, one of the attorneys draw up a court order, has it approved by his or her adversary, and it is submitted to the judge for his or her signature. It is very important for the impartial expert to have the court order *before* beginning the evaluative process. Without such an order the examiner's position as an impartial expert may be compromised. Especially during the litigation may this prove to be the case, and the evaluator will then be sorry that he or she did not await full court sanction before proceeding.

It often happens that one party is very desirous of bringing me in as the impartial expert and the other side refuses. In earlier years I refused to involve myself unless both parties *voluntarily* agreed to invite my participation. I took this position because of my belief that a meaningful evaluation would not be possible with an individual who was not motivated to participate. A few years ago an attorney strongly urged me to serve as an impartial in a situation where one of the parties was being ordered to participate and the other was willing to do so voluntarily. With reservations I agreed to conduct the evaluation. To my surprise, I found that there was no difference between the two parents with regard to the amount of censoring that they were doing. I had come to expect a significant amount of censoring in parents who had come voluntarily and had assumed that it would be even greater in parents who were ordered by the court to involve themselves. I found that the level of censoring was so high in the voluntary parents that it was hard for the involuntary parents to exceed it. Accordingly, I have changed my position and have agreed to conduct evaluations upon court order regardless of whether the parties appear voluntarily or involuntarily. I have come to appreciate that it makes little difference. In both cases there is a significant amount of lying and censoring. (In Chapter Four I will describe the specific techniques that the evaluator must utilize in custody evaluations in order to collect meaningful data under these special circumstances.)

Sometimes the court will be willing to order a reluctant party to participate in a custody evaluation. At times, the court will not support the request of the petitioning attorney for such an order. In such cases, there is no way that I can serve as an impartial. There is still the possibility that I may serve as an advocate. However, there are certain strict provisos that must be satisfied before I will be willing to *consider* serving in such capacity. I first require that the attorney of the parent who wishes to enlist my support write a letter to his or her adversary requesting cooperation in bringing me in as an impartial. Following receipt of that letter of rejection I require that the attorney make a formal request of the court to order participation by the unreceptive party. Upon receipt of a written statement that the court has refused to issue such an order, I will then agree to *consider* involving myself as an advocate. I then see the parent, with no promise beforehand that I will support his or her position. I promise, however, to come to some conclusion regarding whether I can provide support *with conviction* within a few sessions. If I can do so, then I proceed with a more detailed inquiry. If I cannot, I remove myself from the case. When I have considered involvement to be warranted, I can now do so without the fear that I will be subjected to the kinds of cross-examination described previously in which the impartial was made to look foolish because he was stating that one parent was *better* without having seen the other.

When submitting reports in such circumstances, I make it clear that I made every reasonable attempt to serve as an impartial, but that such attempts were not successful. I directly state my awareness that my position is weakened by the fact that I did not have the opportunity to evaluate directly the party whose position I am not supporting. However, I make reference to powerful data (hospital reports, letters, etc.) that support my conviction for coming in as an advocate. In short, I do not take the position that the evaluator should always insist upon coming in as an impartial. I am only saying that he or she should make every reasonable attempt to do so and consider the possibility of coming in as an advocate *after* attempts to serve as an impartial have proved futile.

An impartial expert who frequently appears as an advocate is probably not a wise choice as an impartial. He or she is under suspicion of being someone who is a "hired gun" and will support whomever will pay the price. The parents should also be wary of someone who does evaluations in a short period of time—such as three or four sessions. Such evaluations are likely to be compromised. Custody evaluations are very complex. They at least involve interviews with the parents alone, interviews with the children, and various combinations of the family members. Often other interviews are desirable: one or two stepparents, a housekeeper, a prospective stepparent, a live-in parental surrogate, etc. In addition, the parents should be wary of using an individual who works for a fixed fee for all cases. One cannot tell in advance how protracted the litigation is going to be, how many interviews are going to be required, and whether or not court appearances are going to be necessary. The person who works for a fixed fee is likely to compromise his or her commitment and involvement if the case becomes complex and drawn out.

Lewis (1974) believes that it is unwise for the judge to appoint the impartial expert. The main danger here is that the judge will appoint someone who shares his or her own biases. Unfortunately, I know a number of situations in which this was clearly the case. How often this occurs would be impossible to determine. The problem for parents appearing before such judges, however, is that they may not agree to appoint the parents' choice if they suspect that this impartial will not support their own views. These are the kinds of cases that sometimes require appeals to higher courts if the parents are to get a fair hearing.

On occasion, the impartial expert may be invited to serve by the *guardian ad litem*. The guardian ad litem is generally an attorney who is appointed by the court to serve as guardian of the children in order to act on their behalf in litigation. He or she has free access to all information pertinent to the custody litigation and can present to the court information that either party may be interested in withholding. The guardian ad litem can initiate investigations (including psychiatric evaluations), introduce evidence, and cross-examine witnesses with regard to the custodial decision.

Although the guardian ad litem serves the children in a capacity similar to the way in which the parents' attorneys serve them, their functions are not entirely parallel. The guardian ad litem does not have the right to appeal, whereas the attorneys of the parents do. The guardian ad litem is paid by one or both parents. Because funds for attorneys are generally limited (except in the cases of the wealthy), there is generally less money available to pay the fees of the guardian ad litem than there is for the parents' attorneys. Accordingly, he or she is likely to spend less time with the children than the parents' attorneys are spending with them. Therefore, the children are not given the same degree of representation as the parents.

Although the guardian ad litem has access to information from both sides, I would consider it inappropriate for the impartial expert to request information from the guardian ad litem. First, he or she is an attorney in the case, not a client. In addition, information obtained from the guardian ad litem must be considered hearsay, in that it was acquired from other sources or, at best, relates to his or her (not the evaluator's) observations. Although of no value as a source of information, the guardian ad litem can be extremely valuable to the impartial evaluator *after* the submission of the final report. My experience has been that the guardian ad litem is generally supportive of my position. Since the guardian ad litem has the judge's "ear," so to speak, his or her support can be invaluable. When I come in on the side of the mother, for example, the judge hears support for her position from her attorney and from me. If there is a guardian ad litem involved, and if he or she supports my position (more often the case than not, in my experience), there are now three professionals supporting the mother's position and only one supporting the father (his own attorney). Recognizing this valuable role of the guardian ad litem, I am very pleased if I learn that one has been appointed and will routinely send him or her a copy of my final recommendation.

THE THERAPIST AS THERAPIST VS.
THE THERAPIST AS IMPARTIAL EXPERT

The kind of evaluation described in this book will be seriously comprised if the impartial expert has had any kind of involvement with any of the involved parties prior to the initiation of the evaluation. Any previous contact at all will generally preclude true impartiality. The impartial must really come in "clean," with no previous information that might conceivably "tip the scale" in one direction or another. The principle is similar to that which holds for judges who are expected to disqualify themselves from any litigation in which they have had some relationship with either party.

When the Therapist is Presently Treating
One of the Children

On a number of occasions, while a child has been in treatment, one (and on occasion both) of the parents has requested that I either serve as an impartial expert or (more commonly) provide a recommendation to the court regarding who would be the preferable parent to have custody. In such situations it behooves therapists to explain to the parents that conducting such an evaluation and then providing testimony supporting one parent over the other will almost invariably jeopardize the child's treatment. Such testimony cannot but cause the nonpreferred parent to harbor deep resentment against the therapist. The parents should be helped to appreciate that when a parent is significantly angry at a child's therapist it is almost inevitably communicated to the child. Often the parent will express such resentments openly to the child. But even when attempts are made to hide them, the child will sense the hostile feelings that the parent harbors toward the therapist and will feel caught in the middle of a tug-of-war. Such a situation cannot but compromise the child's positive feelings toward the therapist—feelings crucial to have if therapy is to be meaningful. The child placed in the middle of such a conflict will, in the vast majority of cases, side with the parent's position. And the child must. The parents, their problems notwithstanding, are providing the child with food, clothing, shelter, and probably much more love and affection than the therapist is—in spite of the latter's professions of interest, concern, affection, etc. I generally go further with such parents and tell them that I cannot stop them from requesting that I submit information to the court (I will elaborate on this point below), but if they do so there is 99 + percent chance that the therapy will become practically worthless. If this happens they will have no one but themselves to blame. Accordingly, I advise them to bring in another person to serve as impartial and "leave me out of it."

Borderline Situations
Regarding the Therapist's Role

The therapist does well to clarify his or her role in any situation where there appears to be any question regarding this issue. In the initial telephone conversation, prior to the first appointment, the therapist may detect come confusion on the parents' part as to exactly what is being requested, i.e., which role is being sought: therapist for the child, advocate for the caller, or impartial expert. It is crucial that the therapist make clear to the caller that each of these is a very separate role and they *cannot* be combined. It would be unwise for therapists to invite the parent to discuss the matter in session because if the decision is made to request that the examiner serve as an impartial expert, such participation will have been precluded by the earlier contact with one parent. If the parent decides that therapy, and only therapy, is being requested then, of course, an appointment can be made. However, even at that point, because the question of litigation has already been presented, the therapist should impress upon the parent that if there is a decision later to involve the therapist in litigation the child's treatment would be seriously compromised, if not destroyed.

If the parent states on the phone that he or she is looking for an advocate, I inform the parent that I generally do not serve as an advocate and will only be willing to consider serving as an impartial in custody litigation. If the parent is willing to consider my participation as an impartial I send the aforementioned material (Appendix I and Appendix II) so that the parent will be in a better position to understand the rationale for my approach and the steps that must be taken to bring about my participation. Last, if the parent decides that the impartial role on my part is being sought, I also send the aforementioned information.

At times a child will ostensibly be brought for treatment when actually a custody determination is desired. Sometimes parents may really believe that treatment is the only thing they want, or they may say that treatment is what they want, but will know that the custody consideration is also very much on their minds. They may withhold this from the therapist at the beginning because they fear that he or she will not want to be involved in the legal aspects of the case, or they may fear that the therapist will refuse to take the child into treatment at all if he or she learns that appearance in court is also being considered. Such parents may know of our reluctance to go to court, but may not appreciate the dangers that such appearances pose for therapy. They may consider our hesitation to stem from many factors unrelated to the desire to avoid the inevitable compromise to treatment that such involvement entails. (Of course, many therapists also avoid involvement in litigation because of the indignities and duplicities they may be exposed to.) The parents may have been turned down by a series of therapists who refused to get involved once they suspected that their services were being requested for the purposes of litigation. The parents may not appreciate that the therapist cannot but be indignant, finding him- or herself forced to testify in a case that was initially presented without any reference to the litigation plans. Such resentment compromises the child's treatment. And this resentment beclouds the therapist's objectivity and may affect his or her decision—specifically by the inevitable prejudice toward the parent who was dishonest.

Accordingly, when the litigation motive becomes disclosed I inform the parents that I cannot refuse their request that I provide information to the court. I inform them that they have the power to preclude my involvement, even if one or both attorneys are naive enough to request it. Finally, they should know that such involvement on my part is likely to ruin their child's treatment and they will only have themselves to blame.

Forced Involvement of the Child's Therapist in the Custody Litigation

In spite of the above warnings, there are parents who will still insist that the therapist be involved. A parent may be so filled with rage and bent on vengeance that he or she will be blind to the consequences of demanding the therapist's involvement in the litigation. Or the parent may have deep self-destructive tendencies which involve the children as well. When the therapist's services are so enlisted, it is important to make it clear to the parents and the court that a formal custody evaluation has not been conducted and so the therapist's contribution to the court regarding which of the two parents would be *preferable* for the children must be compromised.

This legal point is best understood by utilizing an analogy to an automobile accident. A woman, for example, drives past the scene of an accident. She slows up, glances at the scene (just as dozens of others may be doing), and then drives on. It is possible that she may subsequently receive a subpoena to appear in court and provide information. In fact, to refuse to appear may place her in contempt of court and subject to punishment. Once in court she may be asked questions such as whether or not it was raining that day, whether the streets were slippery, whether she saw any bodies on the street, whether she saw any blood, how many people were lying on the ground, was it day or night, and how many cars were damaged. All these are questions that can be answered by any reasonably observant passerby. They do not require any expertise. Such a person would not be expected to answer questions like: "What was the length of the skid marks?" "About how many miles per hour was a particular car going prior to the impact?" "Were any of the participants inebriated?" "Did any of the automobiles show evidence of mechanical defects?" and "How deep were the treads on each of the tires on each of the cars?" The latter group of questions can only be answered by experts after proper expert investigation.

A therapist who is treating a child and/or members of a family that subsequently become involved in custody litigation can generally only serve as a provider of facts, like the lay passerby in the aforementioned automobile accident example. Under such circumstances, the therapist can be asked questions like: "Did either of the parents use

corporal punishment? If so, describe the method(s), frequency, etc."
"Who, to the best of your knowledge, made the children breakfast each
morning?" "What were the sleep patterns of each of the parents?"
and "To the best of your knowledge, how many nights per week on the
average did Mr. Jones not return to the home at all?" These questions,
of course, provide information regarding parental capacity, but they
do not specifically ask the therapist to make a direct statement regarding which of the two he or she believes to be the preferable parent. The
therapist who has only served as therapist and not as an impartial
evaluator should not be asked the question: "Who would be the better
parent to have custody of these children?" The primary focus of treatment was therapeutic, and the therapist has not conducted a formal
evaluation to answer this question. In such cases the best answer is: "I
cannot answer yes or no." However, the therapist may have enough information to answer this question. If the therapist provides this information, he or she is most likely to destroy the child's treatment—if he
or she has not done so already by having answered questions that make
it obvious that one particular parent is preferable to the other.

An additional question is that of confidentiality. One parent may
not be willing to allow the therapist to provide information when the
other is very desirous of having him or her brought in (the therapist's
protestations notwithstanding). States vary regarding what rights
parents have under these circumstances. Some states deny privilege
under the best interests of the child presumption. In these states a parent cannot prevent the therapist from revealing any and all information to the court that is pertinent to the child's welfare. The court may
order the therapist to provide the information in accordance with the
statutes or legal precedents. The therapist, in such states, need not be
fearful of the threat that he will be sued for malpractice. In short, in
these states, privilege is automatically waived by any party who
actively contests child custody. There are other states, however, in
which both parents must provide the therapist with their consent for
him or her to testify. If either parent refuses to give such consent, the
privilege must be honored. In such situations, the therapist may be
required to testify about the parent who has provided consent, but
must strictly avoid making any comments about the parent who has not
provided such consent. Of course, that parent's position is being somewhat weakened by the failure to have provided release for the divulgence of the information. (People who plead the Fifth Amendment are
rarely viewed as innocent and merely exercising their constitutional
rights on principle.)

In order to avoid charges of unethical conduct or malpractice
suits the therapist should consult an attorney if he or she has any ques-

tion regarding laws that prevail in his or her state. This is not a situation in which one would want to get some quickie free advice from one's lawyer brother-in-law or cousin. One does well to consult an attorney who is specifically knowledgeable in this area. In addition, one should seek the advice of one's malpractice insurance company. My experience has been that the malpractice insurance company is most receptive to such inquiries in that they much prefer to help their clients *before* the malpractice charges arise. In fact, I would go further and state that the malpractice insurance company is probably the best source of advice in such situations.

Besides the legal issues here, there is an ethical one. In states where a parent can invoke privilege and prevent a therapist from providing information about him- or herself, this particular ethical issue does not arise. However, what about the state in which a parent is automatically considered to waive privilege under the best interests of the child presumption? When testifying in such situations, therapists are certainly obeying the law; however, they are not fulfilling their ethical obligations to respect the parents' confidentiality. If therapists decide that the ethical consideration is more important or higher than the legal, then they are likely to find themselves in contempt of court. Under such threats, most comply with the law and justify their possibly unethical position with the arguments that they are law-abiding and doing what is in the best interests of the children. Those who cannot accept these justifications may choose to defy the law and suffer the consequences of such defiance. If the court wishes to invoke its power, such therapists can literally be put in jail. Although their professional societies may provide them with psychological support and even be willing to enter some cases as an amicus curiae, it is not likely that such support will be financial (although voluntary collections might be taken up). Therapists have little choice in such situations but to hire their own attorneys and assume the cost of such litigation (which may be formidable).

Some readers may be wondering, at this point, what I personally would do were I in such a situation. As a matter of fact, most of my experiences as an impartial expert have been in two states, one of which holds that parents' privilege is lost in custody litigation and the other holds that privilege must be respected. Specifically, in the state of New Jersey (where I live and practice) the parents' privilege must be respected in custody litigation. However, in the state of New York (where I teach) a parent's privilege in custody litigation is not honored under the best interests of the child presumption. Accordingly, I have no ethical conflict with regard to my testifying in the state of New Jersey, because my failure to testify about one parent is in compliance with that parent's request and the law's support. Practically, my experience has been that the unreceptive parent usually does not invoke privilege because of the recognition that such invocation may be viewed by the judge as a cover-up (and properly so) and thereby compromises that parent's position.

Although I have not been put to the test in the state of New York (I testify less frequently there), my guess is that I would not be a "hero" and defy a court order to testify in order to protect a parent's privilege. This is not simply related to a fear of jail and horrendous legal fees (although these certainly play a role). I believe that the arguments for giving the best interests of the child presumption priority over automatic submission to a parent's invocation of the privilege is a justifiable position. A parent who insists upon the therapist's strict adherence to his or her rights under privilege is generally hiding something that should be revealed and I am therefore happy to have the court's support for such revelation.

With such a position, one could argue that I should also reveal information in the state of New Jersey—even if such revelation involves my revealing information against a parent's wishes and defying the law that protects the parents from my providing such revelations. My conviction for what I have said is not that strong that I would be willing to expose myself to the double legal danger [a malpractice suit from a parent for unethical conduct and a contempt of court citation from the court) that would be entailed in such revelation. I recognize that there are no final answers to any of these issues. (There are no final and "right" answers to most issues.) I recognize, as well, that there are readers who would not agree with my position and would act differently. As mentioned, my own position was stated here because of my expectations that at least some readers would be curious about how I would deal with this very controversial issue.

The aforementioned discussion focused on the situation in which the therapist is asked to testify while a child is in treatment and contact with the family is present and recent. There are times, however, when all contact with the family has been discontinued, for varying lengths of time, and the therapist's involvement is then sought or even ordered by court subpoena. Sometimes the situation is one in which the child was treated while the parents were married and the divorce decision came after the termination of contact with the therapist. The custody litigation, then, was generally not even remotely considered by the therapist during the course of the treatment. This may not deter parents, attorneys, and judges from inviting, and even ordering, the therapist to testify. Of course, the issue of compromising the child's treatment is not relevant. The aforementioned legal and ethical issues, however, are still operative. My previous comments regarding whether or not to testify (the state laws, ethical issues, the malpractice threat, etc.) still apply.

On occasion there may be an exception to the caveat that one cannot serve both as a therapist and an impartial expert. This happened to me on one occasion when, five years after I had served as an impartial, the father asked me if I would treat his daughter. As is my practice—whether or not the parents are divorced—I try to involve both parents in the child's therapy, especially when the child is embroiled in the middle of the parental conflict. Such was the case in this situation. Because I had supported the father's position in the custody conflict, he was friendly toward me and I saw no problems from his side. However, I anticipated that there might be difficulties with his ex-wife's relationship with me. Accordingly, I was initially surprised when she was quite friendly to me. This was not simply a matter of "let bygones be bygones." Rather, I recall that she basically did not want the children anyway. She was fighting for them because she could not allow herself to accept the fact that she really did not want to have custody. Therefore, I had done her a service by recommending that her husband gain custody—thus the lack of animosity.

Accordingly, in this case, I was able to serve as a therapist *after* the custody litigation had been completed. However, the aforementioned warnings with regard to the therapist trying to serve *both* as impartial expert *and* therapist at the same time still hold, and I have not yet seen an exception to this warning. There is another situation which may appear to be an exception to the rule that one cannot serve both as therapist and impartial expert. One parent may be totally uninvolved, and even antagonistic, to the therapist. If legal and ethical considerations allow the therapist to provide testimony in support of the involved parent, the therapy will probably not be compromised any further than it has been by the noninvolvement of the hostile parent. No love has been lost by the therapist, because there was no love in the first place.

FINAL COMMENTS

On occasion, I have received telephone calls from attorneys inviting me to answer hypothetical questions in custody litigation. Either my involvement as an impartial is not being requested or one side wishes such involvement and the other refuses. Generally, the invitation has come from one side. Although the attorney initially denies that he or she is requesting that I appear as an advocate, the failure of the other

side to support my involvement as a provider of hypothetical information (the usual case) supports my supposition that I am basically being
invited to serve as an advocate. Although a provider of hypothetical
answers may not be formally designated an advocate, he or she will
certainly be treated as one in the court. In addition, ours is an inexact
science and is more properly still viewed as an art. Accordingly, answers to hypothetical questions are not likely to be as useful in our
field as they might be in others. Providing such testimony, therefore,
may be a disservice to the court and the families involved. For these
reasons I have not yet seen fit to accept such an invitation and consider
it most unlikely that I will do so in the future.

Rothschild (1978) holds a similar position, his main argument
being that each case is so complex and so different that the usefulness
of hypothetical answers is questionable. The therapist does well to give
serious consideration to these factors before accepting an invitation to
provide such testimony.

Levy (1978b) describes a case in which he met together with both
attorneys (without the parents present) as a step toward resolution of a
custody conflict. Although this method certainly has arguments in its
favor in that it is another way of reducing adversarial conflict, I have
certain reservations about its advisability. I generally am against
"secret discussions" in the course of my work whether they are diagnostic, therapeutic, or evaluative (the situation in custody conflicts).
They cannot but evoke distrust of the evaluator and questions like
"Why does he have to talk behind my back?" In addition, many attorneys and judges might consider such a practice to be intrusive into the
judicial process. Judges frequently meet alone with attorneys in their
chambers in order to bring about compromises. Although the therapist
and the judge have different training, the structure of the interview
and its purposes are identical. These criticisms notwithstanding, I am
not suggesting that the practice be ruled out altogether. Any reasonable approach to the resolution of a custody conflict in a nonadversarial setting deserves our attention and respect. It is only with further
experience with such procedures that we will be in a position to
comment on them more definitively.

Ten to fifteen years ago, when I recommended that therapists serve
as impartial experts, and not as advocates, I generally received a hostile response from most attorneys. In fact, I recall specifically a conference held under the auspices of the New York Bar Association in which
I was part of a panel discussing custody litigation. The panel consisted
of a law professor, a judge, an attorney well versed in matrimonial law,
and myself. My suggestion that attorneys consider the impartial expert
alternative were literally met with boos and jeers. (This was not an un-

sophisticated audience. Many were graduates of prestigious law schools.) The matrimonial lawyer on the panel, in a heated rebuttal, literally stated that I was no better than "Richard Nixon," "Adolf Hitler," and others of such ilk. (I concluded here that this gentleman was probably a Democrat.) I suspected that the antagonism toward my recommendation rested not so much on theoretical issues as on the financial, because one of the purposes of my recommendation was to shorten divorce litigation. Because some of the group were already on the edge of violence, I was ambivalent about throwing out for their consideration this possible explanation for their antagonism. After some ambivalent deliberation, stemming in part from fear (which I consider to have been realistic), I decided to throw out my speculation for their consideration. Dozens were simultaneously ranting and shouting, and if there were rotten eggs and garbage available, I am sure that some would have come my way.

It has been a great source of gratification to me to note that, over the years, there has been a general change in the legal profession's attitude regarding its receptivity to the notion of bringing in therapists as impartial experts rather than as advocates. This is the time of enlightenment on the part of the legal profession in this area and altruism, as well, in that the long adversary proceedings are far more remunerative than a conflict cut short by the recommendations of an impartial expert. But the legal profession still has a long way to go in this regard, and it is my hope that this book will play some role in shortening the time until there is general realization of the preference for the impartial expert over the advocate in custody litigation.

2

Preliminary Steps

WHO IS GOING TO CREATE THE GUIDELINES FOR CUSTODY EVALUATION— THE LEGAL PROFESSION OR MENTAL HEALTH PROFESSIONALS?

I do not quickly agree to involve myself in custody litigation. This does not relate to any reluctance to involve myself in such litigation. Although this was certainly true in earlier years, as my experience and knowledge have increased my fears and resistances have diminished significantly. I now find such involvement generally rewarding and gratifying. The main reason I do not so readily involve myself is *caution*. Over the years I have learned about so many pitfalls that I have had to increase the number of stipulations to be satisfied before I am willing to involve myself. These stipulations have increased over the years as I have learned (often the hard way) that not making them risks my compromising the evaluation. In this chapter I will discuss in detail these stipulations. I recognize that many attorneys and/or parents will not be willing to agree to all of them. I recognize, as well, that I have a reputation in my area as being somewhat "hard-nosed" with regard to my reluctance to involve myself in custody litigation when these provisos are not satisfied. However, those who are in agreement with me that they are warranted have also found that they make sense and are conducive to the evaluator's providing the most objective and useful kind of recommendation.

It is important for the reader to appreciate that, at the present time, there are few if any formal legal guidelines or laws dictating or controlling the way in which a custody evaluation should be conducted. We are totally free to refuse to involve ourselves in cases where there has been no previous contact. And even when involved, the courts and attorneys have little control over us regarding the ways in which we conduct our evaluations. Of course, once we have involved ourselves with patients— whether as therapists or as evaluators—we are obligated to give testimony in court, even when we may consider such testifying to be psychologically detrimental to a child's treatment.

Accordingly, methods for conducting custody evaluations are "open territory." Considering the present burgeoning of such litigation, it is likely that certain procedures will become more commonly used than others. At the present time, we in the mental health professions are the ones who are deciding how to conduct such evaluations. If we do not actively conduct them in the ways that we consider warranted, then we may find ourselves submitting to rules, regulations, laws, and constraints that compromise us. If most members of the legal profession had their way, most of us would be involved as advocates. If all of us insisted that we would serve only as impartials (with rare and specific exceptions), they would have just two choices: 1) use us as impartials or 2) dispense with our services entirely. I am quite sure that the first alternative would be chosen by the overwhelming majority of the legal profession. They recognize our value, but we must insist that they take us on our terms. Otherwise, we risk doing our patients a terrible disservice as well as compromising our professional integrity.

There is an old bit of advice which states that if you want to do something that may not be acceptable to your superiors, it is sometimes preferable to go ahead and do it rather than ask for permission. The argument runs that if you ask for permission and are turned down, you will have no opportunity to pursue your course. However, if you don't ask permission, you may very well have your way and no one will ask any questions. On the other hand, you may be stopped if the particular course comes to the attention of authorities and they order or require that you discontinue the particular practice. I am not recommending this approach as a routine to justify *any* unconscionable act. I am only suggesting it in certain situations, when the course of action is a reasonable and humane one and when the individual suspects that his or her superiors will be unreasonable in their refusals. And this is the course of action that I recommend mental health professionals *consider* taking when introducing new techniques in conducting custody evaluations. The courts, although not strictly speaking our superiors, do have the potential to control us (as when they subpoena us even though we deem it psychologically detrimental). On a number of occasions I found the aforementioned advice useful. I have not asked the court permission to introduce what I considered an atypical, but nevertheless justifiable, procedure in the course of my evaluation. At times such procedures have been met with raised eyebrows and incredulity, but I have not yet been put in jail nor have I even been told to cease and desist. At worst I was told that my services would not be enlisted if I insisted upon certain provisos. And even then, there were others who recognized how judicious these were and continued to enlist my services.

THE PROVISIONS FOR MY INVOLVEMENT IN CUSTODY LITIGATION

For a number of years I gave thought to the question of whether I should have parents sign a written statement regarding their willingness to subscribe to various provisions prior to my involvement in custody litigation. For many years I thought the most judicious approach was not to make up a formal document. I imagined that if I got a team of contract lawyers together and they made up what they considered to be the best possible document for this purpose, there would still be other attorneys who would find loopholes in it and interpret it in ways that would be antithetical to the custody evaluation. In accordance with this view I did not, for many years, require a formal written statement. Rather, I went over the provisions verbally before initiating the evaluation. As the years went on, the number of provisions grew, and the time consumed in communicating them all to two attorneys and two parents became inordinate. In such discussions I not only found myself presenting these provisions, but the rationale for each as well. In addition, I found that no matter how clearly I had stated them, there were quite frequently misunderstandings and misinterpretations.

Accordingly, I recently decided to formally document the provisions and require parental signature before proceeding with the evaluation. Although I did not enlist the aid of a team of contract lawyers, I did ask a few attorneys I knew to review the document and suggest any changes they thought might be warranted. To my gratification, I found that there was nothing legally inappropriate in it and the modifications they recommended were minor. The complete list of provisos is to be found in Appendix II. Each parent is sent one and both must sign a statement not only agreeing to the provisos, but indicating as well that the provisions have been discussed with their attorneys. I did not consider it judicious or warranted to require the attorneys' signatures as well. It was not only unnecessary from the legal point of view, but might produce complications if a parent changed attorneys in the course of the evaluation (a not uncommon occurrence). In addition, I send out a reprint of an article of mine, "The Psychiatrist as Impartial Expert in Custody Litigation" (Appendix I). This provides the basic rationale for my evaluation, as well as a description of it. After reading these two documents, the parents and their attorneys have a very good idea about what is to take place if they agree to enlist my services.

The Initial Telephone Call

Generally one of the four parties (one of the parents or one of the attorneys) calls to invite my participation. If the party is receptive to considering inviting me as an impartial expert, I send the aforementioned documents. I let it be known that there will be no further involvement on my part until I have a signed statement from each of the parents. The usual procedure, then, is for me to call both parents, inform them that I have received signed statements from both parties, and suggest that they have their attorneys ask the judge to mail me a court order.

Even at this stage, important information can be obtained. This is well demonstrated by an experience I had with a man whom I will call Mr. Adams. He was divorced and remarried. His first wife had not remarried. They were involved in very vicious custody litigation. Mr. Adams made the initial telephone call and was very desirous of inviting me in as an impartial. Accordingly, I told him that I would send him copies of the aforementioned documents and that he should discuss the matter with his ex-wife. If she was equally receptive to my involvement, then I would have to receive a telephone call from her informing me of her decision. I would then send her the same documents. Upon receipt of the signed documents from both parties, I would then be available to proceed (after, of course, receiving the court order from the judge).

About two weeks later, my secretary informed me that a Mrs. Adams had called and told her that she could be reached at a particular telephone number. I called the number (only five minutes after the call had come through to my secretary) and said, "I'd like to speak to Mrs. Adams please." The woman at the other end coldly stated, "There's no Mrs. Adams here." I apologized and said that I was sorry, that I had probably dialed the wrong number.

This time I more carefully redialed the number jotted down by my secretary. Once again the same woman answered and I once again asked for Mrs. Adams. Again the woman stated that there was no Mrs. Adams at that number. I then asked the woman if her telephone number was the one that my secretary had jotted down. She replied that it was, but that there was no Mrs. Adams there. I explained to her my confusion and told her that only a few minutes previously my secretary had received a telephone call from a woman who stated that she was Mrs. Adams and that she had left that particular telephone number. The woman then asked me who I was and I identified myself. At this point she replied, "Oh, it's Dr. Gardner. You want to speak to Ms. Adams. Mrs. Adams is my former husband's new wife. I'm no longer Mrs. Adams. I'm Ms. Adams. I'm the one who called." My first thought at that point was "I already know who's likely to get custody." Although I would certainly not let my irritation here make a significant difference regarding the person I would consider to be the preferable parent, I had learned something about the extent and depth of this woman's hostility and her capacity to provoke.

The Introduction to the Provisions

Prior to listing the specific provisions that must be satisfied before I will agree to involve myself, the following introductory statement is made:

> Whenever possible, I make every reasonable attempt to serve the court as an impartial expert, rather than as an advocate, in custody litigation. In order to serve optimally in this capacity I must be free to avail myself of any and all information, from any source, that I consider pertinent and reasonable to have. In this way, I believe I can best serve the interests of children and parents involved in such conflicts. Accordingly, before agreeing to serve in this capacity, the following conditions must be agreed upon by both parents and both attorneys.

The proviso includes a very general statement that "I must be free to avail myself of any and all information, from any source, that I consider pertinent and reasonable to have." This is purposely worded loosely so that I may have the greatest flexibility of interpretation should there be any question about my right to a particular piece of information. The stipulation includes the term "any and all"—a term that attorneys are very partial to, although it is one that I find grammatically distasteful. Strictly speaking, it is a redundancy in that *all*, by definition, must include *any* item that is subsumed under the rubric *all*. But attorneys like redundancy, believing that it enhances the power of their position. (I am in agreement that a certain amount of redundancy does so, but there is a point beyond which it serves just the opposite purpose, i.e., it weakens the argument.) In spite of this hesitation over the use of the term, I decided to use it so that should there be any question about my availing myself of any particular information, I could point to the "legal terminology" justifying my availing myself of it.

The value of this wording was well demonstrated by a recent experience of mine. During the course of the evaluation of the parents, a father mentioned that he had secretly made a tape during an argument that he had with his wife. He asked me to hear it during a future session (he did not have it with him at the time), because he felt that it would confirm many of his allegations against his wife. She immediately brought up the fact that her lawyer had been successful in preventing her husband from submitting the tape as evidence in court and that I, therefore, had no right to listen to the tape either. I informed her that both she and her husband had signed statements in which they had agreed to allow me full flexibility to conduct the evaluation in any way I saw fit. In addition, I reminded her that the statement she had signed indicated that she had discussed the provisos with her attorney before placing her signature on the document. I explained that I considered my listening to the tape not only reasonable, but desirable, and I therefore had every intention of hearing it. However, I told her that I thought it should best be played at a time when both she and her husband together could discuss it with me. I therefore set up an appointment to hear the tape with the two of them.

The following day I received a telephone call from the mother's attorney ordering me not to listen to the tape. I told him that he was interfering with my evaluation and that he had no power to impose such a restriction on me. He threatened to get a court order signed by the judge which would prevent me from listening to the tape. I responded that if such a court order were forthcoming, I would remove myself from the case on the grounds that I was being hindered from conducting the evaluation in the way that I saw fit. The following day I received a telephone call from the judge in which he informed me that he had ruled that the tape could not be submitted in evidence. I told him that I was not in a position to judge the legal justification for his position. However, I informed him that I was in a position to judge the psychiatric aspects and that it was my opinion that preventing me from listening to that tape would compromise the evaluation and that if he ordered me not to listen to it, I would discontinue the evaluation. The judge reluctantly acquiesced.

This vignette is not only presented as an example of how my loosely worded statement served to justify my gaining access to information that the court (for reasons which are beyond my comprehension) chose not to allow in evidence. My "hard-nosed" attitude toward both the attorney and the judge (both of whom were trying to control and coerce me) is not simply related to this particular tape incident. I felt I was contributing to establishing myself as someone who is not going to let the judicial process dictate or prevent me from pursuing what I considered to be a psychologically indicated course of action. This is one of the examples of the principle (mentioned previously) that we in the mental health professions must establish guidelines and traditions ourselves before the courts do. Otherwise, we will find ourselves submitting to restrictions that not only hamper our evaluation but may be psychologically detrimental to patients.

Stipulations Regarding Free Access to All Involved Parties

The first proviso states:

1. I will have available to interview all members of the immediate family—that is, the mother, father, and children—for as many interviews (individual and in any combination) as I consider warranted. In addition, I will have the freedom to invite any and all other parties whom I would consider possible sources of useful information. Generally, these would include such persons as present or prospective parental surrogates with whom either parent may be involved and the housekeeper. Usually, I do not interview a series of friends and relatives each of whom, from the outset, is particularly partial to one of the parents (but I reserve the right to invite such parties if I consider it warranted).

The stipulation specifically allows me the greatest flexibility regarding the collection of information from all pertinent parties. As stated, I generally confine myself to evaluating the parents, parental surrogates (present and potential), and the children. I am reluctant to interview a string of relatives and friends, each of whom is predictably going to provide me with glowing accounts of the party being supported. These tend to cancel one another out as each parent selects only those who are predictably going to provide the greatest support. Rich people have the opportunity to bring such a parade of individuals into court. I have generally found it a waste of time to interview these people. However, I am not so rigid with this proviso that I have never interviewed such persons. I just must reserve the right to decide whether or not I wish to extend an invitation to them.

As will be discussed in the next chapter, I invite the parents to suggest to me persons they wish me to interview. I will not allow the other parent to have veto power over my extending the invitation. I will, however, listen with receptivity to the other parent's objections. It is important for the evaluator to appreciate that the court order generally indicates that the impartial interview the parents and the children. Other parties are optional and the impartial has no power to require their participation. Impartials can only extend invitations and these are most properly done through the parents—particularly the party who recommended the name in the first place. I consider it professionally unethical for an evaluator to call up a person with whom there has never been any previous contact and invite that individual to come to his or her office for an interview—even if such interview is associated with custody litigation.

Confidentiality in the Custody Evaluation

The confidentiality stipulation is:

> 2. In order to allow me the freedom of inquiry necessary for serving optimally families involved in custody litigation, the parents shall agree to a modification of the traditional rules of confidentiality. Specifically, I must be given the freedom to reveal to one party what has been told to me by the other (at my discretion) so that I will have full opportunity to explore all pertinent points with both parties. This does not mean that I will not respect certain privacies or that I will automatically reveal all information provided me—only that I reserve the right to make such revelations if I consider them warranted for the purpose of collecting the most meaningful data.

Clearly, this stipulation guarantees my full flexibility in conducting the evaluation. It prevents me from being restrained in any way from gathering information from any party. It protects me from being in the position where one party has provided me with information that he or she does not wish me to reveal to the other. For example, a wife may complain bitterly about her husband's drinking problem. He, however, may have said absolutely nothing about this. This proviso enables me to freely bring the subject up without waiting for him to do so himself. I am even free to introduce the subject with a comment like, "Your wife has complained to me that you drink excessively. I would like to hear about this from you." (The reader should note here that I have carefully refrained from accepting the wife's statement as valid. I merely open the issue and invite his response to the allegation.)

In the course of the evaluation a party may tell me that there is an important issue that warrants disclosure in the evaluation, but the party fears that such revelation might compromise his or her legal position. In such cases, I tell the parent that I do not automatically reveal everything said to me to the other party. However, I will not promise beforehand whether or not I will reveal the information and so revealing it to me, therefore, involves a risk. I do not try to coerce the parent into providing the information. I do, however, inform the party that to the degree that I have all pertinent information, to that degree I am in the optimum position for making the most judicious custody recommendation. The parent has to decide which is more important: the children's best interests or the legal situation.

A good example of this kind of a conflict occurred with a father who told me that he had information that he was hesitant to reveal because he feared my divulging it might weaken his legal position. I presented him with the pros and cons of his revealing the information to me and left it completely up to him to decide what he wanted to do. He decided to take the risk involved in telling me. He then revealed that he had a woman friend and that he had been having an affair with this woman prior to separation. He had no reason to believe that his wife knew anything about this relationship. In addition, he informed me that, even though separated, his lawyer had advised him not to reveal the relationship (past or present) to his wife until after the divorce was finalized. The father also informed me that he planned to marry this woman soon after the divorce process was complete. I told him that I considered there nothing to be gained by revealing the nature of the past relationship to his wife. However, I also informed him that this involvement enhanced somewhat his chances of gaining custody because his work schedule was a heavy one and this woman was a homemaker. I explained to him that for the purposes of the evaluation it would be useful for me to interview her. Obviously, I could not include such information in my report without simultaneously divulging his "secret" to his wife. In this case I let the man decide whether or not he wished to disclose the information and told him that if he chose not to, I would not reveal what he had told me to his wife, either verbally or in my report. In a subsequent session the man told me that he had decided to reveal this woman's identity to his wife because he felt that the advantages to be gained in the custody litigation far outweighed the losses that might be entailed in the other issues over which there were conflicts.

The vignette is presented as an example of how I use this special dispensation in the custody evaluation. As mentioned in the formal statement of this proviso, I do not automatically reveal information to other parties; I merely reserve the right to do so at my discretion. I certainly invite input from the parent whose information I might divulge; but I do not give that party veto power over my doing so. And I do not put direct pressures on people to reveal anything to me. I do, however, try to clarify for them the pros and cons of their divulging important information to me.

Permission to Release Information

The proviso regarding the signing of permission slips to release information states:

> 3. The parties shall agree to sign any and all releases necessary for me to obtain reports from others, e.g., psychiatrists, psychologists, social workers, teachers, school officials, mental hospitals, etc.

The "etc." covers any unforeseen sources of information not covered formally in the stipulation (the aforementioned tape being a good example). As I will discuss in further detail in the next chapter, I do not automatically exercise my right to obtain such information. But I do exercise my right to require the *freedom* to request it if I consider it useful.

It is important for the reader to appreciate that such information, although it may initially seem valuable, is not generally very useful. It is hearsay information and so should not be directly quoted. To do so compromises the evaluation and the evaluator opens him- or herself up for criticism during cross-examination. Therapists should use such information as a point of departure in their direct inquiries with the parents. Even if one obtains a hospital record which states that a mother, for example, was committed with a diagnosis of paranoid schizophrenia, the information may not be particularly useful. The mother may have been grossly psychotic at the time of the hospitalization, but her present psychiatric status is much more important—although her past history is not totally irrelevant. As I will discuss subsequently, the therapist's own observations of the manifestations of psychopathology—rather than the *diagnostic* category—are the more important factors to be considered in the evaluation. Furthermore, schizophrenia does not necessarily compromise one's maternal capacity for all ages of children. Lastly, the extent of the father's psychopathology in this case—especially with regard to symptoms that compromise his paternal capacity—must be weighed against the mother's before coming to any conclusions regarding parental preference. When one considers these additional factors, the hospital report becomes less meaningful.

I generally do not request reports from therapists who have a meaningful relationship with a parent at the time of the custody evaluation. If such a therapist were to provide information that could compromise the parent's problem in the custody litigation, it is likely to have a detrimental effect on the therapist-patient relationship. I am less reluctant to request such information from past therapists, especially if the relationship was not a particularly deep one.

My experience has been that about 20–25 percent of all requests for such information are never responded to. I think this is related to the fear the recipients have of involving themselves in the litigation. On other occasions I have suspected that the recipient of my letter wanted to protect one party from a divulgence that might compromise his or her position in the litigation. Such "protectionism," although often benevolently motivated, is usually misguided. It usually stems from some prejudicial preference for one parent over the other without having had the full opportunity to hear both sides. Whatever the motivation of the non-responder, I have not yet seen fit to press the issue with further letters or any kind of coercive maneuver. As mentioned, such information is generally of low value in the evaluation and serves best as a point of departure for the evaluator's own inquiries.

The Not-Inconsequential Issue of Payment for the Evaluation

The stipulation describing the terms and methods of payment states:

4. My fee for conducting a custody evaluation is $100 per full hour of my time. This not only includes time spent in interviewing, but in report preparation, dictation, pertinent telephone conversations, court preparation, and any other time expended in association with the evaluation. My fee for court appearances is $150 per hour while in court and $100 per hour travel time to and from my office. During the course of the evaluation, bills will be sent to the payer(s) every Friday. In order to insure that the evaluation is neither interrupted nor delayed because of nonpayment, each bill must be paid no later than one week from the date of billing.

Prior to the initial interview (with both parents together) the payer(s) will deposit with me a check (in my name) for $1500. This shall be deposited in the Northern Valley-Englewood Savings and Loan Association branch in Cresskill, New Jersey, in my name, in a day-to-day interest bearing account. This money (with accrued interest) shall be returned to the payer(s) *after* a final decision has been made regarding custody and after I have received a letter from the court, or either of the attorneys, that my services are no longer being enlisted.

This payment should not be viewed as an advance retainer, in that the aforementioned fees will not be drawn against it, unless there has been a failure to pay my fee. It usually serves to reassure the nonpayer that my objectivity will not be compromised by the fear that if I do not support the paying party, my fee will not be paid.

The average total cost for an evaluation is generally in the $1000-$2500 range. It is very difficult, if not impossible, to predict in advance the cost of a particular evaluation because I cannot know beforehand how many interviews will be warranted and whether or not I will be asked to testify in court.

One reason therapists in private practice often hesitate to involve themselves in custody evaluations is the high rate of default on payments. Most often the party who pays is the father. New trends in father custody notwithstanding, the mother is still given custody in the large majority of cases. Accordingly, the father is the one who usually ends up angry. And what better way to express his resentment than to ignore the bills of the person most instrumental in depriving him of his children? I will not detail the various unpleasantries—to speak euphemistically—resulting from my involvement in such situations. To avoid the repetition of such indelicate (and personally humiliating) interchanges between the defaulter and myself, I now insist on an advance payment to help buffer and absorb such defaulted payments. The requirement that payment be made weekly (instead of my usual monthly payment plan) also protects me from default on a large bill. As mentioned, this plan is often welcomed by the nonpayer in that it is reassuring to that person to know that my objectivity is less likely to be compromised by the fear that I will not be paid if I do not support the side of the payer. In effect, it lessens the likelihood that I will be viewed as a "hired gun."

The reader may view this payment program as very distrusting on my part. I am in full agreement that it suggests just that. Such distrust does not come from nowhere. It comes from a number of bitter experiences—including having to engage my own attorney (at my expense, of course) in order to obtain my payment.

The reader may also consider such a payment plan antitherapeutic in that it says to the patient from the outset: "I don't trust you." Were I to utilize such a payment plan in my work with patients, it would indeed by antitherapeutic. One cannot have a meaningful therapeutic relationship in which the distrust element is paramount. Parents being seen in custody evaluation are not patients. The program cannot be viewed as antithetical to their therapy, because there is no therapy. From the outset they are censoring and from the outset they are distrustful of the therapist. They fear that any disclosure may compromise their position in the litigation. They are often counseled by their attorneys to selectively reveal what will enhance their positions and selectively withhold that which will compromise their arguments. By no stretch of the imagination is this a therapeutic situation. Nothing, therefore, is to be lost therapeutically by such a program and much is to be gained in the proper conducting of the evaluation by utilizing it.

Other therapists I have spoken to have also expressed their frustration over the difficulties they have in collecting money from dissatisfied parents involved in custody evaluations. There is general agreement that following the submission of the report, the most common and effective way of expressing resentment is to withhold payment. Some therapists deal with this problem by informing the parent at the outset that the report will not be sent out until full payment is received. In my view there are two drawbacks to this plan. First, it is unethical—at least for the physician. A physician cannot refuse to send a report on a patient because of nonpayment. Although a custody evaluation is not the same as a medical diagnosis and although preservation of life and physical health is in no way involved in a custody evaluation, such differentiations are not applicable for the physician. For the physician, the parents are still basically patients, the differences between custody evaluations and treatment notwithstanding, and the evaluator is generally a psychiatrist, a medical specialist. The physician who withholds a report because of nonpayment is subject to reprimand by his or her medical society and might even be sued for malpractice. (It is probable that evaluators in other professions are not at such great risk if they send their reports contingent upon prior payment.)

The second drawback to this arrangement is that it can only work if the results are unknown to the parents at the time the report is ready to be sent out. As I will discuss later in this chapter, I routinely inform the parents of my findings and recommendations *prior to* preparing my final report. If the payer is the nonpreferred parent, then it will behoove that party *not* to pay and thereby hold up distribution of the report. In such situations nonpayment to the therapist would be reinforced by the therapist him- or herself. To circumvent this problem, the therapist would have to refrain strictly from divulging his or her findings prior to sending out the final report. As I will discuss in greater detail later in this chapter, such a practice is medically contraindicated because it increases unnecessarily parental anxieties and tensions. It is for these reasons that I strongly discourage this practice.

Documents from the Attorneys

The proviso regarding submission of documents by the attorneys states:

> **5.** Both attorneys are invited to send to me any material that they consider useful to me.

Of all the information provided the evaluator these documents are the least valuable. This is especially true of the affidavits that each side prepares in which the various complaints are listed about the other party. Even if the parent him- or herself has not exaggerated, the attorney can generally be relied upon to do so. Many attorneys do not seem to appreciate that the more adjectives one utilizes to modify a noun, the weaker the noun becomes. Some of the allegations appear "canned." One gets the feeling that if a mother, for example, tells her attorney that her husband beat her on one or two occasions, this appears in the affidavit as an extended paragraph in which are included "cruel and inhumane punishment," "mental cruelty," "sadism," and references to various other horrendous indignities. The therapist does well to take such hyperbole with a grain of salt and to recognize that they are typical legal maneuvers designed, in part, to improve one side's position over the other in the legal conflict as well as to impress the client with the lawyer's pugnacity. These documents, however, are not without some value, in that they may serve as points of departure for inquiries in the course of the evaluation. To refer to them directly in one's report would be a foolish mistake on the evaluator's part. They are hearsay and such quotations cannot but compromise the impartial's status.

Discussing the Findings with the Parents

The stipulation regarding my revealing my findings to the parents states:

> **6.** Upon completion of my evaluation—and prior to the preparation of my final report—I generally meet with both parents together and present them my findings and recommendations. This gives them the opportunity to correct any distortions they believe I may have and/or alter my opinion before it becomes finalized in my report. In addition, it saves the parents from the unnecessary and prolonged anxiety associated with wondering what my findings are. Following this session the final

report is prepared and then simultaneously sent to the court, the two attorneys, and the two parents. When a guardian ad litem has been appointed by the court, he or she will also be sent a copy of the final report.

In the early phases of my involving myself in custody evaluations the judges routinely indicated that I was to submit my reports directly to them and inform neither the attorneys nor the clients of my findings. I naively submitted. After all, if a *judge* tells you to do something, you do it! I realize now that this submission related to residua of my childhood view of judges as being both omniscient and omnipotent. However, I became increasingly guilty over the fact that it was often many months (usually between six and twelve) before the parents found out what my recommendation was. During this period they suffered further tension, which added unnecessarily to the heavy psychological burden they were already bearing. Other judges instructed me to send my report to them and to the two attorneys, but strictly advised the attorneys not to reveal my report's contents to the clients. This, of course, was very naive in that the attorneys invariably told the clients my basic conclusions, even though they might not have shown the report directly to them. Here I still was uncomfortable because I suspected that the clients were not being given accurate information about my findings. I believe that lawyers were not fully appreciative of many of the psychological subtleties and I, myself, could do a far better job of explaining the significance of my report and answering any questions they had about it. In addition, I felt that the nonpreferred parent had the right to discuss directly my findings with me, and there was a "cop out" quality to my not having a face-to-face discussion with that parent. Of course, it was the court that was dictating this removal from confrontation and it was the court that was allowing it only many months later, in the courtroom where the nonpreferred parent's attorney, rather than the parent him- or herself, was the confronting party.

In subsequent years I came upon the idea not only of telling the parents my findings but, in addition, giving them the chance to discuss them with me *prior* to the preparation of my final report. In this way they would be the first to learn what my recommendations were and would therefore be spared the extra burden of wondering about my findings over a significant period of time. In addition, they would have the opportunity to change my opinion prior to the submission of my final report. And this would certainly lessen the sense of impotence they felt under the aforementioned earlier plan.

The idea came to me while involved in a custody evaluation with

parents who were particularly anxious people and who were deteriorating significantly under the stresses of the divorce and custody litigation. My initial impulse was to ask the judge who was presiding over
the case for permission to implement this new plan. However, in accordance with what I had said earlier regarding not asking for permission
when you expect the potential permitter to turn you down unreasonably, I decided to go ahead and do just what I thought was best. I
would then take a "wait and see" attitude. At the completion of the
evaluation I told the parents my findings and recommendations and
provided them with the opportunity for feedback. I then sent my final
report to the judge, the two attorneys, and the two clients. During the
week following my mailing out these reports, I continually expected a
letter or telephone call from some irate person—the judge or one of the
attorneys. But nothing happened. In fact, over the next five years, nothing happened! I kept sending out my reports (in recent years I have
added the guardian ad litem to the list, for reasons already mentioned),
and no one objected.

A few years ago, however, three local judges did invite me to
lunch to discuss this practice with me. Their position was that I was
court appointed and that my report should only go to the court and no
one else. I asked them if there were any laws or statutes indicating that
I was *required* to do this. They replied that there were none, but it was
"legal tradition" that a court-appointed professional should submit his
or her report *only* to the court. When I explained to them that this tradition was causing patients unnecessary anguish and grief, one saw my
point and two did not. The two who remained unconvinced were so
steeped in what I believe to have been an illogical tradition and so
inflexible with regard to the capacity even to consider the possibility
that another method might have merit, that they could not see their
way clear to being receptive to any reasonable alternative. The third
recognized that my procedure might have merit. The other two insisted
that they would no longer refer clients to me if I maintained my stand. I
responded that my first obligation was to do what I considered to be
ethically in the best interests of my patients (the judges kept calling
them clients) and to refrain from any act that might be psychologically
injurious to them. Because I considered the unnecessary waiting to be
exactly in that category, I felt that I had no choice but to refuse their
request. I consistently used the word "request" with them in order to
get across the point that they had absolutely no power over me in this
particular area.

Here again we see an example of a situation in which we can contribute significantly to making the "rules" if we wish to; or we can
submit. I no longer maintain my childhood view of the omniscient and omnipotent judge. As the above vignette well demonstrates, judges are

neither. They are as human and fallible as the rest of us and their powers are very well defined and circumscribed. At the present time, many of the techniques used in custody evaluation are beyond their control. We in the mental health professions do well to keep it that way. There are few, if any, rules or statutes that require us to conduct ourselves in any particular way in the course of the evaluation. If we are in agreement among ourselves to do what we consider to be psycho-therapeutically indicated, the courts will have the choice of going along with our procedures or dispensing with our services entirely. I think there is every reason to believe that they will choose the former course. If we *all* refuse to serve as advocates, the courts will have no choice but to use us as impartials. If we insist upon telling our patients our conclusions (when *we* consider it in their best interests psychologically), and all of us follow this procedure, the courts will again have the choice of going along with this procedure or dispensing with our services. I have little doubt that they will choose to let us have it our way with regard to this issue.

There is a fringe benefit to the therapist in discussing the findings and recommendations with the parents prior to writing the final report—a benefit that I had not anticipated when I decided to introduce this procedure into my evaluation. Specifically, it helps the therapist avoid placing errors in the report, errors that crept in in spite of the evaluator's attempts to be meticulous. I have rarely found these to be major. However, minor errors are the ones the cross-examining attorneys will focus upon if they do not think they will be successful in refuting my major arguments. The therapist may have thought that a particular relative was a sister when, in fact, she was a sister-in-law. An age of a significant person may be incorrect or a time duration miscalculated. The year in which the evaluator states a particular event occurred may be off slightly. In the interview in which the findings and recommendations are presented the parents often correct these minor errors, the nonsupported party not realizing that he or she is contributing (admittedly in a very small way) to the strengthening of the document that heavily supports the other parent's position. At times, in the preparation of this presentation, I have not been clear myself regarding some of the small points. This interview provides me with a good opportunity to ask questions, the answers to which enable me to clarify these points.

From Report Time to Court Time

The procedures I follow after the submission of my report are outlined in the next stipulation:

7. Following the submission of my report, I strictly refrain from any further communication with either parent or any other party involved in the evaluation. However, I am willing to discuss any aspect of my report with *both* attorneys at the same time. And such communication may occur any time from the submission of my report to the end of the trial. This practice enables me to continue to provide input to the attorneys regarding what I consider to be in the children's best interests and this may be especially important during the time of litigation. However, in order to preserve my status as impartial, any information I provide either attorney is only done under circumstances in which the other is invited to participate.

In the course of the evaluation I want to give each parent full opportunity to communicate everything that is pertinent. I make it a point, as the evaluation nears the end, to ask each parent repeatedly, "Is there anything else you wish to tell me?" I explain that I do not want to conclude the evaluation with either parent leaving with the feeling that he or she was not given the opportunity to communicate any relevant point. And before concluding with the evaluation I will ask them both, in the presence of one another (I like a witness here), if they are satisfied that I have given them both full opportunity to present their positions. I remind them, as well, that following the session in which I present my findings and recommendations for their consideration, I will have *absolutely no* contact with either of them. Accordingly, it is extremely important that they tell me everything they consider pertinent prior to that time.

My reason for the total moratorium on direct communication with the parents following the submission of my report is that to do otherwise could significantly compromise the evaluative procedure. There are always afterthoughts. There are always new things happening. Allowing such communication will most often involve back and forth telephone calls, continual efforts to change my mind, new allegations, new refutations, etc. These could be endless. And these could place the examiner in the position of ever attaching addenda to the report. Such revisions cannot but lessen the evaluator's credibility.

One might argue that important events might occur subsequent to the submission of the report which might indeed change the evaluator's position. If this is the case, then one or both attorneys should make a recommendation to the court. If the judge then feels that further involvement by the impartial expert is warranted, especially with regard to a reconsideration of the conclusion, then it should be the court's position to request such an update of the evaluation.

For a number of years I experienced significant frustration with one aspect of the impartial expert's role. Although formally still referred to as an impartial by the court and two of the attorneys, I was treated very much as an advocate. I was viewed as a "friend" of the side whose position I supported, and as an "enemy" by the side whose position I did not support. Although basically treated as an advocate by both attorneys, I did not enjoy all the benefits and prerogatives of such status. Traditionally, the court allows the attorney whose position I do not support the widest flexibility in cross-examination. He is viewed as being at a disadvantage and is given every opportunity to convince the court that my position is not a valid one. Were I truly an advocate, however, during breaks I could advise the attorney whose position I supported. I could suggest questions he or she might ask me that would enable me to elaborate on points made by the adversary. The adversary, generally, confines me to yes-no questions and does not give me the opportunity to elaborate. Even the most skilled attorneys, in my experience, do not generally have the sophistication to pick up all the implications and nuances of each issue posed by their adversaries. And even their adversaries are often naive with regard to the psychological implications of the matters on which they are questioning me. And my experience has been that even the more sophisticated attorneys, whose position I supported, were not likely to meticulously follow through with every issue they might have. Accordingly, they did not give me the optimum opportunity to elaborate upon and refute issues focused upon by the cross-examining attorney who limited me to yes-no responses. It was during the lunch breaks, especially, that I felt particularly frustrated. It was not uncommon for me to eat alone during the lunch breaks while observing each attorney consulting with the clients at other tables. I felt strongly that I had valuable input that would be in the best interests of the children, but I could do nothing. "There must be a better way" I recently thought. The better way came to mind after a particularly frustrating experience.

It is often the case that after I submit my report, the nonpreferred side quickly brings in another psychiatrist or psychologist as an advocate. Without seeing the parent whose position I support, this individual sees nothing inappropriate about testifying that the party who is enlisting his or her aid is the *better* parent. As mentioned, these so-called "hired guns" are, in my opinion, a disgrace to our profession.

In a recent case the father, whose position I did not support, saw a psychiatrist who was willing to testify that he was the better parent, without having seen the mother. Prior to the trial, a copy of this psychiatrist's report was sent to me by the mother's attorney. I found significant weaknesses in it. However, I was not in a position to communicate these to the mother's attorney, but assumed that pertinent questions would be asked that would give me the opportunity to refute many of this psychiatrist's arguments. (This was not difficult to do, because they were based on blanket acceptance of the father's allegations without any input from the mother.) When the attorney whose position I supported examined me on the stand, he failed to ask many crucial questions which would have significantly weakened the father's psychiatrist's testimony. It was clear to me that he was not psychologically sophisticated enough to pick up many of the unreasonable statements made by the advocate psychiatrist. In the lunch break, especially, I was particularly frustrated. At one table, in the court dining room, the advocate psychiatrist was freely consulting with the father and his attorney. At another table, the mother and her attorney were consulting. And I sat alone at a third table, feeling totally impotent. I knew that I could be of help to the children if I could speak to the mother's attorney and recommend specific questions for him to ask me when the court adjourned after lunch. But I knew that if I were to do so I would compromise my position as an impartial to such a degree that further testimony on my part would be meaningless. I might even destroy completely the credibility of my full report. And I would risk marring my reputation as being truly impartial in custody litigations in general.

In the period between the end of the trial and the judge's handing down his final decision, I was concerned that the father would win custody and that my failure to have gotten across some important information to the mother's attorney would have contributed. Fortunately, the judge decided in the mother's favor. However, it was then that I decided that I would no longer place myself in such an impotent position. I decided that with regard to that particular case I should have invited both attorneys to speak to me following the submission of the advocate psychiatrist's report and to tell them together exactly what I thought of it—with regard to both its strengths and its weaknesses. In the course of that conversation, I would have suggested to the mother's attorney that he ask certain questions that would enable me to point out the particular weaknesses I considered there to be in the report. Of course, with this information, the father's attorney would have been in a better position to retort. This is perfectly acceptable to me, because he should have such opportunity. It was from these considerations that I added the present proviso under discussion. It enables me to provide such input without compromising my impartial status. It allows me to fulfill my primary obligation—which is to do everything possible to help the children. If one attorney (usually the one whose position I am not supporting) does not wish to involve him- or herself in such a conversation (either personally or via conference telephone call), I will still proceed with my conversation with the other because of the importance of my doing so in the children's best interests. The nonparticipating attorney cannot claim that I have departed from my role as impartial, because he or she has been invited to participate. The stipulation specifically states that: "Such communication may occur at any time from the submission of my report to the end of the trial." This allows me to implement this proviso at *any* time, including the *total course of the trial.*

Again, I asked no one permission to do this. I just added the stipulation to my provisions. I am again in the "wait-and-see" period. Thus far, nothing has happened. And again, I have made a change that I consider psychologically indicated. If any objections come forth, I am certainly willing to discuss them with the objecting party. If I remain unconvinced that a retraction of this position is warranted, I will continue to require it as a provision of my involvement. I believe strongly, however, that the practice is a reasonable one and that it serves better the needs of the children, who are often traumatized significantly during the course of a custody evaluation. Anything that serves to reduce such traumatic exposure cannot but be salutary. This provision is in the service of this goal.

Closing Clarifications in the Provisions Document

Following the formal listing of the seven major provision areas, I include a wind-up statement:

> My experience has been that conducting the evaluation in the manner described above provides me with the optimum conditions for providing the court with a thorough and objective recommendation.

This paragraph is really not essential. It was included in an attempt to "soften" the impact of the formal stipulations and to help impress upon the reader their importance.

The next section provides particulars regarding the steps to take to bring about my involvement:

> After receiving signed statements (bottom of next page) from both parents signifying agreement to the conditions of the evaluation, I will notify both attorneys. I suggest, then, that a court order be drawn up and submitted to the presiding judge. On receipt of the judge's signed invitation, I will invite the payer(s) to forward me the $1,500 advance payment. On receipt of such payment I will notify both parents that I am available to proceed with the evaluation as rapidly as is feasible. I generally cannot promise to meet a specific deadline because I cannot tell in advance how

many interviews will be required, nor can I know how flexible the parties will be regarding making themselves available for appointments I offer.

My experience has been that there is most often one parent who is most desirous of proceeding as rapidly as possible with the evaluation and that the other is in no particular hurry. More often than not, it is the noncustodial parent who is impatient. The custodial parent knows, quite well, that time is on his or her side. The longer the children remain with a parent, the greater the likelihood that they are going to express their desire to remain living with that parent—that parent's deficiencies notwithstanding. Change is anxiety provoking for most of us and even more so for children. Accordingly, one party is eager to accept the earliest appointments offered; whereas the other has a variety of involvements that ever seem to be taking priority or otherwise interfering with my rapidly conducting the evaluation. To agree to meeting a deadline under such circumstances may place the examiner in the position of pressuring or "running after" a parent, and this is not only demeaning and irritating, but may compromise the time available for the evaluation.

It is important for the examiner to appreciate that the noncooperating parent is not necessarily the more impaired. One has to ascertain the *reasons* for the stalling before one can truly determine whether it represents a parental asset or a liability. The staller may indeed be the preferable parent and the stalling is used as a maneuver to entrench and fortify this parent's position. On the other hand, the stalling parent may be the one who has the most to hide and therefore uses time as well as other methods to obstruct the evaluation.

Often the stalling is rationalized. In fact, I have not yet had the experience of a parent overtly admitting to stalling. One hears such comments as, "I waited until after the Thanksgiving and Christmas holidays, because the children are home a lot then." "I didn't think it was a good idea to begin the evaluation just before the summer. It's important that they have a lot of free time to themselves. So I waited until after school started. Now they're very busy, so I can't come here too frequently." "I'm sorry I lost that first document you sent me, doctor. It wasn't until a month later that I realized I'd lost it. Something must have happened in the mail when you sent the second one, because it took three weeks to get to me." "By the way, doctor, I can't come here on Tuesdays because I have my hairdresser's appointment then. And I play bridge on Wednesdays and Fridays. I know you understand." (I certainly did!)

It is for these reasons that I refuse to work under a deadline. Even if there is no stalling, I cannot know in advance the amount of information I will have to collect. To work under a deadline might place pressure on me that would interfere with my objectivity. If, however, a court date has already been set up that appears to be remote enough to allow for the proper conducting of an evaluation, I will advise the parties that I will make reasonable attempts to complete my evaluation before that date, but make absolutely no promises to do so. I am always aware that the longer the litigation, the greater the likelihood that all parties concerned will be psychologically traumatized. I therefore make every attempt to proceed rapidly. I view this as my contribution to the speedy completion of the evaluation. Unfortunately, these efforts are often frustrated by the aforementioned stalling maneuvers.

Upon receipt of *both* signed statements and the advance (security blanket) check, I call each of the parents and set up an initial interview. I make these calls myself, rather than have my secretary make them. My reason is that useful information can be obtained even at this early point. An example of such a situation was given above in the case of Mrs. Adams (pardon me, *Ms.* Adams). Even the simple attempt to find a mutually agreed upon time for the first appointment may present difficulties, so intense are the hostilities. In the course of these back and forth calls, I may present two or three options and also strongly encourage the parties to communicate with one another, rather than my continually serving as the intermediary messenger boy.

As will be discussed in the next chapter, I may serve temporarily as a messenger boy at this stage. However, when I see the parents I make it quite clear that from the first session on I am extremely reluctant to serve in this capacity and expect them to cooperate enough to make mutually agreed upon appointments. Usually they are willing to cooperate then, because each one wants "to put on a good show" and avoid doing anything that might irritate me.

Stipulations for My Serving as an Advocate

Although I firmly insist that I am extremely unreceptive to serving as an advocate, I do not close the door to that role entirely. To do so would be a disservice to many parents and children. However, before I am willing to serve in such capacity, I insist that certain steps be followed. These are spelled out in the provisions document:

> On occasion, I am willing to *consider* serving as an advocate. However, such participation will only be considered after evidence has been submitted to me that the nonparticipating side has been invited to participate and has refused and, in addition, the court has refused to order such involvement. If I do then suspect that the participating party's posi-

tion merits my consideration, I would be willing to interview that party with no promise beforehand that I will support his or her position. On occasion, I have, indeed, seen fit to support the participating party in this manner, because it was obvious to me that the children's needs would be best served by my advocacy and/or not to do so would have deprived them of sorely needed assistance. On other occasions, I have concluded that I could not serve with conviction as an advocate of the requesting party and so have refused further services to that client.

As can be seen, every reasonable attempt is made to get the un-receptive party into my office. As mentioned, there is little difference, most often, between the unreceptive and the receptive in terms of their degree of censorship. Accordingly, if I can get his or her "body" in my office, I feel confident that I can usually get meaningful information.

Actually, a court order requiring that an individual "submit" (a term used by the court, not by me) to a custody evaluation cannot be readily enforced. It is not likely that the judge will put a person in jail for refusing to involve him- or herself. And I have not yet seen anyone fined for refusing. Basically, the court is impotent to require such evaluations of nonincarcerated people. The motivation to cooperate after a court order comes from the realization that not to do so might compromise one's position. And refusing to cooperate implies that one has something to hide. In order not to convey such a notion to the judge, the unreceptive party may, often with the advice of his or her attorney, "cooperate." Although the parent may initially do so with the resolve that he or she will just "go through the motions," my experience has been that the unreceptive party soon becomes deeply involved, no less so than the receptive. There is something about a battle that produces a crescendo of fervor. If one is going to fight at all, one might as well fight to win. Seriously ill people, however, may still refuse—not appreciating the significance of their refusal and how it may compromise their position. This too is information for the evaluator.

If the unreceptive party (and/or his or her attorney) refuses involvement and the judge refuses to order such involvement, I will consider evaluating the receptive party. However, before doing so, I must have written confirmation that the aforementioned steps have been taken. It is extremely important that such confirmation be written so that the examiner has verification in court that every reasonable attempt has been made to serve first as an impartial. This is a protection from the demeaning cross-examination, already described, to which the advocate exposes him- or herself if reasonable attempts have not been made to serve as an impartial. Such verification usually comes in the form of a letter from the attorney of the receptive parent in which there is an itemization of the steps taken and copies of pertinent communications. This usually includes a letter to the adversary requesting involvement of his or her client, a letter of rejection, and a statement that the judge has refused to sign the court order requiring participation by the unreceptive parent.

Upon receipt of this information, I discuss the matter with the referring attorney. Prior to this time I usually have very little information about the family. I strictly refrain from gathering such information because of the risk that it might compromise my position as an impartial. If one attorney learns that I have had lengthy conversations with his or her adversary, he or she would have a justifiable criticism and could raise the question as to whether I was acting in a professionally competent manner regarding true impartiality. Now that there is no risk of such an occurrence, I am freer to talk at length with the attorney of the parent who is eliciting my services as an advocate.

If, on the basis of the information so gained, I suspect that I might be able to support the parent's position, I inform the attorney that I am willing to make an appointment and see the parent about one to three times. I cannot be more specific because I do not know what will be involved. It may be that I can come to a decision regarding my advocacy in only one session; it may take more. During this initial discussion with the parent, I come to some conclusion regarding whether or not I can support the parent's position with conviction. If I can, then I proceed with the more intensive evaluation with the parent and the children (with the drawback, however, of not seeing the other parent). If I cannot, I inform the parent of this decision and the only thing that has been lost has been the time of one to three sessions and the expense of such interview(s).

Upon the completion of such an evaluation, advocates must be sure to outline the steps they have taken to serve as impartials, and they do well to place copies of the aforementioned letters in the report as addenda. They do well to state that no promises were made beforehand, either to the parent or the attorney, that advocacy will be extended. They do well, then, to make a statement that in spite of the compromises attendant to not having access to direct information from the other party, they still consider the recommendations to be valid. Under such circumstances, however, it is extremely important for evaluators to have very powerful arguments and very strong presumptive evidence.

CONCLUDING COMMENTS

I recognize that some readers may consider these provisos somewhat rigid and restrictive. My response is that this was not the way I did things in earlier years. This list of stipulations grew over the years as more and more experiences (some unfortunate, and some even bitter) convinced me that they were vital if I were to provide the most meaningful kind of evaluation. I certainly do not take such a hard-nosed approach with my patients. To do so would be antitherapeutic. Although this more restrictive approach certainly has antitherapeutic elements, it is, I believe, ultimately therapeutic in that it provides the structure within which I am in the best position to determine what would be in the best interests of the children.

3

 The Initial Interview

Usually I require the parents to be present together for the initial interview. In fact, I consider it injudicious to start the evaluation with one party alone and subsequently interview the second in that I want to establish from the outset the notion of impartiality and the idea that both parties are going to be treated equally and fairly. The person who is seen first might be viewed, by the other party, as being the preferred one. I generally do not have the children come for this first interview because they may prove to be a distraction. This is in contrast to my usual procedure in therapy in which I set up a two-hour evaluative session, during which I see the parents and the child in varying combinations as warranted. In the therapeutic evaluation, I generally do not view the children's so-called interferences as distractions from the work at hand. These almost invariably enable me to observe interactions which are useful. In the custody evaluation, however, the amount of "administrative work" that has to be done is significant. It may take an hour, and even more, of the two-hour initial interview. The children here may very well be a distraction, especially if they are young.

PRELIMINARY COMMENTS TO THE PARENTS

I usually begin by expressing to the parents my full appreciation of how difficult this evaluation will be for them and emphasizing that I will do my utmost to make it as painless as possible. Similarly, I express my appreciation that the evaluation may be especially difficult for the children but, again, I will try to be as sympathetic and understanding as I can. Although these introductory comments are not likely to lessen significantly the psychological toll of the evaluation, they may play a role in this regard. Knowing that I am sympathetic to their plight and empathic with the painful feelings they are suffering at this point can be helpful in reducing (admittedly to a small degree) their pains and frustrations. Such comments also have the fringe benefit of our starting off on the "right foot" with the parents and contribute to their forming a good relationship with me—the circumstances of their involvement with me notwithstanding.

In my training I was taught that the ideal way to begin a psychiatric interview was to use the open-ended approach. Specifically, the therapist was advised to limit him- or herself at the outset to an introductory comment that was nonspecific, yet catalytic and facilitative of comments to be made by the patient. Traditional openings included: "So what brings you to the hospital?" "Let me hear what the trouble is." and "So tell me what's on your mind." Although questions such as these are, without doubt, the least contaminated by the specifics provided by the examiner, they are not without their drawbacks. Specifically, they are posed at the most inpropitious time. The patient comes to the initial interview extremely anxious and especially fearful that the therapist will be alienated by what he or she hears. This is particularly anxiety provoking because the patient is so dependent (already) on the therapist for help in the alleviation of the presenting difficulties. In fact, these questions are the most anxiety provoking possible in a situation where the patient is already quite tense. The likelihood, then, of receiving meaningful responses is significantly reduced. The drawbacks of the questions, therefore, far outweigh their advantages at this point. I much prefer to ask a series of simple, factual questions—questions that I know the patient can readily answer—in the initial phase of the interview. These may only take a few minutes, but they can be extremely anxiety alleviating. With each "right answer" the patient feels more comfortable and five or ten minutes later, after these basic data have been obtained, little if anything has been contaminated, but a "different" patient is now answering the open-ended questions. With a decompression of the anxiety, there is now a far greater likelihood that meaningful answers will be obtained.

Recognizing that parents coming for a custody evaluation, although not patients, are likely to be extremely anxious, I will at this early point ask basic data questions for my records. From each parent I get his or her name, address, telephone number, date of birth, occupation, and business telephone number. I then get the names of the attorneys, their addresses, and telephone numbers. I then list the name, age, birth date, school, and grade of each child. I find out whether anyone else is living in the household, especially someone whom I might interview. Most often I will be interviewing other household members, especially full-time housekeepers. (As will be discussed subsequently, the full-time housekeeper can be an extremely valuable source of information and is often an untapped source of information in custody evaluations as well as in child psychiatric evaluations in general.) I then will ask for the date of the marriage, the date of separation, and the date of divorce (if it has already taken place). I ask whether this is the first marriage or if there have been other marriages. If so, I will list the dates of these as well. I then ask if either party is involved significantly with another person, especially if there is someone with whom either parent is living or whom either is planning to marry. These individuals, as well, are important persons to interview.

At this point I tell the parents that the best thing they can do is to try to decide the custodial arrangements between themselves and avoid the psychologically draining and expensive evaluation they are about to embark upon. I try to impress upon them that they know their children better than anyone else, that their children are theirs, and that their fate rests now in their hands. I try to get them to appreciate that any reasonable arrangement for their disposition will generally be approved by their attorneys and the court. I try to impress upon them, as well, how psychologically detrimental custody litigation can be—to the children as well as to the parents. I advise them that if they cannot agree, they are placing the decision in the hands of the judge—a person who must be a stranger or else he or she would be disqualified from involvement in their case. I advise them that this is risky business and that the judges are not famous for the judiciousness of their custody decisions. I remind them that I, too, am not infallible and that there is no recommendation which I have ever made that would be uniformly agreed to by all people. I remind them, what they know already, that my opinion will carry heavy weight in the court and that their involving themselves with me is also risky business.

Unfortunately, by the time parents reach me, they are so deeply embroiled in the litigious process that they are just about incapable of hearing my warning. Accordingly, I have not yet had the experience of parents saying that they would like to interrupt proceedings at that point in order to give further consideration to what I have said. Perhaps such a time will come, but I am not counting the days. In addition, I put in an advance plug for their both taking seriously my final recommendation. I tell them that my experience has been that the nonpreferred party and his or her attorney often reflexly talk about bringing in another psychiatrist or think of other ways to refute my recommendations. I try to explain to them that they have every right to do so and that I consider it part of my obligation to appear in court in order to defend my position. However, I also recommend that they consider the alternative course, namely, considering the possibility that my recommendation might be judicious and that they might do themselves and the children a great service by discontinuing the custody litigation at that point. I am pleased to say that there have been a number of parents who have done just that at the time of the completion of my evaluation. Sometimes even the attorney of the nonsupported parent convinced that parent of the judiciousness of my recommendation.

Following their agreement on the point that they have absolutely no intention of modifying their positions regarding custody, I then impress upon the parents that I have no preconceived notion as to who would be the better parent for their child or children. I emphasize that this will not be an evaluation in which I am going to conclude that one party is the "good" parent and the other is the "bad" one. Rather, the usual situation is one in which both parents are relatively good, capable, and deeply involved and the question is who would be the *better* parent for custody of the children, that is, who has fewer liabilities and greater assets regarding the assumption of the role of custodian.

REVIEW OF THE PROVISOS

Although the provisos have been reviewed by the attorneys and signed by the parents, I have found it useful to review them in detail during the initial interview. This serves to clarify in detail all the provisions, clear up any misconceptions the parents may have (not uncommon, in spite of my attempts to make them crystal clear), as well as to ensure that there will be no problems in their implementation (the parents' signatures notwithstanding).

The Parties to be Interviewed

At this point I make a list of all the parties to be interviewed and discuss problems that may arise regarding exactly who and who will not be involved in the evaluation. I inform the parents that the next sessions will involve my seeing each of them individually. I try to help them appreciate that the best thing they can do for their children is to be open and honest with me regarding the inquiry. I try to impress upon them that to the degree that they withhold information from me, to that degree they compromise my ability to make a judicious decision. If, as they usually claim, they really have their children's best interests at heart, they will give me *all* the information I need to help them in this regard. It is a rare parent who follows this advice. Each generally believes that he or she is the better parent and is not going to really leave such an important decision to me, a stranger. Often the only reason they are talking to me is that the court requires them to. Accordingly, the censoring is usually great and the advice unheeded—professions of agreement and promises of compliance notwithstanding. But I make the statement anyway in the hope that some of it might be heard.

I then inform them that I plan to conduct the evaluation in such a way that when it is completed neither party should be able to justifiably say: "He never gave me a chance to tell him that." I tell them that I will be starting each interview with an open question in which I invite the parent to tell me anything that he or she feels is important for me to know. As will be discussed in detail in the next chapter, the structured questions come only after each parent has exhausted all possible spontaneous comments and statements. The word *exhausted* is applicable here because the amount of information that each party has to give me is often extensive. However, I do not wish to go on endlessly with people who are very verbose and might ramble on for weeks with seemingly endless repetition.

I tell the parents also that I will want to have interviews with each of the children. The nature of my contacts with them will vary with their ages. It is not very likely that I am going to be doing very much individual interviewing with a very young child of one or two, although I will see such a child along with the parents and make observations. I will involve older children (from about 3 and up) in varying depths of psychiatric evaluation, depending upon their ages and degrees of cooperation. Generally, I see children above the age of 4 or 5 two to three times. I inform the parents also that I will want a family interview as well as one or more interviews with the two of them together, after I have completed my individual sessions with each of them. During the individual interviews with the parents I generally get different opinions regarding many issues, and the joint experience with them after my individual sessions helps me clarify to some degree (but never completely) the conflicting renditions.

At times I will want to see other individuals. I may want to interview a housekeeper who has been or will be significantly involved in the care of the children. I recognize that the parent with whom the housekeeper lives, and even the other parent, may be very reluctant to permit such an interview—and the housekeeper herself generally is not too happy about it either. She has to be told that the information that she will be giving me will have to be used at my discretion and that I cannot promise her that some of it may not get back to the mother and father. It is important to provide her with this information. It is only ethical to do so because of the possibility (hopefully small) that she may be compromising her relationship with her employer(s). A housekeeper, by the way, can be a very valuable source of information for the child therapist in general and it is rare that we have an opportunity to avail ourselves of the information that she can provide. She hears the family's squabbles. Often she lives for little but learning about what's going on in the family, and her main topic of conversation with other housekeepers may concern what is happening in their employers' households. On those occasions when I have had the opportunity to interview housekeepers, and when they have been forthright with me at the encouragement of the parents, I have learned many valuable things about the family. Most often housekeepers are quite timid when speaking with the therapist. They may have never been in a therapist's office and may be awed and frightened. On occasion, having one (or even both) employers present at the beginning can help make the housekeeper more comfortable; however, their presence may make her tighten up even more. Because of the extreme anxiety many housekeepers suffer during such interviews, I generally confine myself to one interview.

If there are grandparents who are going to be playing a significant role in the lives of the children, I will request an interview with them, both singly and together. Plans may include their taking care of the children during the day while the custodial parent works. Sometimes a custodial parent may be moving back into the home of his or her parents. There may be some reluctance on the grandparents' part to being interviewed, but the therapist should advise them that their failure to participate may weaken the position of the parent who wishes to enlist their aid in caring for the children. (Again, this is an unfortunate way of getting someone to agree to a psychiatric interview, but it is common and often necessary in custody evaluations.)

There are times when one, or possibly even both, of the parents may be involved with another person and this person may be a potential marriage partner or someone with whom the children will be living. For example, a wife may have met another man with whom she plans to live, and may hope to have the children live with her. She may claim that this will be a good environment for the children because they will have a new relationship with another male. The therapist should not get involved in the moral question of whether or not these people plan to get married. Rather, he or she should simply try to decide whether this man will provide a good environment for the children and be a good surrogate father to help the children compensate for the absence of their natural father from the home. Accordingly, this man should be invited *by the mother* to participate in the evaluation. (I do not invite such "third parties" myself because I consider it to be intrusive and bordering on the unethical.) If he hesitates to come, the wife should be informed that my ability to conduct the evaluation is being compromised and her position is being weakened. In fact, this is the general response I have to those who do not wish to cooperate in the evaluation. Although such "motivation-enhancing" threats may make a mockery of the psychiatric interview, the therapist is often reduced to having to make them in custody evaluations.

I will then ask the parents to suggest any other parties who might be a source of information for me. I inform them that I am receptive to such suggestions and will give serious consideration to objections on the part of the nonrecommending parent. I advise them, at the same time, that I reserve the right to make the final decision regarding whether or not such a person will be *invited* to participate. I emphasize the word invited because I do not have the power to force anyone to participate in the evaluation. I will not give one party veto power over the other regarding extending such an invitation. I will, however, listen with receptivity to any such objections. Generally, I do not interview a parade of friends and relatives whom each side can collect for the purposes of the evaluation. These testimonials elicited from selected friends and relatives generally balance one another out, are likely to be highly biased and exaggerated, and therefore of little value. At this point, I make a list of all the parties to be interviewed. This includes not only the family members, but others who have been recommended and I have agreed warrant an invitation.

Confidentiality

I review this stipulation (sometimes I actually read it) to parents. I emphasize the point that I will not necessarily reveal such information but that I must *reserve the right to do so.* I impress upon them, again, the importance of their being honest with me in spite of this provision. I tell them, as well, that I appreciate that what I reveal may weaken one's position in court; but this may be the price they may have to pay for the benefit of an impartial and objective evaluation. I try to get across the notion that there must be an open pool of information available to me and that I must have the freedom to communicate with all

the concerned parties and not be hampered by a confidentiality obligation. I try to impress upon them that this is only possible if my hands
are not tied by the restriction of being unable to reveal any information. I fully recognize that this provision has resulted in some (if not
many) parents' withholding important information. I appreciate, as
well, that many have probably been briefed by their attorneys regarding what to reveal and what not to reveal. I recognize that without this
provision more information might be coming my way. However, without
it I would be significantly restricted regarding my flexibility. Accordingly, I believe its advantages outweight its disadvantages for the purposes of a custody evaluation.

The Signing of the Release Forms

At this point I list the possible sources of information from other professionals. This includes therapists and counselors, both past and
present. However, I generally try to avoid contacting therapists who
are presently treating either of the parents. It can often compromise
such treatment if the therapist is asked to give information that may be
detrimental to his or her patient. However, on a few occasions, in very
difficult cases, I have contacted such therapists. I have no such reservations with regard to past therapists. Whether one communicates
with a past or present therapist, it is important that the report be in
writing. Folksy telephone conversations have no place in custody evaluations. One wants to have a written report because the material contained therein may become an issue in the courtroom litigation.
Clearly, a written statement leaves little to be questioned regarding
whether or not a particular statement was made. If the therapy involved joint counseling permission from both parents must be submitted. A sample letter is shown in Figure 1. This is accompanied by a
standard printed medical release form, which, of course, is signed by
the parent.
   The signing of such releases may be a sticky point with some
parents. I recall one incident, prior to the time that I submitted the proposals to the parents in written form, that a mother refused to sign a
release for my requesting information from a psychiatric hospital
where her husband claimed she had been a patient. She claimed that I
had never mentioned on the telephone mental health professionals as a
source of information. I knew with certainty that I had and I knew, in
addition, that I had told her attorney this as well. In the ensuing discussion her husband claimed that she was well known to be a "pathological liar" and that I was now observing this firsthand. After a few
more go arounds I informed the mother that I was removing myself

RICHARD A. GARDNER, M. D.
155 COUNTY ROAD
CRESSKILL, N. J. 07626
TELEPHONE 201 - 567-8989

November 10, 1981

Alan Goldenberg, M.D.
1204 Monroe Ave.
Englewood, N.J. 07631

Re: Walton vs. Walton

Dear Dr. Goldenberg:

Judge Jerome Anderson of the Superior Court of New Jersey, Chancery Division, Bergen County, has invited me to serve as court-appointed impartial psychiatrist to render the court my recommendations regarding the custody of Arthur and Michael Walton. Their parents, Ronald and Marcia Walton, are presently litigating for their custody.

Mrs. Marcia Walton informs me that she saw you in psychotherapy from January,1979 to August, 1980. I would be most appreciative if you would send me a report of your findings. I am particularly interested in any comments you have regarding her maternal capacity. For the purposes of the litigation it is important that this information be provided in written form rather than verbally. Enclosed please find a signed release granting you permission to provide me with this information. In order not to slow this matter unnecessarily, I would be most appreciative if you would send me your report as soon as possible.

Sincerely,

Richard A. Gardner

Richard A. Gardner, M.D.

RAG/lg
encl.

Figure 1

from the case. I told her that I was interrupting the interview at that point and planned to write a letter to the judge, with copies to both attorneys, informing them that she had reneged on her agreement to sign any and all (that good old legal term again) releases for pertinent psychiatric information. This was not an idle threat. I arose from my chair as I said it and had every intention of following through. The mother signed.

The evaluator does well to insist that the issue of signed releases be fully clarified before proceeding. On occasion, a parent will hesitate and state that he or she wishes to think about the matter and discuss it with his or her attorney before signing. If this occurs I will point out that the parent has already agreed to sign such a release. However, if the parent wishes to interrupt the evaluation *at that point* I will be willing to do so, pending the decision as to whether or not the form will be signed. However, I make it clear that the interview will be interrupted and that there will be absolutely no further involvement on my part until the release is signed. It is a mistake for the therapist to continue the evaluation (even that particular interview) while such a matter is pending. It becomes ever more difficult to remove oneself as the evaluation proceeds. Evaluators who "run after" parents for a release not only compromise the evaluation per se, in that they may be deprived of important information, but compromise the respect the patients will have for them as well as their own dignity.

As mentioned, I fully recognize that such information is, in the legal sense, hearsay. However, such reports can provide me with useful points of departure for my inquiries. The issues raised in them may not have arisen in the course of the evaluation, and it is in this way that they can be most useful. In addition, they will often lend support and/or credibility to allegations made by one party and refuted by the other. It puts the examiner in a better position to make comments in the report such as: "Although I cannot be completely certain that Mr. Smith is telling the truth with regard to his allegation that his wife abuses alcohol, the weight of the evidence certainly supports his contention. For example, Dr. X, in his report dated . . . . ''

The Financial Arrangements

I then review in detail the payment procedure. Even though clearly spelled out in the written document, misinterpretations and misunderstandings often remain. I explain to both that the bank deposit was placed in an account, in my name, within a day or so of its receipt by me. I tell them that this money, with accrued interest, will be returned after a decision has been made regarding custody and after I receive a letter from an attorney stating that the matter has been settled. At that time, the money will be withdrawn and the check with accumulated interest will be sent to the payer. In addition, I will send a photostatic copy of the bank book. I tell the parents that such a deposit serves two purposes: 1) It protects me from a disappointed payer expressing his or her hostility by not paying my bill. 2) It serves as reassurance to the nonpayer that I will not be a "hired gun" and that my objectivity will not be compromised by the fear that if I come out on the side of the non-payer that the payer will not fulfill his or her financial obligation to me. Whereas in my practice with patients I bill at the end of each month, in custody cases I bill weekly. In this way if there is any problem, there is less of a loss for me. As the reader might suspect, this policy comes from some unfortunate experiences in this regard. There is obviously a distrust element here that would compromise a treatment relationship. However, we are not dealing here with psychotherapy, and the draw-backs of such distrust are more than outweighed by the freedom from contamination that the examiner can enjoy when such a payment pro-gram is a proviso of his or her involvement.

If the evaluator does subscribe to a fee collection program (even if not identical to the one that I use), he or she may learn something about the payer's personality. Specifically, if the payer reneges on the financial obligations, even though these have been clearly spelled out by the examiner at the outset, it may reflect generally upon the parent's honesty and sense of commitment. Even after the aforemen-tioned presentation of the fee program, both in the written document and in the first interview, a parent may feign ignorance of the "rules" of payment. Although one could not use this specific area of "ignor-ance" or attempt to renege as a strong argument against giving cus-tody, it should lead the examiner into other areas of unfulfillment of obligation. Often the other spouse will be happy to provide information in this area that can serve as a point of departure for inquiry. In addi-tion, one might consider such failure to reflect an attempt (either con-scious or unconscious) to lose in the custody evaluation, in spite of professions to the contrary. The parents are generally quite interested in creating a good impression with the examiner up to the point where the final recommendation is revealed. The payer who is strongly moti-vated for gaining custody is generally wise enough to know that reneging on the payment is going to irritate the evaluator and recog-nizes that this may compromise his or her position.

Material from the Attorneys

I advise each parent to ask his or her attorney to send me any material that the lawyer suspects might be of use to me. This includes the various affidavits, dispositions, and other documents pertinent to the separation, divorce, and custody litigation. I will tell the parents that it is unwise for the attorneys to be in touch with me directly and that ideally I should have absolutely no direct contact at all with either of the attorneys other than during my appearance in court, if that is desired. It is rare for an attorney to contact me during the course of the evaluation. Those who have, have generally done so with the intent to press their client's position and otherwise "tip the scales." In such cases I have informed the lawyer that this kind of intervention is inappropriate and that I will make no mention of it in my report if it is discontinued. This statement usually suffices to "help him or her remember" not to call me again. At other times I have advised the caller to place his or her comments in a letter, with a copy sent to the other attorney. This, too, serves to discourage such calls.

As mentioned, the material in such affidavits must not be taken too seriously. It is invariably exaggerated and filled with hyperbole. (Many lawyers seem to work on the principle that the more adjectives there are in a sentence the stronger it becomes; writers and psychologists know better.) Furthermore, the information contained in such documents will be considered hearsay by the court if the therapist presents it. Accordingly, the evaluator compromises his or her credibility by doing so. The impartial expert does best, for both legal and psychiatric reasons, to confine the testimony to his or her observations.

Sometimes I do not receive the pertinent affidavits, pleadings, etc. On occasion this is due to laxity on the part of the attorney (a not uncommon problem in divorce litigation, in this examiner's experience). On other occasions the parent does not remind the attorney. A good attorney, one who is "on top of things," will send this material automatically, especially because the request has already been made in the provisos for my involvement which the client has already discussed with him or her. If, after the initial session, the attorney still has not sent the material, the client is invited by me to remind him or her. I do not, however, pursue the matter further. I consider two reminders enough in most situations. It is rare that I will "bug" a patient for this material. The failure to provide it is a parental deficiency, although generally not a strong one in my deliberations.

The Discussion of the Final Recommendation

The parents are generally pleased to learn that I will not write my final report without discussing with them first my recommendation and my reasons for making it. They usually welcome the opportunity to discuss it with me, correct any errors I may have, and then tend to refute what they consider to be distortions or misguided conclusions. Although I have not yet had the experience of their completely reversing my recommendation by that time, minor alterations in the recommendation have resulted from such discussions. It provides them with a sense of power in a situation in which they basically feel impotent. It is anxiety alleviating in that it shortens the period during which they are kept wondering what my final recommendation will be. Although the judge and the attorneys aren't happy with this step in my procedure, I have deep conviction for its benefits. The evaluator who allows him- or herself to be talked into dispensing with it (with some legal rationalization for doing so) will be doing the parents a terrible disservice in that he or she will be contributing to the psychopathological reactions that are so frequently (if not inevitably) caused by protracted custody litigation.

I take this opportunity to once again impress upon the parents the importance of their avoiding courtroom litigation. I inform them that at the time of my presentation of my final recommendation to them, I will once again advise them to come to some agreement on their own, rather than submit the decision to the judge and give him or her the power to make it.

I also try to impress upon the parents that what will be best for the child will ultimately be best for them as well. The child who is correctly placed will be a happier child, a less scared child, and will therefore be a greater source of pleasure to both parents. As Despert (1953) says: "In the long run the parent who follows a wise course (regarding custody) is rewarded by a better relationship with the child and greater peace with himself." This advice also usually falls on deaf ears—so sure is each of the parents that he or she really knows best. A woman may hate her husband so much that she cannot imagine that her children may do better living with such a wretch. And similarly, the enraged man may not be able to conceive of the possibility that his wife can make an adequate mother for his children.

I also inform them that following this final interview, I will have absolutely no further contact with them (unless, of course, I see them in court). I impress upon them that during the course of the evaluation I will give each every opportunity to provide me with all information each considers appropriate. However, I cannot go on endlessly hearing the various allegations and counter-allegations. It would compromise the evaluation if I were to communicate with either party after its completion. I advise them, however, that if subsequent events warrant my considering a revision of my recommendation, they must work through their lawyers to effect through the judge my further involvement.

Although I suggest to the parents that they be receptive to my final recommendation and consider going along with it, rather than resort to courtroom litigation to resolve their conflict, I impress upon them, as well, that they have every right to bring me to court to be cross-examined. I impress upon them that I consider it my obligation to them to make such appearances and that this is especially the case because I, like all human beings, am fallible.

I then ask the parents if they have any questions about anything that has transpired thus far. Of course, in the course of my presentation they may have asked questions but this final invitation is made to ensure that they are completely clear about the format. Such discussion also has the fringe benefit of reducing anxieties about the evaluation. The more information one has about a feared situation, the less tense one is likely to be. Part of the fear that we have of the unknown relates to our ignorance.

INITIATION OF THE INFORMATION-GATHERING PROCESS

The above discussion of the basic procedure of the evaluation generally takes about 45 minutes to an hour. I then have about an hour or more to devote to a joint interview for data collection. I usually begin by asking the parents about the reasons for the separation. I will generally throw the question out without directing my attention to either parent. At times, the more assertive and/or talkative one will respond very quickly, before the other parent has had a chance to. After one parent has given his or her reasons, I will then ask the other to comment on what has been said. Often there is even disagreement here about what the major problems were. Then I ask the other parent to present what he or she believes to have been the marital difficulties, whether or not they coincide with the first presenter's rendition. It is extremely important for the evaluator not to assume automatically that either parent's rendition is the more likely one. There are exceptions, however, in cases such as alcoholism. Alcoholics typically deny the extent of their drinking (even to themselves) and are well known for their capacity to rationalize. But even here, one does well not to divulge which parent's rendition seems more credible. In fact, throughout the course of the evaluation, the examiner must be extremely careful not to reveal "which way the wind is blowing" or which party's rendition appears more credible. Such a revelation can seriously compromise the evaluation. It will reduce the freedom with which the nonpreferred party will reveal him- or herself. Both parties could justifiably complain that all subsequent hours were unnecessary, and that an added unnecessary expense was incurred. One could argue that further inquiry was still necessary in order to support or refute one's initial impression, but this may not be particularly convincing. I do not go into great detail at this point regarding the various areas of contention in the marital conflict. I merely want to learn about the major issues. And I do not necessarily explore a point to the depth where I am firmly convinced which of the two opinions is more likely to be valid. It is in the subsequent interviews that I attempt to do this (to the degree possible in the course of a few interviews).

I then inquire about each parent's reasons for demanding custody. This question follows the question about the marital conflicts because the reasons for demanding custody are often based on the complaints about the other spouse. Accordingly, one's knowledge of the marital difficulties helps the examiner understand better the reasons for demanding custody. Again, I do not ask each parent to comment in depth on the other's allegations and do not in any way reveal any inkling I may have regarding which parent's complaints are more likely to be valid. Again, I want to deal with the main issues here, not with all the details. It is in the subsequent interviews that I will be getting such information.

I have often found it to be the case that the parent whose position I ultimately do not support has far weaker criticisms against the other parent than the parent whose position I do support. For example, in one case, a mother was strongly critical of her husband for his limited involvement in the home with her and the children throughout the course of their married life. On the average, he would return home at 11:30–12:00 P.M. and even on weekends he would often be away from the home in order to attend to his business. The children had, at a very early age, given up on their father as a source of support, guidance, etc. The father's primary complaint about the mother was that she was "overprotective." When going into this in greater detail I concluded that she was in no way overprotective and that what her husband was calling overprotective were merely the usual manifestations of deep parental involvement. There was no evidence that the mother was trying to infantilize the children, indulge them, or otherwise pamper them.

In another case, the mother was a chronic alcoholic, and the three children had spent many years trying to find hidden bottles of alcohol that their mother concealed in various places in the home. The mother would drink until 4:00 or 5:00 in the morning and then sleep throughout the day. When the children came home from school she was still sleeping. The mother's primary complaints about the father were that he did not take the children to enough museums, plays, and other cultural activities. The father was a very involved parent and preferred to take his children to movies, rodeos, circuses, and sporting events. The mother, herself, was certainly not culturally sophisticated, and the father's somewhat reduced interest in such activities could not be considered a deficiency—considering all the recreational and enriching activities he did engage in with the children.

The interview closes with my setting up an appointment for each of the parents. I inform them that I will see the children subsequently, after I have had a chance to know each of them better. With regard to setting up further joint interviews, I inform them that I will not serve as a messenger boy between the two. Although it may have been somewhat necessary for me prior to the initial inteview, in order to make the first appointment, I will henceforth refuse to play such a role. Accordingly, for appointments that may not have been set up when both have been together, I will give A two possible appointments, and inform A that I must get an answer from either A or B within 24 hours regarding which one is acceptable. If I do not hear from anyone within that period I will hold neither appointment open. If I am called and told that neither is acceptable, then I will give the caller two more appointment possibilities, and so on. The therapist who allows him- or herself to serve as messenger is being used as a weapon. This is not only demeaning and a waste of time, but compromises the examiner's position in the eyes of the parents. Of course, the reader may have another procedure. The important thing is to have a plan that protects oneself from being brought into the marital conflict as a weapon.

4

 Interviews with the
Parents

In this chapter I will detail the techniques I use to evaluate each parent's *parental* capacity. The presentation is lengthy, and it would be unrealistic to expect any examiner to utilize every technique or pose every question in the evaluation of any given parent. I myself have certainly not done so. I have, however, used all the questions and methods presented here at one time or another. My purpose here is to present as much information as possible in the hope that the examiner will find much here that may prove useful in the parental capacity assessment.

RECORD KEEPING

At the outset, I have found it useful to prepare a separate question sheet for each member of the family. These sheets are labeled: questions for father, questions for mother, questions for Bob, questions for Jane, etc. When interviewing mother, for example, I place next to the sheet of paper on which I am taking down information about her, the question sheets for father and the children. Then, when the mother makes an allegation about any of the other parties, I will make an entry on the appropriate question sheet to use as a reference in a subsequent interview. This makes the data collection process most efficient and I avoid losing time searching for particular issues to focus upon—issues related to things one party told me about another in a previous interview. It also has the fringe benefit of making my report preparation more efficient and comprehensive.

For example, during the initial interview, a father may describe a significant alcoholic problem of the mother's. I make a short note on his general data collection sheet (not his question sheet): "Mother has a drinking problem?" Rather than making any further notes on the father's general data collection sheet, I will note on the mother's question sheet the details of the father's allegations. Specifically, I will record his allegations about the times of the day when the mother drinks, the particular kinds of alcohol she consumes, and the amounts. I will ask him about the specific effects of the alcohol on her behavior and any other questions that may help me learn about the true extent of the difficulties. In addition, I will list similar questions on the sheets for the children. If the father has also reported that the mother has encouraged a teenage daughter to join her in her drinking, I will make a note of that on the daughter's question sheet as well. I then leave ample space below the entries for responses by each party during subsequent sessions. The examiner does well not to be too credulous regarding what any party says about the other. When doing custody evaluations, one quickly comes to appreciate how differently two individuals can interpret the same event. One's anticipations and desires play an important role in how one is going to interpret the meaning of an event. This point is well demonstrated by an old anecdote:

> The story is told of a rabbi who dies and finds himself in the hereafter. However, he's not sure whether he's in heaven or hell. He's not feeling very much pleasure; so he concludes that he's probably not in heaven. However, he's not feeling very much pain either; so he decides he's probably not in hell. As he wanders about trying to determine where he is, he suddenly sees walking toward him from the distance none other than Rabbi Abraham Cohen, his mentor from the Talmudic Academy— dead now these thirty years. The rabbi remembered well that Cohen had the reputation of being one of the most pious, dedicated, and humane men ever to grace this planet.
>
> Happily and excitedly the rabbi races toward his old mentor. As he gets closer, he sees that standing by the old man's side is a young, beautiful, and voluptuous woman—obviously the old rabbi's companion. Gleefully the two men embrace one another and with tears rolling down his cheeks, the rabbi tells his old teacher how happy he is to see him and then joyfully says, "It's obvious to me, Rabbi Cohen, that if you are here, this must be *heaven*. A more pious, dedicated, noble individual never set foot on earth. And it's obvious also, Rabbi, that this beautiful, voluptuous, and

gorgeous woman is God's reward to you for the good deeds you did while on earth."

To which the old mentor replies, "Rabbi, I'm sorry to have to tell you that number one, this is *not heaven,* this is *hell!* And, number two, this beautiful, gorgeous, voluptuous woman is *not* God's reward to me. *I am her punishment!"*

The moral of this story, of course, is: with the same data, two observers can come to entirely different conclusions regarding the meaning of a particular event. The story provides an important lesson that is not only applicable to custody evaluations but to other aspects of clinical psychiatry as well. And the aforementioned recording system enables the examiner to collect efficiently data from all parties and assess most judiciously conflicting interpretations of the same events.

It is extremely important for the examiner to keep very meticulous records regarding who was interviewed, on what day, at exactly what time (e.g., 9:30 A.M.–10:30 A.M.), and the fee for each of these sessions. The cross-examining attorney in the courtroom may ask for this information when he or she doesn't have a strong basis for criticism of the *content* of the report. It is one of the things such an attorney may do when "fishing around" in the hope that something might be found to compromise the testimony of the impartial expert.

SPECIOUS MOTIVATIONS FOR LITIGATING TO GAIN CUSTODY

It is important for the examiner to appreciate that the motives for parents requesting custody do not simply stem from love and affection for the children. Often there are much more mundane considerations. The examiner should be aware of this at the outset and should bear this in mind throughout the evaluation—parental professions of love for the children and their fervor to gain custody notwithstanding. People will fight as hard for the reasons given below as they will for love.

The Bargaining Maneuver

Prior to the mid-1970s if a father told his lawyer that his wife's demands were exorbitant and that he was going to retaliate by asking for custody of the children—and then back down on his demand if the wife would reduce hers—the lawyer would discourage such manipulation by advising the father that he had no grounds for such litigation and that it would not be taken seriously by the other side. At that time, only the most obvious and deep-seated deficiencies on the mother's part could cause her to lose custody—defects such as chronic alcoholism, prostitution, gross neglect of the children, severe and obvious promiscuous behavior, drug addiction, overt psychosis (especially with hospitalizations), and other blatant impairments in the mother's capacity to care for the children. Because such gross deficiencies were relatively uncommon, fathers rarely sued for custody from the appreciation that their cases were often hopeless.

It was only in the middle 1970s that courts began to adhere strictly to statutes that were generally passed in the middle 1920s which stated that the sex of the parent should not be a consideration in determining parental preference in custody disputes. Since then, gross negligence has not been necessary to prove in order to gain custody. Rather, the court is asked to grant custody to the parent who is better able to provide love, affection, protection, guidance, and other necessities for the children.

At the present time a father may receive no such discouragement from his attorney. In fact, he may even be encouraged to use the custody litigation threat as a bargaining maneuver. I sometimes use the term bargaining *chip* in such situations because of the implication that the children so utilized are being viewed as practically worthless objects, of little intrinsic value. Their value here is only symbolic, but nevertheless it is real. Such a father may know from the outset that he is not going to press the custody conflict to the point where the final decision will be made. Rather, he will use his custody demand as a weapon, as a bargaining maneuver in the negotiations. He may then finally "give up" on the custody fight when he gets concessions from his wife on such matters as alimony and support payments. A parent who is doing this is not likely to admit it to the therapist conducting the custody evaluation. (This is just one example of the kind of duplicity that the examiner can expect in such evaluations.)

The therapist should appreciate that such a course represents a deficiency in parental capacity. It is a manifestation of the parent's considering personal financial gain to be more important than the children's psychological well-being. Custody litigation is invariably traumatic to children—pulled as they are between parents, lawyers, and other adults. The parent whose desire for personal gain is so great that he or she is blind to these effects on the children reveals a serious defect in parental capacity. Therefore, in weighing the pros and cons of that parent's being given custody, this insensitivity to the children's welfare should be considered one of the arguments *against* being granted custody should he or she change position and seriously seek it.

Financial Gain

Prior to the last few years, the mother was generally given custody of the children, and she remained in the house or apartment while the father moved elsewhere. The basic rationale for this arrangement was the appreciation that children need constancy of environment, and allowing the custodial parent to remain in the home insured such continuity. The children could then remain in familiar surroundings, not only with regard to their home, but in relation to their neighborhood, friends, school, and teachers. In addition, the noncustodial parent (usually the father) was required to provide his wife with alimony and support. In short, with the children came the house and support money. In addition, it is well-known fact that it costs more money to support children in another home than in one's own. Now fathers have greater opportunities for gaining custody. Many envision their remaining in the house with the children and their wives leaving the home. This would result in their spending less on the children's support because, if successful in winning the custody battle they would be living with the children. In short, the person who wins the children, may win the house as well, may not have to suffer the psychological traumas associated with relocation, and can save support money as well. The examiner does well to recognize this important motivating factor on the part of many parents who are suing for custody.

Vengeance

The new interpretations of the law allow a parent to wreak vengeance in a way not previously possible. What better way is there for a disgruntled parent to retaliate for indignities suffered in the course of a marital and divorce conflict than to take away the children—the other parent's most treasured possessions. As mentioned, this is one of the reasons why custody litigation is so vicious. And this is the first time in the history of Western civilization that the parents "start even" when they decide to fight over the children.

Guilt Reduction

Prior to the last few years, a father might say to a child, "If there was any chance in the world of my gaining custody, I would go to the Supreme Court if I had to. But my lawyer tells me that I don't stand a chance of getting custody of you children. He tells me that mothers almost automatically get the children." Such fathers can no longer use this argument. From the outset they are viewed equally by the court with regard to their potential for parental capacity.

A father, for example, who never particularly distinguished himself as a devoted parent, may profess great love for the children at the time of separation and fight viciously for custody. Such a parent, either consciously or unconsciously, may not even wish to be granted custody. What he really wants is to put up a good fight so that he can convince himself and others that he really loves his children. Such a parent may do many things during the evaluation to ensure that he loses the custody battle. Most parents are especially careful to spend maximum time with the children during the time of custody evaluation and litigation in order to impress all concerned with their devotion. Parents who basically wish to lose custody may be oblivious to this common maneuver. Or they may choose a lawyer who is obviously incompetent or neglectful of them. Here the aim may not simply be that of losing the children, but sustaining other losses and disadvantages as well. Such parents are secretly relieved when they are not granted custody, and detecting early this basic desire to lose makes the evaluator's job much easier.

Mothers, as well, may fight for custody in an attempt to assuage guilt. Mothers are supposed to be strongly maternal. In fact, the two words are often used synonymously. But *motherhood* is a biological state, as is *maternity*. However, not all who experience maternity are maternal. For every mother who actually kills her child there are dozens who would like to (not simply occasionally, but on an ongoing basis). There are many mothers who are secretly happy when a child dies, because their goal of having gotten rid of the child has been realized without their suffering any guilt, public rejection, and/or punishment for having killed it. Many mothers cannot admit to themselves and/or others that they would much prefer that their husbands take the children. Accordingly, they may "go through the motions" of a custody fight and hope all the while that they may lose. At least then they can say to themselves (and to others) that they have put up a good fight, and they can blame the judge (and even the impartial expert) for their losing the children. Such mothers are not likely to admit to the examiner their wish to lose. It therefore behooves the evaluator to try to ascertain whether or not such is the situation.

An incident from an evaluation a few years ago is an excellent example of this phenomenon. I was evaluating an English woman who was married to an American. My view of her was that she preferred more to lead a jet-set life than to stay at home taking care of her children, ages 1, 3, and 5. I strongly suspected that she was "going through the motions" of the custody litigation because she could not admit to herself that she really did not wish to have the children. In an interview that took place in early December she asked me what I thought of her going back to England during the Christmas–New Year's holidays. It was one of those rare occasions that I decided to "change hats" and be child therapist advising a parent rather than an impartial evaluator collecting information. Accordingly, I told her that I thought it would be unwise, considering how upsetting the separation and litigation already had been to the children. To this she responded that she was definitely going anyway, because she just couldn't tolerate the idea of not being in England during the Christmas–New Year's season. This is the answer I expected to receive when I switched roles. I do not know whether it was conscious or unconscious, but I do know that at some level she wanted to do things that would compromise her position significantly in the custody conflict.

Other Pathological Reasons for Trying to Gain Custody

There are various kinds of pathological interactions that parents may have with children that may result in their fighting for custody. A parent, for example, may be extremely dependent on a child (especially a teenager) and may view loss of custody with fear of intolerable loneliness. A sadistic parent may need the child as a scapegoat. An overprotective mother may view the child as the main way in which she can prove herself an adequate person. The child is not viewed as an individual who must be ever helped to become more independent. Rather, every attempt is made to prevent such independence and keep the child at an infantile, dependent level of functioning. A father with considerable hostile feelings toward society at large may need a child to act out his hostility. He may have good enough judgment to appreciate the consequences of such acting out, but his child may not. Accordingly, the youngster serves as a perfect vehicle for the expression of the father's antagonism toward the world. The examiner does well to consider these pathological forms of relationships with children and recognize that the loss of the child may be an extremely anxiety-provoking prospect for such a parent.

A very moralistic and/or religious parent may claim that the other parent should not have custody of the children because of "sexual promiscuity." When the examiner makes an inquiry, he or she may find that what is labeled as "promiscuity" may be the normal involvement in private heterosexual activity that a separated or divorced parent today commonly engages in. In such situations, one should ask the complaining parent to specify the effect he or she suspects the other parent's private sexual behavior is going to have on the children. Such a parent may be hard put to provide specific responses, other than to make comments along the lines that the children will identify with such a parent's perversity and will grow up to engage in similar perversions themselves and will therefore be punished by God. Although there are certainly parents who believe with deep conviction that such will be the case, the examiner must appreciate that there are many for whom such moralistic-religious convictions are espoused in the service of vengeance and used as a rationalization for depriving the other parent of the children. Sometimes, the complaining parent was never particularly religious and the "conversion" came right after learning of the former spouse's new relationship.

On occasion a parent, more commonly a mother, will threaten suicide if the child chooses the father. In less extreme cases, the mother will communicate to the child that she will psychologically decompensate, become severely depressed, or exhibit other terrible untoward psychological reactions if the child expresses preference for the father. This is clearly a negative on the mother's part in the custody evaluation and should not be a reason for recommending that the child stay with the mother.

The Attorney's Role in Specious Custody Demands

The attorney may appreciate that the client does not deserve custody, but will nevertheless vigorously support the client's demand. The lawyer may welcome the use of the custody issue as a weapon in the litigation in the hope that pressing this issue will gain concessions in other areas. Using as a rationalization the lawyer's obligation to support the client's position, the attorney may serve as a useful weapon for the parent who wishes to use the custody issue to wreak vengeance, assuage guilt, or extract other concessions.

However, more benevolent considerations are operative on occasion. The attorney may recognize that the client may need the custody litigation in order to assuage guilt over a basic desire not to have custody. In such cases he or she may harbor the hope that the exposure of the client's parental deficiencies in open court may help the parent gain insight into the fact that he or she will be the less desirable custodian. The lawyer may also support the client's demand with future considerations in mind. Although recognizing that the client is presently the less desirable parent, the lawyer may appreciate that future changes may improve the client's capacity or diminish the other spouse's parental ability. Having on the court records the fact that the client has fought for the child may enhance the parent's chances of gaining custody in the future. And the information obtained in the earlier trial may be useful and supportive in such future litigation. A client who has never fought for the children in the past, when he or she had the opportunity to do so, is less likely to gain custody in the future. On the other hand, there is the risk to the client that such litigation may place on the court records information that would weaken his or her case in subsequent litigation, and this may cause the lawyer to be less enthusiastic about the parent pressing the custody issue.

Occasionally a parent will justify cruelty or other forms of inappropriate behavior by claiming that the attorney has recommended such and that the parent is only complying with the attorney's advice. The examiner does well to consider such statements as rationalizations. For example, one father, who was married to a wealthy woman, was not only asking for alimony, but custody of the children and support of them as well. He claimed that under state laws of equitable distribution he was entitled to alimony because he was the financially poorer parent. In addition, he claimed that there was nothing inappropriate about his requesting support—if he were to gain custody—because state laws allowed this. He exhibited no sense of loss of masculine pride as he spoke of his "rights," and he used his attorney's advice regarding what he was entitled to under the law as a rationalization for exploitation. His past life revealed other evidences of his manipulation of others for his personal gain. I considered this father's interest in gaining custody of the children to serve the goal of exploitation of the mother, in that if he were to gain custody of the children he would have more of an excuse to exploit her of her money via child support payments. In such cases the examiner must be careful about using such terms as "exploiter" in the report unless this can be demonstrated clearly. The examiner can, however, get across this point by quoting the mother's comments that her husband is trying to exploit her and then either say nothing or make a comment that her view appears reasonable to the evaluator. This more cautious approach was the one I used here. I was able to get across the message without using the term *exploiter*—thereby protecting myself from questions under cross-examination like: "Have you personally interviewed those persons whom you claim Mr. H. allegedly exploited in the past?" and "Isn't it difficult, if not impossible, to differentiate between taking what is rightfully due us and exploitation?"

THE PROBLEM OF PARENTAL LYING
IN THE CUSTODY EVALUATION

In certain respects therapists tend to be more naive than lawyers with regard to believing a patient's statements. Generally, the therapist expects the patient to be truthful. We are certainly trained to be dubious about what our patients tell us, and our antennae should ever be out sensing for deceptions. But the kinds of deceits that we are most acute in detecting are self-deceptions—things that our patients are trying to hide from themselves. Accordingly, we are quite sensitive to such forms of self-deception as reaction formation, rationalization, and denial. We are also sensitive to the kinds of self-deceptions involved in the formation of many neurotic symptoms such as phobias, obsessions, compulsions, and paranoia. In all of these there is an element of the unconscious attempt to suppress and repress unacceptable thoughts and feelings. But patients most often do not consciously deceive us. They recognize that it behooves them to reveal things that may be difficult and even embarrassing to talk about because they appreciate that such revelations are vital if the therapist is to be helpful.

Lawyers, however, more frequently deal with clients who are consciously untruthful with them, and they routinely assume that their adversaries' clients will be so. Having some experience with duplicity, they may be more astute than the therapist in detecting it. Policemen, judges, and those who work in penal institutions are also more sensitive to conscious duplicity than we are. Accordingly, therapists are handicapped somewhat in the ability to evaluate patients involved in legal proceedings. For example, when we evaluate a parent in a custody determination the parent generally (either consciously or unconsciously) withholds information that might be detrimental to his or her cause. Our expectation of honesty and our inexperience with conscious deliberate deceit may compromise significantly our efficacy here.

It is one of the purposes of this book to assist mental health professionals in conducting this kind of an evaluation more effectively. I will discuss some of the techniques I have found useful in dealing with this problem. Therapists who remove themselves entirely from such evaluations with the argument that psychotherapeutic techniques have never been found to be useful with psychopaths and others who may be routinely deceiving the therapist, is avoiding a social responsibility. Parents in custody litigation do present special problems in the duplicity area, but these are not insurmountable.

In many cases one and even both parents are generally not motivated to involve themselves in the evaluation. The parents know that what they say may literally be used against them, and the person who conducts such an examination must recognize that this consideration pervades the whole atmosphere from beginning to end. One should make the assumption that every verbalization is being screened through an internal censor that asks: "Will the revelation of this information add or detract from the evaluator's view of me as a good and loving parent?" I do not think we should be particularly harsh on parents for taking this position in the custody evaluation. I would go further and say it may even reflect a positive element in that it certainly serves the goal of gaining custody of the children. Alternatively, the parent who is being 100 percent honest may be using such honesty in the service of a strong desire to actually lose the custody contest. I would go further and say that were I in this situation, I would not trust my own objectivity and my own sense of honesty and that I, too, would probably, either consciously or unconsciously, try to alter the truth in such a way that I would minimize my deficiencies as a parent and maximize my assets.

I cannot recall a custody evaluation in which a parent did not accuse the other of lying. How does one differentiate, then, the usual amount of lying from the unusual and/or pathological? Sometimes a parent will state among the complaints that the spouse is a "pathological liar." The examiner does well to inquire about specific examples of such alleged lying—especially in situations that are irrelevant to the custody evaluation (both past and present). A man, for example, complained that his wife would often tell the children to tell telephone callers that she wasn't home, when she really was. On other occasions, she would ask them to involve themselves in similar coverups to visitors to the home. He stated, "She's teaching them to be liars." Although the mother denied doing these things, all three children flatly stated that she did. I had little reason to believe that these children were being actively brainwashed by the father and this information made it more likely that the mother was lying to me in many other areas. With some people duplicity is so deeply embedded in their lifestyle that they hardly realize that they are perennially lying. There are businesspeople, for example, who are ever deceiving. As a matter of course, they add small amounts to bills. They may provide, as a routine practice, a lower weight or number than is stated on the label. They routinely state that an item will be sent out on a particular day, when they know quite well that this is a total impossibility. Accepting cash payments "under the table" to avoid payment of taxes is viewed as "the only way to do business," and those who pay taxes are considered fools. It is unreasonable for the evaluator to think that such individuals are going to be strong subscribers to the Boy Scout oath in the custody evaluation.

Another way of ascertaining whether or not a person is lying is to observe direct deceit in one's own dealings with the parent. I once saw a father who was in the full-time practice of orthopedic surgery in New York City. He was affiliated with a large teaching hospital associated with a prestigious medical school. At that time (the late 1970s) a *low* gross income for people in his position was $300,000 a year. In one session he was complaining to me about his wife's financial demands and stated (without my having asked what his income was) that his gross earnings were $70,000 a year. This was at a time when the orthopedists of New York were complaining bitterly about the fact that their malpractice insurance premiums alone ran from $40,000–$50,000 per year. I did not express my incredulity, but I certainly made a mental note of his duplicity, and it served to make me more dubious about other things he told me. It also told me about his poor judgment in that only the most naive and/or simple-minded individual could believe his statement.

THE VALUE OF THE CLASSICAL PSYCHOANALYTIC APPROACH IN THE EARLY PHASES OF INTERVIEWING THE PARENTS

I generally explain to the parents that I will be conducting a psychiatric evaluation of them as if they were voluntarily coming to me for consultation or therapy. Although I am not a strong subscriber to many of the theories and techniques espoused by the classical psychoanalytical school, I am psychoanalytically trained and believe that there are certainly aspects of that approach that, when used judiciously, have great merit. Such is the case for the early phases of the interviews with the parents.

I will generally begin each of the early sessions with a question such as: "Is there anything you have on your mind that you'd like to tell me?" It is rare for a parent in a custody evaluation to respond in the negative. Most often each of the parents has many things to tell me and each can go on for hours elaborating on the various deficiencies of the partner and the ways in which granting custody to the other party would be a terrible mistake and extremely detrimental to the children. The therapist should not feel rushed to get the more standard questions that I will soon be presenting; rather, he or she should appreciate that this open invitation to the parent to speak clearly may provide the evaluator with the most important information. In this early phase of my interviews I want the parent to "roll," to pour forth a steady stream of information with little or no interruption on my part.

Catalyzing this outpouring serves a number of useful functions in the custody evaluation. It provides the evaluator with detailed information about the various marital complaints and alleged deficiencies exhibited by the other parent. The structured or specific question might not direct itself to the particular issues that carry the greatest emotional charge at that point. Accordingly, such a question might deprive the interviewer of the most important information. It is a good principle of psychotherapy that the issues with the greatest degree of emotional charge are the best "handles" for the therapist to "grab" onto in that they are most likely to lead to the more significant problems. Another value of this approach relates to the nonjudgmental factor. By passively taking in all the information and strictly refraining from revealing any reactions—especially the negative ones—the examiner is likely to be viewed by the parent as being completely sympathetic to his or her position. In short, the complete absence of a negative response is interpreted as positive agreement and support. The evaluator is viewed as being on that parent's side. In such a setting the parent is more likely to reveal deficiencies. In short, the evaluator comes to be viewed as a trusted friend who is in basic agreement with most, if not all, of the complaints. Presumably, such a friend is not going to let the revelations of a few deficiencies affect the basic positive regard. Alternatively, the therapist who expresses disapprobation—ever so slightly—will be viewed as the "enemy" and the patient is likely to "clam up" and reveal few, if any, of the deficiencies that are important for the therapist to learn about. (As I will elaborate subsequently, the parent's own statements about his or her deficiencies are among the most important information the evaluator attempts to acquire.)

I do not wish to give the impression that I remain absolutely silent in the face of this outpouring. I do interrupt, at times, to be sure that I am jotting down accurate information on the data collection sheet of the parent being interviewed, as well as on the aforementioned pages of questions to be asked of the other parties. In addition, if a parent is repetitious (often the case) I will politely interrupt and remind the parent that we do have certain time limitations, that I understand the main point, and that we would do better to go on to other issues. If such interruptions are properly executed, the parent is not likely to object out of the realization that the examiner is trying to save time and money (and, of course, the payer is particularly appreciative of the latter consideration).

On occasion I will interview a parent who has very little to say. He or she enumerates briefly the major complaints and after a few minutes "runs dry." On the one hand, one could view such inability to "roll" as a positive personality trait. The individual quickly "gets to the point" and doesn't waste time with repetition and elaborations that add nothing new. On the other hand, one could argue that there is little emotional charge behind the complaints and the individual is not particularly pained by them. I consider the latter explanation to be the more likely in all of the parents I have thus far seen; that is, the parent who does not fight very hard is revealing a parental deficiency. And this should be taken into consideration in the total assessment.

My experience has been that the average parent needs one or two hours (in custody evaluations I find it more efficient to conduct full-hour sessions, rather than the 45- to 50-minute sessions I set up in treatment) of rolling before "running out of steam." Once that has happened, it indicates to me that I have gained the optimum benefit from this phase of the interviews and I can then proceed to the more structured aspects.

THE CHILDREN'S QUESTIONNAIRE

Whether or not the parent has completed the outpouring process by the end of the first interview, I give the parent a copy of my questionnaire which requests information about the children. One copy of the questionnaire is given to each parent for each child. This questionnaire, which is reproduced in its entirely in Appendix III, is one that I prepared originally for diagnostic/therapeutic purposes. I routinely send it to parents of all children prior to the initial consultation. I have found this questionnaire useful in the custody evaluation as well. The ostensible purpose is to give the examiner information about the children that is of psychiatric significance. However, of equal (if not more) importance is the information it provides about the parent who is filling out the questionnaire. Because each parent is filling out a questionnaire about each child, one can compare the parents' responses. Because they are not likely to be collaborating on filling out the questionnaire (as do parents who are living together), we learn something about each parent's knowledge of the child. This is especially true with regard to such information as developmental milestones, school performance, and past history. The less knowledgeable parent will reveal his or her ignorance on the questionnaire. He or she is not likely to be asking the spouse for help—as is the case when parents are married and filling out together a single questionnaire. And such a parent, of course, "loses points" in the evaluation. Furthermore, one should try to get some idea about the dedication that the parent exhibited in filling out the form. A hastily done, slipshod, haphazard approach says something about the parent's commitment to the child. In addition, it may reveal ambivalence about actually winning custody. Doing a sloppy job is one way to manifest (either consciously or unconsciously) one's basic desire not to gain custody.

For example, on page 4 of the questionnaire the parent is asked to list the ages at which the child reached each of twenty important milestones (sat without support, walked without assistance, recognized colors, etc.). The instructions also indicate that if the parent does not recall the exact time at which the particular milestone occurred, then he or she should merely check off whether it occurred early, at the usual time, or late. One mother (who was litigating for the custody of her two children) recalled nineteen of the twenty items accurately with regard to being able to provide the exact time (to the nearest month). Only one item was checked in the early, usual time, or late column. Her husband, however, could not check any of the items in the exact date column and checked all items in the second column. The same was true for the other child's questionnaire. Another parent never returned the questionnaire at all. I generally make it a practice not to remind the parent to return it and recognize that the failure to do so may be a manifestation of parental deficiency. It is likely that the same lax attitude is exhibited in other aspects of the parent's relationship with the children. It indicates that the other things take higher priority than the needs and interests of the children. On occasion, I suspect that it is done (either consciously or unconsciously) because the parent does not wish to reveal his or her ignorance of the child's life. Or, such failure might reflect the parent's desire not to gain custody, protestations to the contrary notwithstanding.

INDICATIONS OF PARENTAL CAPACITY
FROM THE PAST HISTORY

I begin the more structured phase of the interview with each parent along the lines of the traditional history-taking. I cover typical questions regarding parents, relationships with parents, siblings, relationships with siblings, education at all levels (academic and social aspects), peer relationships, jobs, etc. However, there are certain aspects of the routine evaluation that I particularly emphasize, namely, those that relate to parental capacity.

It is important for the examiner to appreciate that the information gained from the background history is *not* of the highest priority in the custody evaluation, its great importance in psychoanalytic treatment notwithstanding. First, one is much more convincing when focusing on assets and liabilities that exist at the time of the evaluation and in the period immediately antedating it. Also, to argue that a particular childhood experience produced a specific adult behavioral pattern is the kind of speculation (and it *is* a speculation, as much as we may not wish to admit it) that cross-examining attorneys love to seize upon: "Isn't it *possible*, doctor, for a woman to be a good mother even though she was cruelly treated, abused, and neglected by her own mother in childhood?" The answer to this question obviously must be *yes*. But the attorney is not likely to give the examiner the opportunity to speak about its unlikelihood. One might argue, then, that the examiner should not be wasting time in this area. My response is that it is not a complete waste of time in that it does provide information (even though it may not be included in the final report) that can help the examiner come to a conclusion regarding parental capacity. It is information that is placed on the scales that weigh assets against liabilities. It should be viewed as backup verification of the stronger arguments presented in the report—arguments related to the examiner's direct observations and statements made by the parties involved.

For ease of presentation, I will focus on the mother as the interviewee. On occasion, I will make direct reference to the father. However, most of the topics should be covered, to the degree applicable, in the father's evaluation as well. No particular item should be viewed as being of overriding significance; all are taken together in making the decision. Each question and issue focused on is not rated positive or negative simply on the basis of a short answer. Rather, the question serves as a point of departure from which one should try to gain information about the degree of parental capacity that the response reveals. In order to facilitate open discussion, the questions are not of the type that can be answered yes or no; rather, they stimulate more revealing answers.

The examiner should find out about the parents' relationships with their own parents, i.e., with the children's grandparents. One tends to be the same kind of parent that one's parents were. If the maternal grandmother, for example, was a very unmaternal person, if she was somewhat neglectful of or disinterested in her children, the likelihood that the mother herself will be compromised in this area is high. This is especially the case if the maternal grandmother physically abused the mother. This is not invariably so, but one must consider the possibility because she is likely to incorporate her mother's deficient model. Similarly for the father: if his relationship with his father was poor, he is likely to be compromised in his paternal capacity—but again, not invariably.

Reduction in sexual stereotypes notwithstanding, I believe that little girls today are still playing "house" more than little boys. The mothers now being evaluated are likely to have grown up at a time when "house" was even more typically a girl's game. The same is true with regard to doll play. Accordingly, I ask the mother: "What were your favorite games as a girl?" If she describes games like "house," I consider that a positive response regarding her maternal capacity. If she doesn't mention that game specifically, I will ask what her feelings were about playing it. I inquire about her feelings when playing with dolls and how old she was when she stopped. Liking doll play throughout a few years of childhood is positive information. I ask what her feelings were about helping her mother cook and do other work around her home. This does not preclude my inquiring into extradomestic activities and interests. I believe that both of these areas should be evaluated, but the homemaking interests and identifications are an important factor to be considered in determining custody. If she hated it, or her mother hated it, and she most often did it begrudgingly then this would be a negative factor. Although it is unrealistic to expect a child or an adult to relish housework, a certain degree of enjoyment is usually had by many, if not most, girls as they bake cakes, help set the table, and assist in other household activities. Father, also, should be asked questions along these lines. His involvement in such play does not necessarily suggest feminine tendencies (especially if he is young and grew up in a home where sex-stereotyped play was discouraged). Enjoyment of such play, especially if the father enjoyed playing father of the house, is a positive.

Children almost invariably enjoy playing with pets. In fact, the child who does not enjoy pets probably has some kind of psychological problem. The pet serves many important functions for the child. Children readily identify with pets because of the great similarity between the way the pet and the child are treated. Both are dependent on some more competent figure for sustenance and both thrive on tenderness and affection. Much can be learned from children by discussing the fantasies they have when playing with their pets. Although the child may, at times, relate to a pet as a peer, more commonly the child-pet relationship is similar to the parent-child relationship. As Kestenbaum and Underwood (1979) have pointed out, interest in pets in childhood is positively related to strong parental capacity in adulthood. Many children gain their first parental-type experiences in their relationship with their pets.

I ask the parents what their feelings were about helping care for younger children or baby-sitting. Sometimes helping in the care of younger children can be a chore that the child will resist, especially when it is coerced or excessive. However, such activities provide an opportunity for parental expression that I believe the child has the capacity to enjoy—even at ages as young as 4 to 5. A. Freud and Burlingham (1944a and 1944b) described well how children, when separated from their parents, will often assume the role of parental surrogate toward younger children. If a parent has experienced such gratifications, and recalls them with more pleasure than pain, it is an argument in favor of a strong parental interest and capacity.

I ask the parents how many children they envisioned having before they got married. I consider an answer of none or one to be a negative response. (Clearly, the parent who has no children is not coming before me for a custody evaluation. However, a parent may have *planned* to have none and an accidental pregnancy has taken place.) I generally consider a response of two to five or six evidence of strong parental capacity. However, if the parents actually have more than seven or eight children, they show, in my opinion, suggestive manifestations of parental inadequacy. Prior to the last half century, this was not the case. If one wanted four children, one might have to have had eight because of the high infant and childhood death rate. This is not the case presently in Western society. Parents who *today* have seven, eight, or more children show, in my opinion, little respect for the individual needs of children and I lose some respect for such ostensible parental capacity. In such large families children get lost in the crowd and suffer, I believe, from various deprivations. Even when religious conviction is given as a reason for such a large family, I still hold that it reflects an impairment in parental capacity.

I will also ask: "At the time of your marriage, how long did you plan to wait before having your first child?" If the couple did not take into consideration their resources and just went right ahead, this would be a negative. If they waited a reasonable time because there were reality factors that may have caused them to hold off, even factors like wanting to get to know one another better or having a few years of freedom before having children, I would consider the response positive. If, however, there were many years of ambivalence or procrastination, this would be a negative. One does well to go into the question of whether each of the children was planned or accidental and, of course, the planned child does speak for greater parental interest.

The healthy mother has adequate prenatal care and the healthy father is also concerned about this. The failure to be involved in such care is a definite negative, social and economic factors notwithstanding. Even the poorest families have access to clinics where such care is provided. The mother's attitude about her body changes associated with the pregnancy can also give a clue about maternal capacity. If the mother considered herself ugly, rather than beautiful, it is a compromise. The healthy woman is not ashamed of the body changes associated with pregancy; in fact, she is genuinely proud of them. However, it is reasonable that she may not be pleased with facial changes and edema. Similarly, the father who finds his wife repulsive when pregnant is demonstrating an impairment in paternal capacity. The healthy father is not "turned off" by his pregnant wife's physical changes. Again, when there is significant edema, especially of the face, one might modify this position to some degree.

One might ask: "During the pregnancy was there any preference that the child be of a particular sex?" A standard answer here is that the parent had no preference. If, however, the therapist poses the question differently: "Most parents usually have a secret preference even though they may not feel comfortable expressing it. Did you have such a secret preference?" a more honest answer may be provided. When one says, "Most parents usually have a secret preference," it gives some sanction to express what might previously have been considered an unacceptable response. If there was strong and unjustifiable bias in one direction, this would be a negative factor. This might manifest itself in the parent having picked a name for just one sex.

Breast feeding should be discussed. There are those who consider this to be the most important criterion for determining a mother's maternal capacity. I believe this is unfortunate. It is probably true that on a statistical basis, on studies of thousands of women in Western society, the breast-feeding mother would probably prove to be more maternal than the non-breast-feeding mother. However, there are unmaternal women who will breast feed because they have learned a little psychology and have been taught to equate it with femininity and maternal capacity. They will use it as a way of denying basic deficiencies in this area and think that by merely performing this act they are proving themselves highly maternal. Therefore, one must be cautious about the significance of the answers to this question—nevertheless it should be asked. The milk drying up after a short period of time could reflect some impairment of maternal capacity. The mother's tension with the child, an unconscious desire not to feed it, and other psychological factors could cause reduction and even total resorption of breast milk. However, physical factors might also be operative. Accordingly, we do not know enough about these things to be able to say in many cases that it was definitely maternal deficiency that caused the breast glands to stop secreting milk. The father's attitude about his wife's breast feeding should also be explored. Husbands who view it as "animal" or "primitive" are likely to be less paternal than those who are very desirous of their wife's breast feeding. Again, those who read psychology and psychiatry books may learn the "right" answer to this question so the examiner must be cautious before coming to any specific conclusions.

The mother's suffering a post-partum depression following the birth of one or more of the children is an argument against strong parental capacity. Such depressions usually involve deep feelings of dissatisfaction with the maternal role, often preoccupations of a frightening sort involving hostility toward the child, and impulses to throw the child out of the window or kill it. Although these obsessions are frightening and often ego-alien, they still reflect unconscious hostile impulses pressing for expression—impulses that are likely to detract from the mother's healthy involvement with her children.

This book is being written at a time when the pendulum has shifted significantly toward biological explanations for various psychopathological phenomena. A biological explanation for depression is very much in vogue. Although I am in agreement that there are drugs that *probably* (I am not 100 percent convinced) can reduce depression symptomatically, I am not convinced that all depressions are biological in etiology. I believe that in manic-depressive psychosis, the biological factors are probably extremely important. However, I am less convinced about a basic biological cause for many other types of depression and my incredulity extends to post-partum depression as well. One cannot deny that there are massive metabolic changes occurring in the pregnant woman, both during the pregnancy and after the delivery. I am, however, dubious that such changes are of importance in bringing about post-partum depression. Although I am probably in a shrinking minority, I still hold to this position and my comments about its etiology still appear reasonable to me.

When a custody evaluation is being conducted with parents who have adopted their children, one should inquire about the reasons why the parents adopted. Considering our present state of knowledge, I think it premature to conclude that a sterility problem on the part of either parent is necessarily psychogenic. In some cases the argument for psychogenesis seems plausible; in others both organic and psychogenic factors appear to be operating; and in others the organic factor(s) is the more important. In many cases, however, one cannot be certain as to the cause.

Accordingly, it would be a disservice to an adopting parent to conclude, as some psychiatrists might, that the sterility probably has a psychogenic basis. Prior to the adoption it is likely that the parents spent years trying to conceive. When this failed they may have made the rounds among gynecologists, endocrinologists, and other sterility specialists. Such consultations may have involved an endless series of expensive and sometimes painful examinations, tests, and even operative procedures. Years may have been spent meticulously making temperature charts to determine the most fertile period and numerous theories may have been followed as to the best method of conceiving. Finally, when all failed, the parents may have gone through significant ordeals with adoption agencies or other sources before finally being given a child. Such a pursuit is testimony to the strong parental interests of such people, and it is therefore a terrible disservice to dismiss the sterility as psychogenic. In fact, I would go further and say that if they have embarked on this pilgrimage, I would consider it evidence of strong parental capacity.

If, in the process of obtaining the parent's past history, one finds that the parent's recollection of important past events is significantly impaired, one should try to find out the reason for such memory lapses. Unless there is obvious evidence for borderline intelligence, mental deficiency, schizophrenia, or organic brain syndrome, the cause is likely to be psychogenic. Extremely anxious individuals are likely to have memory lapses because tension distracts them from recollections they would otherwise remember. Often disorganization is associated with such chronic anxiety.

Less important than the fact that the parent does not recall important events from the past, is the question of whether such anxiety/disorganization is presently interfering with that parent's capacity to take care of the children. If such is the case, then this would obviously be a parental deficiency. Organizational capacity is not generally considered when one is trying to evaluate a parent's capabilities. However, it is an extremely important factor to consider when one is assessing parental functioning. Not only does the disorganized parent deprive the child of many needs, but the parent also creates anxieties in the child because of the unpredictability of the environment.

EVALUATION OF PARENTAL CAPACITY FROM THE RECENT HISTORY AND PRESENT FUNCTIONING

The Super-parent

It is quite common for a parent (especially a less adequate one), at the time when he or she learns that the custody evaluation will take place, to suddenly become a "super-parent." The parent knows that the examiner is going to make inquiries regarding parental capacity and in anticipation of this may start being a better parent than he or she ever was before. The other parent will usually describe this to the examiner. And the children too will often notice the difference (unless they are very young). One does well to try to detail these changes and, if possible, get the "transformed" parent's admission (to whatever degree possible) that this indeed occurred. Obviously, the parent whose belated involvement coincides with impending custody evaluation is certainly less parental than the one who has exhibited ongoing interest prior to the possibility of there being litigation over custody.

The Parent's Description of the Children

In this phase of the evaluation, I find a useful question to be: "Describe each of your children to me." In the course of answering this question, one wishes to determine whether the parent's description is heavily loaded with negatives such as excessive complaints, derision, and comments that would be ego deflating were the child to hear. One wants, however, not only to focus on negative distortions but positive distortions as well. I believe that the healthy parent distorts somewhat in the positive direction, tends to ignore deficiencies, and views the child as having more assets than the nonparent might observe. To a degree I think this is healthy and a sign of strong parental capacity. We need this extra ego enhancement to serve as a buffer against the undeserved criticism and denigration all of us receive at times in life. I believe that the child who has a parent who is completely objective regarding his or her assets and liabilities loses the extra support and denial of deficiencies that are vital (to a reasonable degree) to healthy growth and development. However, with regard to such positive distortion, one must be sure that the parent is not denying deficits to a pathological degree or exaggerating assets to the point where the child is not confronted with liabilities. The better the therapist knows the child, the greater will be the likelihood that he or she can determine whether such denial and/or exaggeration is occurring.

If in response to the aforementioned general question about the children, the parent has not focused on specifics the therapist should elicit such particulars. One can ask such questions as: "Tell me each of your child's assets and liabilities, his or her strong points and weak points." Or one might ask, "What are the things about each of your children that you like and that you dislike?" If a parent cannot think of significant assets, this is a parental liability. One way in which this happens is that the parent immediately describes liabilities and, when the examiner then asks the parent to discuss assets, the parent shifts quickly back to liabilities. A parent might consider a child's refusal to eat what is prepared to be a liability. On further inquiry, the examiner learns that such power struggles over eating are related to the parent's inflexibility regarding allowing the child a reasonable amount of choice before the preparation of a particular food. A related example would be the child whose refusal to practice a musical instrument is described as a liability. The child's wish not to play the instrument is not given reasonable consideration. The problem here is much more that of the parent than of the child. A parent might consider a liability a child's interest in watching an occasional violent movie on television. The parents who protect their children from the so-called detrimental effects of *occasional* exposure to such fare are, in my opinion, only seemingly benevolent and only ostensibly concerned with their children's best interests. I view such an attitude, especially when rigidly enforced, as a manifestation of overprotection: "I would never let *my* child see such a film." And like other types of overprotection, it generally relates more to hostility, manipulation, and insensitivity than it does to love. Elsewhere (Gardner, 1973a) I have elaborated on my views on the effects on children of watching violent programs on television.

The order in which the parent discusses the children may also provide useful information. This is especially the case if the order of presentation is not in accordance with the chronological ages (oldest to youngest or youngest to oldest). The child who is favored may be selected first for presentation and much more detail is given about that child than the others. Favoritism of one child over the others is generally a parental defect. The nonfavored children, then, will feel like "second class citizens." And the favored child generally does not feel too happy either with regard to the favoritism. I suspect that such a child senses, at some level, the fact that the parent who places a child in a secondary position is not as strongly parental as one who doesn't. The less favored children generally feel rejected and this is a valid observation. The favored child is likely to reason: "If she can reject them, she can probably reject me also."

The parent who answers the question "Describe each of your children" with an emphasis on physical characteristics (especially when there is no particular quality worthy of such emphasis) may be doing so in order to avoid touching on psychological issues. There are individuals who are extremely threatened by discussion and revelation of personal, psychological, or emotional factors in human relationships. They are much more comfortable with the concrete. Such an inhibition (seen in extreme form in schizophrenia) is a definite parental liability. This kind of parent serves as a model for the development of such inhibitions in the children and contributes, thereby, to the development of various forms of psychopathology in them. I recall a father, a physicist, who was just about incapable of discussing any issue in which emotions might arise. He was a tight, tense, monotonous kind of person who at best would be diagnosed as obsessive-compulsive, but who was more likely a borderline psychotic. (He exhibited no evidences at all of overtly psychotic symptomatology.) He confined himself to physical descriptions of the children and, although I invited him to discuss their personalities in each of three interviews, he found it just about impossible to do so. He stated, "I was never good at talking about emotional things. They confuse me. I don't understand them. I'm much better talking about things I can see, touch, and measure. I guess that's why I became a physicist." In this particular case I recommended that the mother have custody. One important (but certainly not the only) reason for my doing so was this significant liability on the father's part. At no point in the report did I use such terms as "obsessive-compulsive" or "borderline psychotic." (As I will discuss subsequently, the examiner does well to avoid use of diagnostic terminology.) Rather, I described the aforementioned personality traits and, in addition, noted verbatim the father's own statements regarding these inhibitions. As I repeatedly state in this book, such direct observations and quotations are the most powerful data for supporting the examiner's position in custody litigation.

The Parents' Description of Their Own Parenting Assets and Liabilities

Whereas in the above section, information about parental capacity is elicited via questions focusing on the children, the questions discussed in this section tend to elicit such information from the parent's themselves via their discussing their own parenting assets and liabilities. Here, one requests that the parent talk about his or her own parenting qualities and then discuss the spouse's. One might approach this subject with the question: "No one is perfect. Everyone has both assets and liabilities, both good points and bad points. With regard to parenting, what do you consider your assets and what do you consider your liabilities?" The question is so worded that it makes it acceptable to describe one's own deficits. In fact, it is so posed that the parent who is inclined to deny any liabilities would find it difficult to do so because such a statement would suggest atypicality.

Most people equate atypicality with unacceptability. The parent in the custody evaluation generally does not wish to risk such a designation. Accordingly, he or she is likely to answer this question with a revelation of deficiencies. This is a very important principle in posing questions in the custody evaluation. The general message one wants to get across is: "Everybody exhibits such and such, from time to time. Under what circumstances do you exhibit these qualities?" "Such and such" is generally an undesirable quality which the parent would generally not wish to admit. However, phrased in a context in which such and such is presented as a universal phenomenon, the parent is far less likely to deny sharing this deficit with the rest of mankind.

In assessing the responses to this question, one must attempt to ascertain whether the particular liability is truly one. Most often there is a continuum from the normal to the abnormal, and it may be very difficult, at times, to determine whether or not the parent exhibits the particular deficit to a degree that would be considered pathological. For example, a mother may say that she screams too much at the children. Healthy mothers, in my opinion, should *at times* be screaming at their children. A softly worded request will often not work. The blood-curdling shriek has much more clout. Children, very early, differentiate between these two types of parental demands. They generally feel that they can ignore with impunity the type-1 demand. With the type-2, however, they recognize that the parent "means business" and they'd better "get on the ball." Only by getting further information about the frequency of the type-2 demands, whether or not they work, whether the children respond most often or ignore them, whether there is follow-through, etc., can one determine whether there is a parental deficit in this area. Often the children's input will help the examiner determine whether the particular pattern is indeed a deficiency.

Sometimes a parent will confirm a deficiency described by the spouse or children. For example, one father complained that his wife was more interested in breeding dogs for shows than raising the children. He described numerous weekend absences when she was off to dog shows. The children, as well, complained that they thought that their mother loved the dogs more than she loved them. In response to the personal assets/liabilities question, this mother responded, "I guess I am into dogs too much. But you know, German shepherds are beautiful animals. But they take a tremendous amount of work. They're not like kids who can grow up by themselves. They're basically still animals." Another mother stated, "I'm just not the mother type. To me, a mother is a cow. She's a tit, nothing more. Maybe I never should have had children. I resented every minute in the house when they were very young. My husband was good about it. He would let me go out a lot, so I wouldn't go crazy. When I was with them, I used to scream too much. I was on top of them for every little thing. I guess it was because I was so frustrated because I had to take care of them. If we could have afforded a full-time maid, they would have been better off and I would have been happier. But, you know, he's no 'father of the year' either...." Another way of posing this question is: "In the course of each of your children's growth and development, what do you consider to be the best things you've done for them?" And "In the course of each of your children's growth and development, what do you consider to be the greatest mistakes you've made?"

The examiner should ask the parent's opinion about what the spouse thinks of him or her with regard to parental capacity. Useful questions are: "What comments has your husband (wife) made about the way you handle the children?" "What does he (she) consider to be your strong points with regard to child rearing?" "What does he (she) consider to be your weak points regarding child rearing?" Some of these criticisms will probably have been mentioned in the initial interview. It is here, however, that one should go into them in depth. Another question that might provide information about the parent's view of his or her own assets and liabilities with regard to child rearing is: "How would you describe your relationship with each of your children?"

There is another question that I have mixed feelings about, but which can occasionally be useful: "If the judge decided upon a split custody arrangement, that is, one in which the children would be divided between you and your husband, and told you that the decision would be yours regarding the split, what would you do?" One could say that this is an unfair question and that it is extremely unlikely that any judge would do such a thing. Decisions made with a "gun at one's head" are not necessarily the same as those one would make in a freer atmosphere. On the other hand, the answer can, on occasion, provide useful information. It is especially useful if the therapist is considering the split custody arrangement. One mother answered: "I've always been better with my daughter than my son. Although I love Jim very much, I often don't know what's going on inside his head. Sara and I are on the same wave-length. I guess I'd choose Sara, but it would tear my heart out if I had to lose Jim. As I told you, I never had tremendous criticisms of Mike as a father, until he met that whore, Gail...." In this case, I ultimately recommended the split custody arrangement with the mother taking her daughter and the father taking the son.

Inquiries Relevant to Child-Rearing Practices in the Infancy-Toddler Period

A crucial element in the child's learning to talk is parental feedback. When the child first babbles and coos, it is crucial that there be environmental response. Otherwise, the verbalizations (as primitive as they are) will not be reinforced and it is unlikely that the child will then proceed to more advanced levels of speech. One should inquire into parental feedback to the child's verbalizations from the earliest months of life.

A most valuable question is: "Are (were) your children the kind who liked to come into your bed in the morning, especially on weekends and holidays?" I believe that the psychologically healthy child likes to do this—at least up to the age of 5 or 6 (and often even until the prepubertal period). Parents with strong maternal and paternal capacity enjoy such morning cuddling immensely. I assume that all children enjoy such cuddling, and a child described as not enjoying it usually reflects the discouragement of one or both parents. If the parents want their sleep, don't like the kicking, or find it uncomfortable, a deficit in their parental capacity is strongly suggested. I consider this one of the most valuable questions in the evaluation, and it warrants full discussion.

The reader will note the question is posed in the nonthreatening manner previously described. It suggests that there are two kinds of children: those who like to come into the bed and cuddle in the morning and those who do not. In a sense, this is true. Severely retarded, autistic, and schizophrenic children probably aren't interested in climbing into their parents' bed in the morning. Assume, however, that other children are interested, and if they are disinclined, it is because their parents have been so. The question implies that the interest arises in the child, and if it is not present it is just a manifestation of common, normal variation and a defect in the parent is not suggested. Accordingly, the parent need not feel embarrassed or guilty when answering in the negative.

Another factor in the bed situation that warrants inquiry is that of the parents' own enjoyment of cuddling. If the parents have separate beds it is likely that their desire for cutaneous gratification is small. If the parents don't like to cuddle with one another, it is not likely (but still possible) that they will want to cuddle with their children. Separate beds can, therefore, be an argument against strong parental capacity—but this criterion must be used with caution, because there are exceptions.

I ask the mother what kinds of feelings she has when she sees a new baby. If the mother is the kind of person who likes cuddling new babies, gets a heartwarming response when doing so, and spontaneously describes this, this would be a positive factor. Or I might ask specifically: "Are you the kind of woman who likes to cuddle babies?" Again, the question is so worded that it implies that there are two kinds of women: those who like cuddling babies and those who don't. I ask the question in a way that attempts to imply that I am equally receptive to a positive or negative response and that neither is preferable to the other.

I generally inquire into the amount of time the parent spends alone with the child in recreational and other activities not strictly crucial to child rearing. Does the mother, in addition to preparing meals and taking care of the house, set aside time to sit alone with the children, read books, and play with them? Admittedly, this is not easy for some mothers, especially when there are many children, and for most parents these activities may be a little boring—at times very boring. There is a limit to the amount of children's stories that the average adult can take. But the healthy parent enjoys them to some extent, primarily because of the pleasure the child derives. One does well to get specific information about the nature of the interaction between parent and child during the reading activity. Does the child sit on the parent's lap while being read to? Is there cuddling? At bedtime, is the child lulled into sleep with stories? Afterwards, does the parent lie down and cuddle with the child to help him or her fall asleep. If done, these are obviously positive factors.

Similarly, I inquire into the father's involvement with the children when he is not at work, especially with regard to such activities as reading, sports, and doing mutually enjoyable things together. One must take into account that the father, after a full-day's work, may have limited capacity for such involvement. However, his fatigue notwithstanding, most healthy, involved fathers do find gratifications from such activities and will give them high priority.

A number of mothers have reported to me that they have refrained from cuddling with and lying down in bed with their sons after they reach the age of 2 to 3 because they had been warned that the boys would develop Oedipus complexes. First, I think that this is very unfortunate and misguided advice on the part of the person who dispensed it. The Oedipal theory is, as the name states, only a theory. To recommend that a mother not cuddle with her son after the age of 2 to 3 because he might develop an Oedipus complex is a most unfortunate bit of advice. Physical contact and sexual seductivity are not necessarily the same. (I am in full agreement that it is psychologically deleterious for a mother to sexually stimulate her son—regardless of his age.) I believe that healthy mothers do not take such misguided warnings seriously, and they continue to cuddle their children—even their sons. Mothers who do subscribe to such advice are probably receptive to it because it provides them with a rationale for removal from physical contact. I believe that we certainly should reduce the amount of physical contact with our children as they get older, but there should be no age at which there is absolutely none. Even when they become adults, embraces are important and healthy.

The examiner does well to inquire about parental involvement in the child's illnesses. How upset does each parent get when the child is ill? What priority does illness take for each of the parents? Which parent takes the child to the pediatrician? One must, of course, consider job obligations before making judgments on this question. In the traditional household, the mother is generally much more available than the father to involve herself in the children's illnesses. However, this does not preclude active interest on the father's part (calls from business or office, visits to the doctor with the child in off hours, and spending time with a sick child after work). It also does not preclude psychological involvement and concern.

A useful area of inquiry is a child's nightmares. Most children, especially between the ages of 3 and 9, have nightmares on occasion. Only when they are severely anxiety provoking and frequent (more than three or four times a week) would I consider them to be pathological. In the context of discussing the nightmare, I will ask a number of questions related to their frequency, content, whether the child awakens the parents, and what is said to the child in response to them.

Actually, for the purposes of the custody evaluation, I am less interested in the content of the nightmares (they are most often stereotyped: a monster, menacing form, etc.) than I am in the person whom the child calls and what is said to the child. I want to learn which parent more frequently is called and which parent more commonly responds. I am also interested in the degree of warmth and sensitivity exhibited in the attempt to console and reassure the child. I will also ask the child questions that can provide me with information in this area.

I often ask the question: "What things do you like doing *most* with the children?" If the parent has difficulty answering this question and cannot think of something he or she likes doing most, it reflects negatively. Then I ask: "What things do you like doing *least* with the children?" If the parent denies there is anything that he or she doesn't like doing, that there is so much love and affection that everything done with the children is enjoyed (including getting up at three in the morning and changing the diapers), then the examiner knows that the parent is being deceptive. He or she should then be somewhat incredulous of answers to other questions and take this duplicity into account when making the final recommendation.

In the context of this question, as well as many others, the examiner should direct attention to parental *patience.* Raising children can be a very frustrating endeavor at times and the good parent generally exhibits a degree of patience with his or her own child that others would not have. The devoted parent has the patience to shop for their clothing, bathe them, help them with their homework, teach them, and engage in games that might not be completely stimulating. The involved parent has a toleration for dialogue with the child that others would find boring.

If the parent has had all the children that were planned, I ask whether he or she occasionally feels a strong craving for another child. The healthy parent generally has such feelings and it is even normal, in my opinion, to describe the squelching of such feelings because of their impracticality. I think it is healthy for a parent to have some lingering feelings of wanting more children after the family is complete. When it is no longer possible or practical to have more children, then these fantasies are gratified through anticipation of grandparenthood. If one elicits these, it speaks for strong parental involvement.

Availability

A father who works full time, or a mother who works full time, is not likely to assume optimally both the obligations of breadwinning and child rearing. The parent who has more time available for the children has an edge over the other. Although this may be considered by some to be "unfair," it is nevertheless a reality that must be considered in the custody evaluation. Of course, *quality* as well as *quantity* of the time with the children must be taken into consideration. But even here the parent with the full-time job is likely to be compromised as far as child-rearing capacity is concerned in that the parent who is exhausted after a full-day's work is not in a good position to provide optimum parenting. This is probably one of the main drawbacks for fathers who are trying to gain custody of their chidlren. This is especially the case when the mother is a homemaker. Although *quality* of parenting must certainly be taken into consideration in all cases, a mother's greater availability is a strong point in her favor when there is a custody conflict in a traditional household.

Disciplinary Techniques

This is an important area of inquiry from which one can learn much about parental capacity. Again, the questions are best posed in a non-accusatory way and one does well to begin with general questions on the subject and then proceed with more specific ones. A good general question is: "Most parents have some problems in the upbringing of their children. What problems have you had with yours?" Again, saying "most parents have some problems" gives the parent sanction to discuss those that the child may have as well as parental disciplinary and punitive techniques. Without such acceptability to respond with a description of difficulties, the mother in a custody evaluation would tend to deny them. Depending upon the nature of the problems and how the parent handled them, one tries to learn something about parental capacity.

One can learn still more about the parent-child relationship with the question: "What things do you find you have to punish the children for?" Notice again how the question is posed: "things...*you* have to punish the children for." The implication is that punishment is appropriate—that the parent does it only because he or she gets backed into a corner. I do not agree with those who believe that in a healthy household one need not resort to discipline and punishment. (The proponents of this view have either not had children or, if they have had, could not possibly have been truly involved with them.) There are times to punish and discipline a child and implementation of such measures does not necessarily reflect negatively on parental capacity. (In fact, the failure to do so might very well be considered a deficiency.) One should learn about the kinds of punishment utilized, the severity, and whether there was cruelty involved. I might say here that spanking, in my opinion, is not necessarily a cruel punishment. There are times and places when, used judiciously and benevolently, it has a place. My personal view is that it should be used mainly in the 2-to-4-year period, that the pain inflicted should be primarily psychological, that the site is best confined to the backside, and that it be the punishment of last (not first) resort. Because of the view generally held by laymen that therapists deplore spanking, one does best to load the question with a high degree of sanction: "How often do you find you have to spank the children?" or "Most parents find that at times they have to spank their children. How has this been the case with you?" Such license is especially important for parents who are being evaluated in custody litigation, because they are ever on the alert to censor information that may be detrimental to their legal position.

Another useful question is: "Who do you think is generally more effective in getting the children to behave, you or your husband (wife)?" In evaluating the response, one should appreciate that *effectiveness* does not only mean getting results, but utilizing methods that do so in the most humane and reasonable way. The cruel and insensitive parent may get results much more frequently than the "softer" one, but obviously the latter parent's approach is preferable.

If the aforementioned general questions do not provide the examiner with signficant information, more specific questions should be used. However, these too must be carefully posed in order to avoid an accusatory implication. Of particular value in this regard is a questionnaire designed by A. Gardner, et al. (1980; Appendix IV). Although designed for research purposes, some of the questions from this protocol are useful in the evaluation of maternal and paternal capacity as well. For each question the parent is asked how he or she would handle the situation in which the child has exhibited a particular type of undesirable behavior. Following the parent's response, the interviewer will request a second method if the first doesn't work, and again a third if the second didn't work as well.

The questions are of particular value because they depict situations in which all parents find themselves with their children, and there is no single "right" response. The questions may put the parent "on the spot," but the answer can be very revealing. Often the first response will be a stereotyped one that the parent suspects is the anticipated answer. The second and third choice reactions are then likely to be more revealing and useful. It is often difficult for the parent to know exactly what kind of a response would reflect parental deficiency. They are analagous to the Rorschach with regard to the examinee's ignorance of the significance of an answer. Of course, the parent is in a slightly better position with regard to understanding the significance of a response to questions here than to Rorschach responses, but there is still a significant element of doubt.

For example, question 10 asks "_____ has broken a very important possession of yours. When you're asking for an explanation, he(she) denies having done it. You know he(she) is lying. What would you do?" The parent may respond, "I'd tell him that if he tells me the truth I won't punish him." This is a common response and the parent may believe that the examiner is impressed here with the parent's benevolence and good sense. However, such a parent may not appreciate that this method of handling lying encourages further lies because the parent is not providing meaningful deterrents to their repetition. The child is essentially being taught that all one need do is confess that one has lied and there are no repercussions. No social system could possibly survive if judges were not to inflict punishment if the alleged criminals were to confess.

Question 11 states, "_____ refuses to go to bed when you tell him(her) to. What would you do?" A parent may respond with a restrictive or punitive answer such as "I tell him that he can't watch television tomorrow if he doesn't go to sleep or that he doesn't get ice cream tomorrow if he doesn't go to sleep." Although such an answer might be reasonable after the third attempt during the same evening, the healthier parent tries to lure the child to bed, and then to sleep, by such seductive activities as reading, cuddling in bed together, listening to soft music, singing lullabies together, etc.

Question 16: "You are in a store. _____ reaches up on the counter, takes something, hides it in his(her) pocket, and walks away. What would you do?" The healthy parent, in my opinion, takes the child back to the store and either gets the child to return it to the owner or returns it to the owner in the child's presence. In either case, the child is made to suffer a certain amount of embarrassment over the transgression. The parent who merely returns the object, without informing the store-keeper of the theft, is depriving the child of an important learning experience. Such a parent is teaching a child that such transgressions are without significant repercussions. To punish the child in a reason-able way for the theft is certainly an acceptable punitive measure. However, it is preferable that the person upon whom the "crime" has been perpetrated be involved directly with the child while he or she is being required to make amends.

Many of the questions in the A. Gardner protocol are generally referrable to the 2-to-5-year-old child. There are other questions that I have found useful. Some of these are much more applicable to older children. As is true for the A. Gardner protocol, I try to get one or two alternatives if the first suggested response doesn't work. Each question essentially asks the parent how he or she would deal with or handle a particular common childhood problem. They are all problems for which there is no single good answer. One basically wants to know whether the parent will handle the situation malevolently or benevo-lently, reasonably or irrationally. Some sample questions:

What's the best way for a parent to handle a child's temper tan-trums?

What would you do if a child cheated while playing a game with you?

What do you do with a child who sucks his or her thumb?

How do you handle a child who uses profanity to a parent?

What about a child who uses profanity in front of a parent, pro-fanity that is not directed toward the parent?

How do you handle the situation when a child refuses to finish supper?

What's the best thing to do when a parent catches a child in-volved in sex play with a neighbor's child?

How do you handle children's fighting, especially when it be-comes fierce?

What do you do when a child steals and then lies about having stolen?

What's the best thing to do when a child refuses to do homework?

What's the best way to handle a child who refuses to do house-hold chores, such as taking out the garbage or making the bed?

What is the best thing for parents to do if they find out that their 14- or 15-year-old daughter is pregnant?

For each of these questions, the examiner might wish to make it more personal and direct the question to the parent's actual experiences in handling his or her particular child with regard to the aforementioned problems. Sometimes the direct reference to the parent's own child is useful. On other occasions, such a direct reference may not be applicable. In such cases, the general speculation on how the parent would handle the situation, if he or she were to have a child who did such a thing, can also provide valuable information. If the parent responds with a statement like "My child would never do such a thing," or "I've never had any such experiences," the examiner should encourage the parent to *speculate*. Some of the responses that are generally inappropriate (and reflect thereby negatively on parental capacity) would include: failure to punish, when punishment is appropriate; bribing; excessively harsh punishments; prolonged isolations; prolonged withdrawal of affection; prolonged ignoring of the child; excessive reliance on reasoning and getting the child to understand; empty threats; and delegation of authority. Responses that generally suggest good parental functioning include: distracting the child; short-term withdrawal of privileges; short-term isolation; short-term withdrawal of affection; parental expression of disappointment; a short explanation which attempts to help the child understand; firm command; reasonable threat, especially when there is a high likelihood of follow through; and recognition of praise and reward as useful preventive measures. The reader who is interested in a detailed description of the disciplinary techniques that I consider preferable, might wish to refer to the Reward, Discipline, and Punishment chapter of my book on child-rearing practices (Gardner, 1973a).

Receptivity to the Encouragement of Healthy Peer Relationships

One should ask about each parent's receptivity to friends in the home. A parent's attitude toward the children having friends in the home can provide significant information about parental capacity. The healthy parent recognizes the importance of such visits and is willing to tolerate the discomforts attendant to them. The healthy parent recognizes that noise, mess, discomfort, disruption, fighting, and other annoyances are a small price to pay for the tremendous advantages accrued to the child by having friends. One father answered, "The house is no place for children to play. Kids just make a mess. Also, I don't like kids on my lawn because it kills the grass. Kids should play in the street where they belong." This response, of course, is quite revealing of this parent's significant deficiencies as a father. Furniture and grass to him are far more important than his child's psychological development. One mother responded to the question with this response: "My parents never let me have friends in the house. They always wanted it very quiet and were afraid that things would be broken. I promised myself that I would never treat my children that way, and I haven't. I always welcome their friends and treat them very nicely—even when it's trouble. I can't ever remember sending a friend out of the house." The children corroborated their mother's statement.

The examiner should inquire about what efforts the parents make to bring the children to others, especially in situations where they may not be readily available. For example, if the child lives in a neighborhood where there are few if any potential playmates, one should ask about what efforts each parent has made to bring the children to distant friends and make appointments for them. Of course, the mother has far more opportunity for this than the father in most traditional homes. One mother in this situation stated that she would love to have her child visit other homes, but that she was afraid to drive and that this phobia resulted in the child's visiting far less than he might have otherwise. This mother's driving phobia was only one manifestation of a generalized dependency problem on her husband, and it was only one of the many ways in which her psychological problems were compromising her child's growth and development. Overprotective parents will often consider their children "too young" to visit the homes of others, at ages when other parents feel quite comfortable with such arrangements.

It is useful to inquire into the friendships that the parents themselves have, both as a couple and individually. The parent who has no social relationships is likely to be impaired as a parent. One could argue that there are parents who are so involved with their children that their failure to have friends provides them with more opportunity for time with their children. On the other hand, I believe that the person who cannot relate meaningfully to other adults has significant personality problems and that these are likely to affect one's child-rearing capacity. One cannot serve as a good model for children if one cannot relate to adults, because the ultimate aim of child rearing is to help the child become an independent functioning adult who can relate well to other adults. In addition, the particular personality problems that compromise the parent's capacity to relate to other adults are also likely to be filtered down to the children. For example, the parent who is distrustful (not necessarily paranoid) is likely to communicate this quality to the children. The parent who is anxious in social situations is basically communicating the message that there is something to be afraid of in one's relationships with others. Accordingly, a detailed inquiry into the reasons why the parent does not have social relationships can very quickly bear on the issue of parental capacity. Asking questions about what each parent does on Saturday night is a good starting point for this inquiry.

Attitudes Toward Children's Use of Profanity

The parent's attitude regarding the child's using profanity can provide important information related to parental capacity. I believe that profanity is one of mankind's greatest inventions. Of the various ways with which an individual can express hostility, what could be more innocuous than using certain words that the society has designated for this purpose? To the best of my knowledge, there is no language that does not have such words. There is no question that they play an important civilizing role. It is reasonable to speculate that without them people would have to resort to more damaging ways of expressing their resentments. This basic concept is epitomized in the old aphorism: "Sticks and stones may break my bones, but names will never harm me."

The healthy parent generally recognizes the basic validity of what I have just said and will not be particularly punitive when the child's profanity is confined to the street with his or her friends. The healthy parent, as well, will generally react negatively to the child's use of profanity in the home, especially when it is directed toward the parents. However, such a parent will differentiate between words and deeds and is much more likely to discipline the latter than the former. A certain amount of reasonable castigation for the use of profanity against a parent is a norm in our society ("How dare you speak that way to your mother!"). I think this is justified in that such disapprobation helps preserve such words' utilization as an innocuous hostile weapon. To allow the free use of these words would soon cause them to lose their clout as aggressive vehicles and the child might then have to resort to genuinely harmful methods of hostile expression.

I generally open the topic with the question: "What do you think about children using profanity?" With the aforementioned guidelines, the parental response can be put in perspective. One father answered, "Those words make me sick to my stomach. They make me vomit. I can't believe it when my son uses them. I tell him he's a bum, an ignoramus, and that he's a good-for-nothing. But even that doesn't stop him." I consider this response to reflect an extremely punitive attitude on this father's part. This was only one way in which he was contributing to his son's severe self-esteem problem. Such denigration for the use of profanity was clearly unwarranted and reflected a definite deficit on this parent's part.

A mother once answered about her son, "It's good for him to get anger out of his system. So when he gets angry and uses dirty words, I encourage him to tell me more." This mother, although seemingly "enlightened" and "modern," was doing her son a disservice. She is not making her social contribution to the perpetuation of the "sanctity" of profanity. In addition, she is not helping her child adjust well in a world that does not subscribe to these rules. Accordingly, he will be viewed as atypical and subject to unnecessary and avoidable ridicule. She is thereby compromising her child's capacity to adjust to life. Both of these parents exhibited parental deficiencies with regard to the use of profanity. One was far too rigid and the other far too free. As is true with most things, the moderate position is generally the preferable.

Commitment to the Educational Process

Each parent should be evaluated with regard to his or her commitment to the educational process. In our modern technological society a good education is crucial. A central element in the child's commitment to and motivation for education is the parents' *genuine* commitment, not their *professed* commitment (Gardner, 1977). The overwhelming majority of parents will claim that they are very interested in their children doing well in school. But the degree to which they will involve themselves in the child's education varies greatly. I am not referring here simply to physical involvement, but to psychological as well. A girl, for example, comes home from kindergarten and proudly shows her father that she has learned how to write her name. One father responds: "Don't bother me now, I'm watching the ballgame. Would you please get me another beer." Another responds: "This is terrific! Does your mother know? I'm going to hang this on the refrigerator and we'll show grandma and grandpa when they come on Sunday." One wants to learn about each parent's receptivity to helping the child with homework. The child here will often give valuable information in this regard. The parent who essentially does the homework for the child, to protect him or her from receiving a low grade, is generally doing more harm than good. Such a parent is probably overprotective in other areas as well. The parent who is always fighting with the child while "helping" with the homework is probably doing the child a disservice.

We all gain a certain amount of vicarious gratification through our children. Our children can serve to compensate for deficiencies and failures that we ourselves may have suffered. A certain amount of this need for vicarious gratification through our children is normal and healthy. In fact, I often say that if not for this phenomenon we might all still be living in caves. However, when it becomes an obsession with the parent then the pressures and coercions are unhealthy.

In addition to an inquiry into the parents' involvement in the formal academic program, one does well to learn about involvement in other aspects of the school situation. I cannot overemphasize the importance of an inquiry into this area. One wants to know about attendance during "open-school week." The parent who is "too busy" is insensitive to the importance of this school visit to the child. One should also ask about conferences with the teacher. It is unfortunate, but most teachers state that generally only one parent (usually the mother) attends such conferences even though the teacher may be willing to accommodate a father by coming in very early in the morning. The most important school activities about which to make inquiries are school plays, dances, concerts, and other artistic performances. Children often work many weeks in their preparation and they are extremely important to the child. Attendance at such activities should be extremely high priority for the parents. In my opinion, there are very few "excuses" that are acceptable for not attending them. There are a few areas that are highly sensitive indices of general parental capacity and attendance at school performances is one of them. In fact, I do not believe that I have ever found a parent who was disinterested in attending such performances ultimately to be the one whom I recommended for custody of the children. This is not to say that such a defect should automatically deprive a parent of the examiner's recommendation. (If that were the case, then all we would have to do would be to ask this one question.) I am only saying that this particular interest is, in my experience, highly correlated with parental capacity.

Interest in Enrichment

The healthy, involved parent is not only interested in the child's academic and social life, but is interested in enriching the child as well. By enrichment I refer to the wide variety of experiences that could make a child more interesting, both to him- or herself and others. One should inquire into parental involvement in such activities as music lessons, dance, visits to museums, visits to historical sites and other places of interest, and involvement in sports. One must be careful to differentiate between the parent who does these things out of duty, with little commitment or conviction, and the one who has a genuine interest in and enjoyment of these activities. As mentioned, the examiner should inquire as to whether the child is being coerced into lessons as opposed to being facilitated and encouraged. Of course, many of these activities are expensive and not available to all. However, even the poorest children can avail themselves of many of these if the parents are willing to take the trouble to find out which facilities in the community will make them available.

I am a strong proponent of the summer camp experience for children. It is an ideal way for the child to take his or her first steps toward independence. In a sense, we are teaching our children to become independent of us from the earliest years of life. Sleeping over at a friend's house is another important step in this direction and summer camp also serves this purpose. There are parents who rationalize not sending their children by claiming that those who do so are neglectful and are using the summer camp as a way of getting rid of their children. Although this certainly may be the case, it need not be. Although parents can certainly enjoy the vacation from the children that summer camp allows, the sleep-away camp experience can be extremely salutary for children. Committed parents are willing to make reasonable sacrifices for it because they appreciate its importance.

"Children Talk"

We have come a long way from the Victorian tradition of the after-dinner conversation in which the men retire to talk business and politics, and the women separately discuss their children and homes. I think, however, that there are residua of this tradition in modern society and that healthy women still like to talk about their children with other women. I ask the mother if she enjoys talking about her children with other mothers. The woman who says, "I prefer talking to the men; I have enough of children all day long," may be healthy, but may also be reflecting some deficiency in her maternal capacity. In our society, new job opportunities for women notwithstanding, more men are still deeply committed to and spend more time with their jobs or businesses than women. Accordingly, they generally have significantly more investment in the extra-domestic world than their wives. The healthy man, however, still enjoys spending some time talking about his children. However, not to be interested in doing this, as much as his wife, should not be viewed as a defect at this time.

Wallet and Purse Pictures of the Children

I ask the parent if he or she has any pictures of the children. This can be especially useful in the initial session with the parents when I could reasonably have good justification for asking to see such pictures. I might even provide a rationale with a comment regarding the fact that it would facilitate my talking about the children if I could see a picture or two. Although this is certainly a fringe benefit of the request, my main reason is far more important. The involved parent generally carries such pictures and will speak of the children with pride when showing them. Accordingly, carrying such a picture in his or her wallet or purse weighs in the parent's favor; while failure to do so might be considered a negative—but certainly not strongly so. If a picture is produced, one tries to get a sense of the amount of pride the parent has when showing it. One may make a positive comment in order to elicit such a response in the modest, for example: "They're very good looking children." One then observes whether there is a reaction of pride and beaming. The parent who looks at the examiner with a blank stare after such a comment does not know the pride experience (but that parent is not likely to have a picture anyway).

Dreams About the Children

I ask about dreams the parent may have had about each of the children. I must emphasize that this is not a very accurate source of information, considering our present state of ignorance regarding the meaning of dreams. It is often very difficult to understand the meaning of a dream of a person who is in analysis. It is even more difficult to be certain about the meaning of the dream of a person who is almost a stranger. If the mother is having repetitious dreams in which the child is dying, or falling out of a window, or having an accident, the chances are that this reflects unconscious hostility. Or if the parent is preoccupied with thoughts that something will happen to the child—some injury, some harm—then an inordinate degree of unconscious hostility is probably present. *Occasional* dreams and preoccupations of the aforementioned type are within the norm, in my opinion, and should not be considered a negative factor in determining maternal capacity. I must warn the examiner here that even if the parent falls into the category of having dreams that are considered reflective of low parental capacity, one should be extremely cautious regarding including this finding in the report, as well as using this information in court. As I will discuss in detail in the next chapter, using information based on projective techniques is extremely risky in custody evaluations, especially when giving testimony in court. Dream interpretation is very much in this category. One may wish to use this information to confirm other conclusions, but one should be extremely careful about including dream interpretations as a major argument in reaching one's conclusions in the final report.

Parental Psychopathology

One should evaluate, to some degree, for the presence of psychopathology not directly related to parental capacity. Many forms of psychiatric disturbance can interfere with parental capacity. These include anxiety, hysteria, depression (with or without elation), obsessive-compulsivity, hypochondriasis, and of course, various kinds of psychotic states. I must warn the evaluator here that he or she does well not (I repeat *not*) to include a diagnosis of any of the people interviewed in a custody evaluation. Basically, the court is asking who is the preferable parent. It is not likely that a diagnostic label is going to add a significant amount of information here. Is the schizophrenic a better or worse parent than a psychopath? Is the hysteric a better or a worse parent than an obsessive-compulsive? These are absurd questions. In addition to comparative diagnoses being of little value, they open the examiner to criticism under cross-examination. For example, the cross-examining attorney might ask the examiner to define the word *schizophrenia*. Following the presentation of the definition, the attorney may produce a standard psychiatric dictionary. The attorney may then ask the examiner if he or she recognizes that particular dictionary as one of the authoritative texts in the field. The likelihood is that the examiner will say *yes*. The lawyer will then read the definition of schizophrenia provided by that volume. Even if the examiner were to be an internationally famous authority on the subject and even though the definition in the dictionary might have been written by a librarian, the court is likely to view the written definition as having greater validity than the examiner's verbal one. (After all, everyone knows that things in print are more likely to be true than things that are said!) Accordingly, there is much to lose, and little if anything to gain, by using diagnostic labels.

What one should do is to describe those symptoms and behavioral manifestations that interfere with parental capacity—regardless of the diagnostic disorder of which they are a manifestation. For example, in one report I stated, "A family interview was conducted with the Smith family on September 23, 1978. As the parents and the two girls entered the room, Jane (age 3) tripped on the threshold. She fell down and began to cry. She quickly got up, however, and ran to her father and put her head in his lap. As she sobbed he caressed her head and made reassuring comments such as 'Don't worry baby, everything will be all right' and 'Daddy will kiss it and make it all better.' Following a few such kisses and caresses Jane stopped crying, but remained sitting next to her father while her head rested against his arm.

While this was going on Mrs. Smith sat staring into space, seemingly oblivious to what was going on. This observation tends to confirm Mr. Smith's allegation that, when he leaves his home in the morning, his wife is sitting in the living room watching television and that when he returns at the end of the day, she is still in the same position, with no evidence that the house has been taken care of or the children tended to to any significant degree." As I am sure the reader can appreciate, such descriptions have far more clout than the diagnostic term schizophrenia. It is very difficult, if not impossible, for a cross-examining attorney to do anything with such a statement. This attorney will just have to let it rest as one of the strong negatives against his or her client and hunt for other issues on which to focus.

Others have come forth with the same caveat. Saxe (1975), for example, warns against the use of diagnoses in custody proceedings and discusses how misleading they can be and how they may complicate rather than elucidate the issues under consideration. For example, he points out how the use of such diagnoses as *schizophrenia* or *psychosis* may mislead a naive court into believing that these disorders are invariably associated with inability to function as a parent. Bazelon (1974), a well-known judge, deplores the psychiatrist's penchant for diagnostic labeling and describes how it can narrow options for the patient once he or she has been put into a particular niche by a diagnosis.

Involvement with Grandparents

A healthy parent recognizes the importance of the children's having good relationships with their grandparents. Child therapists do not give the relationships between grandparents and grandchildren the attention it deserves. Although parents will, on occasion, idealize their children, grandparents are much more likely to do so. They have fewer of the irritating and frustrating experiences that compromise such idealization. The enhanced positive regard that grandparents have for their grandchildren contributes to building the children's self-esteem. In addition, it serves to help them tolerate and more effectively deal with the inevitable criticisms (sometimes undeserved) and rejections (often unwarranted) that all of us suffer, as children and as adults. Accordingly, grandparents serve as an important buffer. A strongly parental parent will recognize this and do everything to foster good relationships with the grandparents, even after divorce. Inquiry about the grandparents should not only be conducted with the parents, but with the children as well. The children should be asked about the grandparents in an attempt to ascertain which ones are the more involved and have better relationships with the children. In addition, one can often learn from the children which parent makes greater efforts to foster good relationships between grandparents and the children. Of course, there are some grandparents who are strongly parental and others who are not. One must therefore try to learn whether a poor relationship between a grandparent and a grandchild is due to grandparental defect or parental discouragement of the relationship (or both). It is important for the examiner to appreciate that I am not presenting this as a strong point in the evaluation, merely one that should be taken into consideration.

Although I do not have conclusive confirmation of this, I believe that the better parent usually has better parents him- or herself. This should not be surprising. Healthier grandparents are going to produce healthier children, so the preferable parent is more likely to have more highly parental parents than the nonpreferred parent. It has been my experience over the years that in the large majority of the custodial cases in which I have been involved, the parent I ultimately recommended to have custody has had more parental parents than the nonpreferred parent. In short, healthier grandparents raise healthier parents who, in turn, raise healthier children.

Visitation and Parental Capacity

For simplicity of presentation, I will generally refer to the father as the visiting parent and the mother as the custodial parent. Even though we are living in a time when fathers are gaining custody more frequently than in the past, mothers are still the custodial parents in the vast majority of households. The reader should appreciate, however, that when I refer to the father as the visiting parent, the issues discussed will be valid for visiting mothers as well, unless otherwise specified.

In a war, it is generally accepted practice to place guards at one's borders and to be suspicious of any strangers who may try to cross them. Specifically, one usually wants to prevent spies and saboteurs from entering one's country and occupied territories. One wants to protect oneself from those who would carry out information to the enemy. In addition, one wants to protect oneself from those who would enter with the intent of destruction. In the war called Divorce, we have a unique situation with regard to those who may cross the border. Whereas the enemies (the parents) have little or no access to one another's territory, the children have free access without being interrogated or searched. In fact, they are most often literally "met with open arms." They serve thereby as convenient spies and saboteurs if either one or both parents wishes to use them as such. And they often are so used.

The two most important issues about which parents wish to gain information are money and sex. The father wants to know if mother's support money is indeed being spent on the children or squandered frivolously. The mother is interested in knowing if the father is squandering money on dates and other "indulgences" while claiming that his funds for alimony and support are extremely limited. Although both parents may be extremely antagonistic toward one another, there is most often residual affection and sexual attraction. Accordingly, although separated or divorced, there may still be significant jealousy regarding involvement with sexual partners. The curiosity associated with such jealousy can be satisfied by information provided by the children. Others, although not actively trying to extract such data from the children, may find it impossible to avoid hearing about these issues.

Johnny returns from a weekend visit with his father and speaks glowingly to his mother about Fran: "Dad's new girl friend, Fran, is terrific. She makes the best pizzas I ever ate and her Hamburger Helper is terrific. And you should see the beautiful gold watch Dad bought her. It has jewels, and everything!" During a weekend visit, Jimmy excitedly tells his father about Dan, his mother's new friend, who has moved into the home: "Dan's a great guy. He's a lot of fun to be with. Because he doesn't work, he has lots of time to play ball with me when I come home from school." There are few parents who could restrain themselves from indulging their curiosity further in such circumstances.

Accordingly, when trying to assess whether a parent is utilizing the children as spies, one does well to try to determine whether it is an active process or a passive one, whether the children are being "briefed" and "debriefed," or whether the parents are more in the category of the passive recipient of the inevitable information that will come their way. It may be difficult for the examiner to ascertain exactly in which category a particular parent lies, but it is worthwhile to attempt to do so. Sometimes inquiry of the children can help in the assessment of this issue.

Using the children to perpetrate "inside jobs" behind the enemy lines is quite tempting. Mother calls father and, in a state of impotent frustration, begs him to speak to the boys in order to use his authority to get them to stop maltreating her and to be more cooperative. Father responds: "They're all yours, baby. You asked me to leave the house. I didn't want to go. You can't have it both ways. You're on your own, kid" (hangs up). Such a father is so desirous of vengeful gratification that he is blinding himself to the effects of such vengeance on his children. He is so pleased with the opportunity they are providing him to wreak vengeance on his former wife, that he does not seem to appreciate that by abrogating his authority, he is contributing to the development of behavior problems in them. They need his super-ego to help them form theirs, and this is especially the case in the situation where the mother appears to have some impairment in exerting her authority. Although this mother's inability to control her children is a parental impairment, their father's active utilization of them as weapons against his former wife is a greater impairment.

Although a rigid visitation schedule is often outlined in the separation agreement, a certain amount of parental flexibility is still necessary for the well being of the children. The evaluator should try to determine each parent's degree of flexibility with regard to the visitation schedule. The parent who rigidly subscribes to it may be doing so as a way of thwarting the other parent and is probably not giving proper attention to the needs of the children. This is illustrated in statements such as, "The divorce decree says you get them Fridays at 6:00 P.M. I don't give a damn what you'll be late for, you're not getting them one second before that. And if you don't have them back here by 6:00 P.M. on Saturday, I'm going to call my lawyer about stopping you from seeing the kids."

A mother who interferes with the visitation, either covertly or overtly, is less sensitive to the children's needs for a good relationship with their father and is thereby compromised in her parental capacity. Such a mother may "forget" to have the children ready and so may thereby thwart the father. On other occasions she may "forget" to bring them home, and he may be kept waiting for them for a indeterminate amount of time—much to his frustration. There are some mothers who will retaliate for their husband's failure to fulfill financial obligations by withholding visitation. Sometimes the courts will support such withholding. Although I am not justifying a man's not fulfilling his financial obligations to his wife and his children, in my opinion this is not a justifiable retaliation. I am fully sympathetic with the privations that such withholding of money can entail. On the other hand, to use the children as a weapon in this conflict will inevitably cause them psychological distress. It is a tempting but injudicious and misguided method of getting vengeance. Requesting the court to garnishee the father's salary or attach his property is a far more reasonable course and is not likely to have detrimental effects on the children.

Soon after the separation the father usually visits with the children alone. However, he may start to combine dating with visitation. This may not be a manifestation of any insensitivity or neglect on his part, but rather the result of the limited free time he has available.

Symbolic of what happens on such occasions is the shifting of the children from the front to the back seat of the car during the visitation period. Previously they sat in the front with him and engaged in active conversation. Now they may find themselves in the back watching the father engage in lively conversation with his date. This can be very painful to them, and the sensitive father is careful to include the children as much as possible when he does combine a date with the visitation. Generally, the father does well to reserve such combined visits for involvements with an important person. If there is a "parade" of dates, a new person for each visit, this is likely to be detrimental to the children. Elsewhere (1977, 1979b) I have described in detail what I consider to be the detrimental effects of children being exposed to a parent's parade of dates.

Many fathers, especially in the period immediately following the separation, will indulge their children significantly during visitation. Visits then may consist of an endless round of entertainment and recreational activities. Homework may be neglected as well as household chores and the normal routine of everyday living. Often, guilt alleviation is the primary motivation. On occasion, such a father may be trying to compensate for feelings of parental inadequacy produced by the divorce. In addition, the father may be trying to compete with the mother for the children's affection by proving that he is the better parent. Whatever the motivations, such a practice is detrimental to the children. It is indulgent and does not provide them with the proper balance of activities—the pleasant *and* the unpleasant, work *and* play. And when there is a custody conflict, additional motives may be operative, e.g., bribing the children into choosing the father as the preferable parent. The examiner should be aware of all of these factors that may contribute to the "good guy" father syndrome, especially when such indulgences are exhibited soon after the separation by a father who was previously not particularly attentive and involved.

Wallerstein and Kelly (1980) make the following statement about the visiting father:

> Men who could bend to the complex logistics of the visiting; who could deal with the anger of the women and the capriciousness of the child without withdrawing; who could overcome their own depression, jealousy, and guilt; and could involve the children in their planning; who could walk a middle ground between totally rearranging their schedule and not changing their schedule at all; and who felt less stressed and freer to parent, were predominantly among those who continued to visit regularly and frequently.

Although this represents an ideal, and there are probably few who could live up to it entirely, it does outline the criteria by which one might evaluate the visiting father (or mother).

Child Snatching

In custody conflicts between parents, the term *child snatching* is used in preference to kidnapping because, strictly speaking, a parent cannot be charged with kidnapping his or her own child. Because a parent cannot be charged with kidnapping his or her own child, the law essentially permits it (Beck, 1977). Time is very much on the side of the custodial parent, regardless of that parent's parental capacity as compared with the noncustodial parent. Accordingly, even if the child-snatching parent is ultimately brought back into court, the longer the children have been with the child snatcher, the greater the likelihood they will state preference for the person with whom they have been living.

The Constitution has specifically left divorce issues to the states, considering them "family matters" that should not justifiably be handled by the federal government. Accordingly, until recently, a parent could take a child across state lines and be immune from prosecution. The parent from whom the children had been snatched was relatively impotent. There was little an aggrieved parent could do if the snatching parent remained in a different state. On occasion, that parent would snatch the children back or engage the services of others to perform this task. In recent years, states have been recognizing and enforcing decisions made in other states with regard to custody. In December, 1980, Congress passed a law requiring all 50 states to recognize and enforce the custody decisions of courts in other states. In addition, the new law requires the FBI to use its resources to help locate parents who have crossed state lines as child snatchers, once arrest warrants have been issued. Accordingly, the child-snatching parent is now considered to be perpetrating a punishable crime, and the FBI can be invited to pursue such a parent across state lines. There is little question that this new law will deter at least some child snatchers.

It is important for the examiner to appreciate that the child-snatching parent is not necessarily the one who should automatically lose custody of the children. It is certainly the case that the child snatcher is being insensitive to the children's need for intensive involvement with the other parent. And this is certainly a negative in the custody evaluation. On the other hand, our court system is not famous for the judiciousness of custody decisions and many have been ill-advised. The child snatcher, then, may be rescuing the children from an extremely detrimental environment, the gravity of which the court did not appreciate. In evaluating such parents, the fact of child snatching is certainly a negative. However, one must also consider each parent's qualities as a parent. In addition, one must take into consideration the desires of the children with the full recognition that their preferences may be related to their having lived a significant period of time with the child snatcher. Sometimes all these factors will balance out in favor of the parent with whom the children lived prior to their abduction. At other times, they will balance out in favor of the child snatcher. I have had two experiences in which I considered the child snatcher to be the less preferable parent in terms of parental capacity. However, the children had lived so long with that parent (partially as the result of court delay) and were so committed to the abducting parent that my ultimate recommendation was that the children be allowed to remain living with the child snatcher. My main point here is that the examiner must have great flexibility in such cases and not automatically assume that the child snatcher is the less preferable parent. In addition, the examiner must appreciate that there are times when the children's desires are so strong and the trauma to them of being removed would be so great that one may end up recommending that they stay with the parent who is intrinsically the less desirable one.

The most extreme example of this kind of situation is the one in which the children live with a paranoid parent. I recall one situation in which the children were living with a paranoid schizophrenic mother. She viewed her ex-husband as the incarnation of all the evil that ever existed in mankind's history. The children were exposed to a constant program of vilification of their father. They, in a kind of *folie a deux* relationship with their mother, developed the same delusions. At the very sight of their father, they panicked and resisted going with him—believing that if they did so they would probably be murdered. Although a paranoid schizophrenic, this mother was functioning adequately in many areas. There was no reason to believe that she could be committed to a hospital and she was certainly not going to voluntarily admit herself. Her paranoid delusional system appeared to involve primarily her ex-husband. Here, I recommended that the children be allowed to remain living with their mother. I suggested to the father that he intermittently try to communicate with the children (via letter, messages from third intermediaries, etc.) in the hope that as time passed the children might ultimately come to see him in a more reasonable light. Although this vignette has nothing to do with child snatching per se, it does demonstrate the principle that the examiner may, on occasion, recommend that the children remain in the custody of the nonpreferable parent because their long-term exposure to that parent would make it psychologically traumatic to them to be removed.

Homosexuality and Parental Capacity

Now to the difficult and controversial subject of homosexuality. No one can say that he or she knows with certainty the etiology of homosexuality. Some claim it is a normal variation and that it is part of the human repertoire. Others consider it a definite form of psychopathology. Still others would say that both factors may be operative to varying degrees and that individuals differ regarding the contribution of each of these factors, that is, the hereditary (or constitutional) and the environmental. The subject, unfortunately, often generates strong emotional reactions. For example, if in a public situation, an authority states that no one knows the cause of schizophrenia, but that he or she believes personally that it is organic in etiology, even those who disagree are not likely to get too heated in their refutations. Similarly, those who claim it is psychogenic are not likely to raise the blood pressures of those who disagree with them. I am sure similar calmness is seen when one talks about organicity vs. psychogenicity for such disorders as migraine headaches, ulcerative colitis, peptic ulcers, hypertension, etc. But if one says publicly in the 1980s that homosexuality is a psychological disorder, the speaker may be pelted with rocks and, if well known, may be the subject of public demonstrations, angry editorials in newspapers, and heated diatribes. Even in university and academic settings, where differences of opinion are supposedly given equal opportunity for expression, those who hold that homosexuality is a psychological disorder may find themselves ostracized. I believe that such strong emotional reaction may be related to reaction formation on the part of those who react with such strong feelings. Certainly, their anger and condemnation are the hallmark of reaction formation and suggest that it is psychologically threatening for many to accept the possibility that homosexuality may be psychogenic. (Similarly, it may be psychologically threatening to some to consider it organic.)

If the examiner is of the belief that homosexuality is a normal human variation, then he or she will probably not consider the parent's homosexuality as a factor in the custody evaluation. Rather, such an examiner will utilize other criteria—having nothing to do with the parent's sexual orientation—to decide custody.

Although this is the common position taken by many examiners in the 1970s and 1980s, this is not my view. I consider there to be a continuum with strong heterosexuality on the one end and strong homosexuality on the other. No individual, no matter how strongly heterosexual, is free from some homosexual tendencies. Similarly, no homosexual individual, no matter how strongly homosexual, is free from heterosexual inclinations. All individuals, therefore, are at some point between the two ends of this continuum. I believe that the person who is an obligative homosexual, who cannot function heterosexually, is suffering with a psychiatric disorder that is primarily, if not exclusively, environmentally induced—although there may be a small genetic (or constitutional) contributing factor. Such an individual has a problem which might readily be classified as a kind of phobia. Specifically, this person is so fearful of functioning with a member of the opposite sex that he or she *cannot* do so even when opportunities are available and the heterosexual partner is desirous of such an involvement. Other psychodynamic factors are operative, e.g., anger toward members of the opposite sex and the desire to express such resentments via withholding sexual pleasure.

My views are less firm with regard to the possible psychopathology of people who are bisexual. Such individuals appear to work on the principle: If it feels good I'll do it regardless of the sex of my partner. Such individuals may enjoy homosexual activities, even when heterosexual opportunities are available. As mentioned, I am less firm in my belief that bisexuals are suffering with psychopathology, but I suspect that they are. Lastly, because of the homosexual potential in even the strongest heterosexuals, I would not consider a rare homosexual act on the part of a strongly heterosexual person to be psychopathological. This would especially be the case when heterosexual opportunity is not available. I view the homosexual capacity to allow for sexual gratification in a heterosexual when heterosexual gratification is not available.

It is important for the reader to appreciate that I am not claiming to know with certainty if the above view is correct. It is the view I hold at this time on the basis of my present understanding of human sexual behavior. It behooves the examiner to have an opinion on the subject if he or she is to be providing recommendations in custody conflicts in which the parent is homosexual. One cannot wait for all the information to come in (it may take hundreds of years). Accordingly, we must make recommendations, recognizing that they have been made on the basis of *hypotheses* regarding the etiology and significance of homosexuality. Although homosexuality is seen in lower animals, it generally manifests itself when heterosexual outlets are not available or as a transient phenomenon. To assume that there are human beings in whom it is the inborn preferential orientation requires the assumption that mankind has departed markedly from the evolutionary pattern. In addition, one must then believe in the existence of a natural sexual variant without the goal of species procreation—another evolutionary innovation, to say the least.

Although I believe that the obligative homosexual is suffering with a psychiatric disorder, this should in no way be interpreted as meaning that I believe that an obligative homosexual (or any other kind of homosexual for that matter) should be deprived of his or her civil rights. One's private sexual life should not be a factor in determining job opportunities, career choice, and so on. To consider a parent's sexual orientation in the custody evaluation is not an infringement of that parent's civil rights. Because I view obligative homosexuality as a psychiatric disturbance, it warrants inclusion in the custody evaluation like any other kind of psychiatric disorder. Even if I were to conclude that the parent's homosexuality was a compromising factor, and even a crucial one in the custodial decision, I would consider it cruel and inhumane to deprive such a parent of opportunities in areas that have nothing to do with one's sexual orientation, such as job opportunity and career advancement. Child rearing *has* something to do with one's sexual orientation.

In the discussion below, where I more specifically discuss how I assess the role of parental homosexuality in the custody evaluation, I will be using the word homosexual to refer both to bisexuals and obligative homosexuals. The more the parent's sexual orientation is in the obligative range, the greater the pathology and the more weight to be given to the homosexual orientation.

In addition, I generally consider the average male obligative homosexual to be suffering with more psychological difficulties than the average female obligative homosexual. This may come as a surprising statement to many readers and I have not seen anything in the literature supporting such a statement. What I say here is my own personal opinion supported, I believe, by these arguments. With rare exception, the primary sexual object for both males and females is the mother. She has carried the children within her own body for nine months, has suffered the pains of their delivery, and has the capacity to feed them from her own body (although she may not chose to do so). The average healthy father, no matter how deeply involved with his newborn infant, is not as likely to have as strong a tie with the newborn child as the average healthy mother. In our society where the mother is still the primary caretaking parent in most families (recent changes in the pattern notwithstanding), the earliest primary attachment for infants of both sexes is the mother. In the normal development of the boy, he transfers his affection from the mother to other girls and ultimately other adult females. The progression is a relatively smooth one for the average healthy boy and does not involve the kind of shift required of the female. The girl, on the other hand, must transfer her sexual involvements from a female (the mother) to a male figure: boyfriends and then adult males. It is reasonable to assume that residua of the attraction to the mother are likely to be present. One confirmation of such residual attraction is the fact that many more heterosexual women are physically attracted to the naked female body than heterosexual men are to the naked male body. Many more heterosexual women purchase magazines depicting naked women than heterosexual men purchase magazines depicting naked men. (The latter are generally only purchased by homosexual males.) For a woman to become a lesbian involves a fixation at an earlier level of development: the level at which she was attracted to her primary sexual object, the mother. Her subsequent lovers are in the same mold, so to speak, and are readily understandable. Blocked in heterosexual gratification, it is reasonable that she may be fixed at or regress to an earlier level.

The male homosexual, on the other hand, has a much more complex course toward his resultant homosexual orientation. He must abrogate mother and all her derivative surrogates. He must shift toward an intense sexual involvement with a father surrogate without any continuity with his previous biological track. The psychological processes involved in such a path are complex and extremely powerful. The distortions of thinking necessary to effect such a transfer are profound. It is for these reasons that I consider the obligative male homosexual to have deeper psychopathology than the obligative female homosexual. And such differences should be taken into consideration in the custody evaluation.

A parent's homosexuality, although a manifestation of psychopathology (in this examiner's opinion), should not in itself be a reason for depriving that parent of custody. It should merely be one factor considered in the decision. It may be an extremely important one, or it may be of little significance. It is important for the examiner to appreciate that removal of the children from a homosexual parent can deprive them of valuable experiences. Homosexuality per se need not make a parent incapable of providing children with most of the benefits of parenthood. Homosexuality need not impair parental capacity. There are many male homosexuals who make very good parents—oriented as they are toward maternal functioning. Although such men may contribute to a boy's becoming homosexual by serving as a model for such an orientation, they do not often exhibit the punitive rejecting attitude toward their sons that may contribute to their becoming homosexual. There is this compromising identification factor, therefore, a factor that may contribute to the son's becoming homosexual; but it is not generally that great that I would suggest that the homosexual father automatically be deprived of visitation and custody rights to which he might otherwise be entitled. Similarly, with the lesbian mother, her homosexuality should not in itself be a reason for depriving her of custody and visitation rights that she might otherwise be granted, even though I believe that her sexual orientation might be a negative factor in making the decision. I would consider it along with other factors, both positive and negative, in making a recommendation.

In custody evaluations involving homosexual parents, I try to determine whether the parent is trying (either overtly or covertly) to raise the child to become homosexual. It can be openly done with the parent directly stating that he or she wants the child to be homosexual. (This, by the way, is rare, in my experience. Most homosexuals I have encountered, if they are to be directly honest, would prefer that their children be heterosexual. Although they claim that they say this because their children's lives would be easier in a society that discriminates so terribly against homosexuals, I believe that it is also stated from the deep appreciation that the homosexual way of life is less potentially gratifying—their professions to the contrary notwithstanding.) More commonly, the homosexual parent encourages homosexuality in the children more covertly, with comments such as "I tell my children that I have no particular preference regarding whether they become homo- or heterosexual." Healthy parents, in my opinion, do have a preference—and strongly so. They want their children to be heterosexual—have no doubts about it—and shudder at the possibility that a child might become homosexual. This has less to do with the social stigma that the homosexual suffers (which, fortunately, is lessening) and more with the appreciation that such a way of life is more likely to be unrewarding and painful than a heterosexual existence—as is true of all life patterns that are associated with psychological disturbance.

Although a homosexual parent provides, in my opinion, an unhealthy model for sexual identification, this fact should not in itself be a reason for refusing such a parent custody if the child is above the age of three or four and exhibits definite heterosexual orientation. By that time the child's sexual orientation is fairly well established and is not likely to be altered unless there is unusual and prolonged indoctrination into homosexual attitudes and behavior and/or environmental factors that can contribute to the development of homosexuality. When involved in custody evaluations of homosexual parents, I examine carefully each child's sexual orientation and look for signs and symptoms of homosexuality and sexual identification problems—both present and potential. For boys, the signs of a potential homosexual problem would include the *frequent* desire to put on the mother's make-up and to wear her shoes, underwear, and other articles of clothing; a preference for the role of mother in playing "house"; and a marked preference for playing with girls rather than boys. These criteria are especially valid when they have taken on an obsessive or compulsive quality. Present uncertainty about traditional male and female roles notwithstanding, I still hold that these criteria are valid. I would recommend that a homosexual father of such a child not be granted custody, unless there were other very powerful counterbalancing considerations. There are also less definite manifestations of a homosexual problem in the male. If a boy exhibits traditionally effeminate gestures and intonations and is *often* called "sissy" or "fag" by his peers, I suspect a potential homosexual problem. Some "momma's boys" may be revealing the kind of attachment seen in the homosexual. Although tomboyishness may reflect a homosexual problem in the girl, it is not a very valuable criterion, especially in more recent years, when girls' involvement in traditional male activities is becoming more common, happily so, in my opinion.

During the prepubertal and pubertal periods special problems may arise that can affect my recommendations regarding custody and visitation. If a homosexual father, for example, is frequently bringing his 13-year-old son together with his homosexual friends, he is providing the boy with a detrimental exposure. Even though there may be no overt invitations to sexual involvement, such a boy is often quite attractive to homosexual men and their feelings toward him will be subtly appreciated by him. A boy of this age normally exhibits a certain amount of homosexual interest. The setting therefore cannot but be a titillating and seductive one for all concerned. Even if the boy exhibits no evidence of homosexual orientation, the atmosphere is bound to be a charged one for him. Although it may not result in his becoming homosexual, it can add to the sexual anxieties and confusions that he will normally have during this period. Accordingly, I would consider such exposures an argument against granting such a father custody. I would certainly, however, encourage visitation, but would recommend that such exposures not be permitted during the visiting times.

If a homosexual parent maintains his or her homosexuality as a private part of his or her life; if he or she is not trying to induce homosexuality in the children or expose them to sexual activities; and if the children are above the age of four and show no evidence of homosexuality or of sexual orientation disturbance, then I would not consider the parent's homosexuality a reason for disqualifying him or her as the custodial parent. Nor would I recommend that there by any reduction or restriction of visitation rights. Although the homosexuality, in itself, would be considered a negative in my considerations, if the above criteria are satisfied, it becomes a small one.

The question of what recommendations to make regarding custody for a homosexual parent who is living with a homosexual partner is a more difficult one. Those who argue that homosexuality is not a psychiatric disturbance would compare such a relationship with a heterosexual one and argue that the same criteria should hold with regard to the granting of custody. If the court would grant custody to a mother who lives with a man to whom she is not married, and if it would grant custody to a father who is not married to the woman with whom he is living (and courts commonly do so today in both of these situations), then, they would argue, the court should not discriminate against the parent who lives with someone of the same sex. I am in agreement with the more liberal criteria that courts have recently been using with regard to the granting of custody to a parent who is living with but not married to a heterosexual partner. Because I believe that homosexuality is most likely a psychiatric disorder, I do not equate heterosexual with homosexual exposure. I believe that a child who lives in a home in which both "parents" are of the same sex is being unduly exposed to an unhealthy psychological environment. The situation is very different from the one in which the homosexual parent does not live with anyone and keeps his or her homosexual life apart from the children. When the parent lives with a homosexual partner, there is an exposure to homosexuality of such great intensity that it is likely to affect the children. I do not believe that the effect is so great that it could reverse the sexual identity of children over four who have already established a heterosexual identity and orientation. Rather, I believe that such exposure could create confusions, anxieties, and compromises in sex role identification that might otherwise not have developed. In addition, as mentioned above, in the adolescent period the titillations engendered in such a situation could not but cause the adolescent significant anxieties. Accordingly, I consider such an arrangement to be a strong negative in weighing the pros and cons for recommending custody. Just as the heterosexual parent who exposes the children to a parade of lovers is, I believe, providing a detrimental exposure, a homosexual parent who frequently brings a partner or series of partners into the home—whether to sleep over or not—similarly compromises his or her parental role. Like all the other criteria I use, no one of these is overriding. I might still recommend custody for such a parent if other factors were present that counterbalanced this one.

In providing a court with recommendations regarding visitation and custody rights for a homosexual parent, the guideline that I use is this: The greater the degree to which the child is exposed to a homosexual environment, the greater should be the restrictions imposed to protect the child from the detrimental effects of such exposure. Homosexuality in itself should not be a reason for reducing a parent's visitation or custody rights. But when there is exposure to homosexuality and imposition of it, one should consider limiting such a parent's privileges.

Joan's situation provides an example of the kind of situation in which I recommended that a lesbian mother not be given custody of her child and that there be a curtailment of her visitation rights. Joan was 13 years old when her parents separated because of her mother's homosexuality. She was an only child. At around the time of the separation Joan's mother became a gay activist. Originally the mother was given custody of Joan, and she moved into an apartment house where there were many other homosexuals who were involved in the Gay Liberation Movement. Joan's mother became increasingly swept up in her political activities, fighting for the civil rights of homosexuals. So involved was she in these activities that she had little meaningful time left over for Joan. Many homosexuals visited the home, where meetings often took place. The apartment was flooded with literature and pamphlets supporting the gay cause. In addition, many homosexual magazines were strewn about the apartment, magazines with pictures depicting various kinds of homosexual activities. On occasion the mother would bring Joan along to gay activist marches and demonstrations, and encouraged her to hand out leaflets in support of the movement. She took a strictly neutral attitude regarding Joan's future sexual orientation. She denied that Joan had ever been invited into sexual encounters with any of her friends. She claimed that although Joan was a little young for such experiences she would have no objection to her having homosexual experiences by her mid-teens if this was her preference.

Joan's father instituted legal proceedings in order to gain custody of his daughter. As the result of my examination of Joan and both parents, I supported his request. Although Joan showed no evidence for a homosexual orientation at that time, I concluded that the intensive exposure to the homosexual environment was sexually titillating and confusing to Joan, but that it was not likely that she would become a lesbian. I considered her mother's intensive involvement in her political activities to be depriving Joan of the amount of attention and affection she warranted. This had nothing to do with the nature of her mother's activities. (In fact, I was in full sympathy with her mother's political activities, believing as I do that there is absolutely no justification for depriving a homosexual of his or her civil rights merely because of the presence of this disorder.) Even if the mother had been involved in activities having nothing to do with homosexuality, her obsessive involvement in a cause resulted in her neglecting Joan. The court agreed with my recommendation and Joan's father was granted custody. The court followed my recommendation that the mother be granted liberal visitation privileges. However, she was not allowed to involve the child in her gay liberation activities or bring her to the apartment where she was living, because of the intensive exposure Joan had there to the homosexual environment.

Before closing this discussion of homosexuality, I wish to emphasize again that I make no claims that my opinion that the obligative homosexual has a psychiatric disorder is "right." I only claim that it appears to me to be the most reasonable conclusion I can come to from my knowledge of and experiences with people who are homosexual. The recommendations I make regarding custody and visitation for the homosexual parent are based on this presumption. Evaluators who do not share my view, and I recognize that they are numerous (although I am not alone either), will, of course, make very different recommendations.

FINAL CONSIDERATIONS

Joint Interviews

It is important for the examiner to appreciate that the joint interviews are more important than the sessions in which the individuals are interviewed alone. This is especially the case for the adults. In the individual interviews each party (parents and children) makes statements about others. These are justifiably called *allegations* by the attorneys. In the joint interview, one has an opportunity to hear the refutations directly (as opposed to their being communicated through a third party—the examiner) as well as observe the interplay between the accuser and the accused. Out of this interplay may come some consensus or even an admission. These admissions and mutually agreed-upon statements are the most powerful parts of the examiner's report. The allegations, moreover, are of practically no value if they are refuted. One of the biggest mistakes an examiner can make is to accept as valid one party's allegation. If he or she does so, the opposing attorney is likely to recognize this weakness in the examiner's report and may make him or her look quite foolish under cross-examination. Generally, I conduct three types of joint interviews: 1) parent-parent interviews, both as an initial interview and after I have collected data from each parent separately, 2) family interviews in which I see both parents and all the children together, and 3) the parent-child interview in which I will see one parent with one or more children. In the interviews in which the total family is present, one can often see whom the children prefer. In the interview with a parent and one or more children, one can observe that particular parent-child interaction.

Verbalizations, gesturing, and all forms of interaction should be studiously observed during these interviews. It is important to appreciate that the parents may try to "put on an act" during these interviews. Accordingly, it behooves the examiner to try to differentiate between playacting and genuine, spontaneous expressions and involvement. However, children—and the younger they are the more truly this can be said—are not going to be able to playact very well nor will the younger ones even try. It is also important to appreciate that the situation is an extremely artificial one and that the parents, especially, are likely to be quite guarded. The tensions and anxieties engendered by the situation are likely to compromise parental spontaneity and relaxation.

The examiner should try to observe how much a child is involved with the mother as compared with the father. Generally, in the first interview the child may be afraid of the therapist, who is a stranger, and may try to cuddle with the parent, hide his or her head in the parent's lap, and/or exhibit other maneuvers which serve to enlist the parent's aid in assuaging the child's anxiety. It is important to note which parent is preferred for such anxiety alleviation. If the parent is caressing and responsive, and if the child sinks comfortably into his or her lap or arms, this is a positive sign. If the parent tends to freeze or stiffen in response, this is definitely a negative. Excessive criticism of the child—"Don't touch that," "Go away from there," etc.—is usually a reflection of some impairment. It is often useful for the evaluator to compliment the child and observe the parent's reaction (just as was done when the child's picture was shown). If the parent responds with pride, this is a positive sign; if not, it is a definite negative.

The way in which the family interview can provide important information was described by the aforementioned case of the schizophrenic mother who stared into space when her child tripped at the threshold. Another example is well demonstrated by my interview with Mr. and Mrs. R and their two daughters, Brenda and Marie. (I present this in the way I described it in the final report in order to provide the reader with the format that I consider most effective for describing such observations.)

On January 7, 1981 a family session was held. When I entered the waiting room to invite the family to my office, Mrs. R was sitting on one side of a partition which partially divides the waiting room, and Mr. R and the two girls were sitting on the other side. There were enough seats on both sides of the partition to accommodate any arrangement. Although it is reasonable that Mr. and Mrs. R might not wish to sit together (divorced people often seat themselves on opposite sides of this partition), the girls chose to sit with their father. Although this is not presented as a major point, it does have some significance with regard to the children's preference.

The family members were seen in the following sequence: First, Brenda was seen alone. Then I interviewed Marie alone. While Marie was sitting in the room, I stepped out into the waiting room and invited Mr. and Mrs. R and Brenda to join us. When Mrs. R entered the room, she sat down in the chair next to the one in which Marie had already been sitting. Mr. R and Brenda sat on a couch opposite to the two chairs which were occupied by Mrs. R and Marie. As soon as Mrs. R sat down next to Marie, Marie got up and walked across the room to the couch in order to sit next to the father. Again the voluntary seating arrangement revealed the children's preference: the two girls with their father sitting on the couch together and Mrs. R sitting alone on the opposite side of the room.

As mentioned, mutually agreed-upon statements and admissions are the kinds of things one wants to focus on in the joint sessions. For example, the mother may state that the father is late for 90 percent of his visitations and that the average lateness is two hours. If the father denies completely that he is ever late, one may not be able to come to any specific conclusions regarding this issue (unless one has some corroboration from the children). If the children are too young or unreliable, then one can do nothing with this information even though one may suspect that the mother is probably telling the truth. If, however, the father does admit to such lateness, but to a lesser degree, then one has more valid data. For example, if the father says that he was late only half the time and that the average lateness was one to one-and-a-half hours, he is admitting a deficiency. In one's final report one can give both parents' accounts and then state that even if Mr. Jones' version is true, it still represents a compromise of his paternal capacity. I cannot impress upon the reader strongly enough the power of this kind of statement in the custody report. A statement made by the deficient party him- or herself is more convincing than any other source of data.

On occasion, a parent will make a statement, present a plan, or exhibit some kind of behavior that he or she considers to reflect well on his or her paternal/maternal capacity. However, without realizing it, the parent is really compromising his or her position. The parent is motivated to discuss the issue with the examiner from the belief that it is an asset. Such a parent will have thereby, as the old expression goes, been hoist "with his(her) own petard". This is an old phrase, not frequently heard these days. A *petard* was a thick iron engine of war, that was filled with gun powder and fastened to gates, barricades, walls, etc., in order to blow them up or, in the case of walls, blow holes in them. The engineer who devised and built such instruments was often directly involved in placing and hoisting the device to the most strategic place. The danger in their use was that the engineer who fired the petard would be blown up by the explosion of his own instrument. In short, the term "hoist with his own petard" has come to mean caught in one's own trap or defeated by one's own plot.

For example, an important factor in deciding who is the preferable parent is the amount of time the parent has available to spend with the children. If a parent works, then the quality of the surrogate caretakers must be examined with care. One father, whom I considered to be the less preferable parent for a variety of reasons related to his personality, was clearly in the less desirable position when it came to providing parental surrogates. His ex-wife was home all day, whereas he had a full-time job as an architect. There were two daughters involved, ages 7 and 9. He lived in a large apartment house with a swimming pool. His plans were to have the two girls come home from school each day and be taken care of by a group of high school and college girls who worked as lifeguards at the swimming pool. They would rotate their baby-sitting days with their lifeguard duties. He provided me with the names, addresses, and telephone numbers of each of the girls (there were five) and insisted that each one was highly maternal (he had interviewed them himself) and promised to be available for at least a few years.

In my report I described how I considered the plan an impractical one for a number of reasons. I suspected that the likelihood that it would work out would be poor and that these teen-agers could not be relied upon to dedicate themselves to the care of these children in a predictable fashion. In addition, I considered it extremely unlikely that these girls would be available over a period of years, considering the usual turnover of such positions. One year later, when the case came to trial, none of the five girls was still working at the swimming pool. The plan that this man had submitted to strengthen his case was basically a poor one and, as I had predicted, it was not likely to succeed. In court he "lost points" because of his obvious impracticality. In short, he was "hoist on his own petard."

The Examiner's Confusion
and Ambivalence

In the course of the evaluation, one may become quite confused. When speaking with the mother, the examiner may feel quite confident that she deserves to have the child. The indignities she describes herself to have suffered at the hands of her husband and the neglect that he has exhibited toward the children appear to be formidable. Then, during the interview with the father, the examiner may wonder how he could have been naive enough to consider, even for one moment, recommending custody to the mother. The father provides convincing arguments that the mother's view of the situation is entirely distorted, possibly even to the point of paranoia. And so, back and forth the arguments go—producing in the therapist mounting confusion and ambivalence. Generally, the joint interviews, as well as input from the children, help the examiner to determine which of the two views are closer to the "truth."

My experience has been that my best evaluations have been those in which I have experienced the most confusion and ambivalence. In such cases, I have had to be "on my toes" and have been therefore highly motivated to extract as much information as possible from all concerned parties. This indecisiveness has sharpened my inquiry and contributed to my ultimately formulating the most comprehensive and convincing evaluation.

It is important for the examiner to appreciate that just as one element in obsessive love is a reaction formation to unacceptable hostility, so excessive hatred (as witnessed in divorce conflicts) can serve, in part, as a reaction formation to underlying, lingering affectionate feelings. It is unreasonable to believe that two people who have been living together for a number of years and who have reared together one or more children do not still have residual feelings of affection and even love. They may have to deny these in order to enable themselves to separate successfully. They may have to exaggerate the hateful feelings in order to provide themselves with the strength to sever the marital bond. And such exaggerations are likely, if not inevitably, going to exhibit themselves in the litigation and in the custody evaluation. Accordingly, exaggerations and distortions are the rule, rather than the exception, and the evaluator must be ever alert to this element during the interviews.

On occasion, it becomes apparent very early in the evaluation which parent is going to be supported. The evaluator should not interrupt the evaluation immediately in such cases, but should at least get full histories on all parties and whatever information is necessary to support adequately his or her conclusion. One does not want to be in the position of not having done a complete evaluation. The parents too are entitled to at least full history taking and reasonable collection of data because of the small possibility that new information may arise that would change the examiner's conclusion.

The Evaluator as Evaluator
vs. The Evaluator as Therapist

In the course of the evaluation, examiners should make every reasonable attempt to restrict themselves to the primary goal: collecting data in the service of making the best possible custody recommendation. The combination of therapy and data collection in a custody evaluation is a poor one. Therapy, among other things, involves providing advice. When one provides advice there is the risk of producing anxiety and alienation of the parent—and such feelings can contaminate unnecessarily the evaluation. Such advice may give the parent a hint as to "which way the wind is blowing," because it may imply: "You are doing things wrong and this is the right way to do them." Although transferential reactions are bound to arise in the most conservative evaluations, once the examiner starts doing therapy the likelihood of such responses occurring increases immeasurably. All kinds of feelings may then come forth: anger, fear, sexual attraction, and so on. These may be very useful to investigate in therapy, but they are not only less useful to investigate in the custody evaluation, they may actually compromise it. One could argue, on the one hand, that such data are also in the realm of what the examiner should be interested in. On the other hand, they are generally of less value than the kinds of "facts" one is searching for, and they may contribute to all kinds of criticisms and accusations that the parent may communicate to his or her attorney. They may provide the attorney with "ammunition" in court if he is sophisticated enough to appreciate that the examiner is involving him- or herself in therapy.

Accordingly, the best and safest position for the examiner to take is that of the strictly neutral data collector who is ever asking questions. This does not mean that the examiner must be an automaton or a data-collecting computer. The evaluator can be human, sensitive, and benevolent in the inquiry. He or she can still be sympathetic to the parents' plights and the pains they are suffering in the course of the evaluation. The evaluator can be sympathetic to the fact that "old wounds" are being opened and are intensifying the psychological trauma of the divorce and custody conflict.

These warnings notwithstanding, I do on occasion provide minor bits of advice in the course of the evaluation. Sometimes the parents' responses provide me with useful information. For example, on a few occasions, a mother has refused to let the children visit their father as long as a new woman friend was present. This is especially the case when the woman friend would sleep over in the father's bedroom in the course of the visitation. In those cases where I determined it advisable (and one must be judicious here), I commented to the mother that I considered her position psychologically inappropriate and that she was not acting in the best interests of their children. I described how such a position could deprive the children of important contact with their father. Some mothers used moral principles and religious teachings to justify what was really vengeful acting out on their parts. (Most of these women were not particularly religious.) Their rage at the thought of the father's being with another woman was so great that they were willing to sacrifice their children's visitation benefits in the service of hurting the father and/or interfering with his new liaison. Some ignored my advice and rigidly held their position—contributing thereby to their children being deprived of freer involvement with their father. Others were willing to modify their position from the recognition that my explanation was a reasonable one. In short, the advice was given en passant, and the reactions provided useful data in the custody evaluation.

To reiterate, evaluators do well to restrict themselves to providing advice on rare occasions only and then only to a limited degree. Under no circumstances should they become involved in an ongoing therapeutic experience in the course of the custody evaluation. And, for reasons to be discussed in Chapter Seven, the examiner should not become involved in providing therapy following the evaluation.

CONCLUDING COMMENTS

My primary purpose in this chapter has been to present to the examiner a compendium of the questions and techniques that I have found useful in evaluating parental capacity in custody litigation. As mentioned, it would be unreasonable to expect the examiner to use all these methods and questions with any particular parent. The evaluator will generally not require all of them in order to come to a conclusion. It is well to pursue those areas that show promise of providing the most meaningful information, to exclude questions that provide little promise for useful or new data, and to discontinue the interviews when enough information is available to draw meaningful conclusions and recommendations.

5

△|△ Evaluation of the
Children

THE PROBLEM OF THE CHILD'S CREDIBILITY

Evaluating the child in a custody evaluation presents the examiner with one of his or her greatest challenges. The primary difficulty relates to the children's credibility (or lack of it) and the criteria that children may utilize to support their arguments. For example, a 6-year-old boy might say, "I want to live with my daddy. My mommy is mean. She makes me get up every day to go to school and she makes me go to sleep early because she says there's school the next day. My father is nicer. When I visit him on weekends he doesn't make me go to sleep early and he doesn't make me get up in the morning to go to school. I want to live with my father." Although no competent examiner would use such a statement as a reason for recommending that this child live with his father, the statement is a good example of the reasoning processes that might be utilized by the child to determine parental preference.

Another problem that faces the examiner is that children tend to be fickle and change their preferences from day to day. Their memories are shorter than adults' and they may utilize their most recent experiences as the primary criteria from which to make their preference. On different days the examiner may get different answers. In

151

addition, because children's reasons are so superficial, they are likely to change their minds as well. Because of the fickleness of children, I often suggest that they be seen twice. One may get an entirely different story in each of the two interviews. If the child gives the same information on two successive interviews, it is to be taken more seriously.

Wallerstein and Kelly (1980) hold that, prior to adolescence, children's preferences regarding parental choice should not be taken too seriously. They were particularly impressed from their studies over the intense hostility that children from the 4th to 6th grades (ages 9 through 11) exhibited in association with their parents' divorce. They are angry at the parent whom they hold to be responsible (regardless of the accuracy of their blame). They are willing to take sides and involve themselves as weapons in the parental conflict. They tend to split the parents into the "good parent" and the "bad parent." In adolescence they may be sorry for their impassioned responses. Such anger makes these children's preferences suspect. Although this examiner has certainly seen many children who exhibit hostility toward the parent whom they consider to be at fault, there are others who will prefer to live with that parent. Many of these children appear to be operating in accordance with the mechanism of *identification with the aggressor* in which they basically follow the principle: "If you can't fight 'em, join 'em." Their preference is based on fear of being on the losing side in what they consider to be an unequal battle. In order to protect themselves, they join the more powerful party and this becomes their primary criterion for deciding parental preference. This is clearly not a healthy criterion, especially in situations where the preferred parent exhibits overt sadistic behavior.

In considering children's input into the custody decision, the question is often asked: "At what age should a child's opinion be taken seriously regarding parental choice in custody conflicts?" I am in agreement with Siegel and Hurley (1977) that there is no such age. Every child is different. There are some children who will give important information at very young ages and there are others who at much older ages are not to be relied upon. Each child must be evaluated separately with regard to his or her competence to provide useful information. Accordingly, no arbitrary age standard should be utilized, but rather the mental development of the child should be assessed in order to ascertain how much weight should be given to the particular child's preference. It has been this examiner's experience that verbalizations made by children under the ages of 4 or 5 have little credibility. One should, however, give weight to one's observations of such children's interactions with each parent. One wants to observe for such things as cuddling, affectionate expressions, glances, gestures, and the general level of tension and anxiety of each parent when with the children. At the other extreme, in the adolescent period, one should generally give great weight to what the youngster has to say. Siegel and Hurley (1977) describe a number of cases in which the courts have given great weight to the adolescent's preference. However, courts are often impotent to do anything but comply with an adolescent who does not wish to live with the assigned custodial parent if the noncustodial parent is receptive to taking the child in. In the middle period, between ages 6 and 12, there is a gradual progression of increasing credibility as the child gets older.

The following vignette demonstrates well how careful the examiner should be with regard to a child's statement of preference:

> Sarah was 7 years old at the time of the evaluation. She and her 5-year-old brother were caught in the middle of vicious custody litigation. Sarah was an extremely bright and articulate child and could carry on a conversation with the examiner in a convincing fashion. There seemed to be no need to gain information through disguise and surreptitious channels. In the first interview she stated quite openly and directly that she wished to live with her father. She enumerated a host of reasons for this, including the fact that her father was much more patient with her, could read stories to her at length, would sit on the floor and play with her, would take her to the zoo and other places her mother was disinclined to visit, and was much more cuddly with her physically. In her second interview with me, as well, Sarah spoke at length about her preference to live with her father.
>
> My evaluation of the parents revealed them to be, with minor exceptions, both dedicated and committed parents. As was to be expected, Sarah's mother denied that she was deficient in the areas that Sarah had described. However, her father stated that his observations of the mother matched those of Sarah. As the evaluation proceeded, I became increasingly closer to the conclusion that the mother was indeed a dedicated and good mother and that the father, although also an involved parent, could not provide Sarah and her brother with the attention that the mother could because of his full-time work as an architect. The mother, on the other hand, was not employed outside the home and was totally available for the children. However, Sarah's descriptions of her preference made me uneasy about making a final decision to recommend that her mother have custody of the two children.
>
> Sarah and her younger brother were being seen in therapy by a psychologist. In addition, the mother was also being counseled by him with regard to helping the children deal with the divorce and litigation. The psychologist only saw the father on one occasion. My original decision was not to get information from the psychologist, in accordance with my policy of hesitating to involve therapists who are seeing the parents or children at the time of my evaluation. I do not wish to put them in the posi-

tion of possibly compromising the child's treatment by providing information to the court that might strengthen one parent's position over the other in the litigation. However, in this case, because of my indecisiveness, I decided to get a report from the psychologist. To my surprise, he reported that Sarah had repeatedly told him in interviews that she wished to live with her *mother* and had given many convincing arguments for this decision. In addition, Sarah told her therapist that she had told *me*, as well, that she wanted to live with her mother. Incredulous, I called the psychologist in order to confirm this and he indeed stated that at no point had Sarah ever veered from her fixed position that she wanted to live with her mother and had told him that she had definitely told me that she did not want to live with her father.

In a joint interview, I presented this information to the parents to see if their comments could clarify what was going on. Each parent immediately offered to provide an explanation. The father stated that Sarah really wanted to live with him and had told him so. However, it was clear to him that Sarah was telling her therapist that she preferred her mother because she knew that this information would be transmitted to her mother through the therapist. He considered Sarah to be afraid to tell her own therapist her true feelings lest she appear disloyal to her mother, whom she assumed would be party to the preferences stated to her therapist. He concluded that Sarah was fearful of expressing her preference for her father because she might alienate her mother. However, he believed that she was stating her true preference to me because she appreciated the importance of my role in the custody determination.

Sarah's mother, on the other hand, stated that Sarah viewed me as her father's confidant. She was aware of the fact that her father was paying me and that her mother was paying the psychologist. She suspected that Sarah assumed that everything that she told me would be transmitted to her father just as everything she told the psychologist was transmitted to her mother. She viewed each professional as the ally of the payer and considered each to be serving as the vehicle for the transmission of just that information that she suspected each parent wanted to hear. And this was the reason she had come out so strongly in favor of her father as custodial parent.

Both explanations seemed plausible. Although the parents certainly solved the dilemma of Sarah's providing two different renditions of her custodial choice, the problem of what Sarah's *real* preference was could not be determined. Accordingly, I discounted her stated preferences entirely (both those made to me and to her therapist) and based my final recommendation on other factors related to the family situation. In this case, I recommended that the mother have custody (my original inclination, as described above), but recommended extremely liberal visitation with her father, whom I also saw to be an excellent parent.

This vignette has been presented here because it demonstrates well the importance of the examiner being cautious with regard to giving great credence to a child's statement about parental preference. However, it also demonstrates the importance of the joint interview discussed in the last chapter. Had I not thrown this dilemma out to the parents, and asked their opinions and explanations, I probably would not have solved the problem and resolved the conflict. Their input was crucial in enabling me to understand what was going on with Sarah.

CONFIDENTIALITY IN THE INTERVIEWS WITH THE CHILDREN

Whereas I tell both parents at the outset that I must be free to use my judgment regarding respecting their confidentiality, and that I insist upon the freedom of divulgence if it will serve the purposes of the evaluation, such "courtesies" are not generally extended to the child. Specifically, I do not routinely tell children, from the outset, that what they tell me may, at my discretion, be revealed to their parents. Rather, I say nothing at all about confidentiality and divulge what I consider appropriate. However, if the child does ask me whether what he or she says to me will be revealed to parents, I will respond that I may very well do so if I think it is important and I make no promises about what I will or will not reveal. However, I also advise the child to tell me what he or she wishes me to withhold and I will give it serious consideration. The main difference between my approach to the child and that of the parents is that for the child I do not bring up the issue, but I do so with the adults.

One could argue that this is deceitful to the child and that he or she has the right to know in advance that disclosures may be made. My response to such a criticism is that I approach the situation in a manner similar to the approach I use in my purely therapeutic work. There, I have found it most useful *not* to bring up the confidentiality issue and attempt to establish the general pattern that all information is put into the common pool for consideration by all interested parties. I want to promulgate an atmosphere of open communication. Bringing up the confidentiality issue tends to squelch revelations. Hopefully, this experience will help the child and parent communicate better with one another as these important issues are brought forth. It is far better for the child to tell the parental preference openly than to hide in fear with regard to it. Usually, the parental repercussions for such preference will not be as punitive as the child anticipates.

In addition, the nonpreferred parent usually knows anyway his or her status in the child's mind. Actually, over the many years in which I have been doing custody evaluations, I have not found the confidentiality issue to be a problem with the overwhelming majority of the children I have interviewed. (In fact, I have not found free divulgence to be a problem with the vast majority of children I see in therapy.) Children generally expect me to reveal what they tell me to their parents. Even though they may have been hesitant to make such revelations themselves, they recognize that making them to me is important if they are to do everything for themselves to live with the parent of their preference.

It is a common practice for judges to interview children in their chambers and try to elicit from them information regarding their custodial preference. Judges are basically not trained to conduct such difficult interviews. Nor do they generally have the time to gain the important information in the more relaxed and nonthreatening way that is desirable (and even necessary) for gaining meaningful data. Accordingly, their interviews are often inept—their professions of sensitivity to the child notwithstanding. It is not uncommon for judges to promise children that their confidences will be respected and that their preferences will not be communicated to their parents. However, my experience has been that judges will often reveal such preferences, completely oblivious to their promises. Often what the children have said becomes part of the court record. This is obviously a disservice to them. It can be disillusioning and can contribute to their feelings of distrust of authority.

On the other hand, when the judge sees the child in chambers and does not reveal what is said to the attorneys and to the parents, the parents are being deprived of information that may have been vital to the decision. This, in my opinion, is unfair to them and, I suspect, could be proved illegal in that a decision has been made without their being given all the information that contributed to it. The child may provide the judge with false information which the parents have had no opportunity to refute, and the judge's decision may have been based heavily on these errors (Selby, 1973).

INTERVIEWING THE CHILD

As mentioned, this may be the most challenging and difficult part of the evaluation. Some of the techniques I will present are standard; others I have developed over the years in order to deal with the special problems the examiner has in interviewing children involved in custody litigation. In these interviews the examiner wants to gather information about the child's feelings about each of the parents, especially as they relate to that parent's parental capacity. In addition, the evaluator is interested in the child's preference. Obviously, the latter question is not one that the examiner should be posing early in the interview(s). Because it is the most anxiety-provoking question and the one that the child may not initially wish to discuss (he or she may not wish to discuss it at all), it is best left to the end in most evaluations. Accordingly, I will describe in this section how I proceed from questions that are seemingly remote from this issue to those that get closer to it. Finally, for the child who is willing to discuss this issue directly—my experience has been that about half of the children I see are willing to do so—I will discuss the specific ways in which I broach this subject.

In my training in the late 1950s I was taught that the best question to begin an interview with was the open-ended one: "So what brings you to the hospital?" "Tell me, what are the problems?" and "So what's on your mind?" Such questions have the advantage of providing answers that are "uncontaminated" by any of the examiner's specific questions or comments that may elicit particular associations. As reasonable as this approach may seem, it has definite drawbacks. The most important of these is the fact that such open-ended questions are being posed at the most injudicious time. When a patient is new to the therapeutic situation, it is most likely that he or she is quite anxious. And when people are anxious they are not likely to process information in the most accurate way. They are more likely to misinterpret, distort, and be defensive. Accordingly, the answers one receives at such times are likely to be unreliable.

On the other hand, if one begins with specific questions to which the patient is likely to provide ready answers, anxiety levels are bound to be reduced. General questions pertaining to name, address, age, school, occupation, and so on, only take a few minutes to ask. Getting the "right" answers makes the patient more comfortable. After a few minutes of such "structured" questions, an entirely different patient is available for answering the more anxiety-provoking, unstructured questions such as "What brings you to see me?" And this principle is useful in the custody evaluation as well.

Accordingly, I will generally begin with the child by asking specific questions about his or her name, age, birth date, grade level, school, teacher, siblings. But even in the interview itself, I proceed from the more concrete and less anxiety-provoking questions to the more general and higher anxiety-level questions. And I leave to the end the most difficult question, that is, the question of specific parental preference. In fact, with some patients I may decide *not* to ask that specific question because I recognize that the child may not wish to answer it and/or because I already have received my answer in less direct, but nevertheless useful ways. After obtaining the name-and-

address type data I may, in some cases, ask the child if he or she understands the purpose of the evaluation. Older children generally do.
Younger children (under 5 or 6) generally do not. If the child's response
suggests that he or she believes that I make the final decision, I will
correct this misunderstanding and inform the child that my job is to
advise the judge and that *the judge makes the final decision.*

Inquiry About the Physical Aspects of the Home and Neighborhood

In the realm of concrete questions, I find it useful to begin with
questions about the physical aspects of the mother's and father's
homes. The focusing on descriptions of *things* (as opposed to *people*)
takes the child away from the more anxiety-provoking issued related to
parental preference. However, from the description of the homes one
can often gain useful information about the child's feelings about each
of the parents. One might begin this section of the inquiry with an introductory statement like: "I understand your parents are no longer living
together." (This question, of course, is only applicable if the separation
has not already been discussed.) If the child answers in the affirmative, then the examiner can continue with questions regarding with
whom the child is living, what part of the week is spent with each of the
parents, and then a description of the two homes. (If the subject of the
separation has already been discussed, then the latter inquiry regarding the two homes can serve as the starting point of this section of the
inquiry.)

Asking questions about the physical characteristics of the home
may provide useful information about parental capacity. The child may
find focusing on the concrete aspects of each of the parent's homes less
anxiety provoking than talking about the parents themselves. However,
in the course of such description the child may provide important information about the parents. One could pose the question: "Tell me about
your house," or "Describe your home." One could then follow up with
questions like: "Tell me things about your house that you like," and
"Tell me things about your house that you don't like." In addition to
eliciting a description of the home in which the child lives, one should
also ask about the home that the child visits.

It is important for the therapist to appreciate that many children
may state a preference for living with the parent with the larger home,
especially if that home has more space and play equipment. Obviously,
this should not be an important consideration in the custody recommendation. It is the parent, not the woodwork, that is going to play the
most important role in the child's growth and development. A child, for

example, might say, "I want to go live with my father because he has a swimming pool." In such circumstances, one does well to ask a child, "Would you still want to go live with your father if he didn't have a swimming pool?" One does well to remove, one by one, all the concrete and material items that attract the child in order to focus more clearly on the personality qualities that are the crucial elements in the evaluation.

A question I have found useful to ask a child is: "What would you do if your father moved into the house where your mother is presently living and your mother moved into the house where your father is now living?" "If you were allowed to go wherever you wished would you stay where you are or would you move?" In other words, the child is asked if the two parents were to switch domiciles, what would he or she then do? This helps the examiner differentiate between choices made on the basis of home, neighborhood, friends, school environment, and familiarity and those based on the personality of the parent. If the child says that he or she would stay in the same home regardless of which parent lived there, the response suggests that parental emotional ties are less strong than the ties to school, neighborhood, and friends. However, if the child states that he or she would want to go with the parent who moves into the other domicile, then the bond with that parent is probably quite strong, and this consideration is being given preference over the aforementioned "externals."

Some Questions About Siblings as a Source of Information About Parental Capacity

Asking the child to discuss his or her siblings is often a good source of information about the parents, without the child necessarily recognizing that he or she is providing such data. Again, this is an area of inquiry which is not directed specifically toward the child being interviewed and so it is less anxiety provoking than the more direct inquiries to be discussed subsequently.

One might ask the child how each of the parents gets along with each of the siblings. Many children are much freer complaining about how a particular parent treats siblings than discussing how that parent treats themselves. An older child might be asked about a mother and a father's involvement with a younger sibling, especially a baby. Questions about who changes the diapers, who makes breakfast, or who likes to cuddle more with the baby can provide useful information about which of the two parents is the more strongly parental.

Even more revealing information can be obtained when the child is asked to discuss each siblings' preferences (except his or her own) with regard to which parent the sibling would like to live with. In this way the child need not describe his or her own preference, but significant information may be gained about the parents. If Mary, for example, says that her brother Jimmy wants to live with his mother, the examiner might ask, "Why does Jimmy want to live with your mother?" One can go further and ask Mary what she thinks about Jimmy's preference. Again, Mary is not being asked specifically to say anything about her own preference. One 6-year-old boy, who stated at the outset that he would never tell me his preference, told me in this phase of the interview that his brother definitely wanted to live with his father. He then told me again how he had no strong preference, except that he did not wish, under any circumstances, to be separated from his brother and then described in great length how close they were, how much they had in common, and how much fun it was to be with his brother. He then sadly described how terrible it would be if he were to be separated from his brother and if they were to live in different places. After extracting as much information as possible about sibling preferences and the child's feelings about them, one might broach the subject of where the child wants to live him- or herself. However, if the examiner senses that this would be too anxiety provoking for the child, he or she should avoid this direct question.

Information About Parental Capacity Derived from a Discussion of Visitation

It is useful to get specific and concrete details about the visitation. Older children will often be able to give such information, but even younger children can provide much useful data. In discussing the visitation the examiner should try to assess how excited the children are in anticipation of a forthcoming visit. One must be cautious here, however, because weekend visitations are still more fun than going to school, doing household chores, and adhering to the regular routines of the custodial parent's household. Questioning the children about the reasons for wanting to visit can also provide useful information about the nature of the relationship with the noncustodial parent. One tries to differentiate here between visiting for gifts, indulgences, and freedom from obligation and visiting for human warmth and deep relationship gratification.

The examiner should try to get information about the visiting parent's punctuality and reliability. Does the parent show up on time? Does the parent show up at all, after having made an appointment? Has the child expressed resentment over such lateness or failure to arrive? Is the child fearful of expressing such anger? Or, if expressed, has this proved useful? Was the noncustodial parent frequently late before the initiation of the custody litigation (and evaluation) and is that parent suddenly proving to be punctual? The child's comments about such deficiencies in the noncustodial parent may differ from the visiting parent's rendition of the visits, but both opinions should be recorded. Better yet, if the visiting parent admits to such deficiencies, then, for reasons given previously, the examiner has very strong evidence for the court report.

The examiner should inquire as to whether the child wants to go on the visit. If the child wishes to, one should learn the reasons why. Is the child happy to be free from the custodial parent's reasonable restrictions? Or, is the child happy to be free of the custodial parent's pathological interactions with the child? If the child states that he or she doesn't want to go and gives reasons such as fatigue, nonspecific illness, "too much homework," or "I just don't feel like going," it is likely that these are rationalizations and that basically the child does not wish to be with the visiting parent. In such cases the child is probably fearful of expressing this overtly and so resorts to the aforementioned excuses.

If the child is not visiting with the noncustodial parent at all during the time of the evaluation, the examiner does well (if the situation warrants it and if there is little or no risk) to suggest that the child be given a trial of visitations with that parent. In this way the child will have actual living experiences upon which to base his or her thoughts, feelings, and reactions. It also gives the examiner better data for coming to conclusions about the relationship with the noncustodial parent. If the child reacts negatively, one should not immediately assume that the experience was a detrimental one. Changes are anxiety provoking for all of us, and especially for children. The duration of trial visitation may not have been long enough to allow the child to overcome initial anxieties. I am in agreement with Goldstein, Freud, and Solnit (1973) that such trials may do more harm than good in situations where, for example, a foster child, who has been living with the foster parents for many years, is moved into the home of biological parents, who have belatedly decided they want him or her returned. This is more likely to be traumatic than the situation I have described above, in which the transfer is from one known parent to another.

It may sometimes be possible to recommend, during the course of the evaluation, that the child actually live with the preferred parent if he or she is not doing so at that point. Rather than just theorize about what it *might* be like living with the other parent, the child will then have firsthand, living experiences to assist in making a more judicious choice. If the evaluation is long enough to reasonably provide such an opportunity, the information then given by the child is likely to have much greater credibility. Unfortunately, most evaluations are not as prolonged that the child is given the opportunity for an extended living experience with the other parent. In addition, school involvement and work situations often make such a trial difficult, if not impossible. However, when the therapist does have the opportunity to make such a recommendation he or she should do so. Of course, such trials are much more reasonably and feasibly accomplished in the counseling situation when there are no court pressures and where accommodations can be made in a much more relaxed and natural fashion.

Information About Parental Capacity Derived from the Child's Comments About the Parents

Discussion of the Divorce.   At this point (if it has not come up already), I will ask the child why his or her parents are getting a divorce. If the child has not been told, this represents a deficit on the part of both parents. The healthy parent appreciates the importance of providing the children a reasonable amount of information about the divorce. The parent who gives rationalizations for not providing such information ("He's too young." "They wouldn't understand." "It would only upset her more.") are compromised in their parental capacity. One must be careful, however, to verify with the parents that the child has not indeed been told. There are many children who will say that they were told nothing when, in fact, they were given detailed explanations. If one of the parents has been providing information, and the other not, then the provider is exhibiting what I would consider to be good parenting and the nonprovider just the opposite.

If the child does provide the reasons, one may get information about parental capacity in the context of such a discussion. For example, if a girl says that her mother no longer wishes to live with her father because her father has been "very mean" to her and the other children, I will ask the child to describe the kinds of mean things. And I am particularly interested in the child's own observations regarding the justification for her mother's allegations. If the "meanness" includes, for example, vilifying and beating the mother, and the child has directly observed such behavior, this would be a very significant parental deficiency. Asking the child to describe in detail the nature of the parental conflicts may provide further useful information in the evaluation. Such descriptions can give useful information about parental preference, provided through the vehicle of discussing reasons for the divorce.

Asking children about their specific reactions, thoughts, and feelings about the breakup of the parents' marriage will often provide information about parental preference. One girl said, "I'm glad my father's not living in the house any more. He was always starting fights with my mother and he was always picking on me and my brother. It's really quiet in the house, now that he's gone. I don't even miss him. Last week I missed him a little bit, but then I thought about all the mean things he did to us and then I stopped missing him." This child had not been directly asked which parent she preferred to live with. However, she clearly stated her preference in the context of her response.

The more common response to the question of the child's reactions to the separation is that of sorrow about the parents having split up. In addition, most children (at least in the early phases of the separation) will wish that the absent parent once again returns to the home. Children generally take the position that if the departing parent truly loved them, that parent would suffer the indignities and pains of the wretched marital relationship. Not being able to project themselves into the position of the suffering parent, they can only consider how the separation affects them. In such cases, the question about their feelings and reactions to the breakup may give little information about parental preference or parental capacity.

In the context of the explanation about the causes of the separation, the child may reveal the parent who is believed to have been at greater "fault." Elaboration of this issue may give the examiner important information regarding custodial preference on the child's part. The more detailed the inquiry, the greater the likelihood the examiner will obtain such information. It is important, however, for the evaluator to appreciate that the parent who has left the home is often viewed as the one who was at fault for the marital breakup. That parent is often viewed as the "abandoner," regardless of how justifiable the leaving of the home may have been. Some children view the parent who has remained in the home as the one who has driven out the other parent and, no matter how justifiable the ejection, these children may view the custodial parent as the worse of the two and the one who was "at fault." Accordingly, such information about who was to blame must be put into context and considered with other data. In fact, every bit of information collected in the custody evaluation (especially data provided by the children) must be viewed as part of the larger picture. Serious errors can result if the therapist places too much weight on one bit of data, no matter how compelling.

Children of divorce are most often angry over the separation. It is only in those cases where the departure of one of the parents has been a relief for the child and decompressed the psychologically traumatic situation that the child will view the separation positively. Although some children suppress the anger they feel over the divorce, many others act it out. Many children direct such hostility more freely toward the custodial parent. In most cases this is the mother. It is as if the child reasons: "I'd better be careful about expressing my anger to my father. He's already left the home. If I tell him how angry I am, I may see even less of him. In fact, I may never even see him again. I'd better be careful. My mother, on the other hand, has proved herself to be loyal. She hasn't left the house. She's a safer target for my hostility. I know she'll be loyal to me no matter what I do. If I have to get this anger off my chest, I might as well direct it all toward her. She's the far safer target." In such a case, the child may expound at length about all the indignities he or she suffers at mother's hands: being made to get up early in the morning to go to school, being pressured into eating breakfast, suffering television restrictions, bedtime curfews, and so on. The mother may describe passive-aggressive and uncooperative behavior at home. The father, on the other hand, may describe model behavior. In such cases, the examiner should be extremely careful before deciding that the parent toward whom the child is expressing the greater amount of anger is, indeed, the less preferable one. The mere fact that the child is more hostile toward one parent should not, in itself, be a reason for recommending the parent with whom the child has the less hostile relationship. One must attempt to ascertain the causes of the hostility—and whether or not it is justifiable—before coming to any conclusions regarding parental preference.

The Description of the Typical Day. It is useful to ask the child to describe in detail exactly what happens on a typical day, from arising in the morning until bedtime. One can lead the child along here and ask specific questions; however, it is preferable to start with a general question like: "I'd like you to tell me about your whole day, from the time you get up in the morning until the time you go to bed at night." After the child has given his or her own description, the evaluator should then proceed with more specific questions. The spontaneous responses, unsolicited by the evaluator, are the more meaningful. For example, if in answer to the original general question the child states, "Before my daddy left the house, he always used to wake me up because my mommy slept late. He always gave me my breakfast because my mommy didn't want to be waked up in the morning. Now that he's gone my mommy sometimes forgets and I've been late for school a lot." Such a response obviously gives much meaningful information about this mother's maternal capacity. However, if such specifics were not provided in the child's general description, the examiner might ask

questions like: "Do you wake up yourself in the morning or does someone wake you up?" "Who wakes you up?" "Who helps you get
dressed?" The main purpose of these questions is to learn about the
child's depth of involvement with each of the parents and the parents'
commitment to the child's rearing.

The questions should cover the wide variety of experiences the
child has during the day. Because they will usually be posed at a time
when the parents are already separated, the examiner should direct
the child to the time *prior* to the parents' separation. It is important to
appreciate that a parent who was involved in a particular acitivity is
not automatically the one who was most desirous of such involvement.
It may be that the other parent was reasonably not available. For example, if a father's job required him to leave the home before the children awakened, it is unreasonable to penalize him if the mother was
always the one to wake up the children. In fact, in the traditional
household, the mother will generally have been the one involved in
many of the daily activities with the child. If it was always the mother
who greeted the children when they returned home from school, and
the father was, with rare exception, working, it would be most unreasonable to penalize such a father for not being available on the children's return from school. It is in the evening, however, when both
parents are generally available, that one can make the best comparisons. One might ask about the homework situation: "Who helped you
with your homework at night?" One should determine not only which
parent was more often involved, but the children's feelings about the
nature of the parent's involvement. One child stated, "I never wanted
my father to help me with my homework because he was always
screaming at me. My mother had much more patience." In the inquiry
one tries to determine whether a parent is doing the homework in an
overprotective way, i.e., doing it for the child, rather than helping the
child learn how to do the homework him- or herself. Besides homework,
one wants to inquire about recreational activities with the child during
the evening. The working father who rarely spends such time with the
child is generally compromised. Similarly, if such a father spends every
evening with paperwork, this is also a parental deficiency, even though
his work or business may have warranted such extra obligations. The
healthy father knows his priorities with regard to profession vs. child
rearing.

A particularly useful area to explore is the bedtime scene. The
strongly involved parent enjoys sitting with the child at bedtime and
reading bedtime stories. I am not claiming that the healthy parent will
invariably love reading these stories endlessly, but he or she will
derive enough pleasure from them to make it a common activity. In

addition, the examiner should try to determine whether the parent enjoys cuddling with the child while engaged in reading such stories. The strongly involved parent will also enjoy lying down with the child and cuddling as well. There are parents who will refrain from such cuddling practices (especially with opposite-sexed children) because they have been told that this will give the child an "Oedipus complex." As mentioned previously, the parent who follows such advice (often given by professionals such as psychiatrists and psychologists) may be using it to rationalize noninvolvement. The healthy parent does not take such advice seriously, the qualifications of the "expert" notwithstanding. The wise parent appreciates the difference between occasional cuddling and sexual stimulation—the former need not be associated with the latter.

Lastly, one should inquire about typical weekends prior to the separation. What was done? Who initiated recreational activities with the children? Who went with them? Who was more patient with the children in these activities? Who was willing to go to more inconvenience in order to involve the children in these weekend activities?

As mentioned, it is important to make every attempt to ascertain what the situation was prior to the separation, and especially prior to the initiation of custody litigation and evaluation. It is quite common for parents to become "super parents" when custody conflict is brewing. In addition, it is important to get parental response and comment (from both sides) regarding each of the children's descriptions of the parents—especially those that reflect negatively on a parent's parental capacity. The examiner who does not do this may justifiably be criticized on the stand by a cross-examining attorney for accepting the description of a young child as valid. It is in the joint interviews, especially, that one has the opportunity for parental input into the child's descriptions. When the parent admits that the child's criticism is valid, one is provided with very powerful information for one's report and testimony.

The Descriptions of the Parents.   Here I describe direct questions to the child regarding the parents. My aim here is to obtain concrete descriptions of parental assets and liabilities without asking the child specifically which parent he or she would prefer to live with. Of course, the information obtained relates directly to parental preference. Again, I start with general questions before proceeding to more specific ones. I might ask at this point: "Tell me about your mother (father)." or "Describe your father (mother)." These are far better questions than: "Do you love your mother?" "Does your father love you?" or "Who loves you more, your mother or your father?" The latter group of questions will provide yes or no answers or one-word responses. The former will generally elicit descriptive, concrete information that is much more valuable for the purposes of the custody evaluation. After the child has given as much information as possible, one can then proceed with questions like: "Everybody is a mixture of both good and bad parts. No one is perfect. Tell me some good things about your mother." When one has exhausted this possibility, the therapist should go on with questions like: "As I have said before, everybody is a mixture of both good and bad parts. Tell me some bad things about your mother. What things about your mother don't you like?" A similar inquiry should then be pursued with regard to the father. Another question in this category might be: "What's the best thing you can say about your mother (father)?" "What's the worst thing you can say about your mother (father)?" One must try to get the child to elaborate upon simple, short answers in order to get as much mileage as possible out of the responses.

Then, a similar inquiry should be pursued with regard to other significant adults who may be involved in the child's upbringing, as for example, a stepparent, a friend with whom a parent is living, and so on. It is important to get information about these individuals to the degree that they may be serving as parental surrogates. In the course of such an inquiry the therapist should make an attempt to learn about the duration of these involvements. Of course, younger children are less likely to be able to provide accurate information about the passage of time. In the joint sessions, however, one can get parental input into this issue. Clearly, the parental surrogate who has enjoyed a longer salutary involvement with the child is going to be in a stronger position for custody than the person whose more meaningful involvement may be of more recent origin (a common situation in custody evaluations).

The evaluator must appreciate that what the child may consider a "bad" quality on a parent's part may indeed be an asset. For example, if a child says, "He makes me turn off the television set in order to go to sleep," and if the sleep time is a reasonable one, this "criticism" is actually an asset and a point of credit to the father in the evaluation. Obviously, the father who lets a child stay up late watching television (especially on school nights) is compromising his paternal capacity.

I have found it useful to ask children whether their parents slept in one bed or two separate beds. If the parents slept in separate beds, I will ask the children whose bed they went into when they would crawl into a parent's bed to cuddle when they were younger. Or, if the parents slept in the same bed, I will ask on whose side they would more frequently enter in order to cuddle. I sometimes go further and ask, "If you were in the middle, between your mother and father, with whom did you cuddle the most when you were younger?" If there was no bed-entering and cuddling at all, this reflects a deficiency on the part of both parents. The healthy parent enjoys such cuddling experiences and welcomes the child's involvement, especially on weekends and holidays. The child who is not "interested" is one who has been rejected from such involvement and has "gotten the message" that overtures for such cuddling are unacceptable.

Questions About Friends.   I have found useful an inquiry into each parent's attitudes toward the children's friends. The healthy involved parent is very respectful of the importance of friends and tries to encourage friendships from the earliest years of life. The devoted parent is willing to tolerate some of the discomforts, noise, mess, and fighting that is usually entailed when visitors come to the house. The committed parent recognizes that these inconveniences are a small price to pay for the tremendous advantages gained by the child in having friends and relating well to others. The parent who does not appreciate this is definitely compromised. Accordingly, I will ask the child about each parent's attitudes toward having friends in the home. One child answered, "When my father's home, he never lets me have my friends in the house. He says they make too much noise and so he can't sleep or watch television. When he's not at home, my mother lets the kids come in and play. But she usually makes them go home before my father gets home because he'll get very angry and make a fuss. I think she's scared of him." Although this mother's fear of her husband and her compliance with his wishes is a deficiency, she clearly recognizes, far more than her husband, the importance of the children having friends. I consider the failure to appreciate the importance of friendships to be a significant deficiency on the parent's part.

In addition to inquiring about each parent's receptivity to having friends visit the children, one should inquire about the interest the parent has in bringing the children to visit friends elsewhere. One should try to determine who makes efforts to bring the children in contact with others and how extensive these efforts are. Of course, the mother, usually being at home more, is more likely to be available for this. On the weekends, however, when both parents are usually home, one may get a better idea regarding which parent is more receptive and willing to go out of his or her way for the child's involvement with peers. Here again, however, one must be careful in that the father may feel more obligated to extend himself in this regard because of the mother having done so to a significant degree throughout the week. In such situations, of course, one gets little information about relative parental capacity. An important point here is that the healthy parent recognizes the importance of involvements with friends and is willing to inconvenience him- or herself in order to facilitate such involvements.

It can sometimes be useful to ask the children what their *friends* think of each of the parents. Sometimes children will be freer to express parental negative qualities through the vehicle of a companion than to do so themselves. Sometimes the comments of friends will corroborate what the child has said. For example, the child of an alcoholic mother said, "My friends don't want to come to the house. My mother never wears nice clothes. She's always dressed in that old housecoat, and she's usually cranky. She's not nice to them. And they say that she's mean and that she's a mess." Another child said, "My friends like to come to the house when my mother's there, but they don't like to come to the house when my father's there. My father's always kicking them out and saying that they make too much noise. My mother doesn't seem to mind them. Kids will come to the house and say, 'Is your father home yet?' They just don't want to come to the house when he's there." Because friends' comments are not generally made directly to the examiner, they should be used with caution. Strictly speaking, they are hearsay. Nevertheless, they are useful information to have as supporting quotations.

Grandparents. One does well to try to find out about each of the parent's commitment to involving the children with the grandparents. The healthy parent recognizes the importance of children's relationships with their grandparents. We in the mental health professions do not generally appreciate the importance of the relationships between grandparents and their grandchildren. The adoration that grandparents often have of their grandchildren can be very esteem-enhancing for the children. They can serve as a buffer against the unwarranted criticisms that children (as well as the rest of us) inevitably receive in life. One should try to find out from the children who calls the grandparents, who invites them to visit, and who seems to be proud of the children's accomplishments vis-a-vis the grandparents.

In some situations the grandparents may be serving either directly or indirectly as parental surrogates. This is direct when, for example, a mother may move back into her own parents' home with her children. In such cases, the examiner should interview the maternal grandparents. In other cases the grandparents may serve indirectly as parental surrogates, especially during visitation. Unfortunately, it is often the case that after a divorce children become estranged from the noncustodial parent's parents, that is, the grandparents on the side of the parent with whom they do not live. An inquiry into the children's relationships with each of the grandparents can provide information about the two extended family settings which the evaluator is trying to compare. Although the primary persons being compared are the parents, comparison of the grandparents warrants the evaluator's consideration—even if these parties are not interviewed directly. An inquiry (with the children and the parents) into the children's relationships with each of these persons provides useful information in the evaluation. The parent who would provide the children with the most meaningful involvement with the grandparents—especially with the preferable grandparents (if such is the situation)—gets "extra points" in the custody evaluation. However, this "edge" should not be given great weight in that it is of much less importance than qualities possessed by the parents themselves. An additional reason for making such an inquiry is that healthy grandparents are likely to produce healthier children and the preferred parent is more likely to have healthier and more parental parents than the nonpreferred parent.

A good way to start such an inquiry is with the concrete. One might ask the child to list each of the grandparents and to tell what name is used when referring to each one. Then one might proceed with a more specific inquiry into each grandparent's assets and liabilities. One can use such questions as: "What are the things about your grandmother (grandfather) that you like the best?" "What are the things about your grandfather (grandmother) that you don't like?" One should try to get information about the frequencies of the visits of each of the four grandparents (or the number that are alive). Other questions should be asked like: "Which one likes to hug you the most?" "Who is most proud of the things you do?" "Who seems to enjoy being with you the most?" At times I have asked the child to list all the grandparents in order of preference: "Put on the top of the list the name of the grandparent you like the most and then put at the bottom of the list the name of the grandparent you like the least. Then put in the middle the names of the others."

The Guardian ad Litem.   In some cases a guardian ad litem may have been appointed by the court. To date I have had no direct contacts with a guardian ad litem during my evaluation. This is probably preferable in that information so provided might be considered hearsay and, in addition, he or she might justifiably be criticized by one of the parents for trying to influence the impartial evaluator. However, the children's comments about their relationship with the guardian ad litem may provide some useful information in the custody evaluation. For example, three children I was evaluating in a custody conflict referred to the guardian ad litem as *their* lawyer. Their view was that he truly represented them and that they could go to him with their complaints. The youngest boy stated, "My father hasn't sent me my allowance this week. I'm going to call my lawyer!" Here, the guardian ad litem was certainly playing an important role in this child's life. The boy's reference to his involvement with *his* guardian ad litem provided information about the father with regard to the latter's reliability in sending his son his allowance. Of course, I did not automatically assume that the father did not send the allowance. I spoke with the father, in a joint session with the boy, and invited his input on this matter. He admitted that he had been defaulting in this regard, stating that he was quite busy and had forgotten. In addition, he denied having received any of the messages the boy left with the father's secretary "reminding him" to send the allowance. As mentioned, open admissions of deficiencies are the most powerful tools the examiner can use in the custody evaluation.

The Direct Question About Parental Preference.   All of the above approaches, although providing significant information about parental capacity, are designed to studiously avoid placing the child in the position of directly stating his or her parental preference. For children who do not wish to state such preference, the examiner will generally have a significant amount of information provided by the above questions. For children who are willing to state a preference, the above questions can help ease the child into the discussion. They have served to desensitize the child to the issue and thereby will make it easier to discuss this sensitive area. But even here, I may not directly "get to the point." Rather, I may ease into the issue by posing questions that may be less anxiety provoking.

The question is sometimes asked whether there is a particular age at which a child's opinion regarding parental preference can be given credibility. I do not believe that there is any such cut-off point. Younger children, of course, are less credible than older ones and the more intelligent the child, the greater the likelihood his or her reasons will be valid. When giving credence to a child's preference, the examiner may wish to have an intelligence test administered. This can often provide information about how seriously a child's preference should be taken. For example, if a 6½-year-old child's IQ indicates that he is functioning in the 9½-year level, this would be important information to include in any statement about how much credence should be given to the child's stated preference. If the WISC-R intelligence test is utilized, one might wish to look particularly at the Comprehension and Picture Arrangement subtests, both of which are particularly sensitive to the child's social judgment capacity and common sense. If time and money do not permit the administration of the WISC-R, I have found the Slosson Intelligence Test (Slosson, 1961) to be useful. Whereas the services of a trained psychologist are generally necessary to administer the WISC-R, most mental health professionals are qualified to administer the Slosson. As will be elaborated upon subsequently, I do not recommend projective tests such as the Rorschach or the TAT in the custody evaluation. An intelligence test would be the only formal psychological test that I would consider to be warranted in a custody evaluation. (Later in this chapter I will elaborate on this point.) Levy (1980) quotes a judge who stated, "I'll be damned if I will let an 8-year-old tell me what to do." The judge's statement implies that he is not giving any credibility to the statements made by the 8-year-old child. This is unfortunate. Although an 8-year-old child's comments should not be the overriding determination with regard to custodial placement, the comments made by most 8 year olds may be useful to the examiner—the youth, credulity, naiveté, and suggestibility of the child notwithstanding.

A type of question that can ease the child into discussing himself or herself is one that encourages discussion of others: "With which parent is it best for a boy(girl) to live, the mother or the father?" Here the child is not being asked specifically with whom he (or she) would like to live, but a general question about children. This type of question makes it easier for children to reveal themselves because they are speaking about "third parties." In addition, many children, after discussing the general question of parental preference, will begin to talk about their own preferences. Although there is a projective element in this question, it is far more understandable to the court than the more traditional projectives that tap deeper layers of the unconscious. I will, on occasion, use this kind of material in my report whereas, as mentioned, I would hesitate to use the "deeper" types of projective material.

Another way of talking about "third parties" is to ask a series of questions about the preferable custodial parent for boys and girls of various ages. For example, when interviewing a 7-year-old boy, one might ask the following series of questions: "With which parent should a 1-year-old baby live, the mother or the father? Why?" "With which parent should a 3-year-old boy live, the mother or the father? Why?" One can then repeat this question for a 5 year old, 6 year old, 7 year old, and so on. One can then ask the same boy the same series of questions, but this time with regard to a little girl. In interviewing a girl, one could similarly present the series, first with one sex and then with the other. My experience has been that when one gets to the age of the child being interviewed, children will generally shift into a discussion of themselves. This not only provides the examiner with a direct statement about parental preference, but it avoids the possible (but small) risks of using projective material.

Another useful way of getting the child to reveal parental preference, without directly asking, is to pose what the legal profession refers to as "theoretical questions." The best ones I have found for this phase of the custody evaluation are those which begin "If the judge said . . . , "If the judge decided . . . , "If the judge asked you . . . ." This is a particularly useful phrase when introducing various "touchy" questions, for example, "If the judge asked your brother whom he would wish to live with, what would be his answer?" "When the judge asks you which parent you wish to live with, what are you going to answer?" "Whom do you think the judge is going to decide to give custody, your mother or your father?" and "Whom do you think the judge is going to think is the better parent, your mother or your father?" These questions are often less threatening for children to answer than a direct one about their preference.

Another way of avoiding the direct confrontation with a request for an overt preference is to use questions that relate to the stated parental preference: "Why does your father want you to live with him?" "Why does your mother want you to live with her?" "Why does your mother think that she's a better parent than your father?" And "Why does your father think that he's a better parent than your mother?" The child should then be asked whether he or she agrees or disagrees with the parental reasons. Here again, such inquiry often leads directly into the child's own statement of parental preference. Sometimes a child will actually state that the parent's motive is vengeance, keeping the house, or saving money by gaining custody. Here, however, one must be careful to differentiate between the child who is parroting a parental statement and the one who has a genuine conviction for the reason being given. At times, of course, such differentiation may be difficult, if not impossible. (I will discuss subsequently in this chapter ways of differentiating between the "brainwashed" child and the one who is speaking with genuine conviction.)

All of the above indirect questions not only are posed in the attempt to protect the child from the feelings of anxiety and disloyalty associated with stating a direct preference, but serve to desensitize the child and prepare the way for a possible direct statement. It is the direct statement that is the most powerful and the strongest in the face of cross-examination. My experience has been that about 80 to 90 percent of all the children I have seen in custody evaluations are willing to give me a direct statement. In such cases I do not simply stop the inquiry after a statement of preference. Rather, I ask the child to elaborate at length the reasons for the preference. I take careful notes during such elaborations. I then make every attempt to encourage the child to state these reasons in a joint interview with both parents. Although some children are too fragile and fearful of such confrontation, my experience has been that most are willing to do this. In fact, the "revelation" usually comes as no surprise to both parents in that they generally know each child's preference prior to the initiation of the evaluation. I do not put great pressure on the child to state the preference and reasons in the joint session, but encourage him or her to do so. This encouragement is only partially done for the purposes of the evaluation. It is also done for its fringe therapeutic benefit because I believe that open communication of these issues is the best way to reduce the problems that invariably arise when they are not directly discussed. In the joint interviews one has the opportunity to correct distortions that the child may have as well as to get statements of admission from the nonpreferred parent. The child's statement and the parental input become important parts of my final report to the court.

Earlier in this chapter I presented a discussion of sibling preferences and how this can contribute to understanding the child's own preferences as well as parental capacity. Once the child has stated a preference, the examiner may use "sibling questions" to get even further information, especially if there is some confusion regarding what the child really wants. One can often get further information in such situations with questions like: "You say you want to live with your father and that you want your brother to live with your father also. If the judge said that your brother must live with your mother, but that you could choose to live with either your mother or your father, what would you do then?" If the child says he or she would still want to live with the father, even though it means separation from the brother, it is a strong statement of preference for the father, because the child is willing to give up the fraternal relationship in order to live with him. On the other hand, if the child switches preferences and no longer wishes to go with the father but rather to live with the mother and brother, we learn something about the strength (or more properly, weakness) of the child's attachment to the father. Specifically, it tells us that the bond with the brother is so strong that he is willing to give up the father. There is also some implication here that the maternal option was not that weak in the first place.

Even the child who adamantly refuses to express a preference throughout the course of my interviews will often give me significant information about his or her preferences. At times the preference will be "slipped in" as the child leaves the final interview. It is as if the child did not wish to leave the consultation room without giving some indication of preference—lest he or she be assigned to the "wrong" parent. In such cases the child might make a statement like: "I don't care who I live with, but I don't mind living with my mother." Or "I don't want to make either one of my parent's feel bad, so I'm not going to say who I want to live with. But, if the judge makes me live with my mother, I'll do it." Sometimes the child, in the closing minutes of the evaluation, will make a statement that one parent is "a teeny-weeny, little bit better." It is important for the examiner to appreciate that the child may want the examiner or the judge to take the "blame" for making the decision. In this way the child may be freed of guilt feelings over disloyalty and safe from the feared retaliation from the nonpreferred parent. The child will then be able to say to the nonpreferred parent, "I really wanted to go with you, but that (explicative) Doctor Gardner told the judge that I should live with Mommy (Daddy)." The examiner does well to allow him- or herself to be used for such purposes.

THE "BRAINWASHED" CHILD

I believe the examiner should work on the assumption that just about all (if not all) children involved in custody litigation are being "brainwashed." Of course, parents routinely deny that they are involving themselves in such a nefarious practice. The child knows quite well that each parent has serious criticisms of the other that are likely to be transmitted to the child, either overtly or covertly. This would be the minimal amount of brainwashing that the child is exposed to. At the other extreme is the more overt program of systematic vilification of the other parent with the intent of so alienating that parent from the children that they will choose to live with the vilifier. Most cases fall in between these two extremes. It is the examiner's job to try to ascertain approximately where on this continuum the brainwashing lies. The closer the parent is to the active program of defamation, the more compromised is that parent's parental capacity.

Elsewhere (1970, 1971a, 1976, 1977, 1979b) I emphasize the importance of parents telling children the main reasons for the separation. There are many benefits to be derived from such discussions and to refrain from them may cause a variety of psychological difficulties in the children. However, implicit in such confrontations is criticism of the other parent. Even though these may be balanced by a presentation of the assets, criticisms are still being made. These can easily be viewed as brainwashing by the parent who is being criticized. Even those parents who do not subscribe to the advice of providing the children with this information are not likely to withhold from the children all the faults they see in the spouse. If they were to do so the child could only wonder why they are getting separated if they have no complaints about one another. But such mystification is rare. Usually a significant number of the complaints is communicated to the children, both overtly and covertly. It is easy to see how the derogated parent can cry brainwashing by the other party. Sometimes separation agreements and divorce decrees will order a parent to stop criticizing the other parent to the child. This is naive because it does not take into consideration the aforementioned factors which make such denigration almost universal.

When a mother tells a child that she cannot afford to buy new clothing because father has not sent enough money, she is derogating the father—regardless of how justified this statement is. In counseling such parents I will even advise the mother to tell the child that the father is not fulfilling his obligations. There are many therapeutic justifications for such advice. However, it is easy to see how the criticized father here might complain that his wife is brainwashing. A father may consider himself to be strongly adherent to the proverbial advice that one should never criticize the absent parent to the child. Such a father may say, "Have I ever criticized your mother to you, even once? You know that I haven't. I'm too good a person to stoop that low. There are things I could tell you about your mother that would make your hair stand on end, but I don't think it's proper to tear down a parent to a child." Such a father is involving himself in an insidious form of denigration of his former wife. His comments cannot but engender fantasies of heinous crimes committed by the mother. Accordingly, in custody evaluations, it is only the severest forms of overt brainwashing that must be taken seriously. It is only when there is an active program of systematic denigration that one considers there to be a compromise in parental capacity.

In custody conflicts each parent is essentially saying that the other is less worthy of taking care of the children. Each parent considers the other to have *serious* deficiencies with regard to child rearing. Otherwise, they would not be involved in a custody conflict. Even though the child may not learn what these deficiencies are alleged to be, he or she is well aware of the process (unless very young) and is likely to view one, or even both, of the parents as significantly deficient. In interviews with the examiner such children may provide criticisms that have been surmised (because of lack of accurate information) or may verbalize those that the child has learned from one of the parents. A crucial question for the examiner is how to determine, via interview with the child, whether an active program of vociferous condemnation is underway. Sometimes there is an artificial quality to the child's verbalizations. It is as if the child has memorized a script. The criticisms are made in an automaton-like manner. Sometimes the child will repeat verbatim the comments of the parent and one can detect adult phraseology and terminology—unlike that of the child. Sometimes the child's mannerisms, mode of delivery, and speech contents are clearly imitations of the brainwashing parent (Duncan, 1978). These manifestations suggest the kind of programming referred to as brainwashing.

The child who presents the examiner with a litany of complaints about the nonpreferred parent may very well be repeating, in parrot-like fashion, criticisms fed to him or her by the preferred parent. However, the examiner must consider the possiblity that another process is operating here. Specifically, some children may have genuinely realistic and appropriate reasons for their choice. In order to ensure that they leave no stone unturned to be assigned to the preferred parent, they may have partially memorized their list of criticisms in order to provide the examiner with the most powerful arguments to support their position. They may appreciate that they have limited time with the evaluator and may also appreciate how important the examiner's comments will be to the court. Accordingly, they may do their homework well and be sure that they present the most complete list possible. In addition, after interviews with many professionals involved in the litigation, they may have gotten their speech "down pat." Differentiating between this kind of litany and the litany of the programmed child may be extremely difficult, if not impossible. In such cases, other aspects of the interview with the child must be given greater credence in order to make a meaningful recommendation.

The evaluator should be wary of a child who describes one parent as having all assets and no liabilities and the other parent as being the incarnation of all of mankind's evils. Of course, there are some parents who may very well have such great deficits that the child's totally negative view is close to accurate. However, in most cases this is not true and such a child may have been excessively programmed (that is, brainwashed beyond the usual amount) or may be denying the hostility that he or she feels toward the parent who is described as practically perfect. Most often the parent who has left the home is viewed as an abandoner and as the cause of the divorce. Accordingly, there is often excessive hostility toward this parent, regardless of how justified leaving the home may have been. With this view of the parent, the child may harbor formidable anger, with little ambivalence. The differentiation between this kind of one-sided view and that of the programmed child is often made by the degree of conviction with which the child speaks of his or her anger. When these feelings are genuinely and spontaneously felt they are often expressed with a greater degree of conviction than is usually seen in the brainwashed child.

A. Levy (1978a) divides children's statements regarding parental preference into certain categories which can prove useful. I will discuss each of these in detail because of their importance in the custody evaluation. The categories are:

I. The child who will not take sides.
II. The child with an ambivalent preference.

III. The child with a seemingly unambivalent preference.
    A. The realistically unambivalent.
    B. The pathologically unambivalent.

I. The child who will not take sides.   Such children have genuinely warm relationships with both parents and their statements of such involvement are credible. If they had their choice, they would choose to divide their time equally between the two parents. They are hesitant to overtly express hostility to either parent, not so much out of any kind of anger inhibition problem, but more because of their desire to avoid hurting each parent's feelings. Levy holds that the parents of children in this category are usually the healthier ones—parents who are less frequently embroiled in years of neurotic litigation. These are the cases that are more likely to be settled out of court. These are the cases also, in this examiner's opinion, that are more likely to profit from a joint custodial arrangement.

II. The child with an ambivalent preference.   These children overtly express a preference for one parent. However, they are in the midst of a loyalty conflict and secretly have positive feelings for the other as well. These positive feelings toward the ostensibly nonpreferred parent may be expressed through exaggerated condemnation of the nonpreferred parent. Their reaction formation, thereby, is a manifestation of their ambivalence. Or they actually tell the psychiatrist many positive things about the nonpreferred parent. When they are with the preferred parent, they are openly loving and openly critical of the nonpreferred parent. When with the nonpreferred parent, they express some warmth and affection, but do not let the preferred parent know of the positive feelings toward the nonpreferred. The ambivalence of these children is partially related to the loyalty conflict and partially related to the pressures placed upon them by the parents to express a preference. The parental pressures enhance the polarization that naturally occurs in most children.

III. The child with a seemingly unambivalent preference.   These children under all conditions make statements in which they claim unequivocal desire to be with one parent and state that they have no desire to live with the other. Levy divides these children into two categories: (A) the realistically unambivalent and (B) the pathologically unambivalent.

> (A) The realistically unambivalent. Children in this category have a clear view of the nonpreferred parent and, to the best of the examiner's knowledge, are justified in not wishing to live with that parent. They do, however, appreciate

assets of the nonpreferred parent as well. Their choice is a sad resignation to the situation. The parents of the children in this subgroup have unequal degrees of pathology with the nonpreferred parent being the sicker one. "The child's preference is related to a need to escape from an unempathetic, somewhat hostile and unavailable parent. The nonpreferred parent is, in effect, pushing the child toward the preferred parent, who is exerting only a minimal pull." The examiner's decision making, in this situation, is not difficult. Generally, even the parents agree that the child's preference is the judicious one.

(B)   The pathologically unambivalent. These are the so-called brainwashed children. "Children in this group are voluble; their statements seem well-rehearsed, almost programmed; and the words they speak are stilted and inappropriate, often repeating the exact phraseology used by the preferred parent in meetings alone with the psychiatrist. They can be described as having been brainwashed by that parent. Their parental choice and their assignment of blame for the divorce are emphatic. They have no hope or wish for parental reunion, and they may even refuse to visit the nonpreferred parent. Their facade is so artificial as to be unbelievable and their statements, however equivocal, cannot be taken at face value."

In these cases the nonpreferred parent is generally not as terrible as the child proclaims. "The preferred parent, moreover, is engaged in an attempt not merely to destroy the other parent but to make the child join in this process. The preferred parent exacts as the cost of his or her love the destruction of the child's empathy and identification with the other parent, forcing the child into open but ambivalent conflict with that parent.... The emotional relationship with one parent is totally ruptured and the child's developmental needs are ignored. The preferred parent usually overidentifies with the child, has an aggressive personality, is manipulative and sadistic, and shows a strong need to be the sole parent."

Levy proposed two possible solutions to this dilemma:

1.   The child should live with the preferred parent and the nonpreferred parent should be encouraged to "let go" and resign him- or herself to the unfortunate reality and to accept the fact that no court can order the child to be meaningfully involved with a parent toward whom there is such strong antagonism.

2. The nonpreferred parent should be awarded custody and the custodial parent have total control over visitation with the preferred.

I do not agree entirely with either of these recommendations and would propose a third. With regard to the first, I agree that at times the child should be allowed to live with the preferred parent (obvious deficiencies notwithstanding) from the recognition that the court cannot order a child to break down reaction formations and other neurotic defense mechanisms. The nonpreferred parent, however, should not be advised to "let go." Rather, he or she should be encouraged to continue to maintain contact, in whatever way possible, in order to communicate to the child the basic feelings of affection that are still present. Whether by telephone, mail, presents, and continuing reasonable attempts at contact, the child will still know that the supposedly nonpreferred parent is still involved. Hopefully, as the child matures, their relationship may once again be established. I have actually seen this happen in a few cases.

With regard to the second recommendation, that the nonpreferred parent have total custody and control, I am in sharp disagreement. The nonpreferred parent may now deprive the child of total contact with the preferred under the guise of breaking the pathological tie. There are probably still healthy elements in the relationship with the preferred parent (brainwashing notwithstanding) which may then not be gratified for both the preferred parent and the child. My own recommendation is a modification of Levy's first, namely, that the child be allowed to stay with the preferred and that the nonpreferred be encouraged to continue contact.

Furthermore, I would divide Levy's category B, the pathologically unambivalent, into two subcategories:

1. The truly pathologically unambivalent, and
2. The seemingly pathologically unambivalent.

Levy's category B children would be in the first category, in that they are truly pathologically unambivalent. In the second category, the seemingly pathologically unambivalent, would be those children who also appear to be brainwashed. However, their litany is not the result of brainwashing but the result of having memorized a "spiel" to present to the various mental health professionals, attorneys, and judges, who may have interviewed them. They come on with their main ammunition and zero in very quickly on the particular criticisms that they know will most impress the examiner. These children are basically not pathologically unambivalent. They are really in category A, the realistically unambivalent. Their litany is not a recording of statements of the preferred parent, rather it is a statement of actual and realistic criticisms they have of the nonpreferred parent. It may be difficult for the therapist to differentiate between these two subcategories of the pathologically unambivalent child, but it is important to try to do so. The most important determinant as to whether the child's lack of ambivalence is pathological is what the realities are with regard to the nonpreferred parent. And it is only by the detailed evaluation of that parent that the therapist is in a position to answer this crucial question.

As I hope the reader will appreciate, the question as to whether a child has or has not been brainwashed is generally a meaningless one. The examiner should communicate to the court that *all* children are brainwashed to a certain degree and that one must try to ascertain the degree to which a child is being brainwashed, that is, how vicious and systematic is the vilification. Minimal amounts of brainwashing are the norm; extensive degrees of brainwashing represent a serious compromise in parental capacity. It is a waste of the examiner's and the court's time to address the question whether the child has or has not been brainwashed. When a pathological degree of brainwashing is possibly present, it behooves the examiner to try to ascertain just how pathological was the brainwashing.

THE JUDICIOUS USE OF SELECTED PROJECTIVE MATERIAL

As I have already mentioned on a few occasions, the examiner should be extremely cautious about using projective material in the custody evaluation. One does well to compare such data to dreams. Most would agree that dreams, per se, are of little diagnostic significance. The dream of the healthiest person utilizes the logic of the psychotic. In the dream there is a bona fide break with reality in which we actually believe that our dream experiences are really occurring. In fact, one useful way of understanding the psychotic state is to consider it a dream in the waking state. Even the healthiest person will have dreams that are not significantly different from the dreams of the psychotic. Accordingly, not only are dreams of little, if any, diagnostic significance, but they are not well correlated with clinical behavior.

Dreams do, however, *at times* provide us with useful psychodynamic information. They can tell us something about why a person is behaving in a particular way. This is especially the case if we have the opportunity to elicit the free associations of the dreamer and to utilize his or her assistance in analyzing the dream. In short, then, the dream has great potential for telling us something about *why* a person is thinking and acting in a particular way, but it is of little, if any, value in providing us with information about depth of psychopathology and degree of impairment in the real world. Accordingly, it is of little value in telling us something about such functions as parental capacity. I am not stating that it is of absolutely no value in this regard. If a mother, for example, describes repetitious dreams of murdering one or more of her children, there is the *possibility* that she may be harboring homicidal impulses toward her progeny. On the other hand, the dream may have nothing to do with such impulses. The children, as extensions of herself, may very well symbolize qualities of her own that she may wish to get rid of. One must know the patient well and have full opportunity for analytic work (generally over a long period of time) before one is in a good position to come to definite conclusions about a dream's meaning. And even then one could only state what is the most probable interpretation. One certainly could not get up in a court of law and say that there is definite "proof" about the meaning of a particular dream, even a repetitious one.

The *Rorschach Test* (Rorschach, 1921) is one of the most widely used and respected projective tests. One does well to view the projections facilitated by the inkblots to have much in common with the dream. Like dream interpretation, there is a wide variety of opinion among psychologists about the meaning of these projections. I agree with those who hold that they can provide useful information, in many cases, about underlying psychodynamics. The Rorschach is probably a better source of information about diagnosis than the dream. However, it certainly has drawbacks in this regard as well. (But diagnosis, as has already been mentioned, is of little value in the custody evaluation.) And as far as a predictor of behavior the Rorschach, like the dream, leaves much to be desired. I am not claiming that it is of no value in this regard; I am only claiming that it is of little value because of the highly speculative nature of the predictions and the correlations between Rorschach response and clinical behavior. Accordingly, it is of questionable value in the custody evaluation where we are trying to learn something about parental capacity. As I described above for the dream, repetitious Rorschach responses in which there is a high frequency of sadistic and even murderous impulses toward children does not necessarily mean that the adult wishes to torture or kill his or her own children. Such productions might relate to feelings about such aspects of one's self (as just one possible alternative explanation).

The *Thematic Apperception Test* (Murray, 1936) is another widely used projective test. Here the patient is presented with a series of pictures and is asked to create a story that is suggested by the cards. Although the pictures are designed to be nonspecific, they certainly restrict and contaminate fantasies. Bellak and Bellak (1949) subsequently developed the *Children's Apperception Test (CAT)*, which follows the same principles. However, the pictures, although again nonspecific, tend to elicit fantasies that are more relevant to the lives of children. I view these tests to have definite value in providing the examiner with psychodynamic material. They have less value (but are not of no value at all) in providing diagnostic information in terms of the specific diagnostic category in which the patients' problems may best be described. However, conclusions about parental capacity derived from these cards are highly speculative and are not likely to hold up well in court. Shneidman's *Make-A-Picture Story Test (MAPS)* (1947) has certain advantages over the TAT and CAT in that the patient is presented with a series of scenes (in which there are no figures, either human or animal) and an assortment of human and animal figurines. The patient is asked to create his or her own picture. The stories obtained thereby are less contaminated by the external facilitating stimulus and are more truly revealing of underlying psychological processes. However, I have the same reservations about the MAPS as I have with regard to the aforementioned projective tests with regard to their value in legal proceedings. Buck (1946) introduced the *House-Tree-Person Test* in which the child's drawing provides useful psychodynamic information. One not only analyzes the drawings per se, but the fantasies the child creates around the drawings. Subsequently, Mackover (1949) published her techniques for analyzing children's drawings which follows similar principles. Buck's and Mackover's contributions have been the subject of significant controversy, and there is no question that there is a high degree of speculation involved in making interpretations in these two tests. Nevertheless, there is no question, in my opinion, that these are useful instruments for learning something about psychodynamics, are less useful with regard to diagnostic information, and are of little value in the courtroom.

The way in which the utilization of projective material can compromise an examiner's position in court is well demonstrated by this vignette. A 6-year-old boy, in the course of the custody evaluation, is given a piece of drawing paper and crayons. He is invited to draw anything he wants and then to tell a story about what he has drawn. This is standard procedure in child diagnosis and treatment. The child draws a house and then draws a man in the middle of the house. The man is drawn in black crayon and as the boy fills in the human outline (again with black) there is a vigorous and intense quality to his work. He then takes a red crayon and says, "The whole house is burning down and so is the man." Again, there is a frenetic quality to his work as he covers the whole drawing with red lines. He then says, "The whole house is burned down. Everything is ashes. Even the man is ashes." The child is then asked how the house caught on fire. The reply, "The boy's friend, who lives next door, burnt it down. He was angry at the man who lived in the house. He didn't like him because he was mean."

Most therapists would agree that the drawing and its associated story reveal that the child is extremely angry at his father. Depicting his father as completely black, and drawing him frenetically suggests that the child views his father as a fearful and ominous figure. He views his father as anxiety-provoking and dangerous. Most would agree, as well, that the friend next door is merely a convenient device for assuaging guilt over his hostility. It is not he who kills his father, but his friend (his alter ego) next door. His hostility toward his father is being released through a drawing in which he totally destroys the father by burning him to death.

Now let us imagine the situation in which the evaluator has included the above material in his or her report and considers the child's massive hostility toward his father as one argument (among many) for recommending that the mother be given custody of the child. The husband's attorney, during cross-examination, could ask the impartial expert to show the court the picture and explain what he considers to be its meaning. Following this, the attorney could ask the following questions to which only yes-no answers could be required:

> *Attorney:* "Is it possible, Doctor, that this child watched television before drawing this picture, either on the same day or one or two days previously?"
> *Expert:* "Yes."

The expert has no choice but to answer yes. If the evaluator answers no, he or she looks silly, because a "no" response essentially says that there is absolutely *no* possibility that this child watched television over a three-day period. Even if there is no television set in the home, there would still be the possibility that he watched in another child's home. The attorney then continues.

> *Attorney:* "Is it possible, Doctor, that the child observed a program in which a building burned?"
> *Expert:* "Yes."

Again, the expert has little choice but to answer yes, because to say that there was *no* such possibility makes him or her look absurd. This is especially the case because most news programs routinely describe the major fire of the day. The attorney then proceeds.

> *Attorney:* "Is it possible, Doctor, that such a program depicted people being injured and even killed in such a fire?"
> *Expert:* "Yes."

Once again, the expert has to answer yes to preserve his or her credibility.

> *Attorney:* "Is it possible, Doctor, that the picture that you've just shown us was suggested by his watching such a television program, a program in which a fire was described, a program in which people were burned to death in the fire?"
> *Expert:* "Yes."

If the expert tries to follow the one-word response with an explanation, he or she is likely to be interrupted by the attorney who will instruct the testifier to confine responses to yes or no. This is likely to frustrate the expert because the deep-seated conviction that such environmental suggestions play a small role, at best, in producing such pictures and fantasies. The examiner firmly believes that it is the internal pressure of psychodynamically meaningful material, rather than external suggestive stimuli, that play the most important role in creating such fantasies in the child. But a skilled lawyer will not permit the testifier to provide this explanation. Even if the examiner were permitted to give it (and sometimes the judge might ask for it), the attorney could still extract a statement that such an explanation is still "theory" and not "fact." And the attorney could then proceed with further inquiry designed to weaken the explanation:

> *Attorney:* "Is it possible, Doctor, that your explanation is incorrect?"
> *Expert:* "Yes."

If the expert claims that there is no possibility that the explanation is incorrect, his or her credibility is seriously compromised. So, once again, the examiner has no choice but to answer in the affirmative. The examiner has no choice but to agree that the explanation may be incorrect and there may be no opportunity to elaborate and explain that the possibility of being incorrect is extremely low, that well-established psychological principles would highly support such an explanation, and so on.

The lawyer whose position the examiner is supporting may provide an opportunity for a presentation of the rationale for the explanation. But it is important for the expert to appreciate that the judge may be extremely unsophisticated when it comes to understanding such psychological processes. And the cross-examining attorney may fully convince such a judge that the expert's interpretations are totally speculative creations, not worthy of consideration. In order to avoid such compromises of one's position, the evaluator should avoid the use of such projective material. In fact, I would go further and suggest that it not even be elicited for the evaluator's own personal information. Once in the files, there is always the possibility that the drawings and notes will be brought before the court. The opposing attorney may ask to look at the evaluator's files (which the competent examiner should bring to the court). If the picture is found, the attorney may not only ask for the explanation but, in addition, ask the evaluator why he or she did not see fit to include it in the report. There is no good explanation. The real answer would have to be that the evaluator wanted to avoid the kind of misguided and misleading interchanges that the revelation of such material might involve. The cross-examining attorney might encourage the evaluator's providing such an explanation because it involves the assumption that the judge is naive with regard to understanding psychological processes. Although, unfortunately, this is sometimes the case, the evaluator is certainly not going to improve his or her position in the judge's eyes by questioning the judge's intelligence or competence. Accordingly, the safest procedure is not to elicit such projective material at all and rely on more objective information that is far less likely to cause embarrassment in court—information that will be understood by even the most psychologically naive judge.

There are judges who will order psychological tests on both parents and/or the children. As mentioned, this is a manifestation of naiveté on the judge's part. It reflects the judge's view (promulgated by mental health professionals) that these tests are "objective" and that they provide information that is much more accurate than clinical observations. The judge here has probably been duped into the belief that there is something more objective and scientific about an instrument such as the Rorschach than the clinical interview. Such a request is probably also related to the judge's belief that these tests are more efficient and can get to the "roots" of the problem more efficaciously than clinical interviews. There is no question that they can often provide much extra information in an expeditious way. But, in my opinion, it is very unlikely that they are of greater value than clinical interviews in custody evaluations. Accordingly, examiners who cooperate in such cases by complying with court dictates are doing their patients and the court a disservice. Unfortunately, such utilization of psychological tests is widespread and contributes, thereby, to each party bringing in a parade of professionals who are going to provide different explanations for the same projective data.

In spite of my strong criticism of the utilization of projective materials in the custody evaluation, I do not refrain from their use entirely. There are a few projective techniques that I do utilize, but I am careful to use them only as a vehicle for obtaining more objective and "hard" data. In short, I utilize instruments that allow themselves to be points of departure for the obtaining of overt statements that can be more useful in custody litigation. For example, I described above the series of questions that I will often ask a child about where would be the best place for a one-year-old child to live, in the mother's home or in the father's home. I then proceed with asking the same questions for children of older ages. Ultimately I hope the child will shift into a discussion of his or her own situation. The earlier responses are of little value in court; the later ones can be very useful.

The projective instruments that I will now describe are in the latter category. Although they do not tap the deeper unconscious material that is obtained from instruments such as the Rorschach and TAT, they do provide a vehicle for obtaining objective responses that may be very useful in courtroom litigation.

"The Talking, Feeling, and Doing Game"

The author's *Talking, Feeling, and Doing Game* (Gardner, 1973b) was designed primarily to elicit meaningful psychodynamic material from children who are resistant to talk directly about their problems or reveal their psychodynamics through play fantasy. The game has proved useful, however, as an additional therapeutic modality for those who are freer to reveal themselves as well.

In this game each player in turn throws the dice and moves the playing piece along a path of colored squares (Figure 2). Depending upon which color the playing piece lands, the player takes a Talking Card, Feeling Card, or a Doing Card. If the player can respond to the question or directions on the card, a reward chip is given. As their names imply, the Talking Cards elicit material of a cognitive nature; the Feeling Cards attempt to evoke emotional responses; and the Doing

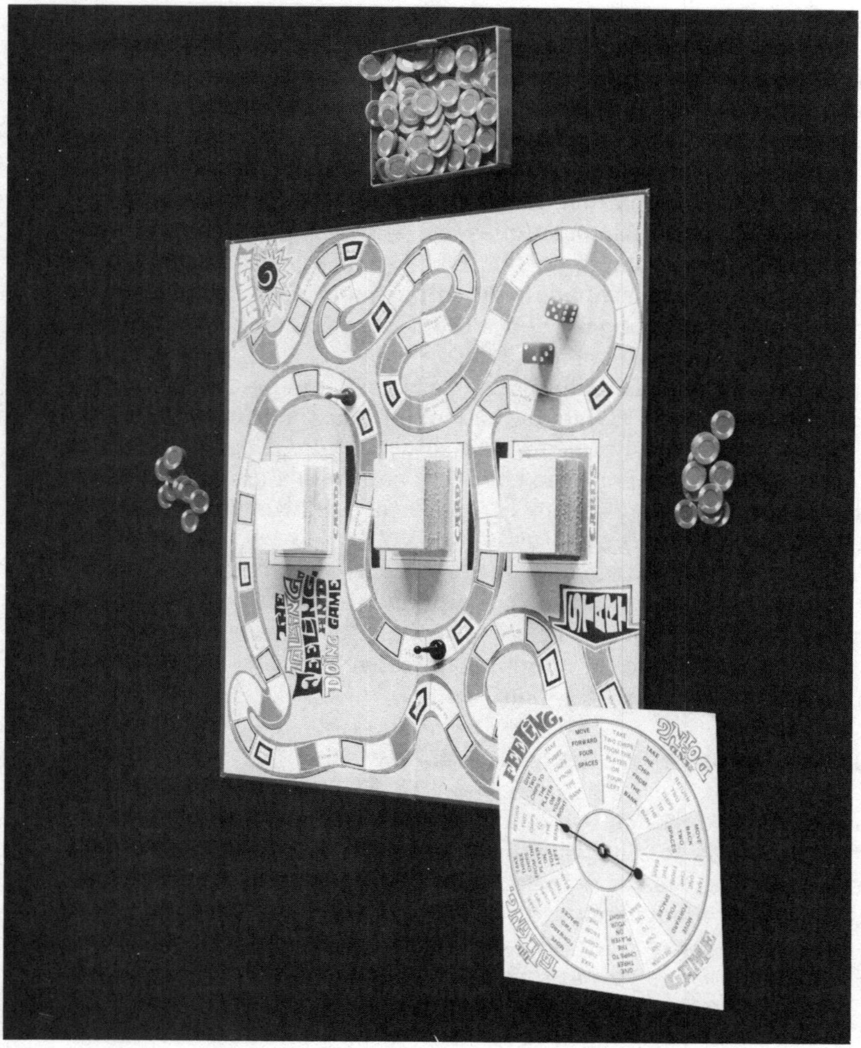
THE TALKING, FEELING, AND DOING GAME
START
CARDS
MOVE FORWARD FOUR SPACES
MOVE BACK TWO SPACES

Figure 2

Cards encourage physical expression. None of the cards attempts to obtain responses that would be as anxiety provoking as free fantasy expression or the relating of self-created stories. The cards range from the low anxiety provoking ("What is your address?" "What present would you like to get for your next birthday?" "Make believe you're blowing out the candles on your birthday cake." "Make a funny sound with your mouth. If you spit, you don't get a chip.") that just about any child can answer and thereby get involved in the game, to the moderately higher anxiety provoking ("Someone passes you a note, what does it say?" "Make up a message for a Chinese fortune cookie." "Suppose two people were talking about you and they didn't know you were listening. What do you think you would hear them saying?" "What's the worst thing a child can say to his mother?" "A boy has something on his mind that he's afraid to tell his father. What is it that he's scared to talk about?" "Everybody in the class was laughing at a girl. What had happened?" "All the girls in the class were invited to a birthday party except one. How did she feel? Why wasn't she invited?")

The playing piece may also land on "Go Forward" and "Go Backward" squares which direct the player to move the playing piece a specific number of squares, as well as on squares directing the player to spin the spinner (which can result in gaining or losing chips or squares on the playing path). These elements of the game do not generally bring about revelation of specific psychodynamic material; rather, they enhance the child's involvement in the game and thereby reduce resistances to the therapeutic activity.

Some of the cards ask the child to directly talk about him- or herself ("Tell something about your mother that gets you angry."); others request information about "third parties" ("A boy was scared to make a telephone call. What was he afraid of?"). In response to the first category of cards, children are likely to talk directly about themselves. In response to the second category, the examiner can often shift from a discussion of third parties to a discussion of the children themselves.

Many of the questions provide information that can be useful in the custody evaluation. For example: "A boy has something on his mind that he's afraid to tell his father. What is it that he's scared to talk about?" "A girl is ashamed to tell her mother about something. What is it?" "What is the worst thing a parent can do to a child?" "What do you think about a boy who curses at his father?" "Act out what you would do if you found that you had magic powers." "Tell about something scary that once happened to you." "What's the worst thing that ever happened to you?" "What is the most important thing that can make a family happy?" "When was the last time you cried? What did you cry about?" "Name three things that could make a person angry."

"Tell about a time when your feelings were hurt." "Was there ever a person whom you wished to be dead? If so, who was that person? Why did you wish the person to be dead?" "What is the worst problem a person can have? Why?" "Make believe that you were told that any three wishes you made would come true. What would you wish for?" "People are a mixture of both good and bad, that is, everyone has good and bad parts. Say something good about someone you don't like." "Of all the places in the world, where would you like to live the most? Why?" "If you became mayor of your city, what would you do to change things?" "Tell something about your father that gets you angry." "What's the worst thing a child can say to his mother?" These are typical questions and, as the reader can appreciate, they can give the examiner information about the child's feelings about the parents that might not otherwise be so readily obtainable. The board-game structure and token reinforcement facilitate the child's revealing this vital material.

For the purposes of the custody evaluation, it is crucial that the examiner select from the child's responses those statements that are directly relevant to the parents themselves, rather than indirect reference via discussion of third parties and people in general. The former kind of information is very valuable in the examiner's testimony; the latter is risky to use in that it opens the examiner to criticism under cross-examination and may compromise his or her credibility.

Verbal Projective Questions

A traditional verbal projective question that children are often asked is what animal they would choose to be if they had to be so transformed and why. Kritzberg (1966) has elaborated this type of question into a more comprehensive series of verbal projective questions that he has found useful in gaining psychodynamic information from both adults and children. For the purposes of the custody evaluation, I have found some of the children's questions to be particularly useful as points of departure for discussions that may provide useful information. I generally start by asking the child the question: "If you had to be changed into an animal—any animal in the whole world—which animal would you choose?" After the child has chosen an animal, I will ask why he or she has chosen that particular animal. After I have extracted as much information as I can from the response, I go on with second and third choices and the reasons why. Then I ask: "Of all the animals in the world, which animal would you not want to be? Why?" Again, I request second and third choices. The same series of questions is then repeated but this time I ask the child what object, that is, what nonliving thing the child would choose to be if he or she had to be so transformed. Again, I ask for first, second and third choices, both positive and negative and the reasons for each choice.

Generally, one isolated response is not as useful as a trend in which there is the same theme repeated in various forms. For example, if the child chooses animals that are described as getting a lot of attention and care, I might suspect that the child is suffering some emotional deprivation. If I can then get the child to shift into a discussion of the parents and the issue of deprivation in the relationship with them, I may have some meaningful material for my report. If I cannot accomplish this, I will not speculate in my report about the deprivational element (at least not from data provided by these particular questions).

Actually, the aforementioned animal and object questions are merely lead-ins to the more important ones regarding the parents. Specifically, I will ask the child "If your mother had to be turned into an animal, what animal would be a good one for her to turn into? What animal would be like her? What animal suits her personality? Why?" I then elicit first, second and third choices, both positive and negative and the reasons for each choice. I then ask a similar series of questions about which animal would suit (and which would not suit) the father's personality. I then proceed with: "If your mother had to be turned into an object, something that isn't alive, what would be a good object to turn her into? What object would be like her? Why?" Again, three choices are elicited, and the reasons, and similar questions are presented for the father. This is a very valuable form of inquiry. In a nonthreatening way it provides answers to the therapist's questions about how the child really feels about the parents. Furthermore, it is fun for children and most involve themselves enthusiastically. It generally is not difficult to get the child to elaborate upon his or her feelings about the parent after the animal or the object has been selected. Using this projective information in this way, the examiner can obtain direct information without having to resort to the kinds of speculations one usually utilizes when describing information derived from projective instruments.

Discussion of Selected Pictures from "The Boys and Girls Book About Divorce"

Another method I have found useful for eliciting information from children is to ask them to relate the fantasies and stories that come to mind when viewing each of a series of pictures selected from my *The Boys and Girls Book About Divorce* (Figure 3). I have found particularly useful for this purpose the pictures on pages 26, 27, 69, 78, 86, and 119 of

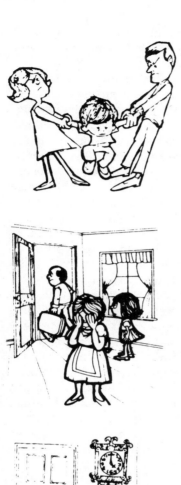

Figure 3

192

the hardcover edition (1970) (pages xxx, xxxi, 49, 61, 70, and 111 of the paperback edition (1971a). The children are presented a picture and asked to tell about what they think is going on. The elicited comments and stories can be a useful source of information about the children's view of the parents and their feelings about them. Some children will speak about the pictures in general and not make direct reference to their own parents' situation. In such cases the examiner must shift the discussion into a direct one regarding their *own* parents, if he or she is to use the information in the report. Other children will start directly discussing their parents' difficulties and then, of course, the examiner's work is much easier.

Sentence Completion Tests

Sentence completion tests are another form of projective test often included in the psychologist's diagnostic battery. Used judiciously these can be of value in the custody evaluation, as long as the examiner makes sure to translate the responses into direct conscious awareness of the child's own situation. As is true of *The Talking, Feeling, and Doing Game,* some of the questions ask for general responses and others make direct reference to the child's own feelings and situation. The Holsopple-Miale Sentence Completion Test (1954) is one of the more commonly used such tests. The questions in this instrument that I have found most useful are:

> Children are usually certain that...
> The hardest decisions...
> Fathers should learn that...
> The most pleasant dreams...
> One can repair the damage caused by...
> The nicest thing about being a child...
> If only people knew how much...
> To be a good liar one must...
> A mother is more likely than a father to...
> A father is more likely than a mother to...

The questions that I usually add when administering these questions to children being evaluated in custody litigation are:

> There would be fewer divorces if...
> The best of fathers may forget that...

> Mothers should learn that...
> I wish that...
> The worst thing that could happen to a family is...
> The best kinds of homes are the ones that...
> Mothers often...
> Fathers often...

Again, only when the child's responses can be directed into particular statements about each of the parents should the information elicited here be used.

It is important for the reader to appreciate that my caveat about projective tests should not be construed as a warning against other kinds of psychological tests. An IQ test may be very well in order. For example, a 12-year-old child with a very high IQ could be said to be functioning intellectually at the 14- or 15-year level. The preference expressed by such a child should be given far greater credibility than a 12-year-old with an average or below-average IQ. In addition, the Comprehension and Picture Arrangement subtests of the WISC-R can provide the examiner with information about a child's social sensitivity and values. Pointing out that the child achieved particularly high scores on these subtests suggests that statements about parental preference should be given greater credibility than a same-age child with lower scores on these subtests.

CONCLUDING COMMENTS

I have presented much more material than one would reasonably want to include in the evaluation of any single child. As mentioned, my purpose in this chapter has been to provide the examiner with a wealth of material from which he or she might draw when conducting the custody evaluation of the child. Many examiners rely heavily on projective material when evaluating a child. I hope the reader will agree that the use of such material in the custody evaluation is risky and that it may seriously compromise the evaluator's testimony. Some examiners may find it difficult to refrain from using these instruments. Therefore, I have provided such examiners with a variety of nonprojective material for utilization in custody evaluations. Another aim has been to demonstrate how rich a source of information children can be in custody evaluations, their youth notwithstanding. Evaluating this information, however, presents the examiner with a formidable challenge. I have sought to assist examiners in assessing optimally this valuable source of information in the custody evaluation.

6

Information from Other Sources

The information from the sources discussed in this chapter is generally less valuable than that which has been obtained from the parents and children. However, information from other individuals can serve to corroborate what has been obtained in the interviews with the primary family members. In addition, it may open up areas of inquiry not previously explored although much of it must be considered hearsay and subject to all the dangers of utilizing such information in one's testimony. Whereas the parents and children *must* be seen in order to conduct an impartial evaluation, these individuals cannot be required by the examiner to be interviewed.

Accordingly, in my statement of provisions for involving myself in custody litigation (Chapter Two), I speak only of my right to *invite* such individuals to see me. Such invitations are best extended through the parents because direct invitations could justifiably be considered by the recipient to be intrusive, coercive, and even unethical (especially for the physician). The degree of receptivity of each of the parents to extend such invitations is often very revealing of the parents' true commitment to be open and honest in the inquiry. And this should be taken into consideration when discussing with the parents the extending of these invitations. Hesitation, delays, and rationalizations for not agreeing to invite a particular party are best viewed as attempts to prevent the disclosure of information that would be damaging to the recalcitrant parent. As mentioned in the discussion of the provisos (Chapter Two), I generally take a conservative position regarding interviewing the assortment of friends and relatives that each parent may wish me to see. The testimonials generally cancel one another out because each has been selected to support the particular parent's position. Also, I do not allow one parent to veto the other parent's request that I see a particular person. I do, however, hear both sides out and reserve the right to make the final decision regarding whether the invitation should be extended.

THE HOUSEKEEPER

Preliminary Considerations

Of all the interviewees, the housekeeper can probably provide more useful information than any other person. She lives in the home, is party to what goes on, and may spend more of her time thinking about what happens between her employers than many other things in her life. She is often a surrogate parent and plays an important role in the children's growth and development. If this is the case, the question as to whether or not she will be involved in the children's upbringing is an important one, and the kind of person she is—especially with regard to her maternal capacity—is an important consideration for the examiner.

Unfortunately, the housekeeper may be very hesitant to divulge information about the family fearing she may compromise her relationship with one or both employers. In addition, she may never have been in a psychiatrist's office before. She may be petrified over the prospect of seeing a psychiatrist, may believe that a psychiatrist can read her mind, or she may just be generally fearful of his or her authority. It is likely that the impartial expert has become an even more formidable figure to her because of what she has heard regarding the evaluation. Also, she may appreciate that each parent has placed the examiner in a position of great authority and power.

It is important for the examiner to advise the parents that the housekeeper be told, at the time the invitation is extended, that the examiner must have the freedom to reveal to her employers, at his or her discretion, any information she provides in the interview. It is only ethical to do this. However, such a statement is likely to increase her fears. Sometimes her resistances to revealing information can be over-come by suggesting that the parents impress upon her that if she really loves the children she will provide the information. Some may consider this "low" and that stooping to guilt evocation as a method of getting the housekeeper to come is beneath the dignity of the impartial expert. My answer to this criticism is that I have found the housekeeper a very valuable source of information and that it genuinely is in the children's best interests for her to see me. Although the approach is not in the highest tradition of psychoanalytic interviewing, the communication is basically valid, and I have not lost any sleep over the fact that I have utilized it.

The housekeeper's anxieties can be further assuaged by the parents' telling her that she does not have to tell me anything she does not wish to and that I will not coerce her into speaking about any topic which she expresses definite reluctance to discuss. They should also advise her that it might be detrimental to the children if she lies to me. (Unfortunately, this warning has not discouraged many from providing me with the most absurd fabrications.) They are also advised to tell her that, at my discretion, I must have the freedom to reveal (or not to reveal) what she says to me about the parents and children. However, they should impress upon her that I will not necessarily reveal every-thing and that I will not automatically be a channel of communication between her and the parents.

It is important for the examiner to appreciate that in the common situation, where the housekeeper is living with the mother, she is more likely to side with the mother in order to preserve a good relationship with her. This situation also gives the mother more opportunity to "brainwash" the housekeeper and instill in her the fear that if she pro-vides information that compromises the mother's position, that her job may be at stake.

Although it is becoming increasingly common for judges to see children in chambers and not divulge what the children say, I have not heard a situation in which the judge speaks to a housekeeper. Whereas I do have the obligation to reveal to the parents information the house-keeper provides me that is important to my determination, the judge does not have this obligation. Although this is an important reason for the judge interviewing the housekeeper, she may be even more fright-ened of seeing the judge than me. Accordingly, the information she pro-vides him may be even less useful than that which she provides me. This drawback to the judge interviewing her notwithstanding, I would strongly recommend that judges attempt to conduct such interviews, because as mentioned, I believe the housekeeper is a most valuable and untapped source of information in custody litigation.

The Interview with the Housekeeper

At the beginning of the interview I do everything possible to try to make the housekeeper more comfortable. I recognize that she is probably more anxious than the majority of people I interview in my office. I generally will begin with a simple everyday interchange about things like whether she had difficulty finding the office, the weather, and so on. These everyday, human interchanges may serve to make the atmosphere a more familiar one and are, thereby, anxiety alleviating. As is true of most, if not all, psychiatric interviews it is best to start with "basic statistical data" questions, rather than open anxiety-provoking ones. (Borrowing from military terminology, I call these "name, rank, and serial number" type questions.) I generally will ask the housekeeper her name, address (some do not live in with their employers), and telephone number. I inquire into her marital status. I get other information such as date of birth, and how long she has been in the United States (applicable to foreigners). I find out the date on which she began her employment with the parents being evaluated and the hours of employment. All these questions are usually answered quite readily and serve to reduce anxiety.

I then ask the housekeeper what she understands to be the purposes of the inverview. If there are any distortions I clarify these. When we both know exactly what my purpose is, I then tell her that it is important for her to appreciate that I reserve the right, at my discretion, to reveal to other parties involved in the evaluation (her employers, their attorneys, and the judge) any information that she has imparted to me. However, I am quick to add that I do not necessarily do this. I impress upon her that I appreciate her position and that she may, with justification, fear that her job may be in jeopardy, or her relationship with one of the parents significantly compromised, if she is too critical of either of them. I tell her that out of respect for her position, I will be very judicious regarding what I reveal and that I will not necessarily divulge what she says. In fact, I promise her that I will make every effort not to do so. I have found that I can often keep this promise and actually protect the housekeeper by getting one of the parents to make the same statement or criticism that was initially suggested to me be her. For example, the housekeeper may bring up a criticism about a father that was not previously brought forth. If I can get the mother to make a statement about this criticism I can protect the housekeeper and need not reveal her to have been the original source of information. However, there are occasions on which I need her corroboration to emphasize the point.

I will then ask the housekeeper what plans she has for herself after the separation or divorce. Is she planning to remain with her present employer, switch to the other parent, or leave the employment of the family entirely? In the context of her answer she may provide me with useful information about whom she considers to be the preferable parent. She may say that she is willing to work for whichever parent is granted custody. She may, however, state that she would only work for one parent and not the other. In giving the reasons why, she may focus on the parent's qualities as an employer or she may focus on the parent's qualities as a parent. The latter information is generally useful and the former may be as well.

Sometimes interviewing the housekeeper is like "pulling teeth." It may be necessary for the examiner to make statements and ask her to respond with a yes or a no. Although this approach is not in the highest psychoanalytic tradition, it may be the only way to get meaningful information from a tight-lipped or fearful housekeeper. One must surmise what she is trying to say and recognize that she is being ultra-cautious. As was described in my discussion of interviewing the parents and children, it is generally preferable to proceed from the low anxiety-provoking to the high anxiety-provoking questions. The yes-no questions are in accordance with this principle. Also, I will often ask the housekeeper to tell me the parental preference of each of the children. By talking about the children's preferences I may learn something about the housekeeper's opinion regarding the preferable parent. I focus on each child separately and ask the housekeeper to comment on the child's statements. Through the quotes of the child's comments the housekeeper may be able to express her own opinion without fear of being considered disloyal.

Often carefully chosen specific questions can be less anxiety provoking and more revealing than open-ended general ones. I have found particularly useful certain questions related to the home situation prior to the separation: "Who prepared breakfast in the morning?" "Who changed the diapers?" "Who got up in the middle of the night when the children cried?" "Who more frequently sat on the floor and played with them?" "Who spent longer times playing with them?" "Who had greater patience?" "Who could engage the children in talk for longer periods?" "Who sang songs more often with them?" "Who enjoyed more reading books with them?" Similar such specific questions can provide information about the visiting parent's habits, especially with regard to punctuality and reliability.

I then go into the more general questions, the more anxiety-provoking ones. I might ask the housekeeper to describe her employer. In this general description I might get some useful information. I then might say, "No one is perfect. Everyone is a mixture of both strong points and weak points. Tell me about some of Mrs. Jones' strong points." Then I will ask about weak points and ask similar questions about the father. In the context of such inquiry the housekeeper may make comments that bear on parental capacity without being aware of it. Typical comments in this category: "She's really trying," "She's now spending a lot more time with the kids," "No one is perfect." These comments can be points of departure for exploration in which one focuses primarily on the positive and then hopes to gain some information about the negatives in the context of the discussion.

The housekeeper is more likely to lie than other interviewees in the custody evaluation. However, she is more likely to do so in a primitive fashion because she is generally less well educated and sometimes, but not always, less bright than the parents. The latter factors may enable the examiner to get information from her when she doesn't realize that she is providing it. For example, I once asked a housekeeper, "What can you tell me about Mrs. Jones with regard to her taking care of the children?" She replied, "She's doing better now than before she was in the hospital last September." By focusing on the areas in which she was now doing better (the positives) I was able to learn something about the negatives. The housekeeper thought she was supplying me with useful positive information and thereby not criticizing her employer. However, she did not realize that, in the process of doing so, she was providing me with criticisms as well. A housekeeper may not wish to make a direct comment or openly express parental preference. However, she might make a comment like "I don't want to say which parent would better for the children. However, children are best off with their mothers." In this way she doesn't openly express her disloyalty but, by a general comment, provides her opinion.

I will sometimes ask the housekeeper this question: "Whom do you think the judge is going to give custody to, the mother or the father?" This question is similar to the one I will often ask children. It serves to reduce feelings of disloyalty in that it is the judge, not the housekeeper, who is dictating the decision. I have somethines found useful asking the housekeeper her opinion about splitting the children up. If she has a strong relationship with the children, her preferences may then come out as she will want to protect one or more of the children from going with the nonpreferred parent. It can sometimes be useful to interview the housekeeper with the children together in order to observe their interaction. Comparing the interaction between the children and each parent with the interaction of the children and the housekeeper can sometimes provide useful information. This is especially the case if the housekeeper is going to play an important role as a parental surrogate.

During one evaluation, after I had interviewed the housekeeper (who was brought by the mother), I received a telephone call from the father. He told me that he had spoken to the housekeeper after the interview and it was clear to him that she had not been completely candid with me. He arranged for her to call me on a subsequent day to give me the "true story." In the course of the conversation with the housekeeper it became clear that she had no real new information to provide. It became clear, as well, that she was only making the call in order to protect herself from the father's anger if she had refused to do so. She would not (and probably could not) directly say all of this; I could only surmise it from the fact that she had no information to provide me and spoke generally about how difficult her position was and how she did not wish to alienate either parent. I then asked her some very specific questions:

Examiner: "Am I correct in saying that you have no new information to give me at this point?"

Housekeeper: "Yes."

Examiner: "As you were talking, I began thinking that you really didn't want to make this call, but that you only did so in order not to get Mr. G. angry at you. Is that correct?"

Housekeeper: "Yes."

Examiner: "Am I correct in believing that you still feel that Mrs. G. would make the better parent at this time and that you didn't want to tell Mr. G. that this is your opinion?"

Housekeeper: "Yes."

Examiner: "So you really still believe that the children will be better off living with Mrs. G., but you don't want to let Mr. G. know that this is what you believe?"

Housekeeper: "Yes, that's right."

Examiner: "And you're only making this telephone call so that he'll 'get off your back'."

Housekeeper: "Yes, but please don't tell him that."

Examiner: "As I told you, I can't promise anything regarding what I will reveal. However, I will try very hard not to tell anyone about this part of our conversation."

Housekeeper: "Thank you very much. You're a *nice* man!"

In this case I was successful in not having to reveal all the details of this conversation. The information that the housekeeper had given me supported other observations of mine that the father was a coercive and manipulative person who had little guilt over using people for his own ends. I was able to quote certain comments of hers that were useful. Of course, had I been cross-examined on the stand with regard to every detail of the conversation, both in my notes and what I could recall, I would have had to reveal the above interchange.

LIVE-IN FRIENDS, POTENTIAL STEPPARENTS, AND STEPPARENTS AS PARENTAL SURROGATES

Most custody litigation takes place before there has been a remarriage. Often, the custody decision is included in the divorce decree and so stepparents, in the literal sense of the word, are not usually involved. However, "third parties" often appear on the scene in the form of lovers, live-in friends, and potential stepparents. The parent who is involved with such a person may have an advantage in the custody conflict in that the presence of such a person promises to provide the child with a two-parent home—generally considered to be more desirable than a one-parent home. Although the individual may have had a long-standing relationship with a parent, usually he or she has had only a minimal relationship with the children at the time of the custody conflict.

Because these third parties are presented as parental surrogates (either present or potential), it behooves the examiner to interview them. However, the examiner should appreciate that this person is almost invariably prejudiced against the alienated parent and will present a highly one-sided view, often parroting that of the parent with whom he or she is involved. There may have been little, if any, direct contact with the parent being denigrated, but this does not prevent the detailed description of the alienated party's deficiencies. The examiner who includes such data in the report is risking the criticism of having introduced hearsay material into his or her testimony. Such third parties will often profess great affection for the children. The children, however, most often do not reciprocate. When one compares the depth of involvement between the surrogate parent (at this stage) and the natural parent, the differences are often vast. Although the surrogate may certainly serve as a "second body" in the home, he or she is often just that and little more with regard to the capacity to provide dedicated attention and deep affection. Accordingly, the examiner should be careful about giving too much weight to the parent who presents such a third party at the time of the custody litigation. However, when the litigation takes place years after the separation there may have been a deep relationship formed with such a third party. Then, of course, the above caveats are not applicable.

It is important for the examiner to appreciate that even when one of the parents is remarried, the relationship between stepparents and stepchildren is notoriously a bad one. As I have discussed elsewhere (1982), the view that stepmothers are mean and evil is not derived *from* fairy tales. Rather, fairy tales reflect the ubiquitous antagonism that children have toward stepparents. And this antagonism does not necessarily arise within the children, with the stepparents being the innocent recipients of the children's animosity. Rather, it is the failure on the stepparents' part to have developed deep-seated loving relationships with the children that engenders the children's anger. I am not suggesting that this is necessarily the result of a deficiency on the stepparents' part. Rather, it seems to be the natural state of affairs and it would be hard to imagine the situation to be otherwise.

There is truth to the ancient aphorism that "blood is thicker than water." The natural mother has carried the child in her own body for nine months, has suffered the pains of delivery, and has the capacity to feed the child from her own body (even though she may not choose to do so). Most fathers are genuinely concerned with and psychologically involved in the growth of their children in utero. And both parents generally share (to varying degrees) the child's upbringing, joys and tribulations, gratifications and disappointments. The stepparent appears on the scene after the "rival" has had many years of investment with the child. The natural parent, then, has a formidable advantage over the newcomer with regard to parental capacity and psychological involvement with the children. Often the newcomer is absolutely no match for the real parent and the only thing that can be said in his or her behalf is that there will be a "body" in the home that may potentially prove to be a genuine parental surrogate. The tenuous involvement of stepparents with their stepchildren (protestations to the contrary notwithstanding) is well demonstrated by the low survival rate of stepparent-stepchildren relationships following the dissolution of second and subsequent marriages. Although a stepparent at the time of the break-up of the stepfamily may profess the desire for an on-going relationship with the stepchildren, such continuity is rarely realized. In short, then, lovers and other strangers should be interviewed, but what they say should not be taken too seriously. What they say about the alienated spouse is likely to be highly biased and the love and/or affection they profess for the children is not likely to have a deep basis. However, two bodies are better than one when it comes to assuming the many responsibilities involved in rearing children. Accordingly, the third party should still have a role to play in the custody evaluation.

GRANDPARENTS

The role of grandparents is generally not given the attention it deserves in child psychotherapy. The parent whose own parents are deeply involved with the children has extra "credit," and it is one of the arguments for giving the children custody to that parent. However, it is a far less important criterion than the parent's own personality characteristics and involvement with the child. Grandparents can make an important contribution to a child's feeling of self-worth. A healthy grandparent idealizes the grandchild and such idealization is important to get in childhood as a buffer against all the unwarranted criticisms that one inevitably gets in life.

As discussed in Chapter Four, I attempt to elicit information from the children about their relationships with their grandparents. In addition, I will ask the parents about the grandparents' relationships with the children. I am particularly interested in the proximity of the grandparents, because this may play an important role in their availability to serve in emergencies, as well as to provide surrogate parenting. Although parents embroiled in custody litigation will often provide very different opinions on a number of issues, my experience has been that they are generally in agreement regarding the depth of involvement of the various grandparents.

If a mother- or father-in-law supports a son- or daughter-in-law as the preferable custodial parent over the parent who is the natural son or daughter, this is a very powerful argument in favor of the son- or daughter-in-law. For example, if a mother-in-law is described as preferring her son-in-law over her own daughter, the evaluator should interview directly this woman. Because of the expected preference of a parent for his or her own child, there are usually overwhelming compromises in parental capacity that warrant a grandparent's preferring a son- or daughter-in-law over a natural child. Getting this information from the parents is not nearly as valuable as a direct quote from the grandparent him- or herself. One grandmother once said to me, "There's no question about it, my daughter has a terrible drinking problem. Her husband was telling you the truth when he said he and the children had to go around the house searching for hidden bottles. Last year, after my husband's heart attack, we stayed in the house for about a month. I used to help them look for the hidden bottles. Although she's my daughter, and I love her very much, my son-in-law is right. She's in no condition to take care of the children. She's my daughter and I love her very much, but I feel sorry for her. She needs help, but she won't get it. She won't even admit that she has a drinking problem." The statement, in itself, was a very powerful one. However, coming from the mother's own mother, it was even more impressive and was a heavy argument in favor of the father.

THE PEDIATRICIAN

It is common for a mother to go to a pediatrician and ask for a letter which states that she is a good mother and should have custody of her children. Such a letter is practically worthless to the court and to the impartial evaluator. A pediatrician knows that if such a request were declined he or she might alienate and even lose a patient. There are few who are so noble and/or sophisticated that they would say that they cannot be of service or that they would be willing to provide a similar letter to the father in that their experiences with him (although less) would warrant their providing him with a similar letter. In short, the impartial expert does well to ignore such letters and put them in the same category as testimonies by friends of each of the parents.

TEACHERS AND PRINCIPALS

In general psychiatric evaluations of children, teachers' comments can be very useful. An elementary school teacher may spend five to six hours a day with a child and has many important observations that can be useful to the child therapist. The information the teacher provides about the child's academic performance and behavior is an important contribution to the diagnostic process and is also useful in ascertaining the child's progress while in treatment.

Unfortunately, such information is of little value in custody litigation. If the child is doing well in school, it may very well be the result of both parents having contributed to the child's healthy development. If the child is doing poorly, in either the behavioral or academic area, it may reflect psychopathology. However, this information per se does not tell us *which* parent was more responsible for such psychopathology. Moreover, teachers tend to be very fearful of involving themselves in parental divorce, especially when litigation is involved. They are traditionally very fearful of alienating parents and may not wish to "take sides." My experience has been that many teachers and school personnel have not been straightforward enough to state directly that they don't wish to be involved. Rather, they may paint pretty pictures of the child's classroom situation, denying that there have been any problems at all. Or, they may speak in the particular educational euphemisms that are in vogue. On occasion, a teacher may confirm a parent's statement that one parent has been actively involved in the child's schooling, has typically appeared at teachers' conferences, at school events, plays, etc., and the other has not. If a letter can be obtained which will confirm this, it can be useful in corroborating parental statements regarding school involvement. It is important that the examiner obtain statements in written form (even though this request may produce even more reluctance on the part of the teacher or administrator to cooperate). Otherwise, the information is more likely to be considered hearsay. And, as mentioned, hearsay information is not only of little value in court, but its inclusion is likely to compromise the examiner's report or testimony.

REPORTS FROM HOSPITALS AND OTHER MENTAL HEALTH PROFESSIONALS

I routinely get permission to request reports from hospitals. As mentioned, it is a proviso of my involvement that the parents agree in advance to sign releases that facilitate my obtaining such material. Hospital reports are often useful to confirm allegations of suicidal attempts, drug overdoses, and child abuse. They also provide useful information about the depth of pathology when hospitalization was required. With regard to the latter type of information, the therapist should not fall into the trap of assuming that past psychopathology and/or hospitalization should automatically deprive a parent of custody. It should certainly be taken into consideration, but not be considered of overriding weight in the evaluation. It is the present parenting status that is most important. The hospital documents can be very powerful sources of information, and it is not likely that an opposing attorney will try to refute them. Nevertheless, such information is still, strictly speaking, hearsay in that the examiner has not observed directly the difficulties described therein. Corroborating statements by the parties concerned can strengthen the value of these already important and convincing documents.

With regard to requesting information from therapists, I recommend that the evaluator divide them into two categories, present therapists and past therapists. I generally do not ask for reports from therapists who are presently treating patients, especially if the treatment is analytically oriented or psychoanalytic. This may involve the therapist's providing information about the patient that may compromise the patient's position in the custody litigation. Although such information may be in the best interests of the child, it may also compromise significantly the relationship between the parent and the therapist. Such compromised therapy might result in the child's losing out in the long run, in that the parent then experiences less adequate and less efficient treatment and becomes a less adequate parent. This is another reason why strict and narrow adherence to the best-interests-of-the-child presumption may not always end up to be in the child's best interests. I prefer to be guided by what is in the best interests of *all* parties concerned and try to balance the various interests.

I have less trouble with requests for information from past therapists. This is especially the case when there is little if any likelihood that the parent will be returning to that therapist. Figure 4 shows a typical letter that I send to such therapists. The reader will note that I describe myself as having been "invited" to serve as an impartial, even though the court terms such an invitation an "order." I do this in order not to be party to the notion that people such as myself, with no previous involvement in a family, can be ordered to conduct a custody evaluation. I also make it clear that the court is requesting my "recommendations." This helps dispel the notion that the impartial expert's decision is the final one. In the second paragraph I request the therapist to focus specifically on the parental capacity of each of the parents. Sometimes a therapist will not wish to commit him- or herself to such a comparison and, instead, will provide me with a wealth of information about the various problems that were dealt with in treatment. I emphasize that I want a written report. As mentioned, this is no place for "folksy" telephone conversations. The examiner does not want to be in a position of being accused of having misquoted the verbal report. This just opens up an area of inquiry and possible compromise under cross-examination that can be completely avoided. Unfortunately, therapists all too often are afraid or hesitate to commit themselves in such a responding letter. All too often, I have found my letter is completely ignored. In such situations I, myself, do not repeatedly request a response. I may ask the parent(s) to "remind" the previous therapist to respond. If there is still no response, I make a note of it in my final report so that the judge can subpoena the therapist if the law of the state permits such action and if the judge wishes to pursue the matter.

REPORTS FROM ATTORNEYS

I usually ask both parents to ask their attorneys to forward any material that they and/or their attorneys think will be of interest or value to me. Generally, these include pleadings, affidavits, depositions, etc. I have sometimes found that the party with the stronger case is very

RICHARD A. GARDNER, M. D.
155 COUNTY ROAD
CRESSKILL, N. J. 07626

TELEPHONE 201 - 567-8989

November 10, 1981

Nancy J. Andrews, ACSW
54 Forest Road
Tenakill, New Jersey 07762

Re: Johnson vs. Johnson
Docket No: M-2584-81

Dear Ms. Andrews:

Judge Alan R. Goldberg of the Superior Court of New Jersey, Chancery Division, Bergen County, has invited me to serve as court-appointed impartial psychiatrist to render the court my recommendations regarding the custody of Thomas and Elizabeth Johnson. Their parents, Grace and Frederick Johnson, are presently litigating for their custody.

Mr. and Mrs. Johnson inform me that they saw you in marital counseling from January to August, 1980. I would be most appreciative if you would send me a report of your findings. I am particularly interested in any comments you have regarding their comparative parental capacities.

For the purposes of the litigation it is important that this information be provided in written form rather than verbally. Enclosed please find signed releases granting you permission to provide me with this information. In order not to slow this matter unnecessarily, I would be most appreciative if you would send me your report as soon as possible.

Sincerely,

Richard A. Gardner

Richard A. Gardner, M.D.

RAG/lq
encl.

Figure 4

quick to respond to this request, whereas the party in the weaker position responds slowly or not at all. In other words, the party with the stronger arguments is very happy to send me all kinds of supporting evidence. The party in the weaker position senses this and recognizes that there is not much to be gained by my reading his or her complaints or refutations.

I wish to emphasize here again that it would be foolish (and even self-destructive) for the examiner to quote these documents verbatim. These reports are infamous for the exaggerations and distortions they contain. When one compares the statements made by one party with the statements made by the other, it is hard to believe that the same people are being described. Hyperbole is invariably present, as each party believes that his or her position will be strengthened by it. The threat of perjury seems not to deter either party from introducing the crassest duplicities. Little guilt is felt over including the most humiliating and denigrating allegations. The attorneys themselves often translate their clients' statements into stock phrases and even paragraphs. It is common for a noun to be preceded by a whole string of adjectives, the writer believing that such adjectives strengthen the argument. The examiner, therefore, can only use the information contained in these documents as points of departure for direct inquiry of the parties concerned. He or she can justifiably be criticized for using this hearsay information in the report.

When reading these reports, pleadings, etc., I make entries into the question sheet of each of the parties mentioned. For example, if in the mother's complaint she claims that the father goes to the race track three times a week and loses on the average of $100 a week betting on the horses, I make this entry on the question sheet for the father. If there are older children involved, whose reliability in this regard can be respected, I will also make similar entries on each of their sheets to see what input they can provide with regard to this allegation.

To simplify my referring back to the original document (if this becomes necessary), I initially assign a page number (independent of the original page number on the document) to each page of every document, and these are listed in consecutive order. For example, if one document has 12 pages and another one 25, the first page of the second document is assigned page 13. And I continue in this manner with all subsequent documents. Accordingly, I may end up with 80 or 100 pages in some cases. I then record on each of the interviewee's question sheets the page number of the document on which the original allegation appeared. This saves me time in transcribing all the details of any particular allegation onto the question sheet. For example, if the father describes five or six occasions on which the mother brutally beat the children and lists a series of psychologically detrimental and denigrating comments she has made about the children in the course of such beatings, I will place on the mother's question sheet an entry like: "pp. 23–24—father—mother's beatings and ego-debasing criticisms." Then, when speaking to the mother, I can easily make direct reference to the original affidavit presenting her with the allegation. Similarly, I make equally short entries on each of the children's question sheets for similar discussion. In my final report I make absolutely no reference to the statement in the original affidavit. Rather, I quote only the statements made in my presence by the various parties involved. To quote directly such an affidavit reveals significant naiveté on the examiner's part and will seriously compromise his or her position in court.

INTERVIEWING FRIENDS AND ASSORTED RELATIVES

Solow and Adams (1977) recommend interviewing friends of the parents. I have not found this to be useful. Generally, each parent is able to come up with a list of friends and relatives who can be relied upon to support, in the most glowing terms, each party's position. Early in my career I was naive enough to see such individuals. I subsequently concluded that most came well rehearsed and were not above lying in the service of what they considered to be the more noble end of supporting the parent they favored. I found also that the comments of these friends and relatives tended to cancel one another out and the interviews therefore were a waste of time. Wealthy people can afford to bring a parade of such individuals to the courtroom. The examiner, however, should not be party to such shenanigans, even if the parent can well afford to pay for it. I am not stating that one should uniformly refuse to see such individuals. I am only suggesting that the examiner recognize that such interviews are most likely to be a waste of time, with rare exception.

THE PROBATION REPORT

Often a judge will order an investigation by the local probation agency. Generally, this involves a visit to one or both homes, as well as interviews with the parents and sometimes the children. Generally, a probation officer is not a psychiatrist or psychologist. Some are social workers and others have less formal training. It behooves the probation officer to make a specific recommendation to the court regarding custody. On occasion, however, I have seen a probation report in which the probation officer has provided a wealth of information and then not come forth with a specific recommendation. This, in my opinion, is an abrogation of responsibility. (It would similarly be an impartial expert's abrogation of responsibility if he or she were to avoid making a specific recommendation regarding which is the preferable parent.)

In the past I have on occasion been told that I should not have the probation report available to me. In recent years I have made this a proviso of my involvement in that it would compromise my provision that I must have *all* information available to me. The people who enlist my services will have to trust that I will not be swayed by any individual report, whether it be the probation officer's or anyone else's. Like all other reports, the examiner should view this one as hearsay. However, there may be information in it that may serve as a point of departure for direct inquiry with the parents and children. Often, the probation officer will have spent much time getting details of the past history. As mentioned, such information is not of the highest priority in the custody evaluation (although it should be taken). What is more important in the probation report is the home visit. Most psychiatrists (including this examiner) do not routinely include home visits as part of the custody evaluation. Actually, there is a strong argument for making such visits. However, they are often very time consuming and costly and so they are not frequently made by psychiatrists and clinical psychologists. The probation officer, however, is very likely to visit one or both homes and describe these in some detail in his or her report. Such information is of some value to the examiner.

My overall experience has been that the probation report is of value in my evaluation but not crucial, and I have conducted many evaluations without having one available. Goldzband (1980) recommends that the psychiatrist and probation officer freely communicate with one another. I am in disagreement with this in that there is a risk of undue influence. The probation officer, like the guardian ad litem, although neutral, should not, in my opinion, be discussing the evaluation with the impartial expert. Reading the probation officer's report provides the examiner with an input of information. Discussing the case with the probation officer opens the examiner to the criticism of being influenced by another professional. I am in agreement with Goldzband, however, in his view that if there are differences of opinion between a probation officer and the psychiatrist these should be aired in court and not personally between the two.

7

The Final Recommendation

Examiners conducting custody evaluations may feel that the burden placed upon them in making such crucial recommendations is formidable. This may be especially true in situations that are not clear-cut. Potential guilt over making injudicious and potentially injurious recommendations can be assuaged if examiners remind themselves that the final decisions are still not theirs alone. Many people will have an opportunity to contribute their opinions, and the judge, although he or she will generally take an impartial expert's opinion seriously, is not bound to do so. Furthermore, although one hopes the custody decision will be final (in order to provide the children with the most stable and predictable environment possible under the circumstances), new information and life changes may arise that will justify a reconsideration of the court's decision. Accordingly, if a decision has been an injudicious one, there are still possibilities for its rectification. Lastly, examiners' burdens will be reduced if they can say to themselves after completing their custody evaluations that they have been dedicated to the task, have conducted their inquiries with integrity and fairness, and have made every reasonable attempt to provide the best possible recommendations. This is all the court asks of the examiners; and it is all the evaluators should ask of themselves.

As mentioned in the document outlining provisions for my involvement, my usual procedure is to present my findings and recommendations to the parents prior to the preparation of my final report to the court. This serves the purpose of shortening the period of anxiety between my final interview and the submission of my recommendation. The parents, therefore, are the first ones to learn of my decision, and they are spared the anxiety of learning from the judge what it was. Unfortunately, there are judges who object to this procedure and require the impartial expert to submit the report to the court alone. There may be many weeks or even months between the time of the completion of the evaluation and the judge's communicating to the parents the examiner's findings. There are even situations in which this is never done. This, in my opinion, is cruel and psychologically detrimental, and the ethical examiner will refuse to be party to such a system. The presentation with the parents also provides them with an opportunity to correct distortions and to provide input into the evaluation. It helps them feel less powerless because there is the possibility that even at that late date the examiner's opinion might be changed. The major portion of this chapter will deal with the preparation of the initial presentation to the parents made from the rough draft of my report. Next, I will discuss techniques for presenting the findings to the parents. Then I will discuss further considerations regarding preparation of the final report.

PRESENTATION OF THE FINAL RECOMMENDATIONS TO THE PARENTS

Preliminary Considerations

I believe that it behooves mental health professionals who make themselves available as impartial experts to do everything possible to ultimately come to a specific recommendation regarding who is the better parent. This usually involves weighing the assets and liabilities of each parent and making a specific decision regarding which parent's assets more outweigh the liabilities. Even if the comparison appears to be a very close one, it still behooves the examiner to make a final recommendation as to which is the preferred parent. I am in agreement with Derdeyn (1976b) that the impartial expert must commit him- or herself to an opinion. I am in agreement with him, as well, that not to do so is an abrogation of the expert's responsibility. The clear-cut cases are usually the easiest ones for the court to decide. It is the more difficult ones—the ones in which the parents appear to be equally well qualified—that impartial experts are often invited to contribute. I have seen reports from individuals who have accepted such invitations in which they have concluded that both parents are equally well qualified and that the court should make the final decision. This, in my opinion, is a "cop-out." No two people are equal and a *decision must be made.* No matter how many hairs have to be split in the process of doing so, we are in the best position to make the kind of sophisticated evaluation required in certain custody conflicts. And the examiner who, as a basic principle, never makes a recommendation but only provides the court with information and elucidation is seriously defaulting on what I consider to be his or her obligation to the court. Perhaps the time will come when I will be totally stymied, when I will find it impossible to make a recommendation. Although I have been involved in a number of cases in which my indecisiveness has been somewhat mind boggling, I have still to date always come through with a specific recommendation. My hope is that I will always be able to do so.

Goldstein et al. (1973) use the term "least detrimental alternative" to refer to the kind of decisions that have to be made in custody evaluations. It is a situation in which there is no "good" or "bad" disposition for the child, but rather a choice between two undesirable alternatives. And it is our job to try to ascertain which of the two undesirable alternatives is the less detrimental. Accepting the situation as one in which there is absolutely no happy solution can lessen somewhat the examiner's burden.

The method I have found most useful in formulating my final recommendation is to dictate material from my basic notes under four categories: the mother's assets as a parent, the mother's liabilities as a parent, the father's assets as a parent, and the father's liabilities as a parent. I simply go through my notes from beginning to end and dictate pertinent material under each category. My secretary, in the course of such dictation, must switch the typewritten page each time a new category is entered. Although this is somewhat cumbersome, it does result in four separate distinct categories of material. An additional page of basic statistical data is also dictated. This contains information about the children's ages, the parents' ages, the date of the marriage, the date of the separation, and the date of divorce (if it has already taken place), and the dates and persons interviewed in the course of the evaluation. In addition, other information such as the names and ages of new spouses (or live-in friends) is also included. Of course, the examiner who does not have the luxury of having a secretary may use the same system by writing the material in accordance with the above plan.

The material as formulated above is used as my guideline in the presentation of findings to the parents. During this presentation I may jot down corrections of any errors that may have crept in (thereby protecting myself from possible error and embarrassment in court). I may also ask questions to fill in minor data that might not have been previously obtained.

The same material is useful for the preparation of my final report. I generally instruct my secretary to type the items in each of the four categories on one side of the paper only. I then cut up the material in each category into smaller sections, each dealing with a particular issue. These are then placed in chronological order (or some other meaningful sequence). I then re-dictate the final report from these clippings. Sometimes little needs to be changed from some of the originally dictated material and these can be retyped without alteration. Others are retyped in altered form. I have found this system to provide me with the most logical and comprehensive kind of report.

Factors to Consider
When Making the Custody Recommendation

Of course, the most important factors to consider are the parental capacities of the mother and father. By organizing each parent's assets and liabilities in accordance with the aforementioned plan, the examiner should be able to come to some definite conclusion regarding the custody issue. In Chapters Four to Six I have provided guidelines for collecting and assessing the most important kinds of data to be included under these four categories. One cannot make up a specific score sheet in which one gives an objective assessment of assets and liabilities. Rather, the best one can do is subjectively weigh these factors and attempt to ascertain which parent has fewer liabilities as compared to assets. (Appendices V and VI provide sample reports demonstrating specifically how I present this material in my final report.) Although the comparison of parental capacities is the most important factor in coming to one's conclusions, other considerations must also be made. I will discuss the most important of these.

The Tender Years Presumption.   As mentioned in the introduction to this book, prior to the mid-19th century fathers were generally the preferred parent. One cannot say that fathers were the preferred parent in custody disputes, because there were no disputes. Fathers were the "rightful" owners of their children; mothers had no education, sources of income, or legal rights. What subsequently came to be called the *tender years presumption* appeared in the middle of the 19th century. It was based on the notion that one should not wrest a suckling child away from its mother's breast. There was some feeling that psychological damage might be caused by such separation during these tender years. However, once the child was weaned (usually by age 3 to 4 in the 19th century), the mother's input was then no longer considered vital. Children were then transferred to their fathers, their rightful parent anyway.

As the result of the women's liberation movement, advances in psychology, child labor laws, and other social changes, women became increasingly considered the preferential parents. By the mid 1920s, laws were passed in most states giving mothers equal rights to fathers regarding custodial preference. However, during the next fifty years, mothers were generally favored in custody conflicts. From the 1920s to the 1970s, custody was generally given to the father only if he could prove conclusively that the mother was unfit. To do this, the father would have to demonstrate the mother's incapacitation, gross neglect of the children, or obvious maltreatment of them. In order to prove this, he would have to demonstrate that she was either a chronic alcoholic, a prostitute, was grossly promiscuous, or provide other evidence indicative of significant incapacitation in child rearing. This preference for mothers was a reflection of the court's working under the tender years presumption.

In the early 1970s a "backlash" movement by fathers arose in which they claimed that the tender years doctrine was "sexist," discriminated against fathers, and did not provide them with equal protection under the law—as guaranteed by the 14th amendment of the United States Constitution (*Watts* vs. *Watts*, 1973). Courts then began to appreciate that many mothers, although not grossly negligent, were not the better parents for children to live with. Accordingly, since the mid 1970s courts have been granting custody to fathers without their having to prove gross negligence on the mother's part. However, in spite of this trend the percentage of fathers who are being given custody is still quite small.

Some who have been instrumental in bringing about this desirable change have, I believe, gone too far with regard to their position that the father may be equal to the mother in his capacity to take care of the children. My personal belief (and I think there are many who will agree) is that the newborn infant is probably still better off with the mother—all other things being equal. I believe that by virtue of the fact that the mother has carried the child within her during pregnancy, has suffered the pains of the delivery, and because she has the physiological capacity to feed the infant from her breasts—from a part of her own body—she develops a psychological tie with the infant that is stronger and deeper than that of the father. Certainly during the mother's pregnancy a healthy father, with a strong paternal interest, will develop a psychological tie with the forthcoming child as well.

However, I believe that this tie is not as strong as the mother's, and this may simply be related to the fact that she has certain experiences during the pregnancy that the father does not have. I believe that one can get a sense of the validity of this hypothesis if asked the question: "If you had to make the decision as to who should be given custody of a newborn infant, the mother or the father—and if both proved to be *equally* capable, interested, and loving parents—whom would you recommend?" I think that most would favor the mother, from some deep appreciation for the validity of what I have said about the special tie she develops during the pregnancy, delivery, and neonatal period.

This preference need not be based on any kind of special instinct or innate capacity in the mother—although it certainly may. We do know that in lower animals there is generally some predominance of one sex over the other regarding caring for the young. To assume in human beings an equal capability for caring for the newborn, regardless of sex, is to assume that there has been some departure from the total evolutionary pattern—a departure I do not consider likely. Accordingly, the younger a child is, the more one should consider the mother to be the preferred custodial parent. Other factors, however, should certainly be taken into consideration. I am by no means suggesting that these arguments should automatically dictate that the mother be the preferred parent for the infant. Rather, I am only suggesting that her special experiences be given proper weight and not be ignored as they are by proponents of the equal capability theory. The maternal preference holds, I believe, during the first two years or so. Beyond that, things may even out, especially if social attitudes regarding male and female roles in child rearing keep changing. This would not then be so important a criterion. (I have elaborated on this issue elsewhere [1973a and 1973c].)

The Best Interests of the Child Presumption.   Since the early 1970s, most courts have been operating under the best interests of the child presumption. This doctrine is generally considered to have been laid down by Justice Benjamin Cardozo in 1925 in the case of *Finlay vs. Finlay.* There Cardozo stated that the judge "does not proceed upon the theory that the petitioner, whether father or mother, has a cause for action against the other or indeed against anyone. He acts as *parens patriae* to do what is best for the interests of the child." Unfortunately (in this examiner's opinion), it took approximately fifty years for the best interests of the child doctrine to become widely used. The tender years doctrine is viewed today as discriminating against men and not providing them with equal protection under the law. It is also viewed as being in conflict with the best interests of the child doctrine which is now the predominant guideline for jurists.

Although most psychiatrists and attorneys today subscribe to the best interests of the child presumption, it has never been clearly defined. An attempt to define the term has been made by the State of Michigan's Progressive Child Custody Act of 1970, which provides ten specific criteria for determining just what a child's best interests are. Although those who drafted these criteria were attempting to provide specific guidelines for defining just what factors should be considered to ascertain what are the best interests of the child, I do not believe that they have succeeded. I consider the guidelines to be so vague and ill defined, and so all encompassing, that they have little value for the impartial expert. For example, item 1 consideration: "the love, affection, and other emotional ties existing between the competing parties and the child." Item 2: "the capacity and disposition of competing parties to give the child love, affection, and guidance and to continue to educate and raise the child in his religion and creed, if any." And item 6: "the moral fitness of the competing parties."

Although Benedek (1972) states that the Michigan Criteria for Custody provide very useful and specific guidelines, I, personally, have not found them useful because they are not specific enough. I am in agreement with Beck (1977) who states that with regard to the best interests of the child presumption: "the courts have found it impossible to operationalize this standard, which at worst has been called meaningless and at best inexact. In reality it offers the judge no substantial guidance. Although he may sincerely believe he is acting in the best interests of the child, he may be influenced by his biases and prejudices."

In this book I have tried to provide some of the criteria by which the mental health professional can "operationalize" the inquiry that enables him or her to make a recommendation regarding what would be in the best interests of the child. However, I personally believe that the best interests of the child presumption may be somewhat narrow. I much prefer to view myself as making recommendations as to what would be in the *best interests of the family*. To focus narrowly on what may be in the best interests of the child may, on occasion, cause one to disregard the effects of the placement on one or both parents. Making a recommendation that might be significantly deleterious to a parent might ultimately be to the detriment of the child. Accordingly, I attempt to make my recommendations in accordance with "the best interests of the family presumption." The Group for the Advancement of Psychiatry's Monograph on divorce and child custody (1980) also makes this point. The group recommends that custody recommendations not simply be based on what is in the best interests of the child, but on what is in the best interests of the family.

The Concept of the Psychological Parent.   In the past, biological parents were automatically given preference over adoptive, step-, and foster parents. Such preference was given in accordance with the "blood is thicker than water" concept. In recent years, courts have been much more impressed with the psychological tie as being as important, if not more important, than the biological. *Beyond the Best Interests of the Child*, (Goldstein et al., 1973) was an important contribution that emphasized this point and played a role in shifting the general attitude of the courts in the United States. Prior to that time (and, unfortunately, to some extent today) the legal profession was deeply wedded to the concept that the biological parent should be given priority over anyone else in custody conflicts.

Goldstein et al. discussed the psychological tie vs. the biological tie in the context of a number of possible situations in which adults were fighting for the custody of children: foster parent vs. biological parent, adoptive parent vs. biological parent, etc. The emphasis on the psychological tie has resulted in a certain amount of distortion of this concept (not, I believe, promulgated by the authors) that there is one parent with whom the child has a psychological tie and another parent with whom the child does not. Unfortunately, their emphasis on *the* psychological parent has contributed to this notion. As a result other persons have thereby been precluded from sharing the status of psychological parent.

In their publication on divorce and child custody, the Group for the Advancement of Psychiatry (1980) takes issue with the notion that the child has only one psychological parent. I am in agreement with the GAP that children develop multiple attachments to a host of figures, each of whom may have the position of psychological parent. We do well to attempt to evaluate the *depth* and *extent* of psychological parenting that is provided by the various adults with whom the child is involved. Most often we do well to give priority to the parent who is the strongest psychological parent and recognize that there are others who share this position to a lesser degree. These other persons may have psychological and/or biological ties with the child.

In custody litigation between parents, there may be one or two stepparents with whom the child also has a psychological tie. And such a tie may be of importance in determining which household would be best for the child. It is important for the examiner to appreciate that the emphasis on the psychological tie should not go so far that he or she loses sight of the importance of the biological bond. The biological tie may be at the very foundation of the psychological. As mentioned, the mother who bears the child carries it within her body for nine months. She suffers the pains of its delivery and has the power to feed it from her own body (even though she may not choose to do so). During this time the biological father (if he has been available and involved) is usually quite interested in the child's intra-uterine growth and development and is especially concerned about both the mother's and the child's well-being throughout the pregnancy, the delivery, and thereafter. Such "programming" is also important in determining the depth of the subsequent psychological tie. These experiences cannot but play a role in future psychological involvements with the child and place the biological parent at a certain advantage over others with regard to custody. The examiner should not lose sight of this important contributing factor to the psychological tie that biological parents enjoy and often exhibit. The strength of this factor (or conversely the weakness of the psychological tie when the biological factor is absent) is well demonstrated by the very low rate of involvement that divorced stepparents have with their former stepchildren. In spite of professions for continued involvement, the attrition rate of such relationships is quite high. It is rare, in this examiner's experience, to see a divorced stepparent still involved in a meaningful relationship with a former stepchild a few years or even months after the separation.

I recently served as impartial expert in a custody conflict in which some of the aforementioned points were well demonstrated. Both parents were remarried and their only child, a 9-year-old boy, was living with his mother. The child had a very deep and warm relationship with his stepfather. In fact, I considered it to be a better relationship than the one that he had with his natural father, who had frequently been cruel to him. The boy was openly antagonistic to his natural father and openly stated that he wished to remain living with his mother and stepfather. In spite of these hostile attitudes, there was no question that some warm and tender feelings still persisted toward his natural father and that the child was still capable of having enjoyable times with him and his new wife during visitation periods. I supported the mother's position that the child should remain living with her. I also recommended liberal visitations with the father.

In cross-examination, the father's attorney continued to ask me which one of the two fathers, the natural father or the stepfather, was truly "the psychological father." I persistently responded that I could not choose one or the other. When the mother's attorney gave me an opportunity to elaborate on this point, I explained that the question of which was the psychological father was not a reasonable one because both were psychological fathers. In this particular situation the child was ambivalent in his relationships with both fathers. In his relationship with his stepfather, the loving affectionate feelings outweighed the hostile; in his relationship with his natural father, the opposite was the case. The negative feelings over the positive toward the natural father notwithstanding, there was still a deep psychological involvement with the natural father and he was also, in every sense of the term, a "psychological father." This child had *two* psychological fathers and it was an oversimplification to assume that he should only have one.

Goldstein et al. also emphasized the importance of continuity in the formation of the psychological tie and the detrimental effects of its disruption. The examiner should consider this factor when making a custody recommendation. Unfortunately, there are times when the continuity factor may change the less desirable parent into a more desirable one. This is often the case in the kidnapping situation when the less desirable parent may have spent so much time with the child that he or she becomes the preferable parent because of the detrimental effects of disruption of continuity.

Gender as a Custody Consideration.   Although it is not usually implemented, there are some who hold the view that boys should live with their fathers and girls should live with their mothers. Proponents of this view emphasize the importance of modeling and identification with the same-sex parent as an important developmental consideration. Although I am in agreement that such modeling is important, those who subscribe to this position are not giving proper attention to the importance of learning how to deal with and relate to members of the opposite sex during the formative years. Children need to be intimate with members of both sexes and the child who grows up in a single-parent home is being deprived of this opportunity. It is difficult, if not impossible, to say which of the two losses is the greater, that is, the deprivation of a same-sex parent with whom one can identify or the loss of an opposite-sex parent with whom one can learn something about heterosexual relationships. Until we know more about these two processes the aforementioned recommendation cannot be supported by this argument.

Some classical psychoanalysts hold that boys should live with their fathers and girls with their mothers in order to avoid oedipal problems. They believe that a boy's living alone with his mother is likely to result in his believing that he has won the oedipal conflict and has been successful in driving his father out of the house. A similar argument is made against a girl's living with her father. As I have described elsewhere (1968, 1971b, 1973a), I believe that those problems generally referred to as oedipal have their roots in emotional deprivations during the first two to three years of life and have a breadth and depth that go beyond mere sexual and possessive desires. Such problems, therefore, are not likely to be alleviated by the somewhat simple maneuver of having a child live with a same-sex parent.

In the adolescent period one also hears the same aphorism: a boy should live with his father and a girl should live with her mother. Here, the sexual implications are more obvious in that the subscribers to this dictum want to protect adolescents from being overstimulated by living together with an opposite-sex parent. Others, however, claim that it is important for the adolescent to live with the parent of the opposite sex in order to have this last opportunity to learn how to live with an opposite-sex person before finding his or her own mate. Those who disagree would argue that this places the adolescent in a sexually stimulating situation.

I, myself, do not generally subscribe to either of these dicta. Rather, I believe that other factors—relating to parenting capacity independent of sex—should be the primary considerations. If, however, there is parental seductivity, then I might very well take this factor into consideration (as one among many) in making my recommendation.

It is also important for the examiner to appreciate that whether or not he or she subscribes to any of these theories, the decision may often be made by the adolescent independent of the examiner's (and even the judge's) opinion. The adolescent usually has very strong opinions regarding whom he or she would like to live with, and the court often recognizes its impotence in ordering the adolescent to live where he or she does not wish to. (This is especially true if the noncustodial parent is receptive to the adolescent's living with him or her.) Accordingly, I will give great weight to an adolescent's expressed opinion and use it as an important criterion for making a recommendation. However, there are often complications. The adolescent's wishes may be ill-advised and inappropriate. The desired parent may not be receptive to having the youngster in his or her home. Each case must be evaluated on its own merits. The only guideline that can be given is that the adolescent's wishes should be taken more seriously than those of younger children. To make gender, per se, an important consideration is generally ill advised. It is sometimes invoked in order to lessen the burden of the examiner or judge and to oversimplify what is generally a very complex consideration.

Parental Sexual Behavior as a Custody Consideration.   In past years the sexual behavior of the mother, and to a lesser extent of the father, was an important consideration for the court in determining custody. Although adultery by *either* spouse was (and still is) generally considered grounds for divorce, adultery by the mother (but, interestingly, not generally by the father) was considered grounds for depriving her of custody. The courts would consider the mother's sexual life in great detail: if she was having sexual experiences—even though she was not bringing her sexual partner(s) into the home—her maternal capacity would be questioned. The fact that she was having sexual experiences—even one sexual experience before the divorce was final—was in itself evidence to the court of her unfitness as a mother.

We can appreciate that this was a very moralistic and somewhat punitive attitude to take, and courts in recent years have been much more liberal with regard to using sexual behavior as a criterion for determining custody. I think, however, that it would be a mistake to go in the direction of giving no consideration at all to the sexual activities of a parent. If a separated parent with temporary custody were, for example, to bring into the home a number of lovers and sleep with them overnight (even without direct exposure of the children to the sexual activities), I would consider this behavior potentially deleterious to the children and an argument against such a parent obtaining custody. Counterbalancing considerations, of course, might still result in my recommending that such a parent keep the children. All of the pros and cons I describe are elements to be weighed in relation to others and are not to be taken in isolation.

It is not on moral grounds but out of purely clinical considerations that I believe such behavior to compromise a parent's capacity. It is the *parade* of many individuals through the parent's bedroom that can be psychologically detrimental to the child. A boy, for example, whose mother invites a series of men to sleep over with her is likely to conclude that just about every man in the world shares intimacies with his mother in ways that he does not. Such an atmosphere cannot but produce in him resentments toward both his mother and the men who share her bed. Even though the child has had no opportunity to observe the sexual activity, he still feels resentful. And the sexual excitation that such encounters on the mother's part may produce in him can cause added frustration and resentment. A girl living with a father who similarly exposes her to numerous women friends is likely to react similarly.

If a mother were to bring a man friend into the home to live, I would not necessarily consider this a reason for recommending that she not have custody of her children. In fact, if the children had a good relationship with this man it might even be an argument for her to have custody of the children. She would then be providing them with a father surrogate in compensation for their father's absence. The children can maintain a good relationship with their father as well as with the friend; one need not preclude the other. If such a mother, however, were to enlist the aid of the children in keeping the secret that a man friend was living in the home, then, of course, this would be detrimental to them. Asking them to be party to a conspiracy of silence places an unnecessary burden on them in addition to that which they are already bearing in association with the divorce. Similar considerations would hold for a man living with a woman friend in his home.

An adolescent girl whose mother has a whole string of affairs and who communicates this to her daughter, either overtly or covertly, is likely to behave similarly as she models herself after her mother. She comes to subscribe to the view that the greater the number of men she can attract, the more attractive she is. The youngster is not likely to gain appreciation of the value of more continual and deeper relationships. In addition, her awareness of her mother's activities can be very titillating—as she is stimulated to fantasize exactly what her mother is doing, and this can contribute to her desire to gain similar gratifications herself. She may begin to compete with her mother and such competition may be confined to boys of her own age. However, at times she may seek older men and even her mother's lovers. Similarly, if an adolescent girl lives with a father who exposes her to a series of affairs, a variety of psychological problems is likely to result. In both of these situations the parental sexual life is directly affecting the children in a detrimental way and would be a negative consideration in the custody evaluation. If a father or stepfather were seductive with a girl, or a mother or stepmother were seductive with a boy, these would be arguments for the child's living in the other home. Elsewhere (1976, 1979c), I have elaborated on these issues.

Financial Considerations.   In most evaluations a mother will complain that the father is not providing her with an adequate amount of money. On the other hand, he will often complain that his wife is trying to exploit and even ruin him through financial pressure. The mother may complain that the privations she suffers as a result of her husband's withholding of funds is directly depriving the children. The husband may complain that, although his gross income is large, his expenses and debts are even larger and that he is living on the brink of poverty in spite of his ostensible wealth. The wife may claim that her husband is using various maneuvers, both legal and illegal, to hide money and that his stated income is only a fraction of his true income. Examiners do well to avoid coming to any conclusions regarding the validity of either party's allegations in such conflicts over finances. They should make every attempt to confine themselves to narrowly psychological considerations when formulating their conclusions. It is quite risky to come to conclusions regarding finances and legal issues, because these are beyond the examiners' area of competence and may significantly compromise the evaluations. Such naivete on the examiner's part will readily be recognized by attorneys and may be one of the first areas

focused on under cross-examination in court. These extra-psycho-
logical issues will be considered by the judge and those trained in such
matters. Examiners do best to view themselves as providing only part
of the data under consideration—that data which relate to their area
of expertise.

The examiner should not fall into the trap of giving preference to
the parent who has more money or more attractive facilities for the
child. Although these factors must be taken into consideration, the
most important factor is the relationship between the parent and the
child. Although the child who is living at a bare subsistence level is not
as likely to grow up as healthily as the one who is not in these circumstances, there is little evidence that poorer children (at least those who
are being provided with a reasonable amount of the basic necessities)
grow up any healthier or sicker than richer children. It is the relationship between parent and child that counts, not the luxuriousness of the
home in which the relationship exists.

The Remarried vs. The Single Parent.   The parent who has remarried
(or is living with someone) has an edge over the single parent in custody
litigation. This is the result of the simple fact that two caretaking
adults can provide a child with twice as much care as one. Of course,
the *quality* of the care must also be assessed. Quantity certainly
counts, but quality counts more. It is better to live with one deeply
devoted parent than two who have compromised involvements.

This principle can be especially unfair to a mother who, having
suffered the loss of her husband, now finds that upon his remarriage
she is placed at a disadvantage in the custody conflict. She may find
that she has little choice but to combine the roles of mother and breadwinner. And now, she may suffer the additional burden of risking losing
her child because of the fact that her remarried husband can provide more time than she. However, one must take into consideration the
fact that a stepmother's involvement rarely matches that of a natural
mother and so the aforementioned mother may still not be at a significant disadvantage. In such a situation one must look carefully into the
number of hours that each of the three parties has available for the
children as well as the depth of commitment. Of special importance
here is the question of adult availability during emergencies. One must
compare each household with regard to what provisions have been
made for caring for children during illness, accident, and other situations that require immediate adult attention.

Gettleman and Markowitz (1974) describe one argument for
giving the father custody that is not generally appreciated. When a
father is granted custody, he can often hire a woman to take care of the

children while he is working—thereby maintaining male and female adult figures in the home. A mother with custody, however, is not as likely to be able to hire a male to provide domestic care while she is out of the house and so is not so readily able to provide the family structure that the children were used to.

There are certain similarities between a situation in which a parent kidnaps a child and one in which a parent moves with the child to another state, often for the purpose of remarriage. The situations are similar in that the parent with the child is making the move without the permission of the other parent. In addition, the move is generally considered illegal. The difference, of course, is that in the kidnapping case, the kidnapper strictly attempts to avoid any communication with the other parent. In the out-of-state move, there is generally communication and the whereabouts of the child are known.

In some states there are laws prohibiting the custodial parent from moving outside the state without the permission of the noncustodial parent and/or the court. However, such laws have little "bite" in that there are generally no particular punitive measures automatically enforced, measures such as loss of custody of the child. They do, however, provide the "abandoned" parent with easy access to the legal system to take some action. As is true for the kidnapping situation, time is very much on the side of the parent who has the child, regardless of the legality of the custodianship. That parent can generally rely on court delays with the full knowledge that the longer the child is with the custodial parent the greater the likelihood the child will develop a relationship and prefer to remain where he or she is. The evaluator must be primarily interested in what is in the best interests of the child and should not automatically assume that the parent who moves out of the state is the worse parent. The illegal act should certainly be taken into consideration as a compromise in parental capacity. However, if it is an isolated defect, and is not just one manifestation of a pattern of duplicity and other forms of dishonesty, then it should not carry over-riding weight.

A mother, for example, may have an opportunity for a new marriage to someone with whom she has formed a deep relationship. She may recognize that the move will compromise her child's relationship with her ex-husband. However, she must also think of herself and her own future. In such situations she may choose to marry and move with the full recognition that her child's relationship with the father will be compromised. I cannot say that such a decision is necessarily pathological. The older the woman is at the time the more reasonable the decision may be. A mother who turns down an opportunity to remarry, because it necessarily involves a move to a distant place, may become so resentful and bitter over the restriction that her maternal capacity will be impaired and the child will suffer. Accordingly, considering all factors, the child's best interests are still served by the move. This is another example illustrating the weakness of the "best interests of the child" presumption. I subscribe to the "best interests of the family" doctrine because I believe it will ultimately be more likely to serve the child than narrow and strict adherence to the "best interest of the child" presumption.

One could argue (as might the noncustodial parent's attorney) that the parent who has moved out of the state has broken the law and should therefore lose custody. Adherence to this position could result in the child's suffering for the "crime" of its parent, in that the parent who moves may still be the preferable one. Accordingly, I would not support automatic deprivation of custody for such a parent. However, that parent should not, in my opinion, totally escape some kind of repercussion. The parent might be required to bear the expenses of visitations and be the one to bring the child to the noncustodial parent. The latter has been inconvenienced enough by the loss of the child; he or she should not be made to bear additional discomforts attendant to traveling long distances for visitation. In addition, financial payments made by the noncustodial to the custodial parent might also be reduced (as long as the child doesn't necessarily suffer) as part of the "price to pay" for having broken the law and deprived the noncustodial parent of an active role in the child-rearing process. If a mother, for example, moves out of the state in order to marry a man whose work necessitates her relocating, the father who remains behind will automatically no longer have to pay alimony because of his ex-wife's remarriage. In addition, the court should consider reducing support payments as a "penalty" that the wife should pay for having deprived the father of active involvement in the child-rearing process and for the discomforts attendant to the more infrequent visitations that such a move entails. If the wife's new husband can afford it, the court might even consider cutting off support payments entirely. Of course, one would not want to implement this action if the child is caused significant privation. Without such repercussions the laws become meaningless insofar as they serve to deter such moves.

Considerations Not Included in One's Presentation and Report.   In particularly difficult evaluations I will sometimes utilize methods of inquiry that are somewhat untraditional but useful. I may, for example, try to form a mental image of the children's lives in each of the two situations. I try to gain a feeling of what it would be like living with each of the parents (and other adults who may be involved) and try to determine the reasons for any preferences I may have. Although I cannot include in my report my "feelings" and "hunches," I can try to understand my reasons for coming to this preference. These reasons can be included in the report. Along these lines I sometimes try to project myself into the future and envision the lifestyles of the homes in two, three, five, and even ten years. There are, after all, many feelings we get about interviewees which, although not fully conscious, nevertheless affect us deeply. One way to tap such impressions is to allow one's mind to wander and to try to get a feeling for each situation during such reverie states. Often, in the twilight state between sleep and waking (or between being awake and asleep) one is in an excellent position to get in touch with such thoughts and feelings. We are less absorbed then in reality and are still awake enough to appreciate mental imagery that enters our conscious awareness. Again, only through more objective self-questioning can one record in the report the particular reasons for the conclusions gained in these dreamlike states.

Another way in which I sometimes gain useful information is to ask my wife what she would do if she were in my position as impartial expert. Without revealing the identities of the individuals involved, I will present the major issues under consideration—especially those that are giving me trouble in making my decision. As a man, I recognize that I may be viewing the situation from a narrow vantage point. I recognize that I cannot be without my biases and prejudices. My wife can provide me with the female point of view. Obviously, I cannot include the conclusions of such discussions in my report insofar as I quote my wife, but I certainly can include the information gained from such conversations. Similarly, I have on occasion posed crucial questions to friends. For example, when having dinner with another couple I might present an important conflictive area in an evaluation without revealing the identity of the family. I cannot, of course, state in my report: "When discussing this custody problem with my friends, Bob and Mary, they suggested that. . . ." However, they may certainly come up with some good ideas which may affect my decision.

Custody Recommendations and Predicting the Future.   Often, if not always, a custody recommendation involves a certain amount of prediction regarding what will happen in the future. The evaluator is basically saying that he or she concludes that one parent will provide a better home than the other in the near future. Sometimes such extrapolations are justifiable, because past behavior is likely to persist. There are situations, however, where the future unknowns are so significant and important that an immediate recommendation cannot be made. In such situations a tentative recommendation might be made, subject to review and reevaluation (preferably by the same examiner) at some future point such as six months or one year.

For example, I once served as an impartial examiner in a case in which there was a 3-year-old girl over whom the parents were fighting for custody. My evaluation revealed that the parents appeared to be relatively equal with regard to their assets versus their liabilities. At the time of the evaluation, each parent had been remarried about two months. Both had quickly remarried following the finalization of the divorce decree. It was immediately after the remarriages that the custody conflict began. In accordance with my usual procedure, I also evaluated the new stepparents. Here too, the assets versus the liabilities seemed to balance. The child, however, had lived with the mother up to that point, mainly because the father's single status and full-time job made him an unlikely candidate for custodial parent. Now that he had a new wife who was fully available as a homemaker, he considered himself to be in a much better position to demand custody. At the time of the evaluation both stepparents were relatively unknown to the child, although they were not complete strangers to her.

In this case I decided to recommend no particular decision be made regarding custody at that point. Rather, I suggested that the child alternate two- to three-week periods of residence at each of the two homes over a six-month period, after which time the custody issue would be reevaluated. It was only then, I believed, that one could be in a position to adequately assess the child's adjustment in each of the two situations as well as get information about the kinds of relationships that would be developed with each of the stepparents. With practically no past experience in these relationships, there was nothing to extrapolate to predict the future course of these relationships. The argument that such alternating residence would be psychologically detrimental to a 3-year-old child is not, in my opinion, necessarily valid. Although such transfers are certainly not desirable, I am not convinced that they are necessarily detrimental to the majority of 3 year olds. In my opinion, more important than the domicile in which the child lives are the personalities of the people with whom the child is living. It is not the woodwork, but the human beings who count in terms of whether the child will develop healthily. If the caretaking figures are warm and loving, the detrimental effects of residence change are likely to be small, if non-existent.

The presiding judge considered my recommendation reasonable and ordered its implementation. When seen again after six months, I had much more information to help me make a judicious recommendation. The stepfather appeared to be far less paternal than the stepmother was maternal. In addition, the deficiencies that were originally described in the natural mother became much more blatant over the six-month period. The father's deficiencies, on the other hand, appeared to be reduced during the six-month period. Considering all these factors I recommended that the father have custody of the child and the court supported this as well.

It is important for the reader to appreciate that the aforementioned case is not typical with regard to my recommending a six-month trial period. The examiner should make every attempt to make an immediate recommendation because of the psychologically detrimental effects of protracted litigation. In addition, the trial period adds additional anxieties and tensions that are generally psychologically detrimental. These drawbacks and caveats notwithstanding, the examiner should consider a plan of the aforementioned type in selected cases.

Types of Custodial Arrangements

Sole Custody.   When we speak of one parent having custody and the other having visitation privileges (the traditional arrangement), we are generally referring to the *sole custody* arrangement. This is the most common type of custodial arrangement. The parent with whom the child lives makes most of the decisions regarding his or her life, although both parents usually participate in such major decisions as education, religious training, and vacations. Usually a fairly specific schedule of visitation is included in the separation agreement and divorce decree. Ideally, this schedule should serve as a guideline when the parents are flexible enough to agree to alter it as conditions warrant. Such flexibility requires a certain degree of cooperation between the parents. The traditional visitation schedule is basically unnatural, because it cannot take into consideration all the unpredictablility of life as well as the vicissitudes of the desires of the various individuals involved. When working at its best the sole custodial arrangement blends into a joint custodial pattern (to be discussed below).

When the parents have demonstrated an inability to cooperate significantly with one another, the sole custodial arrangement may be the best available, its rigidities notwithstanding. In fact, its specificity now becomes an asset in that it spells out very clearly what each parent's rights are with regard to the children. It leaves less room for argument as each parent can threaten to enforce through the court what had been mutually agreed upon by both parties and what had been then ordered by the court.

The sole custodial arrangement is the most common one that I have recommended in my services as an impartial expert. As will be discussed in detail below, the joint custodial arrangement (presently very much in vogue) is not likely to be a viable option for people who have gone to the point of utilizing the court to help them resolve their conflict over custody. Such parents have not demonstrated the capacity to cooperate enough to warrant their being considered good candidates for a joint custodial arrangement. They usually need the rigidity of the sole custody decree. In deciding which of the two parents would be the better sole custodian, one factor that should be considered is each parent's receptivity regarding giving the other parent access to the children. I am in agreement with the position of the Group for the Advancement of Psychiatry (1980) that the very possessive parent, the parent who is going to discourage the child from visitation, is likely to deprive the child of important input from the estranged spouse. The healthier parent, divorce antagonisms notwithstanding, recognizes the importance of the continuing tie with both parents. The examiner does well to consider this factor as an important one when the sole custodial arrangement is under consideration.

Split Custody.   In this arrangement the children are divided between the two parents. One or more children live permanently with the mother and one or more live with the father. Most agree that there are many good arguments for attempting to keep the children together. And I am in agreement that this is most often, but not invariably, the case. The children can provide support for one another and a sense of continuity of the family in spite of the parental breakup. As Freud and Burlingham (1944a, 1944b) have well demonstrated, children who have been isolated from their parents tend to form surrogate families in which the older take on parental roles and thereby serve as substitute parents for the younger. Although the authors studied children separated from their parents during the London Blitz, their findings are relevant to children of divorce. An older brother can serve as a father surrogate and an older sister as a mother substitute.

Although the arguments for keeping the children together are compelling, the examiner should not adhere rigidly to the position that it is *always* important to keep the children together. The examiner should appreciate that there is no completely satisfactory solution to custodial problems when there is a divorce. Every option has its drawbacks. Whatever solution the examiner may suggest, someone is likely to be unhappy. One advantage of the split custodial arrangement is that each parent, at least, has some access to one or more of the children. Such division of the children can at least give the parents the feeling that "half a loaf is better than none." However, this consideration should only be one factor in deciding upon a split custodial arrangement. Its drawback of loss of sibling camaraderie and family cohesiveness must not be underestimated.

When considering the pros and cons of the split custodial arrangement, the examiner might compare the following two situations. In one, there are two children, boys aged 4 and 5½. They are very close friends, have much in common, and the younger one admires the older one—almost to the point of idolization. Although they occasionally fight, they are basically inseparable. Most will agree that separating such boys would be psychologically detrimental. Consider, on the other hand, the situation where there is a 13-year-old boy and a 15-year-old girl. Each leads his or her own life at this point. The girl is deeply involved with her friends, and the boy with his. They have occasional squabbles, but for the most part go their own separate ways. If this boy is close to his father and the girl is close to her mother, then a split custodial arrangement might not be detrimental, and, in fact, might be the most salutary recommendation.

I recall one situation in which a mother of two children, a boy and a girl, stated to me, "My father died when I was one. I grew up with my mother and my two older sisters. To me males were like strangers from another planet. I still know nothing about them and can't relate to them. I do know one thing about them, however, and that's that I hate them all." Unfortunately, her husband and even her son were no exceptions to this massive hatred of men. Her boy was openly neglected and used as a scapegoat, and her husband was openly scorned. With regard to her daughter she said, "I can understand my daughter. We're on the same wave length. I know what makes her tick. She's the apple of my eye." In spite of this rejection and sadistic attitude toward her son, she still wanted custody so as not to "split the children up." I recommended that the son live with his father and the daughter with her mother. The court agreed. In this case, I did not have the feeling that the mother's own attorney basically supported her position—even though he ostensibly did so.

I recall another situation in which a split custody arrangement appeared to be the most judicious. In this case, the parents consulted me for my advice and wanted to do everything to avoid custody litigation. (Children would be far better off if there were more parents like this.) The father was a native Australian and the mother was from Denmark. They had met while studying in the United States. When they got married, they both felt that they could comfortably live in the United States for the rest of their lives. Unfortunately, after ten years and two children (a boy and a girl), they both came to the sad conclusion that they still remained deeply homesick for their native countries and could not adjust to living in the U.S. Although their relationship was still a relatively good one, the pains they suffered over living in the U.S. and being away from their families compromised significantly their potential for marital happiness. The daughter was then 8 and the son 6. Both parents were relatively healthy and stable people, and I could find no significant differences between them with regard to parental capacity. Both were deeply involved with and loving of the children and the prospect of living without either one was deeply painful. The children also were psychologically healthy. In this case I recommended that the daughter return to Denmark with her mother and that the son return to Australia with his father. The relationships were such that this seemed to be the more reasonable arrangement. I recommended that meaningful contact between parents and children be maintained. I suggested that there not only be frequent letters, but occasional telephone calls (admittedly extremely expensive) and, when possible, direct visits. Even while making this recommendation I recognized that the likelihood of there being an ongoing relationship between both children would be small. I recognized that the recommendation would probably mean that the children might never see one another again and that early attempts at following my suggestions were not likely to be perpetuated. Under the circumstances, however, I believe that it was the best for this family. It followed the principle of "half a loaf is better than none." The split custodial arrangement is only one example of the many compromises that divorced people must make, both with regard to themselves and to their children. There are no perfect solutions to most of the problems that confront divorced parents. The split custody arrangement is merely one of the more obvious examples of this unfortunate fact.

Divided Custody.   This is a relatively unusual arrangement. Here, the children spend approximately half the time with one parent and half the time with the other. It is also called *shared custody*. Each parent generally has reciprocal visitation privileges. I have had limited experience with divided custody. Generally, it is most workable when the two homes are in the same school district. Otherwise, it involves twice yearly upheavals from both school and neighborhood—a situation that most would consider educationally and psychologically detrimental. I once saw a situation in which the mother lived on the East Coast and the father on the West Coast. The three children spent one year living with their mother and one year living with their father. Not surprisingly, all three suffered with an assortment of moderately severe psychiatric problems. Some of these were caused by their involvement in the divorce hostilities, but the divided custodial arrangement was clearly an additional psychological burden for them.

I have had two cases in which the shared custodial arrangement took rather unique forms. In one case the children remained living in the same house year after year. For six months of the year the mother lived in the home and for six months the father lived in the house. In another situation the father remarried and then brought his new wife into the home during his half-year residence. Of course, this arrangement insured continuity of neighborhood, schooling, and friends. The discontinuity of parental figures in the home did not appear to exert a significantly detrimental effect in these two cases that I had the opportunity to explore in depth. However, in both of these cases, the relationships of the children with *both parents* were good ones. These families demonstrate well the principle that it is the *relationship* with both parents that is the most important factor that determines whether or not the children will exhibit psychopathology. The divorce per se need not cause psychiatric disturbance and even a somewhat atypical custodial arrangement need not be detrimental. If there is healthy input from parents, the frustrations of the custodial arrangement can usually be handled.

Joint Custody.   In the sole custodial arrangement, one parent's decisions have priority over the other parent's with regard to the day-to-day upbringing of the children. When the term joint custody is used, it usually refers to the situation in which both parents have *equal rights and responsibilities* with regard to the upbringing of the child(ren) and *neither party's rights are superior.* Morgenbesser and Nehls (1980) state that the primary purpose of joint custody is to enable the parents to "share the rights and responsibilities for raising their child or children." They point out that the emphasis of joint custody is not on equal time, but on equal opportunity for both parents to involve themselves in rearing the children. In the joint custodial arrangement the children *live* in both homes; they do not *visit* one and *live* in the other (Ricci, 1980).

Other terms for joint custody are *co-custody* and *co-parenting,* although they are not commonly used. An old term for joint custody is *alternating custody.* Although some use the term *alternating custody* synonymously with joint custody, others make a differentiation. Those who make the differentiation emphasize that in both arrangements the child alternates between two homes. However, in the alternating custodial arrangement the parent with whom the child is living exercises most (if not all) rights and responsibilities of child rearing. In the joint custodial arrangement, regardless of where the child is living, *both* parents participate in the child-rearing process. Alternating custody is more like alternating sole custody in that the parent with whom the child is living at the time makes the primary decisions regarding its welfare. Some have used the term joint custody synonymously with *divided* and *shared* custody. As indicated in the previous section, I prefer to use the latter terms to refer to the situation in which there is a half-time division between sole custodial parents. Of course, less important than the terms is the actual living situation of the children. And, of course, there are many situations in which a particular term (regardless of the particular examiner's definition) is not likely to apply.

Since the middle-to-late 1970s we have witnessed a marked upsurge in the frequency with which the joint custodial arrangement is being recommended. In fact, at the time of this book's publication, the arrangement is very much in vogue. One factor in the present-day upsurgance of joint custody has been the changing concept of the role of fathers in the child-rearing process. As long as mothers were considered the preferable parent, joint custody was not considered seriously. In the 1970s, when the parent's sex became less often a consideration in custody decisions, the joint custody option became a more viable one. Since January 1st, 1980, judges in the state of California are required to order a joint custodial arrangement for all divorcing parents unless there are compelling reasons for another arrangement. At the time of this writing, other states are following suit. As will be discussed below, I think more harm than good will come from such laws.

Advantages of Joint Custody. One of the advantages of the joint custodial arrangement is that each of the parents is protected against the terrible sense of loss that comes with the sole custodial arrangement—in which the noncustodial parent feels extraneous, expendable, or an outcast. Neither parent's self-esteem is lowered as much as is the case when sole custody is granted. When there has been a custody conflict, the parent who loses not only loses the children, but self-esteem as well. He or she has been judged the *worse,* or at least, the *less adequate* of the two parents. And such designation has been made by a court—often after serious and prolonged deliberation. But even when the decision has been impetuous and not well thought out by the judge, the parent who loses custody cannot but feel this double loss, that is, children plus self-esteem.

The joint custodial arrangement can protect the parents from such an ego-debasing experience. It is therefore tempting to recommend. However, this should not be a primary consideration. In fact, it should rank very low on the list of considerations when determining which parent should be given custody. In fact, I could easily argue that it should not be a consideration at all in that the decision should be based on what is in the children's best interests, not what is in the parents'. However, if a parent is psychologically fragile and a sole custodial decision would risk significant psychological deterioration, then the children might suffer from such a parent's decompensation. Accordingly, I would not dismiss this factor entirely as a consideration. Rather, I would rank it extremely low and only consider it in those infrequent situations when there is a high risk of parental psychiatric deterioration if the child(ren) are lost. One could argue, even then, that the needs of the parent (to maintain psychological stability) is being given priority over the needs of the children (to be in the best possible home). This is one of those dilemmas to which there is no good answer (like so many of the other important problems in life). My only response here is to reiterate my position that it might be injudicious to remove the parental self-esteem effects of the decision as a consideration entirely, but it should be kept low on one's list and brought into consideration only on those rare occasions when warranted. This is in accordance with my position that custody recommendations should be based on what is in the best interest of the family.

Another advantage of joint custody is that it avoids an element of the sole custody situation that is likely to engender controversy. Specifically, in sole custody arrangements, one parent is placed in a position of authority over the other and this is bound to produce resentment. Joint custody obviates this difficulty (Coogler, 1978). Another aspect of the joint custodial arrangement that may reduce hostility is the noncustodial parent's greater opportunity to be with the children. There is thereby less frustration and less hostility to be vented on the custodial parent. Still another fringe benefit of the arrangement is realized when the noncustodial parent is the primary supporter. A father, for example, who has a joint custodial arrangement may be more motivated to contribute to the support of the child(ren) than when he is a visiting noncustodial parent.

Joint custody also avoids the problem of discrimination between the sexes in that the court doesn't have to award the child to either the father or the mother. In addition, the arrangement allows the child to see the father assuming traditional female roles of housekeeping and child rearing. The children's mother, too, may have to assume work functions outside the home. The children, then, come to view both parents in a more balanced way—each assuming both domestic and extra-domestic responsibilities. The situation increases the likelihood that the children will be comfortable in both of these roles when they become older.

Joint custody reduces the possibility of the father being viewed as the "good guy," the bearer of gifts, the taker to circuses and rodeos, etc. In such a situation the mother may come to be viewed as the "bad guy," the one who imposes discipline. In joint custody both parents share both roles (Eder, 1979).

Joint custody also provides children with certain distinct benefits. First, of all the custodial arrangements it most closely approximates that of the original marital household. Artificial schedules, totally unrelated to momentary desires and the vicissitudes of life, are not utilized. Like the household that existed prior to the divorce, there is a freer flow of involvement with both parents. Children suffer less of a sense of impotence in the joint custody arrangement in that they have some input into what happens to them (of course, the older the child the greater the participation). There is, of course, the danger that the child will try to use the greater flexibility of the joint custodial arrangement to avoid responsibilities and express hostility. A common way in which this is done is for the child to say, "If you don't stop making me do such and such, I'm going to go to my mother's (father's) house." Healthy parents, of course, do not acquiesce reflexly to such a command and still have veto power over the child. They take with serious consideration the child's wishes but certainly utilize their own adult judgment as well. Healthy parents do not allow the children to use their input as a way of fleeing from working through difficulties. They do, however, recognize that at times transfer to the other home can be a useful way of decompressing conflict-laden situations.

The Risks of Joint Custody.   I am in full agreement with attorneys Foster and Freed (1978) who state, "A joint custody award may be a judicial 'cop-out' in order to avoid complex and difficult fact-finding." It is certainly easier for a judge to award joint custody than to consider all the mind-boggling facts often involved in a custody conflict. Such judges may rationalize avoidance of the problem by considering themselves advanced thinkers who are up to date with modern trends. Such thinking may be enforced by reference to newly enacted statutes (the aforementioned example of California being one) that require the judge to award joint custody unless there are compelling reasons for considering an alternative.

The drawback here is that automatic or too frequent granting of joint custody may do children much more harm than good. The system increases the chances that the children will be used as weapons or spies in the parental conflict. There are no restraints on the parents in the joint custody arrangement to utilizing their children in this manner. Although the sole custodial arrangement cannot protect children completely from such utilization, it certainly reduces the opportunities for the parents to involve their children in such maneuvers. It lessens the likelihood of there being arguments over when the children shall go to whose home. Automatic award of joint custody does not take into consideration the logistics of school attendance, and thus it can cause more problems in the educational realm.

Abrahms (1979) points out that joint custody is likely to be more expensive than sole custody. Each parent must maintain full facilities for the children in both homes. This often includes extra rooms, clothes, toys, bikes, facilities for sleepover friends, etc. This consideration, however, should be a minor one for the examiner in considering the joint custodial arrangement. It should be extremely low on the list of criteria utilized to determine the custodial arrangement. Parental personality factors and many other aspects of both parents' life situations should be given much more importance.

A common criticism of the joint custodial arrangement is that it can produce confusion in the child who is shuttled back and forth between different homes in which he or she is exposed to different lifestyles, rules, disciplinary measures, parenting styles, and even socioeconomic milieu. In addition, its critics claim that it is invariably associated with an unpredictability and lack of environmental continuity that cannot but be detrimental. I believe that these drawbacks are most relevant for much younger children, especially those under the age of 3 or 4. Above that age, however, I believe that most children can accommodate well to the arrangement and need not suffer from confusion over lack of continuity.

Dullea (1980) addresses this question by referring to a typical query of joint custodial parents: "Isn't it bad for a child to have two homes and two sets of toys and two sets of clothes?" Parents who are proponents of the joint custodial arrangement will often reply: "It's better to have two parents." The response, in my opinion, is well taken. Whatever drawbacks there may be to having two sets of homes, the arrangement provides the child deep involvement with two parents rather than one. In short, then, I believe that the drawback of environmental discontinuity in the joint custodial arrangement is more than outweighed by the advantage of the children's having access to both parents in a less structured and less artificial arrangement. Further, it is not the shifting scenes that are in themselves the highly detrimental element; it is the parental conflict and impairments in parental capacity that cause the psychological damage.

Who Should Be Given Joint Custody? In my opinion three primary criteria should be satisfied before the examiner seriously considers a joint custodial recommendation:

1. Both parents be equally well suited to assume the responsibilities of child rearing and be equally involved with and affectionate toward the child(ren).
2. The parents prove that they are able to cooperate in the joint custodial arrangement, must demonstrate the capacity to com-

municate well, and be willing to make the compromises necessary to insure the viability of the arrangement.

3. The child's school situation should be such that it would not be
    disrupted by moving from home to home. Accordingly, this is
    generally only possible when both parents are living in the
    same public school district or when the child is attending a
    private school that is reasonably close to the home of each
    parent.

Items 1 and 3 may often be satisfied by parents involved in custody litigation. However, it is extremely rare for item 2 to be applicable. Parents who are warring for custody of their children have
generally proven themselves incapable of cooperating with one another to a significant degree over issues that pertain to the child-
rearing process. Otherwise, they would not be litigating for custody of
the children. Accordingly, the examiner who considers a joint custodial recommendation should only do so if he or she has reason to
believe that such parents will change dramatically in the future and
will be able to cooperate to a degree not presently observed. This is
risky business and I would caution the examiner against making such
predictions, especially when a custodial arrangement is based on
them. It is for this reason that I rarely make a joint custodial recommendation for parents who are involved in custody litigation.

Even when the parents are not litigating for custody, people who
are involved in a divorce conflict generally have some disagreements
over child rearing. Accordingly, when one recommends the joint
custodial arrangement for such parents, i.e., those *not* involved in custody litigation, there is still the predictive element involved in that the
examiner *hopes* that the parents will cooperate more in the future than
they are presently. In addition, there is the risk that they will not do so.
For this reason when I do make a joint custodial suggestion, I recommend that it be temporary and only finalized after a six-month (or even
a one year) trial period.

Benedek and Benedek (1979) suggest that the following criteria
must be satisfied before a viable joint custody arrangement be recommended:

1. Both parents have a clear understanding of what joint custody
    involves and have the desire for such an arrangement.
2. The parents have the psychological flexibilty and maturity to
    make the sacrifices and compromises necessary for the ar-
    rangement to work.
3. Both parents exhibit strong parental capacity.

4. The parents can cooperate significantly well with one another.
5. The parents live close enough to one another so that the travel arrangements do not become cumbersome or unrealistic.

As can be seen, the Benedek and Benedek criteria are basically the same as the author's. Unfortunately, courts are not giving the attention to these criteria that they deserve, and the joint custodial arrangement is too freely being recommended.

Who Should Not Be Given Joint Custody? Parents who cannot communicate well with one another are poor candidates for the joint custodial arrangement. During the custody evaluation the examiner has an excellent opportunity to observe how the parents communicate. If they have trouble in this area it is not likely that they will make good joint custodial parents. A joint session provides the examiner with an opportunity to observe this first hand. The evaluator should not only observe how the parents are communicating in his or her presence but obtain information about their communicative capacity from others involved in the evaluation.

As mentioned, parents who are in active conflict (especially those who are embroiled in custody litigation) are not likely to be good candidates for joint custody. One might argue that a joint custodial arrangement might reduce such parental fighting in that it would remove one of the issues of conflict. In the sole custodial arrangement one parent has great control over the child-rearing process whereas the other is relatively impotent. In the joint custodial arrangement, both have the power to make decisions. However, my experience has been that children are more frequently used as tools in the fighting rather than reducing it when conflicting parents are given a joint custody agreement. Accordingly, it increases rather than reduces the animosity.

There are some who hold that the evaluator should ascertain whether the areas of conflict are within the marital realm and whether there is basically agreement about child rearing. In such cases, they believe that the joint custodial arrangement can still be a viable one in that the parents have been able to separate their marital problems from conflicts over parenting. Although theoretically there may be such people, I have not seen any to date. Generally those who come to the point of custody litigation are involved in an all-out war which includes criticisms of the other party both as a marriage partner and as a child rearer. In fact, if there were no criticisms over child rearing, the parents would not be litigating for custody. Accordingly, we are still left with the basic conclusion that people who are involved in custody litigation are unlikely candidates for a joint custody recommendation.

On occasion, one will see a situation in which one parent wants joint custody and the other sole custody. Here it is likely they are fighting over how much time and control each will have of the child. In such circumstances, it is not likely that the joint custodial arrangement will work. Goldzband (1980) is also firmly of the opinion that parents involved in a custody dispute are not likely to be able to handle a joint custodial arrangement. He too does not consider this a reasonable recommendation to be made frequently by the impartial expert.

The reasons for desiring joint custody must be assessed. The mother, for example, may welcome the joint custodial arrangement because it gives the father more time with the children and leaves her with less responsibility for their upbringing. Sometimes vengeance may be a motive. A father, for example, may recognize the mother to be the preferable parent and realize that if he were to fight for sole custody he would not be likely to win. However, if he tries to gain joint custody he may be successful, and this may serve him well as a way of wreaking vengeance on his wife. Just as one wants to look into the motivations, one also should consider the unmotivated parent. Joint custody should not be imposed on a parent who is unmotivated for it (such as is the situation in California where the judge is required to order it unless there are compelling reasons for considering an alternative). The likelihood that the unmotivated parent is going to assume the degree of responsibility entailed in the joint custodial arrangement is small. Accordingly, the plan may be doomed to failure.

Some parents will request joint custody in order to reduce guilt. A parent may not want the degree of involvement required in a joint custodial arrangement but will request it in order not to appear (both to him- or herself and others) as undesirous of having the children as much as possible. The increasing prevalence of the joint custodial arrangement makes such parents feel even more guilty if they do not request it. Child rearing which stems from guilt rather than love is not likely to be very effective (Salius, 1979).

Joint custody is commonly requested (and even granted) as a compromise. It may appear to be a reasonable course, but this is a poor reason for recommending it. In such situations, instead of the parents having a *joint custodial arrangement*, they have a *no custodial arrangement*. Neither parent has power or control, and the children find themselves in a no man's land, exposed to the crossfire of the parents, pulled apart like rope in a tug of war, and available as weapons for both sides. The likelihood of children developing psychopathology in such situations approaches the 100 percent level.

The lifestyles of the parents must also be considered. Parents with significantly different lifestyles are not likely to be good candidates for a joint custodial arrangement. A father, for example, may be an adherent of the view of traditional roles of male and female with the male the breadwinner and the female the housekeeper. It may be very difficult for such a man to assume household and child-rearing responsibilities merely by being awarded joint custody. He must prove himself capable of the shift before being seriously considered a candidate for these responsibilities. Also, equal exposure of the children to dramatically different lifestyles is likely to be confusing, and the examiner does well to consider this factor. The examiner's own values are likely to contaminate such assessment. This handicap notwithstanding, he or she must try to ascertain what specific aspects of each lifestyle might be detrimental. Hopefully, the less detrimental lifestyle will be seen as preferable and sole custodial arrangement for the preferred parent will be recommended.

One must also consider availability in assessing parents as possible candidates for joint custody. This involves a flexibility of scheduling that may not be possible for a parent with a full-time job, especially a job that requires the parent's continual presence. In most school systems, there are only about 180 school days per year, and there are few full-time jobs in which an employee has the freedom to work only 180 days. In addition, there are the emergencies that inevitably take parents away from their chores and duties. A joint custodial arrangement requires both parents to have significant flexibility in this regard if it is to be viable.

The Prognosis of Joint Custody.   Because the recommendation for joint custody must often be made at a time when the hostilities between the parents are highest, a certain amount of speculation is involved. When the recommendation is made, it is with the hope that there will be a decompression of hostilities and an increase in cooperation. Because of the risk, I generally suggest that the joint custodial arrangement be instituted on a trial basis only and not finalized until after a six month's or even a year's trial. Again, this recommendation is rarely made for parents involved in custody litigation; rather, it is made in situations in which the parents have manifested a definite capacity for compromise and cooperation.

A smoothly running joint custodial arrangement may run into difficulty when one of the parents remarries. The remarried parent then has many more obligations (especially if there are stepchildren on the scene) and may not be able to handle so easily the responsibilities of joint custody. A stepparent may "gum up the works" by not being receptive to all the cooperation with the ex-spouse that is entailed in the joint custodial arrangement. And if both parents remarry, the risk of the joint custodial arrangement breaking down is even greater.

There are other unpredictables that compromise, if they do not destroy, the smoothly running joint custodial arrangement. For example, if a homemaker mother gets a job she will generally not have as much flexibility to assume easily the responsibilities of joint custody. I have mentioned the importance of both parents living in the same school district or the children attending a private school. If one of the parents moves out of the school district or at a distance significantly far from the children's private school, the joint custody arrangements will have to be compromised. I generally recommend that the divorce decree stipulate that the whole custodial arrangement will no longer apply if one parent moves a significant distance away. In fact, there are divorce decrees that stipulate that if a parent moves out of a certain radius that parent will lose custody of the children, whether it be sole, joint, or other custodial arrangement. Parents whose joint custody arrangement is getting into difficulty do well to seek counseling. A mediation service for couples in the joint custody situation might very well be useful. If these services are not utilized or available, it is possible that the couple will have to resort to litigation as a last attempt to resolve their conflict(s).

Visitation

The court is generally not significantly interested in the impartial evaluator's recommendations regarding visitation. It usually makes a distinction between an impartial providing information that may be useful to the court in general and the examiner making recommendations regarding such specifics as the visitation scheduling. The particulars of the visitation schedule are generally worked out among the clients, the lawyers, and the judge. The parents, especially, know their particular needs and life situations far better than the professionals involved, and the nitty-gritty details of the visitation schedule are best worked out by them, with the attorneys attempting to resolve differences when warranted.

However, the attorneys and court may ask the impartial for advice regarding basic principles of visitation, and this may be taken seriously by the court and incorporated into the final plan. For example, I may recommend that a father be given custody but that a mother be granted very liberal visitation privileges. This is a general recommendation; the particulars can be worked out by the parties. Or, I may advise that a few shorter experiences may be better than a longer one. In order to demonstrate the rationale behind this recommendation, I will compare visitation with the frequency of psychotherapeutic sessions. I point out that if a patient has one session a week, he or she may bring in a dream as old as six days. It is generally quite difficult to analyze such a dream because the events that contributed to it may be blurred in memory. However, if a patient has two sessions a week, no dream can be more than three days old (assuming the sessions are evenly spread), and the analysis of such a dream becomes more meaningful because the events that have contributed to it are more readily recalled. Accordingly, twice-a-week therapy is not just twice as good as once-a-week therapy but significantly more effective (although one cannot reasonably quantify it). Similarly, events that occurred six days prior to a session may be quite "stale" and the emotional reactions surrounding the events are dissipated. This is less likely to be the case when an event is two to three days old. In the same way, shorter and more frequent visitations are preferable to fewer and longer ones. This is the kind of general information that the court can find useful. On the other hand, the examiner tends to trivialize and demean his role if he gets involved in the petty particulars of the visitation scheduling, such as whether the father should pick up the children at 5:00 PM or 6:00 PM on Saturdays, or exactly when Christmas Eve should be considered to start. I am not suggesting that evaluation should *never* be involved in the particulars of the visitation schedule. In fact, there are times when the court may specifically request such a recommendation. I am only saying that most often such involvement is unwarranted and unnecessary.

The evaluator should be wary of recommending a custodial and/or visitation arrangement that compromises significantly the children's opportunities for involvement with the noncustodial parent. It is important to recognize the significant role of the noncustodial parent as a source of identification and as a way of learning how to relate to people of that sex. Only when the noncustodial parent is exposing the child to significant psychological and/or physical abuse should there be special restrictions placed on visitation with him or her. When a noncustodial parent exhibits mild to moderate deficiencies that are detrimental, there is often a tendency to "protect" the child from such exposures. For example, if a father is routinely late or unreliable, parents (and sometimes the court) will prohibit visitation in order to protect the child from the anxieties and disappointments associated with such behavior. This is an error in my opinion. The child should be helped to express the feelings attendant to the visiting parent's behavior in the hope that some change will be effected. If this fails, the child should be helped to occupy him- or herself with other activities and not "hang in there" waiting expectantly for that which may not occur. These "living experiences" are much more likely to help the child deal with the visiting parent's deficiencies than artificial cessation of visitation entirely. In such cases, the unreliable parent is likely to seize upon the rationalization: "You know I'd be here every day of the week if I could, but your mother (father) hates me so that he (she) got the judge to stop me from seeing you entirely." The custodial parent then becomes the "bad guy" and the visiting parent the innocent one who is being unjustifiably persecuted. The principle of providing living experiences with a parent who exhibits mild to moderate (but not severe) deficiencies is an important one therapeutically that can be justifiably included in the impartial's recommendations.

Placement Outside Either Home

When both parents exhibit significant deficiencies, some examiners give serious consideration to recommending to the court that the children be taken away from both parents as one possible solution to the problem. They take the position that since both parents are significantly defective the children will be better off in a foster home or in a residential treatment center. Although there are certain situations in which such a recommendation is warranted, I personally am very loath to suggest it. Only when there are *severe* deficiencies on the part of *both* parents should this be considered in my view.

The examiner should appreciate that parents who are involved in a custody conflict, their deficits notwithstanding, are still demonstrating strong parental interest by virtue of the fact that they are willing to expend the time and money attendant to such litigation. The evaluator must appreciate that healthy, loving forces are still operative when parents are in the midst of a custody conflict and that basic affection for the children is probably still present—the previously discussed specious reasons for demanding custody notwithstanding. It is very unlikely that a total stranger is going to provide such a depth of involvement and affection. As deficient as the parents may seem to the examiner, they may be far better for the children than a stranger. If one is going to recommend a foster home, one should get a significant amount of information about the prospective foster parents. Ideally, this should involve interviewing these people. Without comparing the three (there are now three options: the mother, the father, and the foster home) one is in no position to make any statement about which is the preferable. Merely to say that the child should not be in either home but should be in a "foster home" without knowing anything about the foster home is similar to saying that the child is better off with the mother without having seen the father. The basic principle of this book is that custody recommendations involve the examiner comparing the mother with the father and this cannot be meaningfully done without seeing both. When one introduces a third option (a foster home) one must evaluate the people concerned in order to make a judicious recommendation. The same holds true if one is going to recommend the home of a relative. Residential treatment centers should only be recommended when the child's problems (not the parents') result in such severe psychopathology that such treatment is warranted. The treatment center should not be viewed as a dumping ground but rather as a place for providing the child with a psychotherapeutic environment. Again, the evaluator should have specific knowledge of the institution before recommending it.

Preparing the Final Presentation

In the preparation of the final report I generally use a two-phase process. In the first step I go through all my notes and select pertinent material. This is organized and collated into a preliminary report which I use in my presentation to the parents. The basic outline is the same as the final report, but my notes are in crude form. During the presentation to the parents I make any corrections that are necessary and/or rectify any distortions that may have crept in. Following the presentation to the parents I use these notes in the preparation of my final report, which, of course, is better organized and gives greater attention to sentence structure, grammatical detail, etc.

The method that I have found most expeditious in preparing the presentation for the parents is to dictate data from my notes in accordance with a special procedure. (The examiner who does not enjoy the luxury of a dictating machine and a secretary has a more laborious task ahead of him or her, but the principles are the same.) All dictated items are entered onto one of five sheets: 1) Basic Statistical Data, 2) The Mother's Assets as a Parent, 3) The Mother's Liabilities as a Parent, 4) The Father's Assets as a Parent, and 5) The Father's Liabilities as a Parent. As I go through the notes I indicate on which of the five sheets each item should be typed. Accordingly, my secretary is continually switching sheets in and out of the typewriter. Included on the sheet of Basic Statistical Data are the names and ages of all parties interviewed, as well as the dates and duration of each of the interviews. Important milestones are also placed there, such as the dates of the various marriages, separations, and divorces. On each of the other four sheets are placed appropriate material relevant to each parent's assets and liabilities. Especially important are direct quotations. I generally include here statements made by the parents themselves as well as other parties such as the children. Also vital to include here are the examiner's own observations, as opposed to hearsay (which has no place in a custody report).

If a parental surrogate (such as a stepparent or a live-in friend) has been interviewed then that person has a separate sheet for his or her assets and liabilities. (Of course, the amount of material in each category may not fit on one sheet, so that each category may ultimately end up with many sheets.) In addition, the material is typed on one side of the paper only so that I can cut up the sheets and place the items in a certain logical order in the preparation of my final report.

Although the reader may consider the aforementioned plan somewhat laborious, I have found it to be the most efficient and expedient of the various methods I have tried. As mentioned so many times in this book, in the custody evaluation one is basically comparing each parent's assets and liabilities. Organizing all the material into "stacks," in which I have indicated the parents' assets and liabilities, is the most reasonable way to accomplish the task. I am often struck, after compiling the information in this way, how the result, which may have previously been somewhat unclear, becomes obvious. The weight of one category over another may be so great that the conclusion becomes compelling. And the fringe benefit of such organization is that it impresses the reader and thereby increases the likelihood that the recommendations will be taken seriously. On the other hand, the most sensitive and brilliant recommendation may lose some of its efficacy if presented in a disorganized report. (See Appendices V and VI for examples of two typical reports, somewhat altered in order to preserve the families' confidentiality.)

Presenting the Findings to the Parents

As soon as the parents are seated, I will immediately state, without any introduction or explanatory comments, which parent I am recommending. I may say, while looking at the father: "Mr. Jones, I'm going to recommend to the judge that you have custody of the children." I will then quickly turn to the other parent and state: "However, I'm going to recommend that the judge give you, Mrs. Jones, liberal visitation rights." I consider this the most humane approach to providing the parents with my decision. They are invariably quite anxious about the decision and preliminary buildups and other preparatory explanations only increase their anxiety. *After* the statement has been made, I generally pause in order to allow for immediate reactions. Generally, the preferred parent responds with a sigh of relief and some glee. The non-preferred parent is usually irate and upset. I will then tell the nonpreferred parent that one of the purposes of this interview is to provide him or her with the opportunity to attempt to change my opinion. I also state (as I have stated before) that the final decision is not mine but the judge's. I also advise the nonpreferred parent that I consider it my role to appear in court and to testify in order to defend and explain my recommendations. In fact, I go further and tell that parent that I welcome the opportunity to defend my position under cross-examination in that I am not infallible and nonpreferred parents have a right to bring me to court to defend my position.

I then repeat the recommendation made to the parents in the initial interview, namely, that they still have the opportunity to resolve the differences between themselves and not resort to lengthy and psychologically devastating courtrom litigation. I try to impress upon them once again that the custody of their children still lies within their hands and that any reasonable decision that they agree upon is not likely to be rejected by their attorneys (who are best viewed as their advisors and employees, rather than their masters) or the judge. I warn them that the judge is a human being, has his or her own prejudices, and that often injudicious recommendations are thereby made. I emphasize that now *they* have the control; once they go to court they are placing control in the hands of a stranger. I point out to them that they and the children have already suffered significant psychological pain over being embroiled in the litigation and that what they have suffered thus far is small compared to what they will experience if they go to court. In spite of these warnings, I have not yet had the experience of the nonsupported parent accepting this advice. This 100 percent failure rate notwithstanding, I still consider it my role to present the advice. However, I have had a number of experiences in which the attorneys, after receiving my report, encourage the nonsupported parent to go along with the recommendation. Or, a judge will meet with the attorneys in chambers and encourage the attorney of the nonsupported parent to encourage his or her client to comply.

Early in the presentation it is advisable for the examiner to state (if appropriate) that he or she believes both parents to be dedicated, interested, and qualified; that the recommendation is based on a careful weighing of the assets and liabilities of each; and that the person whom the evaluator is recommending to have custody is the one who has fewer liabilities and more assets with regard to the child-rearing arrangement. The parent who loses the children is likely to feel that he or she is being labeled *totally* deficient as a parent. Emphasizing these points may serve to lessen the likelihood that the nonpreferred parent will continue to harbor this ego-debasing self-concept.

Before presenting the specific reasons for my recommendation, I again tell the parents that the interview has three purposes: 1) to tell them my findings at the earliest possible time so that they are protected from the terrible anxieties and tensions associated with not knowing what they are, 2) to give them the opportunity to correct any distortions in my findings, and 3) to provide them the opportunity to change my opinion. This lessons their sense of impotence and provides them with an open forum for expressing their differences. In the courtroom situation they are forced to swallow their rage and suffer terrible frustration as each observes the other making statements that he or she believes to be total lies—fabrications designed to mislead the court. (As mentioned, my presentation also has a third purpose, namely, providing the examiner with the opportunity to correct minor distortions that may have crept into his or her notes, distortions that the cross-examining attorney is generally happy to seize upon in the attempt to compromise the examiner's credibility.)

I then tell the parents that I am going to present my findings from the preliminary notes that will be used in the preparation of my final report. I tell them that I have divided the presentation into four categories: 1) the father's assets as a parent, 2) the father's liabilities as a parent, 3) the mother's assets as a parent, and 4) the mother's liabilities as a parent. I will then describe the rationale for my having made my particular recommendation by balancing these four areas of consideration. I remind them that the session is an open-ended one and that I welcome their interrupting me to correct any distortions they believe I may have. I urge them to express their differences during this session because, as indicated in my statement of provisions, I will have absolutely no contact with either of them between the time of this session and my possible appearance in court. Again, I remind them that I do not want them to leave the evaluation with the feeling that I did not provide both with the opportunity to give me any information that is pertinent.

As the reader may well imagine, such presentations have generally not been placid ones. Crying, pleading, accusations of incompetence on my part, and regret over having agreed to become involved in the evaluation are common. Sometimes, prior to the completion of the evaluation, one or both of the parents has been advised by attorney that the aid of other professionals will be enlisted if my recommendation does not support the particular client's position. Although the parent may find some solace in the prospect of bringing in another person, such comfort is generally naive because it does not behoove the supported party to cooperate in or agree to an evaluation by an additional impartial. Also, the court is not likely to order one. Accordingly, the new professional is then left in the position of serving as an advocate, a very weak position—especially when he or she follows the testimony of an impartial.

In the course of the evaluation, the examiner is likely to find many manifestations of psychopathology in each of the parents. As described earlier, being embroiled in custody litigation is a predictable way of producing such psychopathology and/or exacerbating pre-existing psychological disorder. The therapist should be extremely cautious with regard to recommending therapy. He or she might wish to do this in this final interview because of a moral obligation to suggest treatment that the parent may not realize is needed. However, the evaluator who does so is stepping beyond his or her role as an impartial expert if he or she formally makes such a recommendation in the written report. But even when recommending treatment verbally in the final interview, the evaluator does well to make the suggestion passively and cautiously. The principles here are not very different from those that are applicable to the situation in which I am evaluating a child and observe psychopathology in the parents. The parents have brought the child for treatment and are expecting a specific recommendation as to whether or not the child should have treatment. Although they may expect some counseling for themselves, they have varying degrees of receptivity regarding therapy for themselves. Similarly, parents who come for a custody evaluation, are not requesting an evaluation regarding whether they need treatment. In the custody evaluation they may be more receptive to the examiner's statement about the children's needing treatment, so this can be stated more directly as a fringe consideration of the evaluation.

With regard to the parents, if I do believe that therapy is warranted, I will not come out directly and say to either parent in a direct confrontation that he or she needs therapy and should contact a therapist. Rather, I consider it better to approach the matter with a question such as: "You told me many things about yourself which suggest that you recognize that you have psychological problems. Am I correct?" If the parent agrees, then I might continue, "Have you ever considered going into treatment?" This is a good point of departure for exploring the possibility. The examiner should appreciate that if a person goes into treatment because he or she has been talked or coerced into it, it is not likely that the experience will be a meaningful or productive one. The examiner knows also that treatment can only be meaningful (for an adult) if there is insight into the fact that one has problems and there is motivation to do something about them. If the parent appears ambivalent or lacking in insight to a significant degree, then the examiner might recommend a few consultations and attempts at therapy to "see what it's like." If the parent is receptive to pursuing this recommendation, *it is inappropriate for the impartial expert to provide a specific referral.* The evaluator who does this may very well compromise his or her position in court if asked by an opposing attorney if a recommendation to a particular therapist was made. Although made with the most benevolent intent, there is always the risk of being viewed as one who has used the role as an impartial to "send business to a friend." And even worse in such a situation is the impartial examiner's recommending him- or herself. This would be a serious breach of the role of impartial expert and those who do this might be disqualified or, at least, seriously compromise themselves in court. It suggests opportunism and exploitation, rationalized as helping a sick person.

Another drawback of making such a recommendation in the report is that the court might use it coercively and require a parent to go into treatment or else there might be certain legal repercussions. Some judges, lawyers, and courts tend to be very dictatorial and ordering people into treatment is consistent with this philosophy. Members of the legal profession do not often appreciate the fact that meaningful treatment cannot be mandated, that without motivation and insight it is likely to be a farce. Accordingly, it is safest for the impartial to avoid discussing the question of a parent's need for treatment in the final report, but he or she might cautiously broach the subject in the final interview.

THE FINAL WRITTEN REPORT

Appendices V and VI present examples of my final report. My general format is to begin with the report's title: PSYCHIATRIC CUSTODY EVALUATION. Because the report might be buried in a pile of complaints, affidavits, certifications, and other documents this lets the reader know exactly what is contained in the document. Next, I indicate the date on which the full report was sent to the court, the attorneys, and the parents. Then, I indicate the name and address of the judge. This lets all readers know that it is a direct communication between me, the impartial expert, and the judge who has enlisted my services. I then indicate the particular case to which the report relates by stating: 1) the names of the litigants, e.g., Parker vs. Parker and 2) the Docket Number, e.g., M-2753-81. It is extremely important that the examiner include the docket number. This is what the court clerk will look at when filing the report. Court calendars are so tight and the number of cases so great, that it is unlikely that the judge is going to read immediately the examiner's report. Rather, it will be filed until the time the case comes before the judge, and it may be a few months to a year after the report is submitted. (This has been my experience in the New York-New Jersey area. It may be different elsewhere.) I cannot emphasize strongly enough the importance of placing the docket number in a conspicuous place on the first sheet of the report, as well as any other correspondence with the court. Without it there is the risk that the report will be unfiled or misfiled. (This happened to one of my reports, so I speak from bitter experience.)

I begin by directly addressing the judges as if I were writing a letter to him or her: Dear Judge So-and-So. My introductory paragraph usually follows this format:

> This report is submitted in compliance with your court order dated February 26, 1981 requesting that I conduct an evaluation of the Parker family in order to provide the court with information that would be useful to it in deciding which of the Parker parents should have custody of their children, Thomas and Elizabeth.

The paragraph indicates that I am conducting an evaluation in compliance with a court order—once again affirming my position as an impartial who serves the court. I make it clear that I am merely providing information that would be useful to the court in helping the *court decide* which of the parents would be the preferable one to assume custody of the children. I wish to make it clear to all concerned that it is the court's final decision, that my role is to provide information and not to make the decision.

The next paragraph begins with the statement: My findings and recommendations are based on interviews conducted as itemized below: I then list the date of each interview, the person(s) seen, the duration of each interview, and the *total* number of hours of interviewing. I then add the date and duration of the interview in which the findings and recommendations were discussed with the parents.

I then give a mere skeleton description of each of the parties. Generally this involves the age and place of birth of each of the parents, and important vital statistics such as age at which the parent came to the United States (if foreign born), dates of previous marriages, and usually occupation(s). As mentioned in my discussion of the parental evaluation, I do get some background history of each parent, but do not consider this a vital part of the custody evaluation. I am not saying that such information is totally inconsequential; I am only saying that for the purposes of the custody evaluation it is low priority information. It is high priority information if one is doing psychotherapy or psychoanalysis. For the purposes of the custody evaluation one is much more interested in the immediate past and the present.

I present the date of the present marriage, the date of separation, the birth dates of each of the children, and their present living arrangement, i.e., with whom they are presently living and whether third parties (such as stepparents, live-in friends, grandparents, etc.) are living with the children.

The above information will provide the reader with a concise statement of the present status of the family. A short statement follows presenting my final recommendation. Just as in the interview in which I present my findings and recommendations I begin with a short statement of my conclusion, I follow the same principle in the report as well. Whereas in the interview with the parents its purpose is to lessen parental anxiety, here it lessens the reader's curiosity and helps the reader avoid wondering what my final recommendation is going to be or hunting at the end of the report for it. A typical statement is:

> It is my opinion that Mrs. Susan Parker should be granted custody of both children. My reasons for coming to this conclusion are elaborated below. Although much information was obtained in the course of the evaluation, only those items specifically pertinent to the custody consideration will be included in this report.

This statement covers me for a possible question by a cross-examining attorney as to why I did not include a particular bit of information that he or she thinks pertinent. This is easy to do because the most voluminous report will never include all the possible data that might be considered relevant. Actually, there are degrees of pertinence and I make it clear here that I am presenting only the information that I consider most pertinent.

This is only one example of an extremely important consideration for the examiner when writing his or her report. Specifically, the examiner should always be thinking about the cross-examining attorney interrogating him or her on the stand. The good attorney will scrupulously examine the report and look for any loophole—even a word—that might represent a weakness. Sometimes a poorly chosen word may be enough to provide the opposing attorney with ammunition in the attempt to discredit the evaluator. It is not that the attorney will expect the examiner's entire testimony to fail by pointing out one such defect, but the more such deficiencies the attorney can find, the weaker the valid parts of the report will appear to be. For example, in one report in which I described a mother's extreme ambivalence about her marriage I wrote, "She has left her house countless times in the last few years, only to return after a few days or weeks." Her lawyer picked up on the word *countless* and asked with marked incredulity and associated histrionics if that was indeed the case. "You mean to say, Doctor," he asked in utter disbelief, "she left the house so many times that it would be absolutely impossible to count them?" Actually, the number of such episodes was about ten to fifteen, but I did not consider it important to spend time calculating the specific number. I had to admit it was in ill-chosen word and he managed to get a lot of mileage from this "defect" in my report. The opposing attorney will find flaws that do not in fact exist; the examiner should not provide him or her with real ones as well.

A report that presents one parent as having only assets and the other as having only liabilities is not likely to have much credibility. We are not usually dealing here with a situation in which there is one "good guy" and one "bad guy." We are dealing with human beings who have both assets and liabilities. If a parent is fighting for custody of a child and is willing to expend time (and often a considerable amount of money) in such litigation, the likelihood is that there are strong parental assets, deficiencies and specious motivations notwithstanding.

As stated previously many times, the evaluator's primary goal in the custody evaluation should be to attempt to assess each parent's assets and liabilities in the parental role. Consistent with this goal, the mode of presentation that I prefer is one in which each parent's assets and liabilities are listed separately in four separate sections. Then, a discussion in each of the four sections is presented in which an attempt is made to assess the importance of the various parenting qualities in such a way that the arguments for preferring one parent over the other are convincing. In the preparation of these four sections, I use material prepared for the presentation to the parents. I have found it useful to take these basic data and literally cut the sheets into strips on each of which is some statement about parental assets and/or liabilities. (Having the material typed on one side of the paper only is an obvious prerequisite to this procedure.) Whereas in the presentation to the parents these were presented in a somewhat randomized fashion (as dictated in the preparation of that presentation), here I try to organize them into some meaningful sequence. I then dictate directly from these slips of paper. Of course, each examiner will develop his or her own method. I only present here the one that I have found most effective after having tried others, and I recommend it for the reader's consideration.

In the course of writing the report the examiner should avoid the use of hyperbole. Overstatement and "overkill" generally weaken rather than strengthen a report. As a college freshman, I recall an English professor telling the class, "The adjective is the enemy of the noun." The statement has relevance to the final report. The more adjectives one uses to modify a noun, the weaker the statement becomes. Although the reader may not be aware of this, he or she is likely to respond negatively, either consciously or unconsciously, to overkill. David Lambuth (1923), one of Dartmouth's most revered English professors, often said: "If you have to hit a nail, hit it on the head." There is great wisdom in this statement and it is useful for the examiner to remember it when writing a custody evaluation.

The examiner should avoid referring to parents and other adults by their first names in the report. The parents, of course, will be referring to one another by their first names and over the course of an intensive evaluation the examiner may find him- or herself doing so as well. In the interviews it becomes somewhat artificial and cumbersome to continually refer to the parents as Mr. or Mrs. So-and-so. By the time the final report is being prepared, the evaluator may have spent fifteen to twenty hours with the family, by which point he or she is no longer thinking of the parents as Mr. and Mrs. So-and-so. However, one must repress the natural tendency to use first names in the writing of the report. An attorney may interpret this as a manifestation of condescencion on the part of the examiner. To protect oneself from this possibility, it is safer to avoid such usage. Strict adherence to this practice makes the report somewhat cumbersome when one is repeatedly referring to the parents as Mr. John Jones and Mrs. Mary Jones. This drawback notwithstanding the recommendation still holds. One can, however, use the shortened form: Mr. J. and Mrs. J. if one notes this early with a statement such as: "...Mrs. Jones (henceforth referred to as Mrs. J.)...." I do, however, use first names for children. It would be artificial to refer to an infant as Mr. or Master Smith. It might even produce a chuckle in the reader. I do not think there is a risk in referring to children and adolescents by their first names.

It is a good idea to place in the final report defenses against anticipated accusations. It places on the record the reasonable refutation that the examiner may not be given the opportunity to provide on the stand. In essence, it punctures the balloon before the cross-examining attorney has a chance to blow it up. For example, a mother once complained that it was a sign of serious parental deficiency on her husband's part to have brought their 12- and 14-year-old boys to his attorney in order to make statements and sign affidavits criticizing her. She somewhat condescendingly and gratuitously stated that she would never do such a terrible thing to her children. Although I am in agreement that there are times when utilizing the children in such capacity can be psychologically detrimental to them, it is not always the case. In this situation, the children were strongly desirous of living with their father because their mother entertained a parade of lovers in the home. Although she did not actually have sexual relations in front of the children, they were exposed to a parade of men friends sleeping overnight with her. The mother, however, flatly denied having lovers in the home. The children were the only witnesses to this and the father needed their testimony to support his position. They welcomed the opportunity to provide testimony because of their strong desire to live with their father. In this case, I did not view the father's bringing the children to his attorney to be a sign of parental deficiency (as the mother would have wished me to believe). Rather, I viewed it as a manifestation of his affection for his children and his desire to do everything reasonable and possible to remove them from their mother, who, in my opinion, was clearly the less effective parent.

Accordingly, in this situation, I quoted the mother's criticism of her husband and then stated my own opinion that in this case it was justifiable for the husband to have these boys interviewed by his attorney. I described them as relatively healthy and stable and quite capable of handling the situation in the lawyer's office. I stated that I did not consider the experience to have been psychologically traumatic to them. And I went further and stated that I considered it a psychologically salutary experience for them in that it provided them with a sense of power in a situation in which most children generally feel impotent. Not surprisingly, the mother's attorney asked me no questions about the alleged deficiency on the husband's part related to his having brought his children to his attorney in order to sign affidavits in which they criticized their mother.

The examiner should base his or her strongest arguments on deficiencies on which both parents agree. For example, a father may complain that his wife stays up drinking all night and, when the children return from school the next day, she is still sleeping in bed 90 percent of the afternoons. The wife may deny the drinking, but may agree that she is a "night person" and therefore needs much sleep during the day. She may claim that she is only asleep on 50 percent of the afternoons when the children arrive home. In such circumstances, the examiner should quote each parent's statement. He then might state: "Even if Mrs. Jones' more conservative estimate is valid, it still represents a deficiency in maternal capacity in that she is not available for her children half of the days on their return home from school." These deficiencies, on which both parents agree, are the most powerful arguments and are extremely difficult, if not impossible, for an attorney to refute in cross-examination.

The previously discussed advice to avoid the use of diagnostic terms can extend, at times, to labels that may be generally viewed as signifying pathology. For example, one may even get in trouble using a term like *alcoholism*. As is true for most disorders, there is a gradual continuum between the normal and the pathological, and there is often no sharp cutoff point between the two. Most people become obsessed or "hooked" at times on an idea. And it is within the normal range to become so preoccupied, on occasion, to be unable to "unhook" oneself. Where this degree of normal proclivity for preoccupation ends and the pathological degree begins—the degree that would justifiably be called an obsessional neurotic disorder—is very difficult to define. Accordingly, if one refers to a parent as an "alcoholic" the opposing attorney may ask the examiner to define alcoholism, to state exactly how one diagnoses it, and how much alcohol one must consume in order to be so diagnosed. There are people who can consume huge amounts of alcohol and not have it interfere with their functioning, and there are others who, after very small amounts, become incapacitated. The alcohol ingestion becomes a "problem" when it interferes with functioning in significant areas of life, e.g., work, family relationships, social relationships, etc. Accordingly, one does well to describe the incapacitation that is caused by the alcohol and avoid terms such as alcoholism or alcohol abuse. This may appear to be a very fine distinction to the examiner, but it is the kind of thing that an attorney might want to seize upon in cross-examination. By focusing on the behavioral difficulties that are described to result from alcohol ingestion, one presents a stronger picture. Otherwise, the examiner exposes him- or herself to being asked to define terms like alcoholism or alcohol abuse and to define the so-called "point" where normal alcohol ingestion ends and pathological ingestion begins. One may, however, quote the interviewees who used such terms. By doing so, one "plants seeds" and gets across the message.

I have found this "seed planting" principle to be useful to follow in the custody evaluation. Occasionally, the examiner will have very strong suspicions about a negative personality trait on the part of one of the parents, but will not have enough bona fide evidence to make a definite statement or conclusion about this trait. One way to get such a statement "into the record" and, thereby, plant a seed in the judge's mind is to quote a party who makes the particular criticism. For example, in one case a husband, who was suing for custody of the children, was in a far less stable financial situation than his wife. Under recently passed equitable distribution laws in New Jersey, the assets of the marriage are divided equally between the partners, regardless of sex. Under these laws, a husband can conceivably receive alimony from his ex-wife and, if the children are living with him, support for them as well. Under such circumstances it is even possible for him to remain in the house, especially if it is in the children's best interests to remain there with the custodial parent (the usual case). The examiner might have the tendency to be biased against the husband in such circumstances because it is so untraditional an arrangement and can easily be viewed as exploitation on his part. In this particular case, I was convinced that the husband was exploitive and that his desire for this arrangement was just one manifestation of this trait. However, I could not use his claims for custody and child support as confirmation because he was operating with the blessing of state law and could claim, through his attorney, bias on my part. What I did here was to quote a number of the wife's statements in which she accused her husband of being exploitative. These were statements made to me in his presence. In this way, I was able to introduce the notion without actually claiming that I was supportive of the wife's position.

As mentioned, in the presentation of assets and liabilities, one should strictly confine oneself to direct quotes. These provide the most powerful arguments. In addition, one does well to describe direct observations. It is not likely that the cross-examining attorney is going to accuse the evaluator of duplicity. This is especially the case if the observation has taken place in a family setting where the examiner's observation has been shared by other persons. These quotations and observations are at the heart of the report and are the most important material contained therein.

Following the presentation of parental assets and liabilities I summarize my conclusions in a section entitled *Conclusions and Recommendations*. There I restate my final conclusion and outline some of the main arguments for it. One must be very cautious here regarding accepting as valid what one parent says about the other—no matter how convincing the statements may appear to be. One can use such statements, however, with such qualifications as: "If the court accepts as true Mr. X's allegation that his wife consumes, on the average, one-fifth of a gallon of whiskey a day then I would consider this an argument against her receiving custody of the children." The examiner should use other statements which indicate that he or she considers certain allegations likely, or very likely, but should not commit him- or herself to 100 percent acceptance. Statements like: "The weight of the evidence strongly suggests that Mrs. X's and the children's description of the father's visitation pattern is more likely than Mr. X's. Specifically, although I cannot be certain, the weight of the evidence appears to support their claim that during the last three years Mr. X has visited the children on the average of once a month and that such visitations were unannouned in over 90 percent of the cases. Mr. X's claim of visiting on the average of once every ten days appears, to this examiner, to be the less credible version considering his inability to describe in specific detail the times of such visitations and the experiences he alleges to have had with the children during such visits. Mrs. X and the children claim that Mr. X is 'lying.' Mr. X claims that Mrs. X and the children are involved in a 'conspiracy' against him. Although I am not 100 percent certain, I believe that the weight of the evidence suggests that Mrs. X's and the children's rendition is closer to the truth. If the court agrees with me, then I would consider this an important factor in recommending that Mrs. X maintain custody of the children."

In this section of the report I may make some recommendations regarding visitation. However, I do not recommend specific schedules. This is something for the parents and the attorneys to work out and is not one of the nitty-gritty particulars that the examiner should be concerned with. It tends to trivialize the report and I consider such concerns to be most often inappropriate for the impartial examiner, except when there has been a specific request for such details.

Preparing a custody report is very time consuming, especially when one must review it carefully for accuracy and the avoidance of "loopholes." The ideal report is one in which the cross-examining attorney will find no defects. He will find no "handle" to "grab" to compromise the examiner's credibility. The well-planned report, one that is extremely convincing, may be so powerful in its logic that the parties may avoid going to court because they both recognize that its conclusions are compelling enough to predict the court's decision.

The Face Letter

As mentioned, I send copies of the final report to each parent, each attorney, and the judge. In addition, if a guardian ad litem is involved, he or she receives a copy as well. The report is accompanied by a face letter, a copy of which is shown in Figure 5. I do not routinely send my curriculum vitae or other material describing my qualifications for conducting the evaluation. However, I offer to send such material if it is requested by the judge. Because the attorneys receive copies of the face letter, there is the implication that they too can receive information about my qualifications if they request it. (Some do and some do not.)

As the reader can appreciate, preparing the report of the final recommendations is a time-consuming task. These recommendations, however, may be the most important source of information for the judge. He or she generally has neither the time nor the expertise to conduct this kind of inquiry. The judge usually recognizes the biases of the lawyers and their clients and generally welcomes the recommendations of a qualified neutral party. Because of the weight of these recommendations and the gravity of the decision, the evaluator owes to all concerned the most serious dedication to the task.

RICHARD A. GARDNER, M. D.
155 COUNTY ROAD
CRESSKILL, N. J. 07626

TELEPHONE 201 - 567-8989

February 28, 1981

Honorable Benjamin Carter
Superior Court of New Jersey
Chancery Division
Courthouse
Hackensack, N.J. 07601

Re: Parker vs. Parker
Docket No. M-25713-79

Dear Judge Carter:

Pursuant to your court order dated December 18, 1980, I am enclosing a copy of the report on my custody evaluation of the Parker family.

I hope you find it useful. If you wish information about my qualifications for preparing this report, I will be happy to forward it. Please do not hesitate to contact me if I can provide you with any further information.

Sincerely,

Richard A. Gardner

Richard A. Gardner, M.D.

RAG/cg
encl.

cc: Mrs. Susan Parker
Mr. Thomas Parker
Mark J. Goldman, Esq.
Henry R. O'Brien, Esq.

Figure 5

8

Providing Testimony
in Court

One of the primary reasons, if not *the* primary reason, therapists
hesitate to involve themselves in custody litigation is the fear of a court
appearance. The prospect of being cross-examined on the witness
stand is generally enough to chill the blood of most therapists. Such
dread, in my opinion, is not necessary. The more thorough the investigation has been, the more familiar the examiner is with the family, the
greater will be his or her conviction for the recommendations made.
And such conviction is the best allayer of the aforementioned fears. Of
course, experience also reduces such tensions. And knowledge is a
powerful weapon against fear. The more familiar we are with a situation, the more we know about it, the less likely we are to fear it.

Therapists have heard stories about attorneys trying to compromise the credibility of the testifying expert by such methods as
trickery and hair splitting. They have heard about attorneys becoming
aggressive—to the point of being insulting and sarcastic. They know
that such lawyers are attempting to make them look like fools. They
know about courtroom antics and histrionics. This is one of the reasons
therapists avoid getting involved in testifying if they possibly can. The
therapist may be honest, direct, and convinced that his or her position

261

is a valid one. He or she may be trying to be of service to the family and may feel strongly that the testimony can be helpful. Yet the prospect of being involved in courtroom games—whose main purpose is to degrade, professions of the "best interests of the child" notwithstanding—discourages significantly the involvement of mental health professionals.

Accordingly, therapists avoid testifying—which is unfortunate because we have much to offer. Court calendars are heavy. A judge may have to make decisions on fifteen, twenty, or thirty divorces a day—each one of which may present him or her with a mind-boggling amount of crucial data. No human being can be expected to make judicious decisions under these circumstances. Consequently, any kind of competent information that can be given the court can be useful. These decisions are vital. A custody decision significantly affects the lives of both children and parents. Often it is made within a few minutes and as a result there is frequent misjudgment, causing needless hardship and suffering. Therapists are in a position to help the court avoid tragic mistakes; and it is unfortunate that the present legal system for dealing with custody conflicts often deprives the court of the services of many of us, or uses those of us who do involve ourselves in a most ineffective way. But, as mentioned, these ancient legal traditions should not deter us from fulfilling our social obligations. My hope is that this book, and especially the information that I provide in this chapter, will help assuage therapists' fears and increase the likelihood that they will involve themselves in this important kind of litigation.

It is not uncommon for the side (parent and attorney), whose position has not been supported by the impartial, to immediately engage the services of another mental health professional as an advocate. In fact, it is not uncommon for both sides to have a list of such individuals even prior to the impartial examiner's revelation of his or her findings. In spite of initial professions of receptivity to the notion of giving serious consideration to the findings of an impartial, advocates are already being lined up for the courtroom battle. Of course, the parent whose position has been supported by the impartial is not likely to involve him- or herself in a further evaluation. Accordingly, this new advocate comes to court at a distinct disadvantage. He or she has not had the opportunity to evaluate both sides and this, in itself, is a serious compromise in the testimony. The attorney whose position is being supported by the original impartial is most likely to play up significantly this deficiency. In addition, the new advocate is not likely to have the sanction of the court. In fact, he or she will often be viewed disapprovingly by the court because his or her very presence is a statement of antagonism to the judge's own appointee (the impartial expert).

Unfortunately, such advocates are not hard to find. No matter how obvious the parent's deficiencies, they are willing to come to court and testify on behalf of the parent whom the impartial considered less qualified and even state that that parent is the preferable parent without ever having seen the spouse. The examiner does well to appreciate, however, that the nonpreferred party has every *right* to enlist the aid of such experts. Generally, the nonpreferred parent still believes that he or she would be the preferable choice and that the impartial examiner has erred grievously. The nonpreferred parent's attorney may even believe his or her client's position and therefore brings in such an advocate in the hope that it might help the cause. Sometimes, the attorney of the nonpreferred parent basically believes that the impartial evaluation and recommendation is judicious and that his or her client should not have custody—but still it behooves him or her to bring in such an advocate in the service of helping the client "win," which is what litigation is all about anyway. We see here another example of how the best interests of the child are of lower priority than the wishes of the advocate parent. On occasion, the nonpreferred parent's attorney may request that the court bring in a second impartial. On only one occasion have I had the experience of the court being receptive to this request. (In this particular case I was the second impartial.) Generally, and with good reason, the judge is going to be unreceptive to this request. The judge is likely to view such a request as merely another legal maneuver that cannot but lengthen the litigation. The attorney whose position is supported is most likely to object to his or her client being subjected to yet another exhausting examination and this will lessen the judge's receptivity as well. The judge, however, will generally allow adversary professionals to testify. The spectacle of a parade of mental health professionals, each testifying on opposite sides of a custody case, is certainly not a credit to either the legal or the mental health professions. It certainly says something about how primitive still are our techniques and how subjective are our conclusions. Because the art/science of psychiatry is still so inexact I would still not preclude such displays—our embarrassment over them notwithstanding. However, such parades would be far less common if preliminary mediation and the enlistment of impartials routinely preceded any kind of adversary courtroom proceeding.

Ideally, the impartial's report should be so convincing that the parties will agree not to proceed further with the litigation and to try to implement the recommendation. I have seen a number of situations in which the nonpreferred parent's attorney played an important role in convincing his or her client of the judiciousness of the impartial's report. In addition, if the impartial has a very good reputation with the court, if the judge has the highest respect for the impartial's recommendations, then the nonpreferred attorney may discourage the client from further litigation because of his or her knowledge of the judge's respect for the impartial's opinion. Such "power" on the part of the impartial is not without its drawbacks. Although it may be ego-enhancing for examiners to be placed in such a position, it places an extra heavy burden on them because of the powerful influence of their report. I much prefer not to enjoy such an honor and believe it is preferable that I be asked to testify in court. The impartial's report should not be looked upon as a document handed down from on high. Rather, it is *one opinion* that should be looked upon with respect, but not as *the final word.*

PREPARATION FOR THE COURT APPEARANCE

The examiner should strongly request that his appearance be scheduled for a particular time on a particular day. Law courts are notorious for their lack of concern for witnesses' time and noncourt obligations. Witnesses can literally sit for days outside the courtroom waiting to be called. Whereas I recognize that one cannot know in advance how long a particular witness will be on the stand and that it is necessary to avoid a situation in which the court is available and there is no one standing by to be examined, the courts still show great insensitivity in this area. Although experts are generally afforded a little more courtesy, they still do well to make every attempt to impress upon the court their desire to appear at a particular time. As the reader may recall, in my list of provisos for involving myself in custody litigation, I specify that I will be paid completely for my time in court. There is no differentiation made between time on the stand and time waiting to testify. There are two reasons why my fee is higher for court appearances: 1) testifying is a more draining experience than the custody evaluation per se, and 2) it "helps the client remember" that I am in court and increases his or her motivation to get the attorney to put me on the stand as soon as possible. However, in spite of requests for consideration, the examiner will often find him- or herself sitting in the courthouse for hours waiting to be called.

On the night prior to the court appearance, examiners should review all their material to the point where the major facts are easily recalled. In addition, they should have their notes well organized so that they can quickly refer to particular points. Impartials compromise their credibility if they are disorganized or if they cannot readily refer to the material on a particular issue. An examiner hunting through dis-organized notes strewn in front of him or her does both the supported client and the court a disservice. Ideally, the examiner should be so familiar with the material that little direct reference to written notes is necessary. The most impressive testimony is that which is verbally given, freely and spontaneously. A thorough grasp of the material is one of the best ways to reduce anxieties related to court appearances. And having the full conviction that one's position is valid and that one has compelling support with material which can be readily conveyed is the most predictable way to reduce fears of a court appearance.

One of the questions facing the examiner who is in full-time private practice is how many patients to cancel for a court appear-ance. One cannot know at the outset exactly how long he or she will be required to remain in court. Generally, one can expect to stay longer than anticipated. The method I have found useful is to request that I be scheduled to appear as the first witness in the morning. In this way I lessen the likelihood that my appearance will be delayed by an unpre-dictably protracted testimony by someone appearing before me. Being the first person to testify makes it more likely that I will begin at an appointed time. I generally cancel all of my morning patients because my average time in court is usually two to three hours. I tell all my afternoon patients that I am not certain whether or not I will be back in the office. I advise them to call my office around 1:00 P.M. to find out whether or not I will be back. When the court recesses for lunch I call my office to advise whether or not I will be back to see my afternoon patients. In this way I protect myself from the loss of income that would be entailed if I were to cancel the full day and then find myself re-quired to appear only in the morning. On other occasions, I have can-celed the whole day and used the free time in other ways.

THE COURT APPEARANCE

Once in court the "friend of the court" may find that he or she has fewer friends than anticipated. Certainly the parent who may lose the children because of the examiner's report is likely to be bitter and filled with rage. And that parent's attorney, even if secretly agreeing with the examiner, will often appear hostile—that, after all, is what he or she is being paid for. Even the parent whose position the examiner supports may be dissatisfied. This parent may feel that the therapist has not manifested the appropriate degree of hatred for the spouse and that he or she has not been properly appreciative of the partner's most obvious alienating characteristics. In addition, this supported parent may believe that the evaluator has not gone far enough in his or her recommendations—and this parent's attorney will often reflect these views. Although up until this time the impartial may have done everything possible to remain neutral and above the adversary proceedings, he or she is now very much in the thick of it. As mentioned, I believe there is some justification for this. The evaluator should be available for cross-examination. Both clients should have the opportunity to question the impartial's findings, and the evaluator should have enough conviction for them that he or she has no hesitation defending them by submitting to courtroom examination.

When called to the stand, and throughout the court appearance, the impartial should take a passive role in adhering to the structure of the court routine. He or she should make every attempt to follow court protocol and to comply with all reasonable requests. The evaluator should passively comply with the swearing-in rituals and with requests for such information as name, address, license to practice, and so on. (I generally refer to these as the "name, rank, and serial number" type questions.)

Following this routine introduction, everything becomes pertinent and important—even though not appearing so. For example, at this point a question may be raised regarding the impartial's credentials—especially those which warrant testifying as an expert. This seems an innocuous enough question, but it can be quite loaded. Generally, the therapist will have been asked to provide a curriculum vitae and a list of publications to the court and to both attorneys. If the lawyers are well versed in the significance of these professional qualifications, they will try to find deficiencies in the examiner who supports their adversary's position. A common way of exposing such "defects" is to ask the therapist if he or she has a qualification the lawyer knows full well is lacking. The attorney who can obtain a series of such nos may be successful in lessening the court's respect for the expert witness.

If the impartial expert is extremely well qualified, then the attorney whose client this impartial is supporting will try to elicit the most detailed elaboration of this examiners qualifications. The opposing lawyer may interrupt, even before the therapist has had a chance to begin to list his or her qualifications, and say to the judge: "My client and I accept Dr. X's qualifications. Your honor, I suggest we proceed." At this point the well-qualified expert may not even have had the opportunity to tell the court that he successfully completed the first grade. Accordingly, the court will have been deprived of knowing the expert's qualifications—information I believe the judge is not only entitled to have, but should have if he or she is to weigh properly the testimony of conflicting experts. Following such an attempt to squelch the expert's providing his or her qualifications, the original lawyer (whose position the impartial is supporting) is likely to say to the judge: "I believe, your Honor, that it would be helpful to the court if Dr. X *were* to present his qualifications." While the judge and the two attorneys are trying to decide this question, the evaluator does well to sit quietly in accordance with my previous recommendation that he or she take a very passive role in following courtroom procedure. All would agree that the court has every right to know the qualifications of those who profess to be experts. However, as the reader can well appreciate, this consideration may take second place to an attorney's attempt to lessen an expert's credibility in order to enhance his or her client's position. So from the beginning the interests of the children become less important than the interests of the client in winning the case.

If the expert does have the opportunity to present his or her qualifications, it is preferable that the interrogating attorney present the questions for the examiner to answer. Otherwise there is the risk that the evaluator will appear immodest or boastful. On the one hand, it behooves the examiner to present such qualifications for the court's information. In doing so, there is always the risk of appearing self-aggrandizing or of "overkill." If the attorney, however, asks the question, such risks are reduced. The good attorney, also, will assess the situation and not "overload" the judge with too many qualifications. He or she knows that a reasonable presentation of the most crucial and relevant is the best way to impress the judge. Of course, in many cases the court will have asked for the evaluator's curriculum vitae along with a report so that no new information is being provided during this part of the testimony. I often wonder, then, what a squelching attorney expects to accomplish in such situations, because the judge already knows what the expert's qualifications are.

Although some witnesses are intimidated by a lawyer's pomposity and bombast, I generally welcome such displays. I come to the court after having conducted an extensive and time-consuming evaluation. I have gathered an immense amount of information, am convinced of the validity of my conclusion, and am confident therefore when on the stand. I appreciate well that an attorney's histrionics and expressions of incredulity are maneuvers that are typical of the lawyer whose position is weak. Such displays may be for the benefit of the client so that the lawyer can give the impression that he or she is working vigorously to earn his or her fee. One should take much more seriously the attorney who is well prepared and has logically and consistently thought out his or her arguments. There is a definite plan for the inquiry and the points logically follow one another. The people we should take most seriously in life are generally those who "speak softly and carry a big stick." But even here, if the impartial has done a solid evaluation, there is little to fear.

The impartial's testimony, as well, will gain or lose credibility in accordance with the same principles. The more volatility, the more sermonizing, the more harangues and histrionics, the less credibility will the evaluator have. And if the impartial becomes hostile, it suggests that a "sore point" or "soft spot" has been touched upon by the cross-examining attorney. Such overreaction and defensiveness will give an astute attorney a good "handle" for an effective refutation. The sensitive attorney recognizes that such emotional displays and defensiveness are compensations for basic deficiencies in the testifier's arguments and will exploit this knowledge to full advantage.

On occasion, the impartial will be confronted with an attorney who does not basically have conviction for his or her client's position. As I have discussed, most attorneys will still accept a case and support a client's position even though they may not be in sympathy with it. (They are acting here in accordance with an ancient legal tradition.) Such attorneys are not likely to argue as strenuously or effectively as those who have a deeper commitment to their client's position. Earlier, I described as an example of this an attorney who gave me much greater flexibility during cross-examination than I had ever been given before (or subsequently) and his granting me this was his way of helping his adversary, whose position I supported. He too was "going through the motions" in order to earn his fee and satisfy his client.

There are times when the examiner will have a strong impulse to respond with a joke or wisecrack. This is especially true when one is being interviewed by one of the wild types I have just described. Although the joke may be unusually clever and certain to make everyone in the courtroom laugh, the therapist does well to resist the impulse. The attorney is sure to ask the judge, in a very sanctimonious manner, to direct the examiner to observe courtroom decorum and to respect the dignity of the legal process. The judge will invariably honor this request, and the therapist's position will be compromised—the cleverness of the joke notwithstanding. For example, I recall on a couple of occasions being asked by a cross-examining attorney: "Are you being paid for your testimony, Dr. Gardner?" The implication of the question, of course, was that I was a "hired gun," even though I was brought in by both sides as an impartial. Of course, I had no choice but to answer yes. My impulse was to say, "Aren't you?" or "Why, are you doing this for nothing?" I squelched these responses (even though one wisecrack usually deserves another), because the lawyer would have used it as an excuse to request of the judge that he quickly hit me over the head with his gavel (figuratively, of course) and require me to confine myself to simply answering the questions. I would not give him this opportunity to compromise me with the judge.

It is important for the reader to appreciate that I am not suggesting that the impartial expert artificially "play it cool." Such advice suggests that there may be strong underlying feelings that the evaluator does well to hide. Ideally, impartials should have such a strong command of the material and such convictions for their position that they will be genuinely secure when testifying in court. Under such circumstances, the impartial will have few feelings to hide and will not have to create any false impressions of calmness. Nor am I suggesting that the evaluator ideally be free from tension. A cross-examination is an extremely difficult experience and one must be alert and "on top of it" at all times. The mental health professional, especially, is in strange territory in the courtroom. He or she may be dealing with attorneys with years of experience in cross-examination and they may be quite clever in utilizing maneuvers that attempt to make the impartial look foolish, change his or her testimony frequently, get upset, or exhibit other qualities that will compromise credibility. The evaluator's best defense against such formidable adversaries is to have a firm and full grasp of his or her position, to be clear on the issues, and to be able to state them as calmly and as concisely as possible. Also, the impartial expert can take solace from the appreciation that he or she is more knowledgeable about the case than anyone else in the courtroom because only the impartial has had the opportunity to conduct the most extensive evaluation of all parties concerned.

Early in the inquiry the impartial is generally asked to present the exact dates of the various interviews. The examiner should have such a list readily available to read to the court. It is obviously important that the court have this information. I have read many evaluations in which there have been a total of one or two sessions from which the conclusions have been made. Such paucity of contact with the family is, in my opinion, suggestive of a superficial evaluation. The greater the number of interviews the greater the likelihood the court will be receptive to the conclusions drawn from such contacts. Having this information readily available improves the evaluator's impression on the court. Lastly, lawyers like to dwell on minutiae of this kind. This is often done in the hope that there will be some slip-up on a minor point. An opposing lawyer may try to get much mileage from such an error—again in order to compromise the therapist's credibility.

As I emphasized earlier in this book, the strongest points in the final written recommendation are those based on the examiner's direct observations and direct quotations of the various parties involved. The same principles hold in the courtroom. For example, a strong statement in one's testimony might be: "During my interview with Mrs. X on July 14th, 1981, she stated, 'I never wanted to have children. I always found them a burden.'" The evaluator should avoid using any hearsay information. However, there may be times when it may be judicious to include such data in the report because it might be valid and contributory. To ignore it, in such cases, might very well result in an injudicious decision by the judge. Accordingly, I sometimes use hearsay information, but I am very careful when I do to label it as such and to present it with appropriate qualifications. For example, I might state in my report or state in court: "If the court substantiates Mrs. X's allegations that her husband has beaten the children on at least fifteen occasions during the last year while in a state of inebriation, then I would consider this another reason to deprive him of custody." The reader should note that I leave it to the court to make the final decision regarding whether or not hearsay evidence is valid. No matter how credible it may appear, the examiner does well to avoid accepting it as truth. If the evaluator does so, he or she may be subject to justifiable criticism in court and may look foolish under cross-examination.

Throughout, the examiner should avoid, whenever possible, the use of psychological jargon. There are those who compensate for their feelings of professional inadequacy by using abstruse terminology. There is no concept in all of psychology and psychoanalysis that cannot be understood by the average child of twelve or thirteen. After all, we are only talking about human relations not chemical and mathematical theories. Impartials who use an abundance of such jargon compromise their credibility because the court may sense they are trying to hide ignorance with verbiage. In addition, they expose themselves to another common courtroom ploy. Suddenly, a lawyer may appear with a medical or psychiatric dictionary in hand. The attorney will ask the examiner (often in wise-guy fashion) to define a particular word that he or she has used. It is not uncommon for attorneys in such situations to preface their comments with: "With all due respect, Dr. . . . ." When an attorney prefaces a comment with "with all due respect," it generally means that there is no respect. And the way the attorney says the word "doctor" conveys even less of a feeling of admiration on the lawyer's part. No matter how experienced the examiner may be with regard to that particular word (possibly even more than the person who wrote the dictionary) it is not likely that the evaluator's definition will coincide with that in the dictionary. This is especially true in the field of psychiatry and psychology where things are so vague and undefined. The laymen's inordinate respect for the written word is such that the dictionary's opinion may be taken over that of the expert's. Or, the expert may not be familiar with some of the abstruse minutiae that the dictionary describes. It is rare that a therapist will come out ahead in such a confrontation; therefore, he or she does best to avoid jargon. Again, we see here an example of how the court is used for the purpose of making an expert look foolish, rather than for its ostensible purpose of establishing what is best for the children.

As mentioned, impartial experts do well not to use projective material in their evaluations. There is probably no other place where they are so vulnerable as in the interpretation of projective material. Our field has not reached the point where there is unanimity regarding the interpretation of any ink blot, figure drawing, self-created picture, dream, or fantasy. There is a wide variety of opinion regarding the meaning of such material and the less familiar the examiner is with the patient, the more likely his or her opinion will diverge from that of another. Accordingly, no matter what interpretation the evaluator gives, the attorney is likely to be able to present an alternative that is equally credible to the court—which is often naive with regard to such matters. There are judges who routinely order psychological tests on parties embroiled in custody litigation and they use the findings from projective tests as crucial determinants of their decisions. This is a grave mistake. It is very difficult, if not impossible, to differentiate the dreams of the normal person from those of the psychotic. Dreams may tell much about psychodynamics but they tell very little about diagnostic status and even depth of pathology. In fact dreams, by the very nature of the logical processes they utilize, *are psychotic*. And material elicited in projective tests has the same drawbacks for the custody evaluator. Even the most highly maternal parent will have death wishes, on occasion, toward the children, and these may be symbolically represented in projected fantasies. It is therefore naive and injudicious on the part of courts to utilize such material in custody deliberations, and it is a disservice to the courts for psychologists to provide it.

Most of the questions posed by the attorney whose position the impartial expert supports will be open-ended and will thereby provide the examiner with the opportunity to elaborate on his or her findings and justify the conclusions and recommendations. For example, the lawyer may ask, "Can you state to the court your reasons for recommending that Mrs. X get custody of the children?" or "Can you tell us why you believe that Mr. X should not get custody of the children?" The opposing lawyer, however, will generally pose most of the questions in such form that the therapist will have little opportunity to elaborate on the answers. They are so structured as to warrant, and even require, answers that are simple, short, and often yes or no. The questions are often so worded that the therapist may be required to provide responses that do not reflect his or her true intent or position. The evaluator does well to avoid such distortion of his or her position by not falling into the trap of answering yes or no when the issue is too complex to warrant such a response. The examiner, in such cases, should not hesitate to respond with "I cannot answer yes or no." The examiner should be comfortable with answering in this way as many questions as the lawyer poses which warrant such a response. To do otherwise may result in the court's coming to oversimplified and even erroneous conclusions. In spite of these precautions, questions may be so worded and selective that the evaluator's true intent may be distorted or misrepresented. It is here that the impartial expert sees most clearly how hypocritical is the attorney's statement that he or she is "only interested in what is best for the child."

The examiner may feel quite frustrated on the stand when prohibited from elaborating on responses and clarifying the kinds of misleading conclusions that are often conveyed by the simple yes or no response. If the evaluator tries to elaborate, he or she will be interrupted by both the questioning attorney and the judge and instructed to strictly confine his or her answers to the questions posed. With such questioning the attorney hopes to get the evaluator to selectively present and reveal items and material that will support his or her client's position and withhold from the court that which will weaken the client's cause. For example, I once served as an impartial expert in a case in which I recommended that the mother have custody. One of my main reasons for this was that the father was far more committed to his work than his children. His wife and his children viewed hm as "workaholic"—which he was. In the cross-examination the attorney asked: "To the best of your knowledge, Doctor, is Mr. X an alcoholic?" I answered no. He then repeated the same question with regard to drug addiction, wife beating, gambling, and philandering. Again, I had to answer that he was none of these things. He then continued and asked me questions about whether Mr. X had ever been in jail, committed to a mental institution, received electroshock therapy, or had attempted to kill himself. Again, I continually answered no to all of these questions. The attorney, of course, refrained from asking about any of the deficiencies that his client did have—deficiencies that contributed to my recommending custody to his wife. I suspected that the judge was not taken in by all of this game playing and that the inquiries were conducted for the sake of the client whom the attorney hoped would be impressed by the "brilliance" of this cross-examination.

Another example of how the cross-examining attorney uses the yes-no answer to mislead the court is demonstrated by the case of Mr.

X, a philanthropist, who was quite neglectful of his children. This was an important factor in the examiner's decision to recommend that his wife be given custody. The lawyer was able to elicit a long stream of yes answers from the examiner regarding the various charities to which Mr. X had made generous contributions. He then asked, "You will agree then that Mr. X is a very generous and giving person?" The lawyer here was obviously trying to get the court to generalize from Mr. X's social benevolence and conclude that he was equally benevolent to his children. To such a question the examiner properly answered no—because the statement was not basically true. Or he could have answered, "I cannot answer yes or no." The attorney did not ask the therapist to give the reasons why he could not answer yes or no (the usual situation), because he suspected the therapist would use the question as an opportunity to make a comment along these lines: "In the area of public contributions, Mr. X is, without doubt, a generous man; however, when it comes to the care of his children, I do not consider him generous because. . . ."

The impartial expert should also be aware of the simultaneous presentation of multiple questions presented as a single question for which a yes or no answer is requested. The lawyer here may be trying to sneak in a question that, if asked alone, would receive a different answer. The lawyer may have a question he knows the therapist will answer negatively. By mixing it in with a collection of questions he knows the therapist will answer positively, he hopes to get a yes answer for that particular question as well. If the therapist detects even one misstatement in a barrage of accurate facts, he does well to answer no or state that he cannot answer yes or no. Again the attorney will usually not ask why the examiner has responded in this manner, because he or she suspects that the examiner will use such an open question as an opportunity to focus on the single misleading statement hidden in the series of accurate ones.

Sometimes it is preferable for the therapist to *attempt* to preface a yes or no answer with "To the best of my knowledge. . ." or "At the time of my evaluation, I found no evidence for. . . ." For example, let us take the situation where a woman has not described marital infidelity to the therapist during the course of the evaluation—concluding that such a disclosure would lessen the likelihood that she would be awarded custody. Her husband may not have known of any affairs when this was discussed during the course of the evaluator's examination. However, between the time the impartial expert submitted the report and the court appearance (usually many months later) evidence may have become available strongly suggesting that there was infidelity. Although such information may not be of much significance regarding which parent the evaluator would have recommended for custody, it may have great significance regarding certain legal aspects of the divorce. If the expert has truly been impartial, he or she will have had no contact with either party between the time of the submission of the report and the time of the court appearance. Accordingly, the examiner will not be in a position to know about this new evidence. In court the impartial expert may be asked to provide an answer to a question regarding the mother's marital fidelity. To then provide a definite negative answer to such a question is naive on the therapist's part, compromises his or her credibility, and this may mislead the court. Introductory qualifications can protect the examiner from such embarrassment. If they are not permitted, then the evaluator should provide only a response: "I cannot answer yes or no."

On occasion an attorney will attempt to cause expert witnesses to lose their composure—and thereby compromise their credibility—by asking questions which suggest extremely abnormal behavior that the evaluator did not pick up in the course of the evaluation. For example, the attorney might say, "If you learned that Mr. X had a series of homosexual lovers during the course of his marriage would that have changed your opinion?" "If you found out that Mrs. X had been hospitalized in a mental hospital prior to her marriage, would this have changed your opinion?" "If you learned that Mr. X would undress his 5-year-old daughter and ask her to dance naked in front of male friends, would this have affected your opinion?" These allegations may be gross exaggerations of what had really gone on or may have been invented by the attorney and have absolutely no basis in reality. They are designed to get the examiner flustered and seduce him or her into thinking that he or she has missed extremely important points. The attorney here is trying to compromise the evaluator with such questions, and the examiner should be aware that this is occasionally done in the courtroom.

At times a lawyer may bombard the therapist with a barrage of questions that appear to him to be irrelevant or only peripherally relevant to the issues at hand. In my experience, one of two things is going on in such a situation. The first, and less likely, is that the lawyer really has an important point to make which the impartial expert does not understand. The more likely alternative, in my experience, is that the attorney doesn't know where he is going and is flooding the therapist with questions in the hope that some response might provide him or her with an issue that might be useful for him or her to pursue. One would hope that the judge or the opposing lawyer would interrupt such inquiries very early; unfortunately, my experience has been that they may take considerable time before doing this. Courts traditionally allow wide latitude regarding the length and depth of cross-examination. The defendant, or weaker party, is thereby given the greatest opportunity to strengthen his or her position. In such cross-examination (which can last hours and even days) the examiner should appreciate that the judge is generally not naive and that he or she will not be impressed by the lawyer's antics, misleading questions, attempts to deceive the court, etc.

As described earlier in this book, up until recently, I suffered significant frustration during court breaks when I could not communicate with the attorney whose position I supported. As an impartial expert I suffered all the disadvantages of being an advocate and had few of the advantages. I am no longer in such an impotent position. As mentioned, I have circumvented this problem by making myself available to both attorneys, not only following the submission of my report, but right up through the trial—especially during the breaks in the course of the litigation. However, I strictly adhere to the position that I will not speak to one attorney without the other being invited to hear and contribute. This gives me the freedom to recommend lines of inquiry to either attorney. Of course, the attorney whose position I am supporting is generally quite receptive to my suggestions. As might be expected, the other attorney is generally interested in what I have to say but not too happy that I am providing "ammunition" to the other side. He or she may not even be willing to be party to the conference, but the invitation is invariably extended. If this attorney declines my invitation, he or she cannot claim that it wasn't offered and that I didn't give him or her the opportunity to hear my comments and to participate in the discussion. My status as impartial expert is thereby preserved, and my moral obligation to do what is in the best interests of the children is thereby gratified.

CONCLUDING COMMENTS

The impartial expert is basically serving as an advocate of one side against the other once the report has been submitted. Although the judge may still consider him or her to be impartial, and although the examiner wishes to maintain this view of him- or herself, it is easy to get swept up emotionally in the adversary proceedings. There is often a thin line between serving the children dispassionately as an impartial and serving the children emotionally as an advocate. "Battle fever" tends to be contagious and generals rely upon it for the success of their troops. When one starts fighting, one generally fights hard. The risk here is that the impartial will be reduced to becoming one of the com-

batants who is "out to win." I consider this to be one of the occu-
pational hazards of being an impartial expert. I would not view such
tendencies however to be necessarily neurotic or inappropriate. I
consider them to be natural and would only warn the impartial expert
not to let them get out of hand. To do so may very well compromise his
or her position, because emotionalism and objectivity do not go well together. And this is especially the case on the stand. Should the impartial be unable to place such feeling in proper perspective and control
them to a reasonable degree, it is likely that neurotic factors are operative. For example, a male examiner, who has fought for custody of his
own children, may overidentify with a father involved in such a conflict. He may even support inappropriately the father's position. This is
a risk when serving as an impartial expert if one has been, or worse, is
presently embroiled in a custody conflict oneself. The likelihood of
maintaining one's full objectivity is almost at the zero level. Another
example of the evaluator's inappropriate involvement might result
from sexual-physical attraction. A male evaluator might be "turned
on" by a young, seductive mother. This may not only contribute to his
favoring her over the father but "fighting hard" for her cause. The
evaluator who has significant neurotic problems in relating to either
men or women has no business serving as an impartial evaluator. Such
prejudicial attitudes toward one side over the other is bound to contaminate an impartial evaluation. In short, getting slightly swept up in
the fray of custody litigation is probably normal. But when the evaluator finds him- or herself harboring very strong feelings and preoccupations or fighting very vigorously, the likelihood is that inappropriate
and/or neurotic elements are contributing. As is true in psychotherapy,
such contaminations are a disservice to the patients and are signals to
the examiner that such involvement should be reconsidered until such
time as these problems are resolved.

Fain (1977), an attorney states:

> ...one must always bear in mind that the exercise of discretion by a
> judge is far less a product of his learning than of his personality and his
> temperament, his background and his interests, his biases and his pre-
> judices, both conscious and unconscious.

The same caveat holds for mental health professionals. We, too, are
not free from our prejudices and biases, and we should be aware of
this when conducting custody evaluations. Awareness of our prejudices should make us more modest in conducting custody evaluations.
The mental health professional does well not to involve him- or herself
in evaluations that might be contaminated by such prejudices. Although there are few who are noble enough to make such a decision, it
is an ideal that is still valid.

⚖ Concluding Comments

The reader will be in a better position to appreciate fully my ensuing comments if I define specifically what I mean by certain terms. These terms are sometimes used loosely (and even interchangeably), but they have very specific meanings. I will use the term *mediator* to refer to an impartial person who tries to help conflicting parties resolve their differences by facilitating reasonable communication in a nonadversarial setting. The mediator attempts to help the conflicting parties assess the important issues more clearly and to resolve their differences in a nonadversarial fashion. The mediator may introduce options that the two sides may not have considered and is asked to comment on various solutions that may be proposed. Generally, the mediator is not asked to come forth with specific final recommendations; rather, his or her purpose is to facilitate communication so that the conflicting parties will be in a better position to resolve their differences themselves. Ideally, the parties should have the feeling when the mediation process has been terminated that they, much more than the mediator, have formulated the agreement. Under such circumstances the likelihood is increased that the parties will be committed to the agreement.

I use the word *arbitrator* to refer to an impartial party who, after serving as data collector and mediator, comes forth with specific recommendations. Generally, there are two kinds of arbitration: binding and nonbinding. In *binding arbitration* the two parties agree beforehand that the final recommendations of the arbitrator will be binding upon both, regardless of how much discomfort the final recommendations may cause. Obviously, the parties must have great respect for such an arbitrator's impartiality and fairness if they are to commit themselves to submit to the arbitrator's recommendations, regardless of the content. In *nonbinding arbitration*, the parties agree that the arbitrator's recommendations will certainly be taken seriously (otherwise they would not have engaged the arbitrator's services), but neither party is bound to comply with the recommendations.

At present, when a couple wishes to divorce (even in states with no-fault divorce statutes), each partner is encouraged, if not required, to get his or her own lawyer. In some states it is illegal for one lawyer to represent both parties. In others the practice is generally frowned upon and is considered to border on the unethical. Lawyers are usually advised by their professional societies to discourage clients who come to them as a couple. And there is most often no formal legal apparatus enabling the lawyer to so serve. In short, it is very difficult, if not impossible, in most states at this time for attorneys to serve as mediators or arbitrators in divorce conflicts. However, the laws as well as deep-seated professional traditions dictate the adversary route.

In accordance with my belief that the adversary system—its ancient heritage and merits notwithstanding—can be a source of significant grief for divorcing couples, as well as a cause of psychopathology when litigation is protracted, I believe that the first step for the resolution of divorce conflict should be mediation or arbitration. Only when such efforts fail, should adversary proceedings be utilized. I wish to emphasize that in spite of my criticism of the adversary system, I am not suggesting that we dispense with it entirely in divorce proceedings. It can still prove extremely useful. But I would reserve it as the course of last resort, not first, as is presently the situation.

I believe that attorneys can serve as mediators in divorce conflicts. Such attorneys should preferably be well-trained matrimonial lawyers—well versed and experienced in divorce litigation. They should have the full sanction of the legal profession to involve themselves in such matrimonial mediation. Some lawyers claim that the attorney cannot be objective when serving in the position of the mediator or the arbitrator and that such loss of objectivity may result in favoritism toward one of the contesting parties. The adversary proceedings, they hold, are more likely to bring about the best resolution of a conflict. However, lawyers seem to lose this inhibition to arbitrate when they are invited to serve as arbitrators in commercial disputes and when they receive appointments as judges. Then they quickly and without too much difficulty shift into the role of the mediator or arbitrator. I believe that discouraging attorneys from mediating and arbitrating matrimonial matters has less to do with the fear of loss of objectivity than with their fear of loss of money and/or reputation of being a "winner." Arbitration requires only one lawyer, litigation two. Arbitration may be a short proceeding, whereas adversary litigation is more predictably drawn out and very expensive. Accordingly, this traditional way of handling matrimonial disputes dies hard.

In the course of their inquiries arbitrating lawyers could bring other professionals in for consultation. They might want to seek the services of a social worker, clinical psychologist, or psychiatrist. They might bring in an accountant to help make decisions with regard to the financial arrangements. And they might even consult with a more experienced person in the field of matrimonial law, just as a physician would consulting a specialist in an area in which he or she did not enjoy as much expertise.

In spite of the deep entrenchment of adversary proceedings in divorce conflict at this time, we are seeing the beginning of a new trend—a trend in which mediation and/or arbitration are being appreciated as the preferable first step for divorcing couples in conflict. We are beginning to experiment with a number of plans. I will present here a few that appear most reasonable to me and discuss what I consider to be each one's advantages and disadvantages. Conclusions must be tentative. Only with time and experience will we learn which systems prove to be the most practical and efficacious.

In one system that appears reasonable to me, if a man and woman decide to divorce—and if the decision has definitely been made—they can proceed along one of two paths. The first would be along traditional lines: each would get his or her own attorney and they would attempt to resolve their differences within the structure of the adversary system. An alternative would allow (and even encourage) them to get two lawyers who would serve *in tandem* as nonbinding arbitrators. The first attorney would serve primarily in the early phases. His or her primary goal would be to mediate with the parties in order to help them resolve their differences and then to formulate a separation agreement acceptable to both parties. The second attorney would serve later as a check on the first and would draw up a divorce judgment incorporating the first lawyer's separation agreement as well as any changes that were warranted.

It would be preferable that the second lawyer not be an associate of or be recommended by the first. Rather, the couple should engage him or her through other sources. In this way the second attorney will be less likely to be a "rubber stamp" of the first or be someone with biases similar to the first. If the second attorney detected inequities or manifestations of prejudicial treatment by the first (in spite of the latter's attempts at impartiality), these would be discussed with the first attorney and the clients, in a nonadversarial cooperative vein, in an attempt to resolve these differences. Once resolved, the second attorney would draw up the divorce judgment and submit it to the court. At any point in the process, either of the attorneys might enlist the assistance of a mental health professional, accountant, or specialist attorney well versed in the particular area of difficulty. At any point, as well, either party could discontinue the proceedings and would be completely free to proceed along the traditional adversary lines.

In order for this system to work, the professionals involved in the arbitration proceeding, namely, the arbitrating lawyers, the mental health professionals, the accountant, and any other consulting lawyers who may have been brought in, must be protected from providing furter testimony. If the clients feared that the information revealed in the arbitration proceedings could be freely available in any future adversary proceedings that would ensue if the arbitration failed, it would be less likely that they would reveal themselves. The implementation of this proposal would require protection of all from providing testimony in subsequent litigation. However, I am not suggesting that the arbitrating lawyers, mental health professionals, accountants, or others could not testify if *both* parties agreed that they wanted such testimony brought into court. They have valuable information to offer, and it should be available to the court if at all possible. Lawyers who oppose this system because of its economic implications for them would do well to appreciate that a lawyer who established him- or herself in this role and who gained a good reputation in it would be likely to attract many clients. The potential financial savings and avoidance of hardship that use of his or her services promises is bound to bring many clients. But more important, the attorney would be doing a very humane thing for society at large by keeping more divorce conflicts off the adversary track.

This system could also be useful following the granting of the divorce. If, after the divorce, the couple felt that they wished to reconsider the agreement, that there had been a change in their situation which warranted alteration of their contract, they could go back to the same arbitrating attorney(s) and come to some new agreement. If agreement were not possible, they would be free to utilize adversary methods to help resolve their difficulties.

I believe there are other changes that could take place that would enhance the likelihood of such a system working. One relates to the training of the lawyer. The lawyer's traditional training has been deeply committed to the adversary tradition as a way of resolving conflicts. I believe that the lawyer should also receive more training in the role of mediator and arbitrator. The attorney's knowledge of the law relating to such matters as divorce makes him or her ideally suited to serve in this position. However, legal training in adversary proceedings is so deep that it makes it very difficult for the attorney to do this at present.

Another change that I think would be helpful in making such a system work would be the legal profession's establishing formal specialties—such as exist in medicine. There are presently a few loose specialties in law, e.g., matrimonial and patent law. However, such specialties are unusual and the training requirements for them are not as rigorous as those in medicine. Many lawyers present themselves as being general lawyers and will accept most if not all clients. I believe economic considerations play a significant role in the lawyer's reluctance to form organized specialties. (I recognize, however, that other considerations are operative in the legal profession's hesitance to organize formal specialties: "Who will be the judges of qualifications? What will be the standards? How much credentializing and craft union excluding will go on?") It is somewhat naive on the part of clients to think that any lawyer can be so knowledgeable in all areas of law that he or she can be truly effective. I believe it is a disservice to the public for attorneys to present themselves as being so qualified. A specialty such as matrimonial law, in which there would be rigorous requirements for training and certification, would provide more of the kinds of attorneys that one could want for effective utilization of proposals such as the one I have presented here.

Kubie (1964) suggested that parents would do well to utilize the services of a committee to help them resolve post-separation and post-divorce disputes regarding their children. He recommended that the committee consist of such persons as a pediatrician, a child psychiatrist, a child psychoanalyst, an educator, an impartial attorney, or a clergyman. Kubie was not specific about the number of such individuals he would select for such a committee, but the presumption is that it would be three or four. I consider the proposal ideally desirable, but extremely impractical. Having all these professionals meet simultaneously over a period of time (which is often necessary if one is to resolve meaningfully many custody disputes) would probably be prohibitively expensive. The likelihood of their all being available for all of the sessions is small, and the absence of one or more parties is likely to

compromise the work. Derdeyn (1975) considers the method so complicated and expensive that it would be applicable only to the very
wealthy, and I agree with him.

A panel system that I consider more practical would be one in
which a matrimonial lawyer, well versed in marital conflicts, and a
mental health professional, equally well trained in such matters were
to serve as the mediating panel. Because the attorney is rarely as well
trained in the behavioral sciences as the mental health professional
and because the mental health professional is rarely as well trained in
legal matters as the attorney, the two would complement one another
very well. Both of their services are necessary for a proper understanding of the complex issues before them.

Many professionals (McDermott, Bolman et al., 1973; Goldstein,
Freud and Solnit, 1973) have recommended that children involved in
custody litigation have their own lawyers. Obviously, children so represented are more likely to get proper treatment from the court as well
as from their parents and their advocates. However, I believe that this
recommendation has the disadvantage of further intensifying the problems associated with adversary proceedings. We have enough difficulties dealing with *two* lawyers, each of whom represents a client.
Adding a *third* would compound immeasurably many of the problems
intrinsic to adversary procedings in divorce litigation. The morass of
conflicting data would be even more mind-boggling than it is now. We
have enough trouble with two lawyers doing everything possible to
squelch information detrimental to their clients' positions. Should we
add a third to further confound us? Accordingly, I have serious reservations about this recommendation—in spite of its potential benefits to
the child. I believe that having professionals serve as impartial mediators or arbitrators, as described, is the preferable method for dealing
with such conflicts. Coogler (1977) also takes issue with the concept of
the child advocate. He points out that there are often as many conflicting interests among siblings as there are between husband and wife.
Accordingly, if "justice" is to be done, each child might require a
separate attorney. Implicit in Coogler's statement is the appreciation
that four or five attorneys involved in one custody case would make a
circus of the courtroom and even if there were parents who could
afford to put on such a horrendous spectacle. Coogler and I would
agree that child advocacy is a step in the wrong direction. It increases
adversarial proceedings rather than decreases them and adds immeasurably to the potential psychological damage that families may
suffer.

Another problem with the utilization of the adversary system in
custody litigation is the fallibility of the judge. No matter how brilliant,

no matter how well trained, no matter how attentive, the judge is still basically a human being with his or her own prejudices, knowledge gaps, and limited capacity for absorbing information. The impartial expert involved in custody litigation can take solace from the awareness that the final decision does not rest with him or her, but with the judge. The judge cannot enjoy such solace. Of course, appeals to higher courts can serve as checks on the judge at the trial level (and assuage any guilt or fear he or she may feel), but they are uncommon and add to the financial burden of the parents. If the judge is to take his or her job obligations seriously, the pressure could be formidable. I believe that this problem could be reduced with a two- or three-judge panel or a judge and a six-person jury. Three-judge panels and six-person juries are known to the legal profession in various segments of Western society and so are not without precedent. I recognize that the use of such panels and juries will add to the expense of custody litigation, but it certainly would reduce the chances of injudicious recommendations.

Divorce mediation is currently increasing so much that it is on the verge of becoming a fad. The aforementioned plans are only a few among many being tried in various ways at this time. All of these should be viewed as experimental; definitive judgments should be withheld. There is every indication that the mediation trend will continue to grow, and this should result in a reversal of the present burgeoning of custody litigation. My greatest concern about the rapid development of family mediation relates to the training that mediators are receiving in both law and the behavioral sciences. Marriage is basically a contractual arrangement and a divorce, whatever else it is, is a legal process designed to break the marital contract. The legal aspects of divorce can be too complex to be properly fathomed by someone lacking significant legal education. Yet many mental health professionals are mediating the legal aspects of such disputes—with little appreciation of the fact that they are ill qualified to do so. Obviously, this is a dangerous situation. Individuals may be "mediated into" accepting injudicious financial arrangements or suffer other forms of grief because of the mental health mediator's naivete of the legal implications of the compromise. Similarly, attorneys without proper training are now mediating the psychological aspects of divorce. Many believe that they have some inner knowledge of how to resolve family problems because of their own "intuition," "instincts," and life experiences. This can also be dangerous. Injudicious visitation and even custodial arrangements may be mediated, to the psychological detriment of both the children and the parents.

To summarize our present situation, divorce mediation is rapidly becoming the "in" approach. However, the paucity of qualified mediators results in people of questionable qualifications appearing as self-appointed "experts." When the need is great (which it is) and the supply of well-qualified professionals small (which is also the case), then the vacuum tends to be filled by less trained and even incompetent individuals.

Those of us who have worked for many years toward the goal of removing divorce from the adversary arena, or at least reducing the frequency with which the system is utilized in divorce conflicts, are now closer to our objective than ever before. However, we cannot enjoy our victory because a new menace threatens to complicate the lives of the divorced, namely, mediation by unqualified "experts." Until rigid and stringent standards are set for individuals serving as divorce mediators, divorcing families are likely to encounter a new breed of predators who may deprive them of proper legal protection and provide them with psychologically detrimental advice. Because mediators are being drawn from a variety of fields—law, psychiatry, psychology, social work, pastoral counseling, etc.—it is not likely that such standardization will be achieved in the near future. Consequently, I see a bleak picture for divorce mediation in the next few years, but hope that ultimately the best methods will survive and only the most qualified and trained individuals will be permitted to provide this service.

A mental health professional who serves as an impartial expert takes on a heavy burden indeed. To the degree that he or she is respected by the court, to that degree will the report be taken seriously. A child's whole future may be affected by the examiner's decision. And it is for this reason that the kind of evaluation I have described in this book is so expensive and detailed. The fact that only a small percentage of people involved in custody conflicts may be able to avail themselves of such an evaluation does not lessen its intrinsic value. To the degree that the mental health professional can provide families with such an evaluation, to that degree will their needs best be served. Although evaluations of this kind may be among the most difficult that the examiner is called upon to conduct, these evaluations can also be among the most gratifying. I hope this volume will help my colleagues enjoy the satisfactions—the labor and frustrations involved notwithstanding—that I have gained from conducting such evaluations.

Appendix I

The Psychiatrist as Impartial Expert in Custody Litigation

THE PSYCHIATRIST AS IMPARTIAL EXPERT IN CUSTODY LITIGATION

Richard A. Gardner, M.D.

During the last few years courts have increasingly taken the position that a parent's sex should not be a consideration in custody litigation. Prior to the first quarter of this century, fathers were generally considered the preferential custodial parent — primarily because they were usually in a better financial position to support the children and the concept of a noncustodial parent's supporting the children was generally considered unjust. It was primarily in the third decade of this century, with increasing appreciation of the importance of the maternal role in child-rearing and the efforts of the women's liberation movement, that the present statutes regarding equality of the sexes in custody conflicts were passed. However, during the next fifty years the mother was almost automatically granted custody unless it could be demonstrated that she was grossly unfit to fulfill her maternal role. During this period fathers rarely sought custody, so meager were their chances of gaining it. Since the early 1970's the fifty-year-old statutes are being more strictly interpreted and fathers' chances of gaining custody are increasing. Accordingly, custody litigation is becoming ever more common. (Derdeyn [1976] has written an excellent historical review of social attitudes regarding parental custody, from Roman times to the present.)

Many attorneys and psychiatrists who have been involved in this new wave of litigation have become increasingly concerned that the adversary system, its merits notwithstanding, has certain limitations as a method of determining which is the "better" parent. Psychiatrists serving as advocates most often do not have the opportunity to evaluate both parties, and so their testimony regarding which is the better of the two parents must be weak and suspect. The impartial expert appears to be more suited to advising in such situations. However, most agree that such experts are certainly not free from prejudice and subjectivity. Accordingly, there should still be an open route to adversary proceedings should either party wish to utilize them to question and even refute such experts' recommendations. It is the purpose of this article to acquaint the attorney with the basic operational procedures and rationales of the impartial custody evaluation so that the lawyer may be in a better position to advise clients regarding what they can expect should they or the court choose this method of resolving their differences. In addition, mention will be made of the ways in which the attorney can specifically cooperate with the consulting psychiatrist in order to facilitate the smooth operation of the evaluation.

Preliminary Considerations — Ideally, both attorneys and both clients should be in agreement that the services of an impartial expert would be desirable. It is not reasonable to ask of the clients that such an expert's decision be binding. Impartial experts are not free from fallibility and giving their decisions such power will place upon many such a burden that objectivity may be lost. Rather, the clients should be encouraged to give serious consideration to the choice of the expert so that there will be greater receptivity to complying with his or her recommendations. The attorney who has already decided beforehand which expert he will bring in as an advocate, if the impartial expert does not favor his or her client's position, is not operating within the true spirit of this method of resolving custody conflicts. The attorney's position should be one of receptivity to, but not blanket acceptance of, the impartial expert's findings. If the consultant's conclusions do not support the client's position, the lawyer should be willing to try to help the client change his or her stand, if the expert's report seems credible to him. A reflex attempt to disprove the findings or disparage the expert may not be in the children's best interests.

If only one side wishes to engage the services of the impartial expert, the evaluation may be severely compromised. However, if the court is willing to order the unreceptive party to submit to examination, an evaluation is still possible. From the point of view of the consultant, the best arrangement is to evaluate parties who have exhibited motivation for the consultant's services. To interview someone who has been coerced into the evaluation is certainly a compromised situation; however, it is far better than not interviewing the party at all. Although the unreceptive parent is more likely to censor (not that the receptive one is free from such censorship), useful information can still be obtained.

It is preferable that the impartial expert be someone who has had absolutely no previous contact with either client. Otherwise, preexisting biases are likely to contaminate the evaluation. The person who is treating one or more of the children, even though quite familiar with the family, is a poor choice. Such a therapist's work with the children will almost invariably be compromised after a parental preference has been declared. The nonpreferred parent is likely to become significantly alienated from the therapist. The parental antagonism toward the therapist is usually sensed by the child, places him or her in a loyalty conflict, and weakens thereby the child's relationship with the therapist.

The attorney should be willing to make available to the therapist all records that are pertinent to the evaluation. These include affidavits, separation agreement(s), the divorce decree(s), hospital records, medical and psychiatric reports, psychological tests, etc. Most competent psychiatrists will use such information judiciously. They will use the data contained therein as points of departure for their own inquiries. They would not generally rely on such data to be of primary importance, lest they compromise the expert's testimony by use of hearsay information. The attorney does well to advise the client to cooperate with the psychiatrist by signing releases for the acquisition of such information if this material has not already been obtained by the referring attorneys.

My next point is a difficult one for most lawyers to appreciate. But it is crucial to the successful impartial custody evaluation. Many, such as myself, advise the clients in the first interview that their confidentiality may not be fully respected during the evaluation and, at the discretion of the examiner, information may be transmitted to the other party. The consultant must have such flexibility if he is to discuss with each party the allegations made by the other.

A conflict that the attorney faces when making such a referral is that the procedural rationales of such an evaluation are, at times, antithetical to the basic principles of adversary proceedings. The impartial expert works on the premise that the more information he or she has available, the better will be his or her position to make a judicious recommendation. Accordingly, the consultant will encourage both parties to openly and freely discuss all issues, both with the consultant alone and in joint interview with the other party. The lawyer will often consider such revelations to compromise the client's legal position and may discourage such openness. To the degree that the attorney can encourage such revelations, as they pertain to issues. relevant to the children, the lawyer will be assisting the impartial expert in doing what is in the best interests of the children.

The attorney should also appreciate that the client's wish to gain custody of the children may not simply be motivated by loving interest in their welfare. The client may try to gain custody in order to assuage guilt over "abandoning" the children. Wresting the children from a hated spouse is probably the most effective way of wreaking vengeance. Some threaten such litigation (sometimes with their attorney's suggestion and/or compliance) as a bargaining maneuver — knowing full well that custody is not really desired and that the pursuit will be discontinued when the other side makes certain concessions. Often very mundane considerations are also operative. The parent who has custody does not pay support and is the one who is given preference for remaining in the home, the tradition being that the children remain in the home with the custodial parent.

The attorney does well not to place a time limit on the evaluation. It is very difficult to say in advance how many interviews will be necessary. The expert's decision may have a profound effect on the children's lives and should not be made quickly. The psychiatrist has to get to know the parents and children well, must not work under the pressure of a close deadline, and must be free to pursue any lines of inquiry that promise to provide pertinent information.

The Evaluation: Most consultants meet with both clients together in the initial interview in order to explain the "ground rules" and other aspects of the evaluation. Although some of this information may have already been imparted during previous conversations with clients and attorneys, I usually find it judicious to repeat these so that all are clear regarding the procedures that will be followed during the evaluation. I explain the importance of openness and honesty if I am to truly serve the best interests of the children. I explain to the clients that I reserve the right to reveal, at my discretion, certain aspects of what was told to me by the other party. I try to impress upon them the fact that if I do not have such freedom and flexibility I will be ill-equipped to ascertain the validity of the various conflicting allegations that I invariably hear in such inquiries. I express my appreciation that such revelations may compromise the parents' legal positions, but if they truly have their children's interests at heart they will take such a risk. I inform the parents that following my individual sessions, I will meet with them jointly. In this way I will be able to hear both sides of the story with each one having the opportunity to comment to me on any distortions he or she sees the other to have. I try to help them appreciate that this is more easily done in a private conference with me than in a court of law.

I then make a list of the various parties that I will be interviewing. Generally this involves the parents, each child, and prospective parental surrogates such as a step-parent (present and prospective), grandparents, relatives, or persons with whom the parent is or plans to be living. A housekeeper can be a valuable source of information if her services can be engaged. However, in all fairness to her, she must be told in advance that the consultant reserves the right to reveal, at his or her discretion, whatever the housekeeper may relate. I generally discourage each parent's bringing in friends and neighbors. Their comments are invariably highly biased, overdetermined, and often hearsay. But I will not refuse to see any person who can reasonably provide me with useful information. I also discuss any other joint interviews that appear to be warranted (in addition to the aforementioned joint interview(s) with the parents together). Usually one or more family interviews are conducted and sessions with any combination of family members may also be desirable.

I also discuss the plan of payment. This is not simply for the obvious purpose of learning how I will be receiving remuneration for my services, but it also helps ensure that I will not be operating under the expectation that if I do not favor the payer's position he or she will express disappointment and anger by withdrawing payment for my services. The attorney does well not to underestimate this possible contaminant to the evaluation. A provision in the court order, which originally invited the expert's participation, that directs a particular party to pay can serve to assure the consultant (to some degree) that payment will be forthcoming. Placing the money in escrow is a little more reassuring; but being paid an estimate of the total cost in advance is much more reassuring. The latter provides all with the best protection against such bias. On occasion, I will conduct home visits to each of the domiciles in which the children may potentially reside. There I meet with those who are living in the home and more directly observe the setting in which the children may be living. Conversations with teachers can sometimes provide useful information. I inquire about not only the children's behavior and academic performance in the classroom, but the teacher's encounters with the parents as well.

In the interview, my main aim is to gain information about parental capacity. Such interviews have a different quality from the traditional ones that the psychiatrist usually conducts. Most patients realize that the more open and honest they are with the psychiatrist, the greater the likelihood that they will be helped with their problems. Most patients overcome initial embarrassment and shame in the service of their desire to be helped. In the custody evaluation, however, the parents' primary goal is to keep or acquire the children — the parents' most treasured possession(s). In the service of this goal, each parental answer is censored in accordance with whether the interviewee believes it will strengthen or weaken his or her position. I have described elsewhere (Gardner, 1976) the special interviewing techniques that the consultant can utilize to circumvent such resistances and obtain reliable and valid data.

Generally, I first invite each party to relate to me as much as he or she wishes about anything considered to be relevant. I then proceed to take a traditional family history and life background. Particular questions about the marriage and childrearing are also included. The skilled evaluator learns as much from the attitudes, slips, and emotional reactions as he or she does from actual statements. I am not particularly concerned with arriving at a final diagnosis. The court has asked my opinion regarding which parent would be the better one for the children. A diagnosis per se may not give any valid information in this regard. In addition, it may provide a cross-examining attorney with an opening to weaken the expert's testimony. No matter what definition the consultant gives to any diagnostic label, the attorney is likely to find a source with a different definition (such is the state of the art). One easily protects oneself from such compromising of one's position by avoiding diagnostic labels entirely (if possible).

The most convincing reports are heavily weighted with direct quotations of statements made by the clients to the psychiatrist. Unless one is going to question the expert's honesty, these are hard to refute in cross-examination. Psychoanalytic interpretations of projective material, although valuable to the psychiatrist, may not be impressive information to the court. In addition, such interpretations do not stand up well when subjected to cross-examination. For example, a boy may draw a picture of a man sitting in a house. He may then take a red crayon and cover the whole picture with scribbles while gleefully telling a story about how the house burned down and the man in it was burnt to death. The evaluator may be convinced that the man represents the child's father; that the story reflects great hostility toward him; and that it is an argument (among many of course) for the mother's being given custody. The opposing attorney may ask questions like: "Isn't it possible, Doctor, that the child saw a TV program in which a house burned down?" And then, "Isn't it possible that the drawing was merely prompted by the television experience?" And then, "Isn't it possible that the drawing does not reveal hostility to the father?" To each of these questions the expert (if he is to be worthy of the title) has little choice but to answer yes. He or she has no opportunity at that point to add that such explanations, although possible, are extremely improbable. To safeguard themselves from such compromising of their testimony, many consultants avoid introducing such data or utilizing them to a significant degree.

In the interviews with the children, one may have to resort more to projective techniques — but even here they should be used judiciously. I prefer direct statements and observations of behavior and interactions. The young child is not sophisticated enough to censor and play act for my benefit. The child will put his or her head in the lap of the preferred parent when sitting between the parents in the family interview. The child will snuggle up to the warmer parent when shy and embarrassed in front of the stranger called a psychiatrist. These are the kinds of observations that provide the evaluation with its most convincing data.

Asking the children whom they wish to live with is tricky and requires great skill — not only with regard to asking the question, but understanding the meaning of the response. Some children will come right out and state their preference. Others have a preference, but do not wish to declare it openly lest they appear disloyal to the nonfavored parent. Such children may indirectly reveal their preferences to the psychiatrist, in the hope that such communications will ultimately be transmitted to the judge. Their position then, when with the nonpreferred parent, can be: "It was not I who decided that I couldn't stay with you; it was the judge." The child may express a preference out of fear of reprisals. Or the child may choose to live with the parent who gives him the best time (children are not famous for their appreciation of the importance of learning to do things like homework, getting out of the bed in the morning on time, taking out the garbage, arriving at places on time, etc.). Many may express a preference for the parent they were last with prior to the interview — that parent having just indulged the child in the hope that the youngster will favor the indulger. The child may opt to live with the parent who believes that it behooves him or her to provide the child with the most enjoyable times on a continuing basis. Some children have been brainwashed, even to the point where they share a parent's paranoid obsession against a former spouse. It is in this area that the expert's sensitivity and competence may be put to the greatest test.

Postevaluation Considerations: At the completion of my evaluation I review all my material and make a decision. I try to consider each parent's assets and liabilities regarding parental competence and decide which parent ends up with the best balance — both in the present and in what I would anticipate is likely to be the future. A report describing one parent as having most, if not all, the assets and the other most, if not all, the liabilities, is likely to be biased. Most examiners submit their reports to the court and attorneys, without first discussing them with the clients. This was my position until the last few years. Recently, I have begun to present my conclusions to the clients *before* making up the final report. I do this in order to give them a final opportunity to change my opinion before it is submitted. After the report is submitted, there is little, if anything, I can do to change it. At that time, the parent will usually suffer the frustration of not having access to me outside the artificial setting of the courtroom. Although I have not yet had the experience of changing my basic recommendations in such a discussion, I have had some minor modifications introduced and corrected erroneous material that may have crept into the report. This, of course, improves my report and strengthens my own position under cross-examination. Such an interview, therefore, has the fringe benefit of protecting the examiner when subjected to cross-examination.

The best reports, in my opinion, are free from psychiatric jargon. This not only makes the report easier to understand, but protects the psychiatrist from an examining attorney's attempts to compromise his or her credibility by trying to demonstrate that the expert's definition of a psychiatric term does not coincide exactly with that of a particular dictionary or other authorities. The report should not generally make recommendations regarding decisions of money and property. This is the province of the lawyers and accountants and a psychiatrist who does involve himself is going beyond his own area of expertise. It is not only injudicious to do this but may reflect some bias or lack of objectivity as well. It is appropriate for the psychiatrist to make a general statement about visitation — for example, "Although I believe Mr. X to be the preferential custodial parent, I believe that Mrs. X should enjoy the most liberal visitation privileges." It is inappropriate for the impartial expert to become involved in the nitty-gritty details of the visitation schedule. This is something that is more properly worked out by the clients and their lawyers.

* * *

A divorce may be one of the most psychologically traumatic experiences a person may endure. And extended divorce litigation may add to such trauma. Custody litigation is generally even fiercer and more psychologically devastating than traditional marital conflict. Arguing over money and property is one thing; fighting over children is something entirely different. One's most treasured possessions are at stake; possessions money cannot buy; possessions that may be lost forever. No wonder then that custody litigation is so vicious. Psychological deterioration is common in the course of prolonged divorce litigation and even worse deterioration is the rule during protracted custody litigation. The attorney has it within his power to discourage and prevent such untoward sequelae if he will truly commit himself to the doctrine of doing what is in the children's best interests. To do so he may have to overcome the lawyer's traditional role of doing what the client wishes. Doing what the client wants and what is in the client's and children's best interests may not be the same thing. By carefully selecting an impartial expert — an expert whose opinion is deeply respected — the attorney will be less likely to try to refute this expert's opinion if the recommendation does not support his or her client's position. The attorney will then have a deeper conviction for discouraging the client from further litigation and will be protecting both client and children from the often devastating psychiatric traumas attendant to prolonged custody litigation. And he will be playing a role in doing what is most likely to be in the family's and the children's best interests.

July 24, 1979

Appendix II

Provisions for Accepting an Invitation to Serve as an Impartial Expert in Custody Litigation

RICHARD A. GARDNER, M. D.
155 COUNTY ROAD
CRESSKILL, N. J. 07626
TELEPHONE 201 - 567-8989

Provisions for Accepting an Invitation to Serve as

an Impartial Expert in Custody Litigation

Whenever possible, I make every reasonable attempt to serve the court as an impartial expert, rather than as an advocate, in custody litigation. In order to serve optimally in this capacity I must be free to avail myself of any and all information, from any source, that I consider pertinent and reasonable to have. In this way, I believe I can best serve the interests of children and parents involved in such conflicts. Accordingly, before agreeing to serve in this capacity, the following conditions must be agreed upon by both parents and both attorneys:

1) I will have available to interview all members of the immediate family--that is, the mother, father, and children--for as many interviews (individual and in any combination) as I consider warranted. In addition, I will have the freedom to invite any and all other parties whom I would consider possible sources of useful information. Generally, these would include such persons as present or prospective parental surrogates with whom either parent may be involved and the housekeeper. Usually, I do not interview a series of friends and relatives each of whom, from the outset, is particularly partial to one of the parents (but I reserve the right to invite such parties if I consider it warranted).

2) In order to allow me the freedom of inquiry necessary for serving optimally families involved in custody litigation, the parents shall agree to a modification of the traditional rules of confidentiality. Specifically, I must be given the freedom to reveal to one party what has been told to me by the other (at my discretion) so that I will have full opportunity to explore all pertinent points with both parties. This does not mean that I will not respect certain privacies or that I will automatically reveal all information provided me--only that I reserve the right to make such revelations if I consider them warranted for the purpose of collecting the most meaningful data.

3) The parties shall agree to sign any and all releases necessary for me to obtain reports from others, e.g. psychiatrists, psychologists, social workers, teachers, school officials, mental hospitals, etc.

4) My fee for conducting a custody evaluation is $100 per full hour of my time. This not only includes time spent in interviewing, but in report prepara- tion, dictation, pertinent telephone conversations, court preparation, and any other time expended in association with the evaluation. My fee for court appearances is $150 per hour while in court and $100 per hour travel time to and from my office. During the course of the evaluation, bills will be sent to the payer(s) every Friday. In order to insure that the evaluation is neither interrupted nor delayed because of nonpayment, each bill must be paid no later than one week from the date of billing.

Prior to the initial interview (with both parents together) the payer(s) will deposit with me a check (in my name) for $1500. This shall be deposited in the Northern Valley-Englewood Savings and Loan Association branch in Cresskill, New Jersey, in my name, in a day-to-day interest bearing account. This money (with accrued interest) shall be returned to the payer(s) _after_ a final decision has been made regarding custody and after I have received a letter from the court, or either of the attorneys, that my services are no longer being enlisted.

This payment should not be viewed as an advance retainer, in that the aforementioned fees will not be drawn against it, unless there has been a failure to pay my fee. It usually serves to reassure the non- payer that my objectivity will not be compromised by the fear that if I do not support the paying party, my fee will not be paid.

The average total cost for an evaluation is generally in the $1000-$2500 range. It is very difficult, if not impossible, to predict in advance the cost of a particular evaluation because I cannot know beforehand how many interviews will be warranted and whether or not I will be asked to testify in court.

5) Both attorneys are invited to send to me any material that they consider useful to me.

6) Upon completion of my evaluation--and prior to the preparation of my final report--I generally meet with both parents together and present them my findings and recommendations. This gives them the opportunity to correct any distortions they believe I may have and/or alter my opinion before it becomes finalized in my report. In addition, it saves the parents from the unnecessary and prolonged anxiety associated with

wondering what my findings are. Following this
session the final report is prepared and then
simultaneously sent to the court, the two attorneys,
and the two parents. When a guardian ad litem has
been appointed by the court, he or she will also be
sent a copy of the final report.

7) Following the submission of my report, I strictly
refrain from any further communication with either
parent or any other party involved in the evaluation.
However, I am willing to discuss any aspect of my
report with both attorneys at the same time, either
personally or by conference telephone call. And such
communication may occur any time from the submission
of my report to the end of the trial. This practice
enables me to continue to provide input to the
attorneys regarding what I consider to be in the
children's best interests and this may be especially
important during the time of litigation. However, in
order to preserve my status as impartial, any information I provide either attorney is only done under
circumstances in which the other is invited to
participate.

My experience has been that conducting the evaluation in the
manner described above provides me with the optimum conditions
for providing the court with a thorough and objective recommendation.

After receiving signed statements (bottom of next page)
from both parents signifying agreement to the conditions of the
evaluation, I will notify both attorneys. I suggest, then, that
a court order be drawn up and submitted to the presiding judge.
On receipt of the judge's signed invitation, I will invite the
payer(s) to forward me the $1500 advance payment. On receipt of
such payment I will notify both parents that I am available to
proceed with the evaluation as rapidly as is feasible. I generally cannot promise to meet a specific deadline because I cannot tell in advance how many interviews will be required, nor
can I know how flexible the parties will be regarding making
themselves available for appointments I offer.

On occasion, I am willing to consider serving as an advocate. However, such participation will only be considered after
evidence has been submitted to me that the non-participating
side has been invited to participate and has refused and, in
addition, the court has refused to order such involvement. If
I do then suspect that the participating party's position merits
my consideration, I would be willing to interview that party with
no promise beforehand that I will support his or her position.
On occasion, I have, indeed, seen fit to support the participating

party in this manner, because it was obvious to me that the
children's needs would be best served by my advocacy and/or not
to do so would have deprived them of sorely needed assistance.
On other occasions, I have concluded that I could not serve with
conviction as an advocate of the requesting party and so have
refused further services to the client.

Richard A. Gardner, M.D.

I have read the above, discussed the provisions with my
attorney, and agree to proceed with the evaluation. I agree
to pay ____% of the $1500 advance and ____% of the fees in
accordance with the aforementioned payment schedule.

Date: _____   _____
                                        Parent's Signature

Appendix III

Parents' Questionnaire

RICHARD A. GARDNER, M. D.
155 COUNTY ROAD
CRESSKILL, N. J. 07626
—
TELEPHONE 201 - 567-8989

PLEASE BRING THIS COMPLETED FORM WITH YOU AT THE TIME OF YOUR FIRST APPOINT-

MENT ON_____AT_____

IT IS PREFERABLE THAT BOTH PARENTS ACCOMPANY THE CHILD TO THE CONSULTATION.

Child's name_____Birth date_____Age___Sex_____
              last   **first**   **middle**
Home address_____
              street   city   state   zip
Home telephone number_____
                    area code   number
Child's school_____
           name   address   **grade**
Present placement of child (place check in appropriate bracket):

	Column A Adults with whom child is living	Column B Non-residential adults involved with child
Natural mother	( )___	( )___
Natural father	( )___	( )___
Stepmother	( )___	( )___
Stepfather	( )___	( )___
Adoptive mother	( )___	( )___
Adoptive father	( )___	( )___
Foster mother	( )___	( )___
Foster father	( )___	( )___
Other (specify)	_____	_____

Place the number 1 or 2 next to each check in Column A and provide the
following information about each person:

  1. Name_____Occupation_____
          last   first
     Business name_____Business address_____

     _____Business tel. No. (   )_____

  2. Name_____Occupation_____
          last   first
     Business name_____Business address_____

     _____Business tel. No. (   )_____

Place the number 3 next to the person checked in Column B who is most involved
with the child and provide the following information:

  3. Name_____Home address_____
                                             street
     _____Home tel. No. (   )_____
      city   state   zip
     Occupation_____Business name_____

Business address_____Bus. Tel. No. ( )_____

Source of referral: Name_____Address_____

_____Tel. No. ( )_____

Purpose of consultation (brief summary of the main problems):_____

_____

_____

_____

_____

PREGNANCY
  Complications:
    Excessive vomiting_____hospitalization required_____

    Excessive staining or blood loss_____

    Threatened miscarriage_____

    Infection(s) (specify)_____

    Toxemia_____

    Operation(s) (specify)_____

    Other illness(es) (specify)_____

  Smoking during pregnancy_____average number of cigarettes per day_____

  Alcoholic consumption during pregnancy_____describe, if beyond an occa-

    sional drink_____

  Medications taken during pregnancy_____

  X-ray studies during pregnancy_____

  Duration_____weeks

DELIVERY
  Type of labor: Spontaneous_____Induced_____
  Forceps: high_____mid_____low_____
  Duration of labor_____hours

  Type of delivery: Vertex (normal)_____breech_____Caesarean_____

  Complications:
    cord around neck_____

    cord presented first_____

    hemorrhage_____

  infant injured during delivery_____

  other (specify)_____

Birth Weight_____
  Appropriate for gestational age (AGA)_____
  Small for gestational age (SGA)_____

POST-DELIVERY PERIOD (while in the hospital)
  Respiration: immediate_____delayed (if so, how long)_____

  Cry: immediate_____delayed (if so, how long)_____

  Mucus accumulation_____

  Apgar score (if known)_____

  Jaundice_____

  Rh factor_____transfusion_____

  Cyanosis (turned blue)_____

  Incubator care_____number of days_____

  Suck: strong_____weak_____

  Infection (specify)_____

  Vomiting_____diarrhea_____

  Birth defects (specify)_____

  Total number of days baby was in the hospital after the delivery _____

INFANCY-TODDLER PERIOD
  Were any of the following present--to a significant degree--during the
  first few years of life? If so, describe.

  Did not enjoy cuddling _____

  Was not calmed by being held and/or stroked _____

  Colic_____

  Excessive restlessness_____

  Diminished sleep because of restlessness and easy arousal _____

  Frequent headbanging_____

  Constantly into everything_____

  Excessive number of accidents compared to other children_____

DEVELOPMENTAL MILESTONES

If you can recall, record the age at which your child reached the following developmental milestones. If you cannot recall, check item at right.

	age	I cannot recall exactly, but to the best of my recollection it occurred		
		early	at the normal time	late
Smiled				
Sat without support				
Crawled				
Stood without support				
Walked without assistance				
Spoke first words besides "ma-ma" and "da-da"				
Said phrases				
Said sentences				
Bowel trained, day				
Bowel trained, night				
Bladder trained, day				
Bladder trained, night				
Rode tricycle				
Rode bicycle (without training wheels)				
Buttoned clothing				
Tied shoelaces				
Named colors				
Named coins				
Said alphabet in order				
Began to read				

COORDINATION

Rate your child on the following skills:

	Good	Average	Poor
Walking			
Running			
Throwing			
Catching			
Shoelace tying			
Buttoning			
Writing			
Athletic abilities			

COMPREHENSION AND UNDERSTANDING
Do you consider your child to understand directions and situations as well as other children his or her age?_____If not, why not?_____

_____

How would you rate your child's overall level of intelligence compared to other children? Below average_____Average_____Above average_____

SCHOOL
Rate your child's school experiences related to academic learning:

	Good	Average	Poor
Nursery school			
Kindergarten			
Current grade			

To the best of your knowledge, at what grade level is your child functioning: reading_____spelling_____arithmetic_____

Has your child ever had to repeat a grade? If so, when_____

Present class placement: regular class_____special class (if so, specify)

_____

Kinds of special therapy or remedial work your child is currently receiving

_____

Describe briefly any academic school problems_____

_____

_____

Rate your child's school experience related to behavior:

	Good	Average	Poor
Nursery school			
Kindergarten			
Current grade			

Does your child's teacher describe any of the following as significant classroom problems?
Doesn't sit still in his or her seat_____
Frequently gets up and walks around the classroom_____
Shouts out. Doesn't wait to be called upon _____
Won't wait his or her turn_____

Does not cooperate well in group activities_____
Typically does better in a one-to-one relationship_____
Doesn't respect the rights of others_____
Doesn't pay attention during storytelling_____

Describe briefly any <u>other</u> classroom behavioral problems_____

_____

_____

PEER RELATIONSHIPS
Does your child seek friendships with peers?_____

Is your child sought by peers for friendship?_____

Does your child play primarily with children his or her own age?_____

younger_____older_____

Describe briefly any problems your child may have with peers_____

_____

_____

HOME BEHAVIOR
All children exhibit, to some degree, the kinds of behavior listed below.
Check those that you believe your child exhibits to an excessive or ex-
aggerated degree when compared to other children his or her age.

Hyperactivity (high activity level)_____
Poor attention span_____
Impulsivity (poor self control)_____
Low frustration threshold_____
Temper outbursts_____
Sloppy table manners_____
Interrupts frequently_____
Doesn't listen when being spoken to_____
Sudden outbursts of physical abuse of other children_____
Acts like he or she is driven by a motor_____
Wears out shoes more frequently than siblings_____
Heedless to danger_____
Excessive number of accidents_____
Doesn't learn from experience_____
Poor memory_____
More active than siblings_____

INTERESTS AND ACCOMPLISHMENTS
What are your child's main hobbies and interests?_____

_____

What are your child's areas of greatest accomplishment?_____

_____

What does your child enjoy doing most?_____

_____

What does your child dislike doing most?_____

_____

MEDICAL HISTORY
If your child's medical history includes any of the following, please note
the age when the incident or illness occurred and any other pertinent information.
Childhood diseases (describe any complications)_____

_____

Operations_____

_____

Hospitalizations for illness(es) other than operations_____

_____

Head injuries_____

_____with unconsciousness_____without unconsciousness_____

Convulsions_____

_____with fever_____without fever_____

Coma_____

Meningitis or encephalitis_____

Immunization reactions_____

Persistent high fevers_____highest temperature ever recorded_____

eye problems_____

ear problems_____

poisoning_____

-8-

PRESENT MEDICAL STATUS

Present height_____Present weight_____

Present illness(es) for which child is being treated_____

_____

Medications child is taking on an ongoing basis_____

_____

FAMILY HISTORY - MOTHER

Age_____ Age at time of pregnancy with patient_____

Number of previous pregnancies_____Number of spontaneous abortions

(miscarriages)_____Number of induced abortions_____

Sterility problems (specify)_____

School: Highest grade completed_____

  Learning problems (specify)_____grade repeat_____

  Behavior problems (specify)_____

Medical problems (specify)_____

Have any of your blood relatives (not including patient and siblings) ever

had problems similar to those your child has? If so, describe_____

_____

_____

FAMILY HISTORY - FATHER

Age_____Age at the time of the patient's conception _____

Sterility problems (specify)_____

School: Highest grade completed_____

  Learning problems (specify)_____grade repeat_____

  Behavior problems (specify)_____

Medical problems (specify)_____

Have any of your blood relatives (not including patient and siblings) ever

had problems similar to those your child has? If so, describe_____

_____

Most children exhibit, at one time or another, one or more of the symptoms listed below. Place a P next to those that your child has exhibited in the PAST and an N next to those that your child exhibits NOW. Only mark those symptoms that have been or are present to a significant degree over a period of time. Only check as problems behavior that you suspect is unusual or atypical when compared to what you consider to be the normal for your child's age. Then, on page 12, list the symptoms checked off on pages 9-12 and write a brief description including age of onset, duration, and any other pertinent information.

Thumb-sucking ___

Baby talk ___

Overly dependent for age ___

Frequent temper tantrums ___

Excessive silliness and clowning ___

Excessive demands for attention ___

Cries easily and frequently ___

Generally immature ___

Eats non-edible substances ___

Overeating with overweight ___

Eating binges with overweight ___

Undereating with underweight ___

Long periods of dieting and food abstinence with underweight ___

Preoccupied with food--what to eat and what not to eat ___

Preoccupation with bowel movements ___

Constipation ___

Encopresis (soiling) ___

Insomnia (difficulty sleeping) ___

Enuresis (bed wetting) ___

Frequent nightmares ___

Night terrors (terrifying nighttime outbursts) ___

Sleepwalking ___

Excessive sexual interest and preoccupation ___

Frequent sex play with other children ___

Excessive masturbation ___

Frequently likes to wear clothing of the opposite sex ___

Exhibits gestures and intonations of the opposite sex ___

Frequent headaches ___

Frequent stomach cramps ___

Frequent nausea and vomiting ___

Often complains of bodily aches and pains ___

Worries over bodily illness ___

Poor motivation ___

Apathy ___

Takes path of least resistance ___

Ever trying to avoid responsibility ___

Poor follow-through ___	Little, if any, response to punishment for anti-social behavior ___	Suspicious, distrustful ___
Low Curiosity ___	Few, if any, friends ___	Aloof ___
Open defiance of authority ___	Doesn't seek friendships ___	"Wise-guy" or smart aleck attitude ___
Blatently un-cooperative ___	Rarely sought by peers ___	Brags or boasts ___
Persistant lying ___	Not accepted by peer group ___	Bribes other children ___
Frequent use of profanity to parents, teachers, and other author-ities ___	Selfish ___	Excessively competitive ___
	Doesn't respect the rights of others ___	Often cheats when playing games ___
Truancy from school ___	Wants things own way with exag-gerated reaction if thwarted ___	"Sore loser" ___
Runs away from home ___		"Doesn't know when to stop" ___
Violent outbursts of rage ___	Trouble putting self in other person's position ___	Poor common sense in social situations ___
Stealing ___	Egocentric (self-centered) ___	Often feels cheated or gypped ___
Cruelty to animals, children, and others ___	Frequently hits other children ___	Feels others are persecuting him when there is no evidence for such ___
Destruction of property ___	Argumentative ___	
Criminal and/or dangerous acts ___	Excessively cri-tical of others ___	Always wants his or her own way ___
Trouble with the police ___	Excessively taunts other children ___	Very stubborn ___
Violent assault ___	Ever complaining ___	Obstruction-istic ___
Fire setting ___		
Little, if any, guilt over behavior that causes others pain and dis-comfort ___	Is often picked on and easily bullied by other children ___	Negativistic (does just the opposite of what is requested) ___

Quietly, or often silently, defiant of authority ___

Feigns or verbalizes compliance or cooperation but doesn't comply with requests ___

Drug abuse ___

Alcohol abuse ___

Very tense ___

Nail biting ___

Chews on clothes, blankets, etc. ___

Head banging ___

Hair pulling ___

Picks on skin ___

Speaks rapidly and under pressure ___

Irritability, easily "flies off the handle" ___

Fears
dark ___
new situations ___
strangers ___
being alone ___
death ___
separation from parent ___
school ___
visiting other children's homes ___
going away to camp ___
animals ___
other fears (name) ___

_____ ___

_____ ___

Anxiety attacks with palpatations (heart pounding), shortness of breath, sweating, etc. ___

Disorganized ___

Tics such as eye-blinking, grimacing, or other spasmodic repetitious movements ___

Involuntary grunts, vocalizations (understandable or not) ___

Stuttering ___

Depression ___

Frequent crying spells ___

Excessive worrying over minor things ___

Suicidal preoccupation, gestures, or attempts ___

Excessive desire to please authority ___

"Too good" ___

Often appears in-sincere and/or artificial ___

Too mature, frequently acts older than actual age ___

Excessive guilt over minor indiscretions ___

Asks to be punished ___

Low self-esteem ___

Excessive self-criticism ___

Very poor toleration of criticism ___

Feelings easily hurt ___

Dissatisfaction with appearance or body part(s) ___

Excessive modesty over bodily exposure ___

Perfectionistic, rarely satisfied with performance ___

Frequently blames others as a cover-up for own short-comings ___

Little concern for personal appearance or hygiene ___

Little concern for or pride in personal property ___

"Gets hooked" on certain ideas and remains pre-occupied ___

Compulsive repetition of seemingly meaningless physical acts ___

Shy ___

Inhibited self-expression in dancing, singing, laughing, etc. ___

Recoils from affectionate physical contact ___

Withdrawn	___	Mute (refuses to speak) but can	___	Flat emotional tone	___
Fears asserting self	___	Gullible and/or naive	___	Speech non-communicative or poorly communicative	___
Inhibits open expression of anger	___	Passive and easily led	___	Hears voices	___
Allows self to be easily taken advantage of	___	Excessive fantasizing, "lives in his (her) own world"	___	Sees visions	___
Frequently pouts and/or sulks	___				

As requested above, please first list below symptoms marked with the letter P and next to each symptom give descriptive information such as age of onset, age of termination, and other important data. Then list symptoms marked with an N and provide similar information.

P or N   Symptom   Brief Description

_____ _____   _____

_____ _____   _____

_____ _____   _____

_____ _____   _____

_____ _____   _____

_____ _____   _____

_____ _____   _____

_____ _____   _____

_____ _____   _____

_____ _____   _____

_____ _____   _____

_____ _____   _____

_____ _____   _____

_____ _____   _____

_____ _____   _____

_____ _____   _____

SIBLINGS

	Name	Age	Medical, social, or academic problems
1.			
2.			
3.			
4.			
5.			

LIST NAMES AND ADDRESSES OF ANY OTHER PROFESSIONALS CONSULTED

1. _____

2. _____

3. _____

4. _____

ADDITIONAL REMARKS

Please use the remainder of this page to write any additional comments you wish to make regarding your child's difficulties.

Appendix IV

Maternal Discipline Techniques— Self-Report Instrument

MATERNAL DISCIPLINE TECHNIQUES--SELF-REPORT INSTRUMENT

Typical Child Behavior Problems

ONE OF THE THINGS WE'RE INTERESTED IN IS HOW YOU HANDLE _____ WHEN S/HE MISBEHAVES. I AM GOING TO DESCRIBE SOME DIFFERENT WAYS IN WHICH CHILDREN DISOBEY THEIR PARENTS. I WOULD LIKE YOU TO IMAGINE YOUR CHILD IN EACH SITUATION AND TELL ME HOW YOU WOULD DEAL WITH HIM/HER.

1. You need to take _____ out for an errand and you don't have much time. You call out for him, but he does not answer. After calling a few more times, you begin to look for him. Soon you become worried, but then find out that he has been hiding from you.

First method: What would you do?

Second method: What if he did it again the next day? What would you do then?

Third method: What would you probably do if he did it once again?

2. You're shopping in a store and _____ is with you. He sees something that he likes and asks you if he can have it. You tell him "NO," but he demands to have it and starts crying and screaming.

First: What would you do?

Second: What if she continues crying and screaming? What would you do?

Third: What if she did it once again?

3. You're busy cooking in the kitchen and you tell _____ to stay out for a while. Instead he climbs up on a table and knocks over a bowl, spilling all of the food on the floor.

First: What would you do?

Second: What if she came back into the kitchen and climbed back onto the table?

Third: What if she did it once again?

4. You and your family are in a strange area with lots of people and you tell _____ not to go too far away. However, he soon wanders off and you have to go looking all over the place for him.

First: What would you do when you found him?

Second: What if he wanders off again and you had to go looking for him again? What would you do when you found him?

Third: What if it happened again? What would you do when you found him?

5. _____ and a neighbor's child are playing together in your living room. _____ asks to play with a toy, but th other child refuses. _____ gets angry, hits his playmate, and takes the toy.

First: What would you do?

Reproduced with permission of A. K. Gardner, S. Scarr, C. Schwarz, Yale University, New Haven, Conn.

MATERNAL DISCIPLINE TECHNIQUES--SELF-REPORT INSTRUMENT

Second: What if she did it again? What would you do?
Third: What if the next day, she did it again? What would you do?

6. After being told many times not to go into your closet, you come home to find
   that _____ has be playing there for a while and has made a big mess.
First: What would you do?
Second: What if later that same day you found him in your closet once again making
   a mess? What would you do?
Third: What if it happened again?

7. While playing in another room, _____ accidently breaks a lamp, but does not come
   and tell you. You know that he has done it.
First: What would you do?
Second: What if the next time he broke something, he didn't tell you? What would
   you do?
Third: What if it happened again?

8. _____ is especially rude to one the the grandparents.
First: What would you do?
Second: What if later that day, it happened again? What would you do?
Third: What if it happened again that same day?

9. _____ "acts up" by running around and making a lot of noise while a neighbor or
   casual acquaintance is visiting and talking with you.
First: What would you do?
Second: What if he continues to distract the two of you by making lost of noise?
   What would you do?
Third: What if it happened the next day? What would you do?

10. _____ has broken a very important possession of yours. When you ask him for
    an explanation, he denies having done it. You know he is lying.
First: What would you do?
Second: What if he continues to lie? What would you do?
Third: What if a similar thing happens the next day? What would you do? (Depending
   on the type of punishment described, could be replaced with: What if he still
   continues to lie?)

11. _____ refuses to go to bed when you tell him to.
First: What would you do?

Second: What if he still refuses to go to bed? What would you do then?
Third: What if the same thing happens the next night? What would you do?

12. Instead of eating his dinner, _____ plays with his food and then starts throwing it.
First: What would you do?
Second: What if he continues to throw his food? What would you do?
Third: What if he did the same thing at the next meal? What would you do?

13. You are busy in the kitchen, and you ask him to do you a favor by answering the door. Instead of helping out, he just says "No."
First: What would you do?
Second: What if he still refused? What would you do then?
Third: What if later that same day, you asked him to do you another small favor, and he refused? What would you do?

14. You and your family are outside. When you are not looking he runs into a busy street, falls down and starts crying and calling for you. You pick him up and see that he doesn't seem to be hurt.
First: What would you do?
Second: What if later that day, it happens again? What would you do?
Third: What if the next day, it happens again? What would you do?

15. You're very tired and _____ has been pestering you. You have told him to stop, but he continues to bother you.
First: What would you do?
Second: What if he continues to pester you? What would you do?
Third: What if later that day, he began to bother you again? What would you do?

16. You are in a store. _____ reaches up on the counter, takes something, hides it in his pocket and walks away.
First: What would you do?
Second: What if he refused to give it back? What would you do?
Third: What if the next day, he did the same thing in a store? What would you do?

Appendix V

Sample
Custody Evaluation

PSYCHIATRIC CUSTODY EVALUATION

August 25, 1981

Honorable James K. O'Brien
Supreme Court of New York
New York County
60 Centre Street
New York, New York 10007

Re: Johnson vs. Johnson
Docket No. M–3784–81

Dear Judge O'Brien:

This report is submitted in compliance with your court order dated June 9, 1981, requesting that I conduct an evaluation of the Johnson family in order to provide the court with information that would be useful to it in deciding which of the Johnson parents should have custody of their children Tara, Elaine, and Charles.

My findings and recommendations are based on interviews conducted as itemized below:

July 6, 1981 —	Mrs. Carol Johnson and Mr. Frank Johnson, seen jointly	2 hours
July 7, 1981 —	Mr. Frank Johnson	1 hour
July 11, 1981 —	Mrs. Carol Johnson	1 hour
July 13, 1981 —	Tara Johnson	1½ hours
July 14, 1981 —	Mr. Frank Johnson	1 hour
July 20, 1981 —	Mrs. Carol Johnson	1 hour
July 21, 1981 —	Charles Johnson	¾ hour
	Elaine Johnson	¾ hour

July 22, 1981 —	Tara Johnson	½ hour
	Mrs. Carol Johnson and	
	Tara Johnson, seen jointly	½ hour
July 24, 1981 —	Mrs. Carol Johnson	1 hour
July 27, 1981 —	Mrs. Carol Johnson and	
	Mr. Frank Johnson, seen jointly	1 hour
Aug. 3, 1981 —	Elaine Johnson	¾ hour
Aug. 4, 1981 —	Tara Johnson	¼ hour
	Mr. Frank Johnson and	
	Tara Johnson, seen jointly	½ hour
Aug. 10, 1981 —	Tara Johnson	
	Mr. Frank Johnson and	
	Mrs. Carol Johnson, seen jointly	¾ hour
Aug. 11, 1981 —	Tara Johnson	
	Elaine Johnson	
	Charles Johnson	
	Mrs. Carol Johnson and	
	Mr. Frank Johnson, seen jointly	¾ hour
Aug. 14, 1981 —	Tara Johnson	
	Elaine Johnson	
	Charles Johnson	
	Mrs. Carol Johnson and	
	Mr. Frank Johnson, seen jointly	1 hour
		16 hours

In addition, on Aug. 16, 1981, Mr. and Mrs. Johnson were seen together for the purpose of my presenting these findings and recommendations to them. This interview lasted two hours, bringing to 18 the total number of hours spent with the Johnson family in association with this evaluation.

Mr. Frank Johnson, an airline pilot, is 43 years old. His first wife died soon after the delivery of Tara, who is now 16 years of age. He married Mrs. Carol Johnson when Tara was 2 years old. Mrs. Johnson, a housewife, who was formerly an elementary school teacher, is now 40. Her first marriage ended in divorce. A child of this relationship died soon after birth. There are two children of the Johnson marriage: Elaine, 11, and Charles, 7. Mrs. Johnson adopted her stepdaughter Tara in July 1980. In October 1980, Mr. Johnson initiated divorce proceedings because he felt that his wife no longer respected him and that she was a poor mother for the children, especially his daughter Tara. However, Mr. and Mrs. Johnson are still occupying the same domicile.

Both parents are requesting custody of all three children. It is this examiner's recommendation that Mr. Frank Johnson be granted custody of Tara and that Mrs. Carol Johnson be granted custody of Elaine and Charles. The observations that have led me to these conclusions will be divided into four categories: 1) Mr. Frank Johnson's assets as a parent, 2) Mr. Frank Johnson's liabilities as a parent, 3) Mrs. Carol Johnson's assets as a parent, and 4) Mrs. Carol Johnson's liabilities as a parent. Following these four presentations I will comment further on the way in which my observations brought about the aforementioned recommendations. Although much information was obtained in the course of the evaluation, only those items specifically pertinent to the custody consideration will be included in this report.

Mr. Frank Johnson's Assets as a Parent

Mr. Frank Johnson is Tara's biological father. The special psychological tie that this engenders is not enjoyed by Mrs. Carol Johnson and Tara. It is not the genetic bond per se that is crucial here; rather, it is the psychological attachment that such a bond elicits. Mr. Johnson had already started to develop a psychological tie with Tara while his first wife was pregnant with her. He was actually present at her birth and assumed an active role in her rearing—almost from birth because of the illness and early death of his first wife. This situation prevailed until the time of his marriage to Mrs. Johnson when Tara was 2 years of age. Although Mrs. Johnson has been Tara's primary caretaker since then, Mr. Johnson's early involvement with Tara during these crucial years of her development contributes to a very strong psychological tie between them that has continued up to the present time.

My observations have convinced me, and both parents agree, that at this time, Tara has a closer relationship with her father than her mother. Her relationship with Mrs. Johnson at this time is characteristically a difficult one in that there are frequent battles and power struggles. Although Tara is not completely free of such involvement with her father, such hostile interaction is far less common. In my interviews with Mr. Johnson and Tara I found her to be far more friendly with him than I observed her to be with Mrs. Johnson in my joint interviews with them.

In every interview, both alone and in joint sessions with various members of the family, Tara openly and unswervingly stated that she wished to live with her father: "I want to live with my father. I am closer to him." "When I was younger, my mother did more things; but since I'm older, my father does more things." "My father listens to what I say; my mother doesn't."

Mr. Johnson and Tara both utilize a similar method of communication. Neither feels a strong need to give confirmation or examples to general statements that they make, and they are therefore comfortable with one another. Mrs. Johnson, on the other hand, is much more specific in her communications and this is a source of difficulty, not only in her relationship with Tara, but in her relationship with her husband as well.

All five family members agree that Mr. Johnson spends significant time with Charles, involved in typical father-son activities, sports, games, etc. It is also apparent that Charles has a strong masculine identification and this arose, in part, from his modeling himself after his father.

Mr. Frank Johnson's Liabilities as a Parent

Mr. Johnson states that he would not have involved himself in the custody evaluation conducted by this examiner if he had to contribute to its financing. Accordingly, Mrs. Johnson assumed the total financial obligation for this evaluation. I conclude from this that with regard to this particular criterion for comparing the parents Mr. Johnson's position is less strong than Mrs. Johnson's.

On many occasions Mr. Johnson made general comments about his superiority over his wife with regard to parental capacity. For example, "She's a very poor mother," "She neglects the children," and "If you had all the information you would see that I'm a better parent." However, it was extremely difficult to elicit from Mr. Johnson specific examples of incidents that would substantiate these statements. I not only considered this to be a manifestation of Mr. Johnson's problem in accurately communicating, but also considered it to be a deficiency in his position. One cannot be convinced of the strength of such statements if no examples can be provided to substantiate them.

In the hope that I might get more specific information from Mr. Johnson I asked him, on at least three occasions, to write a list of specifics that might help corroborate some of his allegations. He came to three subsequent interviews without having written anything in response to my invitation. I consider such failure to reflect a compromise in his motivation for gaining custody of the three children. When he did finally submit such a list it was far less comprehensive than that which was submitted by Mrs. Johnson and, in addition, the issues raised had far less significance, e.g., "She's late once in a while," "She's sometimes forgetful," and "She doesn't like playing baseball with Charles."

Although I described Mr. Johnson's communication problem as a factor supporting his gaining custody of Tara, I would consider it a liability with regard to his gaining custody of Elaine and Charles. Tara (possibly on a genetic basis) communicates in a similar way and so, as mentioned, is comfortable with her father when they communicate. Elaine and Charles, however, appear to be identifying with their mother with regard to communication accuracy. Accordingly, intensive exposure to Mr. Johnson might compromise what I consider a healthier communicative pattern.

Mr. Johnson's profession as an airline pilot has not enabled him to have predictable hours. Not only is his schedule variable, but there are times when he is required to work on an emergency basis. All three children agree that Mrs. Johnson is more predictably present. Mr. Johnson's irregular schedule is not a significant problem for Tara who, at 16, is fairly independent and would not suffer significantly from her father's schedule. The younger children, however, are still in need of predictability of parental presence and Mr. Johnson has not demonstrated his capacity to provide such predictability. In my final interview with Mr. Johnson he stated that he would change his work pattern to be available to his children during non-school hours. Mrs. Johnson was very dubious that this could be arranged because his job does not allow such flexibility. Both parents agreed, however, that it had not occurred in the past and that such predictability was not taking place at the time of this evaluation.

Both Charles and Elaine stated that they wanted to live with their mother and not live with their father. Charles stated, "I want to be with my mother. I'd be alone when my father goes to work." Elaine stated, "I want to live with my mother. I'm closer to my mother. I'm not as close to my father."

In a session in which I was discussing his future plans with Mr. Johnson, he stated that he was considering moving to California because he could earn more money there by supplementing his income with certain business ventures that he had been invited to participate in. He stated also that he would still move even if he were only to be granted custody of Tara. Although I appreciate that a higher income could provide Mr. Johnson's children with greater financial flexibility, I believe that the disadvantages of such a move would far outweigh its advantages from their point of view. Specifically, the extra advantages they might enjoy from such a move would be more than offset by the even greater absence of their father who, his liabilities notwithstanding, is still an important figure for them.

In an interview in which I discussed with Mr. Johnson how he would react to the various custodial decisions, he was far more upset about the prospect of losing Tara than he was about the possibility of losing Charles and Elaine. In fact, he appeared to be accepting of the fact that Elaine would go to her mother. Although somewhat distressed about the possibility of Charles' living with his mother, he did not show the same degree of distress as his wife over the prospect of losing the younger two children.

Mrs. Carol Johnson's Assets as a Parent

Mrs. Carol Johnson was far more committed to the custody evaluation than her husband. As mentioned, she was willing to make the financial sacrifices involved in the evaluation. I consider this to be a factor reflecting greater motivation than her husband for gaining custody of the children. Mrs. Johnson is more available to the children during non-school hours than her husband and this is one element in her favor regarding gaining custody, especially of the younger children. Mrs. Johnson is a more accurate and clearer communicator than her husband and this is an asset. As mentioned, the younger children do not seem to have been affected by their father's communication difficulty. Having them live with him might result in their acquiring this maladaptive trait.

During her pregnancy with Elaine Mrs. Johnson suffered with toxemia and associated high blood pressure and convulsions. Most physicians generally discourage women with this disorder from becoming pregnant again because it is genuinely life endangering. However, Mrs. Johnson did wish to have a third child, primarily because her husband, she states, was so desirous of having a son. Her pregnancy with Charles was complicated by the exacerbation of a preexisting asthmatic condition from which she states that she almost died. A less maternal woman would not have become pregnant again.

Elaine stated on many occasions, and in every interview, both alone and with other family members, that she wished to live with her mother: "I'm closer to my mother," "She's home more than my father," "They call my father to do things at work all the time," and "My mother has more feelings for me than my father."

Charles also, both in individual session and in joint interviews, emphatically stated that he wished to live with his mother: "I want to stay with my mother because she doesn't work as much as my father." "If you get sick the father might not know what to do, but the mother does." "My mother knows how to take care of me." "She doesn't work that much." "She reads me books more than my father."

On one occasion Mr. Johnson stated: "Carol is closer to Elaine than I am. They are similar. They're both sore losers. Both get emotional if they don't have their way." Mrs. Carol Johnson agrees that she and her daughter Elaine have these traits, but not to the degree described by her husband. Although there are certainly negative elements regarding the reasons why Mr. Johnson sees Elaine to be closer to his wife, this statement is an admission of his recognition of this preference of Elaine for her mother. The situation is analogous to Mr. Johnson's involvement with Tara. They are closer to one another, yet maladaptive and undesirable factors are contributing to the closeness.

Mrs. Carol Johnson's Liabilities as a Parent

Tara is not Mrs. Johnson's biological daughter. Although she has raised Tara from her infancy, as if she were her own biological child, and although she has adopted her, Mrs. Johnson is at a certain disadvantage regarding the development of a strong psychological parent-child tie. As mentioned, I believe that a biological relationship increases the strength of the psychological bond. Accordingly, Mrs. Johnson is at a disadvantage when compared to Mr. Johnson regarding this aspect of the custody consideration.

Mrs. Johnson and Tara have a poor relationship at this point. In my interviews with Mrs. Johnson and Tara I found the latter to view her mother scornfully and to be openly resentful of her authority. On one occasion Tara said: "She has a lot of nerve telling me what to do." Were this an isolated statement, it would probably not have much significance. However, all agreed that it epitomized her general attitude toward her mother. Although some of the scornful attitude Tara exhibits toward her mother can be viewed as age-appropriate, I believe the extent goes beyond what is to be expected for teen-agers.

Mrs. Johnson cannot provide Charles with the same kind of father model and father-type involvement that her husband can. Although she claims an interest in sports and a greater degree of facility than the average woman, it is still clear that her husband has been far more involved in this type of activity with his son than has Mrs. Johnson.

Mr. Johnson accuses Mrs. Johnson of being excessively punitive and too strong a disciplinarian. Mrs. Johnson claims that her husband is too lax with the children and does not implement proper disciplinary measures. I believe that it is most likely that Mrs. Johnson is a little too punitive and that Mr. Johnson is a little too lenient. However, neither parent exhibits these difficulties to a degree that would be significantly injurious to the children, nor would I consider this to be a factor compromising either of their capacities as parents. It is probable, however, that these differences are playing a role in Tara's antagonism to her mother and her gravitating toward her father.

In every interview, both individual and joint, Tara openly stated that she wished to live with her father. "I would be very unhappy if the judge made me go with my mother." "He can't make me live with my mother. I'd run away to my father if he did."

Conclusions and Recommendations

Weighing the above factors as best I can, I believe that the evidence is strongly in favor of Mr. Johnson being given custody of Tara. I believe, also, that the above evidence strongly supports the conclusion that Elaine should be given to Mrs. Johnson. Although there are certain arguments supporting Mr. Johnson's gaining custody of Charles, I believe that these are greatly outweighed by arguments in favor of Mrs. Johnson's gaining custody. Were the court to conclude that Tara would be better off living with Mrs. Johnson, I believe that there would be a continuation of the present hostilities, and this could be disruptive to the healthy psychological development of the younger children—if they were exposed to such hostile interactions over a long period. I believe that if Mr. Johnson were to be granted custody of Elaine and Charles it is most likely that they would suffer psychological damage. All things considered, I believe he is the less preferable parent for the younger children and, if they had to live with him, they would suffer emotional deprivations that could contribute to the development of psychiatric disorders.

Richard A. Gardner, M.D.

Appendix VI

Sample
Custody Evaluation

PSYCHIATRIC CUSTODY EVALUATION

November 17, 1981

Honorable Roberta Barnes
Superior Court of New Jersey
Chancery Division
Courthouse
Hackensack, New Jersey 07601

Re: Mercer vs. Mercer
Docket No. M-6093-81

Dear Judge Barnes:

    This report is submitted in compliance with your court order
dated September 9, 1981, requesting that I conduct an evaluation of
the Mercer family in order to provide the court with information
that would be useful to it in deciding which of the Mercer parents
should have custody of their two sons Richard and Victor.
    My findings and recommendations are based on interviews con-
ducted as itemized below:

Oct. 15, 1981 —	Mr. Bernard Mercer and Mrs. Gloria Mercer, seen jointly	2 hours
Oct. 16, 1981 —	Mrs. Gloria Mercer	1 hour
Oct. 19, 1981 —	Mr. Bernard Mercer	1½ hours
Oct. 20, 1981 —	Mrs. Gloria Mercer	1½ hours
Oct. 22, 1981 —	Richard Mercer	1 hours
	Victor Mercer	1 hour
Oct. 26, 1981 —	Mrs. Gloria Mercer	1 hour
	Mr. Bernard Mercer	1 hour
Oct. 29, 1981 —	Ms. Dorothy Burns	1 hour
Oct. 30, 1981 —	Mr. Bernard Mercer and Mrs. Gloria Mercer, seen jointly	2 hours

Nov. 3, 1981 —	Mr. Bernard Mercer and Mrs. Gloria Mercer, seen jointly	2 hours
Nov. 5, 1981 —	Mr. Bernard Mercer Mrs. Gloria Mercer Richard Mercer and Victor Mercer, seen jointly	2 hours
		17 hours

In addition, these findings and recommendations were discussed with Mr. and Mrs. Mercer in a 2-hour interview conducted on November 10, 1981, bringing to 19 the total number of hours devoted to this evaluation.

Mr. Bernard Mercer is a 45-year-old president of a computer consultation service. He was born in Mexico, where his father was in the public service. When he was 5, his family moved to Washington, D.C., where he was raised and educated. Mrs. Gloria Mercer is a 42-year-old housewife who was born and raised in Atlanta, Georgia. At 18 she moved to live and work in Washington, D.C. The Mercers have two children. Richard, age 13, born on August 10, 1968, is presently in the 7th grade. Victor, age 12, born on September 18, 1969, is presently in the 6th grade. Both children attend the local public junior high school.

Mr. and Mrs. Mercer were married on March 4, 1966 in Washington, D.C. It was the first marriage for each. In 1970 the Mercers moved to New Jersey where Mr. Mercer began his computer consultation service. He considered his background education in engineering and business to qualify him for this career and his business has done quite well. Mr. Mercer states, and Mrs. Mercer agrees, that he is highly respected in his field for both efficiency and honesty.

Mr. and Mrs. Mercer were separated on April 14, 1981. Mrs. Mercer initiated the separation, requesting her husband to leave the home because she "found his presence there intolerable." She describes him as having been uninvolved in the welfare of the family for many years, to the point where the home was only his "official address." Mr. Mercer states that he reluctantly acquiesced, not wishing to live with someone who considered him "obnoxious to live with." Upon leaving the home Mr. Mercer moved into the apartment of Ms. Dorothy Burns, where he has been living ever since. The children have continued to live with their mother.

Each parent has many criticisms of the other, both with regard to child-rearing capacity as well as other areas of functioning. Each would consider it detrimental to the children if they had to live with the other on an ongoing basis—thus the litigation over their custody. It is this examiner's opinion that Mrs. Gloria Mercer should have custody of both children. The findings and observations that have led me to this conclusion will be divided into four categories: 1) Mr. Bernard Mercer's assets as a parent, 2) Mr. Bernard Mercer's liabilities as a parent, 3) Mrs. Gloria Mercer's assets as a parent, and 4) Mrs. Gloria Mercer's liabilities as a parent. In addition, the comments made by Ms. Dorothy Burns (with whom Mr. Mercer is presently living and whom he states he plans to marry upon the finalization of his divorce) will also be discussed. Finally, the reasons for my conclusions and recommendations will be presented. Although much information was obtained in the course of the evaluation, only those items specifically pertinent to the custody consideration will be included in this report.

Mr. Bernard Mercer's Assets as a Parent

Mr. Bernard Mercer's deep involvement in the evaluation and his strong desire to have custody of the children are a manifestation of his commitment to them. Although his wife and the boys consider vengeance to be an important motivating factor in Mr. Mercer's attempts to gain custody, I believe that loving feelings as well are operative.

Mr. Mercer, despite reduced commitment to visiting his children's schools, has always been and is still highly committed to the educational process. He has masters degrees both in computer engineering and business administration. He has actively been devoted to a business which he founded and which has grown considerably in the ensuing eleven years. He has thereby served as a good model for his children with regard to education and hard work.

Mrs. Mercer and the children describe Mr. Mercer as having always been reliable in paying for family expenses, both prior to and since the separation. When asked to say the best things he could about his father, Richard answered, "Since my father and mother have been separated, he's asked more about our homework and he's caring more about us. Before he left the house, he didn't give a damn." However, both boys describe their father as spending some time with them on most weekends before the separation and that this has continued since Mr. Mercer has left the home. His main activities with the boys have been attending sporting events such as football and hockey and playing electronic games.

Mr. Mercer describes great interest in seeing his children as much as possible at this time. He states that he appreciates that the separation is a deprivation for them and he wants to make up for this as much as possible. However, Mrs. Mercer and the two boys consider this interest as primarily having begun at about the time of the separation and that it is artificial. They all consider it a manifestation of his interest in impressing this examiner and the court.

Mr. Mercer's Liabilities as a Parent

Mrs. Mercer states that for many years prior to the separation her husband had not psychologically been a member of the family. She states that he did not return home until 1:00–2:00 A.M., two to three nights a week, claiming that he had to entertain clients. And such absences began about two years after the marriage. She suspected strongly that her husband was spending time with other women, but he always denied this. However, she considers her suspicions to have been confirmed by the fact that her husband moved into the apartment of Ms. Dorothy Burns immediately after the separation. Mr. Mercer agrees that the home was not psychologically his primary base because his wife so frequently complained about him. He states that she was always criticizing his manners and frequently portrayed him as inept and incompetent. Mrs. Mercer agrees that she did frequently criticize her husband, but believes, as well, that most of her criticisms were warranted.

Mr. Mercer gives religious differences as another reason for his withdrawal from the home. Although both of the Jewish faith, he describes himself as much more religious than his wife and this has resulted in conflict over such issues as keeping a kosher home and the children's religious education.

When Richard was asked about his father's involvement in the family, he stated, "My father never cared much about what happened to the family. He would come home late two or three nights a week, long after we went to sleep. But he was around sometimes on weekends and we would do things with him then. He does care about paying bills. But he hardly ever helped us with our homework. He never took us out to nice places for dinner. Just to places like McDonald's."

When Victor was asked about his father's involvement in the home prior to the separation, he stated, "He wasn't home a lot. He was always out on business; he wouldn't come home 'till very late. When I got sick my mother was always there, but my father wasn't. My father never visited my school; my mother always did. He didn't even know who my teachers were or even my orthodontist. He only went to my school once and that was last year. He's making believe now that he's more interested so he can tell the court that he's a good father. He asks me a lot of questions now so that he'll know what to tell the judge." On another occasion Victor stated, "My father never went to any of the parents' meetings at school or anything like that. Now when we visit with him he asks me a lot of questions about school so everyone will think he knows a lot. He was never interested before."

Mr. Mercer reluctantly agreed with the boys' and his wife's complaints that he rarely attended school functions, such as parent-teacher meetings and school plays. However, he describes more participation in school events than his family describes. He states that there was much more participation on his part in school plays than the children recognize. He states that it was not uncommon for him to arrive late and leave early and this is why the boys view him to be noninvolved. He describes business obligations as the reason for his limited appearances. Mrs. Mercer basically supports the opinion of the children that he rarely attended at all, but she does agree that there were a few such appearances. Both boys and their mother consider Mr. Mercer's statement about coming to school functions late and leaving early to be fabrications—formulated to make a better impression on the examiner. Mr. Mercer gives as another reason for rare attendance the fact that his wife frequently criticized him at such functions and accused him of inappropriate behavior at school. Mr. Mercer seems not to appreciate that he is not providing valid reasons for such absences. His failure to appreciate that he is rationalizing his impaired involvement is a liability with regard to paternal capacity.

Mrs. Mercer describes her husband as slovenly and unkempt in his habits. She states that it was only for his interviews with this examiner that he had taken the trouble to dress in a more tidy fashion. Both boys agree with their mother's complaint about their father's slovenly habits. Mrs. Mercer also complains that her husband embarrasses her at times by telling off-color jokes at inappropriate times. She does not consider such humor to be offensive per se. She only feels that he is injudicious with regard to the situations in which he tells such jokes. For example, she describes his telling off-color jokes to the children's teachers, and especially enjoys telling them to those who appear prim and proper. Mr. Mercer describes himself to have a good sense of humor and admits telling such jokes to the children's teachers, but denies that they were alienated by them.

Both Mr. and Mrs. Mercer come from families that were not particularly religious. However, in recent years Mr. Mercer has become increasingly religious and has placed pressures on his wife to keep a kosher home. She has consistently refused and this has been a source of friction. In addition, about five years ago, Mr. Mercer began to insist that the children be enrolled in an Orthodox Hebrew school in order to prepare for their bar mitzvahs at 13. Again, Mrs. Mercer refused to comply with this request, claiming that she did not wish her children exposed to such a rigorous religious experience. Her own preference would have been that the children not have bar mitzvahs at all and that they not attend Hebrew school. A compromise was arrived at with the children being enrolled in a Reform temple. In addition, Mrs. Mercer agreed to allow the boys to have bar mitzvahs. However, the religious issue was not resolved that simply. Throughout the years Mr. Mercer has continually placed great pressures on the children to involve themselves in great depth in their religion. He places pressure on them to go to the temple when they do not wish to go. At such times Mrs. Mercer intervenes and insists that they not be forced to attend if they do not wish to.

Regarding this issue, Richard stated, "My father is a hypocrite. He's really not that religious. Yes, he goes to temple sometimes, but he doesn't really know what the hell he's doing. He's always trying to get us to study Hebrew, and I just don't like Hebrew. It's boring. I'm glad I had a bar mitzvah, because of all of the presents. But I don't need all of that religious bunk. I wish my father would get off my back."

With regard to the religious issue, Victor stated, "My father's always telling us that we should study Hebrew more and that we should be more religious. He's always criticizing my mother for not keeping a kosher home. He only eats kosher foods in the home, even though my mother will buy nonkosher foods. But he'll eat pork in a Chinese restaurant. He's a hypocrite. I wish he'd leave me and my brother alone with all this religious stuff. I'm going to have a bar mitzvah because it will be a big party. I'm glad my mother protects us when he starts getting on our back with religion."

It is not Mr. Mercer's religiiosity that is in itself a parental liability. It is his coercive qualities that are a paternal detriment. The boys are clearly being placed in the middle of a tug-of-war over the religious issue and Mr. Mercer is not giving them the flexibility that is warranted for children their age.

Mrs. Mercer states that her husband does not respect the boys' privacy when their friends come to the home. Rather, he insists upon joining the group and does not respect his sons' complaints to their father that they be allowed to be alone with their friends. Both boys and Mrs. Mercer consider this to be an important reason why the children's friends refuse to come to the house, and they consider it a factor in Richard's poor peer relationships. Mr. Mercer denies this degree of intrusiveness and describes his involvement as noncoercive. He states that he is just trying to be friendly with the boys. Regarding this issue, Richard stated, "He embarrasses me in front of my friends. He tries to be with my friends when I don't want him to. He asks them about things they don't want to talk about, like sex." Mrs. Mercer also describes her husband as rejecting Victor's friends. Whereas he tries to befriend Richard's friends, he openly alienates Victor's. When Victor was asked about this, he stated, "He never likes any of my friends. He wouldn't let me take any of my friends with us. Often he'll ask my friends to leave." A good parent is sensitive to the importance of children's friendships and is particularly sensitive to the fact that reasonably accommodating friends in the home is important for children's healthy growth and development. Mr. Mercer does not seem to be sensitive to this fact and such insensitivity is a parental deficiency.

Mrs. Mercer describes both children as being afraid of their father. Victor agrees and claims that he is fearful of his father's rage outbursts. This problem exhibits itself in the children's reactions toward their father helping them with their homework. All four members of the family agree that Mr. Mercer spent much more time helping Richard with his homework than he did with Victor. Mr. Mercer states that he often offered to help Victor with his homework, but that he refused. Victor agrees that this was often the case and that he refused because of his father's bad temper and impatience when he would make mistakes. Mr. Mercer agreed that he was often short-tempered with Victor and not typically so with Richard.

All four family members agree that Richard has a problem in expressing hostility toward his father. All four agree, also, that this problem is related, in part, to Mr. Mercer's outbursts of rage. Although the problem is partly Richard's, it also is a reflection of parental deficiency on Mr. Mercer's part. Richard's contribution to the difficulty is his excessive timidity and fear of self-assertion. Mr. Mercer's contribution relates to his volatility and poor impulse control. With regard to Richard's fear of his father, Victor stated, "Richard's afraid to say no to anyone. But he'll say no to my mother because he's not afraid of her like he's afraid of my father."

Both children and Mrs. Mercer are in agreement that Mr. Mercer shows preference for Richard over Victor. Throughout their lives the boys state that their father gave Richard much more expensive presents than he gave Victor. With regard to this criticism, Mr. Mercer stated, "I don't calculate the amount." The mother and boys agree that this preference for Richard over Victor was not simply confined to gifts. From earliest infancy Mr. Mercer was described as having much preferred to cuddle with Richard than with Victor. In addition, the mother and both children agree that when Richard and Victor have a fight, Mr. Mercer is much more likely to put the blame on Victor. Even Richard agrees that there were many times when he recognized that he was the initiator of a fight and yet his father would blame his brother. In response to this criticism, Mr. Mercer stated that Victor was the more aggressive one and therefore got more of the blame. The other three family members all state that this is a distortion on Mr. Mercer's part and that Victor was by no means the more aggressive of the two children with regard to initiating fights. Mr. Mercer did agree, however, that there probably is some preference for Richard related to the fact that he was the first born. He does not appear to appreciate that his reason is a rationalization.

With regard to this preference, Richard stated, "My father's more patient with me. He gives me bigger presents than he gives Victor. I don't feel good when my brother gets a smaller present." Mr. Mercer's preference does not simply show insensitivity to Victor, but Richard does not appear to be reacting positively to the preference either. At some level Richard appears to recognize that such favoritism reflects a parental deficiency.

Each parent was given a questionnaire for each of the two children. This questionnaire is generally given to parents at the beginning of a consultation and is quite comprehensive. It generally takes about an hour to complete. On page 4, the parent is asked to list the age at which the child reached each of twenty important developmental milestones (sat without support, walked without assistance, bowel-trained day, bowel-trained night, etc.). On Victor's questionnaire Mrs. Mercer indicated the exact times for nineteen of the twenty items. Mr. Mercer could not indicate exact times for any of the items, but could only check off under the column "early," "at the normal time," or "late." The same ratio was present for Richard's questionnaire. These responses reflect far greater knowledge of developmental details on Mrs. Mercer's part than on her husband's part.

The boys were asked what visitation arrangements they would like to have if the judge were to grant their mother custody. Richard responded, "I don't like to see him very often, but I go because they make me. He often talks about the family problems and I don't want to talk about it. He often talks about religion and I don't want to discuss it. He asks me a lot of questions about school so he'll have information for the judge. I know that. He makes me feel bad when I say I don't want to go. If I tell him I don't want to go with him he gives me a guilt trip. He'll tell me it makes him very upset and makes him feel bad when I don't want to go. If I saw him once a week, just the one day, that would be enough." With regard to the same question, Victor replied, "I'm supposed to see him every other weekend and once a week during the week, but I don't want to see him that much. I'd like to see him about half of that time. I really don't like to see him that much. He makes me feel bad if I tell him I don't want to go there. I don't like being with that woman he lives with. And I don't want him to talk to me so much about religion. I don't want to see him because I have homework, or I'm busy, or I'm tired, or I just don't want to see him."

In the family interview conducted on November 5, 1981 (the last data-collecting interview of the evaluation), both Richard and Victor appeared to be fearful of expressing criticism of their father. They did ultimately overcome some of their embarrassment and fear. Then Richard stated, "He hasn't been a good father. He hasn't been the kind of father who takes care of his children all the time. He hasn't gone to school presentations or plays or PTA meetings or been home very much. He doesn't treat us nicely. He's always giving us this religious bit and trying to force us to go to temple. He embarrasses me in front of my friends and I don't want to bring them home."

Victor, although initially hesitant to express himself, finally said, "My brother's right, he hasn't been a good father to us. I know he's always preferred my brother over me. He doesn't like my friends and they don't like him. He always gave my brother bigger presents. He never went to school or anything like that. He doesn't even know our teachers. He's always bothering us to go to temple. He's never been a real father in the home."

In that interview Mr. Mercer attempted to defend himself by stating that he removed himself from the home because of his wife's criticisms. He gave the same reason for his poor school attendance. To this Richard replied, "That's not a good reason for staying away from the home so much and for not going to school meetings." It is clear here that Richard does not accept his father's rationalizations for withdrawing from school and home activities.

It was apparent from the family interview of November 5, 1981 that even if some of the children's antagonism toward their father is unwarranted and even if there has been some brainwashing on Mrs. Mercer's part, Mr. Mercer has lost his children psychologically and that to have him gain custody would be detrimental to them.

Mrs. Gloria Mercer's Assets as a Parent

Mrs. Mercer describes deep involvement in the children's interests and activities. And the boys confirm her version of her involvement. She describes herself as being actively involved with the teachers of each of the schools they attended. She describes full attendance at all school concerts, plays, PTA meetings, teacher conferences, etc. She describes her husband as hardly ever attending these and on those rare occasions when he did so, he invariably came late or left early.

Richard openly stated that he preferred to live with his mother: "I don't want to live with my father and his girl friend Dorothy. I don't like Dorothy that much. Besides, she has to go to work all day, while my mother is home when we get out of school. And my father also has to work all day, and he also comes home very late. I'd have to come home to an empty house. My mother is home when I come home from school. My father and Dorothy say that they care for us a lot. But after the divorce they'll not care for me as much as they say. They are only saying that now so that my father can get custody. Now Dorothy's acting nice and trying to do the things I want. I know that after the divorce my father and her will do less of the things that I want. I know that. After the divorce he'll go back to doing the things he did before he decided he wanted us to live with him. He used to scream a lot and he'll start doing it again. He was disgusting to look at in the morning. He didn't bathe or shower very much so his body smelled sometimes. He used to gobble up his food. Now he's putting on a show. He never wanted to do that much with me before. I'd like to stay living with my mother. I'll visit my father once in awhile, but I don't want to live with him. My father would get angry with me if I told him how much I want to live with my mother. Also he'll make me feel guilty. He'll say, 'How can you do this to me? How can you hurt me so much?'" When Richard was asked whom he thought his brother would prefer to live with, he stated, "My brother told me and my mother both that he wants to stay with her. My brother gets into a lot of fights with my father. Also, he doesn't like my brother's friends. My brother is very upset about Dorothy Burns. He doesn't think it's right for him to live that way without being married."

When Victor was asked to discuss his preference, he stated, "I want to live with my mother. She cares more about us than my father does. My father never came to school events. He didn't care very much about us. My mother is much nicer to us and more interested in us. My father is a phony. He's acting like he loves us very much, but I don't think he does. And he's always talking about religion and temple. And I certainly don't want to live with that woman Dorothy Burns. Since he left the house he's trying to be nice only because he wants to get custody. I think he wants to get custody so he can hurt my mother. He's just trying to put on a good show now, but it won't work. I'll never live with him and that woman. My mother's right, she's a tramp for living with him without being married."

Mrs. Gloria Mercer's Liabilities as a Parent

Mrs. Mercer exhibits a moralistic, although not uncommon, reaction to Mr. Mercer's woman friend, Ms. Dorothy Burns. She described at length how psychologically detrimental it is for the boys to visit with Mr. Mercer and Ms. Burns, as long as they are living together and not married. She does not seem to appreciate that denigrating her husband's woman friend compromises the relationship the children have with their father and deprives them of the potential benefits of their relationship with him that they might otherwise have were she not to be so critical. Both children appear to have taken on this highly moralistic attitude regarding their father's living with Ms. Dorothy Burns while still legally married to their mother.

In my evaluations of the children I found nothing to indicate that they were exhibiting detrimental psychological reactions to their experiences with Ms. Dorothy Burns. I believe that Mrs. Mercer is exhibiting a common reaction of wives to their divorcing husbands' new women friends: jealousy and anger. And the children are being used as weapons to vent her rage. Although such reactions are common, it is psychologically injurious to the children if such mothers try to wreak vengeance on the father by discouraging the children's visiting with him when he is with the new woman friend or denigrating him for the new relationship. Mrs. Mercer, however, was willing to go along with my suggestion that she not discourage the children from visitations simply because their father was not married to Ms. Burns. Accordingly, I consider this defect to be less severe than it would be if she were absolutely adamant in her refusal to reconsider her position.

Although many of Mrs. Mercer's criticisms of her husband

appear to be accurate (as confirmed by the children and even Mr. Mercer himself), she does make false criticisms as well—criticisms that unnecessarily compromise him in the eyes of his children. For example, she complained that during each of the visitations her husband prevented the boys from calling her. She states that this was especially the case during a two-week vacation that they took with him to Canada last summer to visit members of his family. Both children flatly deny that their father prohibited them; in fact, they claim that he encouraged them to do so. In addition, Mr. Mercer denies that he discouraged the children from calling their mother during that vacation. In fact, he states that he encouraged it. Another probable distortion is Mrs. Mercer's complaint that Mr. Mercer typically denigrated the children mercilessly when disciplining them—calling them names such as "stupid," "idiot," and "dumb little bastard." Mr. Mercer and the children deny frequent use of such terminology. They can only recall such terms being used on extremely rare occasions.

Mr. Mercer complains that his wife often compared him unfavorably to others and that frequently she made such unfavorable comparisons to the children. He stated, "She'll say that another man is a better father than I am or she'll say, pointing to the other man, 'He's a real man.'" Richard and Victor agree that their mother does make such criticisms about their father in front of them. Regarding this, Richard stated, "She does say things like, 'I wish you kids could have had a father like that.' It makes me think that I wish I had." Although Mr. Mercer has a valid complaint here, both children agree that their mother's basic criticisms of their father are valid.

Mr. Mercer claims that his wife is overprotective of the children and tends to keep them in an infantilized state. He describes Richard as often complaining of minor physical illnesses and tending to exaggerate the slightest physical complaint. He describes his wife as indulging such symptoms and keeping Richard out of school unnecessarily. In a detailed discussion of this issue, I could not conclude that Mrs. Mercer is overprotective. I found no evidence for the kind of indulgence Mr. Mercer describes. However, both Richard and Mrs. Mercer describe Mrs. Mercer as doing just the opposite, namely, forcing Richard to go to school when he complains of minor illnesses. Another example of the overprotectiveness Mr. Mercer describes is his complaint that Mrs. Mercer keeps Richard in bed long after an illness is over, often requiring him to remain out of school three days after he is afebrile. Both Richard and Mrs. Mercer deny this. Victor also denies having observed this. Mr. Mercer describes his wife as excessively concerned about the children's riding their bikes in the neighborhood. Mrs. Mercer admits she has warned the boys to be careful, as any mother would, but does not consider her concerns exaggerated. The children agree that their mother's concerns are no greater than those of their friends' mothers. My basic conclusion regarding the overprotective complaint on Mr. Mercer's part was that there was little if any validity to it.

When Richard was asked about anything he could say about his mother that he would like changed, he answered, "Nothing big comes to mind." He was then asked about small criticisms that he might have about her. He replied, "She used to drink too much coffee—five to six cups a day." Similarly, when Victor was asked about any criticisms he could make about his mother, he was not able to provide any answers. I consider the children's inability to think of meaningful criticisms of their mother not to be a manifestation of significant inhibitions on their part. Rather, it reflects their deep devotion to her and an appreciation of her loving commitment over the years.

Dorothy Burns

Ms. Dorothy Burns, the woman friend with whom Mr. Mercer is presently living, was seen in interview on October 29, 1981. Ms. Burns' primary contact with the children has been short contacts during a few visits. She described Richard as being warm in his relationship with her; however, she describes Victor as having been more aloof.

Ms. Burns is 32 years old and states that she presently lives with Mr. Mercer, who moved into her apartment on April 14, 1981. She states that she and Mr. Mercer plan to marry soon after his divorce is finalized. (In a separate interview Mr. Mercer confirmed this.) She states that if Mr. Mercer gains custody, they plan to buy a house so that she, Mr. Mercer, and the two boys can live together. Ms. Burns is a computer programmer and has a full-time job. She was married once before, at age 22, and separated from her husband 1½ years later. There were no children by that marriage.

Considering the extremely limited contact that Ms. Burns has had with the children and considering the deep involvement that Mrs. Mercer has had with them, as well as the absence of significant pathology in Mrs. Mercer's relationships with the children, it is hard to imagine that the children could relate in any but the most superficial way with Ms. Burns at this time. There was nothing in the interview with Ms. Burns that warranted my concluding that she would be a detrimental influence. Rather, her situation is such that she could only play a miniscule role at this point as a mother substitute, considering the deep and involved investment the children have with their mother.

Conclusions and Recommendations

It is my opinion that the evidence for Mrs. Mercer's retaining custody of the children is formidable. The boys' relationship with their mother is a far deeper one than that which they have with their father. They have many bitter criticisms of their father which date back to the earliest years of their lives. They do not view him as a man who has been deeply committed to the home and Mr. Mercer agrees that this has been the case, but rationalizes his impaired involvement with very weak and unconvincing excuses. The children are particularly bitter over his failure to involve himself in a meaningful way with their school, parent-teacher meetings, school plays, etc. Mr. Mercer does not seem to appreciate how crucial these events are for school children and how pained and disappointed his children were over his failure to involve himself. They, like their mother, view him as a "boarder" in the home. In addition, the boys fear his outbursts of rage, see him as preferring Richard over Victor (both consider this a defect), and find him guilt-evoking and intrusive. Lastly, they resent his coercive religious attitudes.

Their relationship with their potential maternal surrogate, Ms. Dorothy Burns, is at best a most superficial one. Their involvement with her is miniscule compared to that which they have with their mother, and it is reasonable to say that their relationship with her could never approach even a small fraction of the intensity of the relationship they enjoy with their mother. It is not that Ms. Dorothy Burns is grossly deficient in this regard; it is merely that she is a newcomer and it cannot be expected that a relationship that the children can presently have with her could in any way approach the intensity of the one these children have with their mother. Lastly, Ms. Burns and Mr. Mercer have work obligations that necessitate their being out of the home all day; whereas Mrs. Mercer is freely available to be at home when the children return from school, as well as when they have to miss school for sickness, weather, etc.

It is my recommendation that Mr. Mercer be granted flexible visitation privileges. I would not recommend, however, that the children be forced to see their father more frequently than they wish to. At their ages their wishes regarding visitation should be given the greatest respect.

Richard A. Gardner, M.D.

References

Abrahms, S. (1979), The joint-custody controversy. *New York*, June 18, 1979.

Bazelon, D.L. (1974), The perils of wizardry. *The American Journal of Psychiatry*, 131:1317–1322.

Beck, P.W. (1977), The law of child custody. *The Journal of Legal Medicine*, January, 1977, pp. 8CC–8FF.

Bellak, L. and Bellak, S.S. (1949), *The Children's Apperception Test*. New York: The Psychological Corp.

Benedek, E.P. (1972), Child custody laws: their psychiatric implications. *The American Journal of Psychiatry*, 129:326–328.

_____ and Benedek, R.S. (1979), Joint custody: solution or illusion? *American Journal of Psychiatry*, 136(12):1540–1544.

Buck, J.N. (1946), *The House-Tree-Person Test*. Los Angeles, California: Western Psychological Services.

Cardozo, B. (1925), Finlay v. Finlay. 148 N.E. p. 626.

Coogler, O.J. (1977), Changing the lawyer's role in matrimonial practice. *Conciliation Courts Review*, 15(1):1–7.

_____ (1978), *Structured Mediation in Divorce Settlement*. Lexington, Mass.: D.C. Heath and Company.

Derdeyn, A.P. (1975), Child custody consultation. *American Journal of Orthopsychiatry*, 45(5), 791–801.

_____ (1976a), Child custody contests in historical perspective. *American Journal of Psychiatry*, 133:1369–1376.

_____ (1976b), A consideration of legal issues in child custody contests. *Archives of General Psychiatry*, 33:165–171.

_____ (1978), Child custody: a reflection of cultural change. *Journal of Clinical Child Psychology*, 7(3):169–173.

Despert, L. (1953), *Children of Divorce*. Garden City, New York: Dolphin Books, Doubleday and Co., Inc.

Dullea, G. (1980), Is joint custody good for children? *The New York Times Magazine*, Feb. 3, 1980.

Duncan, J.W. (1978), Medical, psychologic, and legal aspects of child custody disputes. *Mayo Clinic Proceedings*, 53:463–468.

Eder, V. (1979), Shared custody—an idea whose time has come. *Joint Custody: A Handbook for Judges, Lawyers, and Counselors*, pp. B22–B23. Portland, Oregon: The Association of Family Conciliation Courts.

Fain, H.M. (1977), Family law—"whither now?" *Journal of Divorce*, 1(1):31–42.

Forer, L.G. (1975), *The Death of the Law*. New York: David McKay Co., Inc.

Foster, H.H. and Freed, D.J. (1978), Life with Father: 1978. *The Family Law Quarterly*, 11:321–362.

Freud, A. and Burlingham, D.T. (1944a), *War and Children*. New York: International Universities Press.

_____ (1944b), *Infants Without Families*. New York: International Universities Press.

Gardner, A.K., Scarr, S., and Schwarz, C. (1980), Maternal discipline techniques—questionnaire. (unpublished manuscript)

Gardner, R.A. (1968), The Mutual storytelling technique—use in alleviating childhood oedipal problems. *Contemporary Psychoanlysis*, 4:161–177.

_____ (1970), *The Boys and Girls Book About Divorce*. New York: Jason Aronson, Inc.

_____ (1971a), *The Boys and Girls Book About Divorce*, paperback edition. New York: Bantam Books.

_____ (1971b), *Therapeutic Communication With Children: The Mutual Storytelling Technique*. New York: Jason Aronson, Inc.

_____ (1973a), *Understanding Children—A Parents Guide to Child Rearing*. Cresskill, New Jersey: Creative Therapeutics.

_____ (1973b), *The Talking, Feeling, and Doing Game*. Cresskill, New Jersey: Creative Therapeutics.

_____ (1973c), Women's liberation, sexual development, and children's play. *Medical Aspects of Human Sexuality*, 2(1):7–12.

_____ (1976), *Psychotherapy with Children of Divorce*. New York: Jason Aronson, Inc.

_____ (1977), *The Parents Book About Divorce*. Garden City, New York: Doubleday and Co., Inc.

_____ (1979a), The psychiatrist as impartial expert in custody litigation. *New York Matrimonial Practice—1979. Course Handbook*, 54:293–307. New York: Practising Law Institute.

_____ (1979b). *The Parents Book About Divorce*, paperback edition. New York: Bantam Books.

_____ (1979c), Intergenerational sexual tensions in second marriages. *Medical Aspects of Human Sexuality*, 13(8):77ff.

_____ (1982), *The Boys and Girls Book About Stepfamilies*. New York: Bantam Books, Inc.

Gettleman, S. and Markowitz, J. (1974), *The Courage to Divorce*. New York: Simon and Schuster.

Glieberman, H.A. (1975), *Confessions of a Divorce Lawyer*. Chicago: Henry Regnery Co.

Goldstein, J., Freud, A., and Solnit, A.J. (1973), *Beyond the Best Interests of the Child*. New York: The Free Press (a division of Macmillan Publishing Company, Inc.).

Goldzband, M.G. (1980), *Custody Cases and Expert Witnesses: A Manual for Attorneys*. New York: Harcourt Brace Jovanovich.

Group for the Advancement of Psychiatry (1980), *Divorce, Child Custody and the Family*. New York: Mental Health Materials Center.

Holsopple, J.Q. and Miale, F.R. (1954), *Sentence Completion: A Projective Method for the Study of Personality*. Springfield, Illinois: Charles C Thomas.

James, R.J. (1978), Psychiatry and the family law bill. *Australian and New Zealand Journal of Psychiatry*, 12:119–122.

Kestenbaum, C. and Underwood, S. (1979), *Mental Health Assessment Form, Addendum: Maternal Attitudes and Adaptation*. New York: St. Luke's Hospital Center.

Kirshner, S.G. (1979), Child custody determination—a better way! *University of Louisville School of Law: Journal of Family Law*, 17(2): 275–296.

Kritzberg, N. (1966), A new verbal projective test for the expansion of the projective aspects of the clinical interview. *Acta Paedopsychiatrica*, 33(2):48–62.

Kubie, L.S. (1964), Provisions for the care of divorced parents: a new legal instrument. *Yale Law Journal*, 73:1197–1200.

Lambuth, D. (1923), The Golden Book on Writing. Hanover, New Hampshire: Dartmouth College.

Levy, A.M. (1978a), Child custody determination—a proposed psychiatric methodology and its resultant case typology. Journal of Psychiatry and Law, 6(2):189–214.

_____ (1978b), The resolution of child custody cases—the courtroom or the consultation room. Journal of American Psychiatry and Law, 6(4):499–517.

_____ (1980), The meaning of the child's preference in child custody determination. Journal of Psychiatry and Law, 8(2):221–234.

Lewis, M. (1974), The latency child in a custody conflict. Journal of the American Academy of Child Psychiatry, 13:635–647.

Lindsley, B.C. (1976), Custody proceedings: battlefield or peace conference. Bulletin of the American Academy of Psychiatry and the Law, 4(2):127–131.

_____ (1980), Foreword to Custody Cases and Expert Witnesses: A Manual for Attorneys, M.G. Goldzband. New York: Harcourt Brace Jovanovich.

Machover, K. (1949), Personality Projection in the Drawing of the Human Figure: A Method of Personality Investigation. Springfield, Illinois: Charles C Thomas.

McDermott, J.F., Bolman, W.M., et al. (1973), The concept of child advocacy. American Journal of Psychiatry, 130:1203–1206.

Morgenbesser, M. and Nehls, N. (1980), Joint Custody: An Alternative for Divorcing Families. Chicago, Illinois: Nelson-Hall Publishing Co.

Murray, H. (1936), The Thematic Apperception Test. New York: The Psychological Corp.

Nizer, L. (1968), My Life in Court. New York: Pyramid Publications.

Ramos, S. (1979), The Complete Book of Child Custody. New York: G.P. Putnam's Sons.

Ricci, I. (1980), Moms House/Dads House. New York: Macmillan Publishing Co., Inc.

Rorschach, H. (1921), The Rorschach Test. New York: The Psychological Corp.

Rothschild, C.J. (1978), Child custody cases: the role of the psychiatrist. Canadian Medical Association Journal, 118:346–347.

Salius, A. (1979), Joint custody. Joint Custody: A Handbook for Judges, Lawyers, and Counselors, pp. B16–B19. Portland, Oregon: The Association of Family Conciliation Courts.

Saxe, D.B. (1975), Some reflections on the interface of law and psychiatry in child custody cases. *Journal of Psychiatry and Law*, 3(4): 501–514.

Selby, D.M. (1973), Custody of children and the law. *The Medical Journal of Australia*, 2:896–898.

Shneidman, E.S. (1948), *Make-A-Picture Story Test*. New York: The Psychological Corp.

Siegel, D.M. and Hurley, S. (1977), The role of the child's preference in custody proceedings. *Family Law Quarterly*, 11(1):1–58.

Slosson, R.L. (1961), *Slosson Intelligence Test*. East Aurora, New York: Slosson Educational Publications, Inc.

Solow, R.A. and Adams, P.L. (1977), Custody by agreement: child psychiatrist as child advocate. *The Journal of Psychiatry and Law*, 5(1):77–100.

Sopkin, C. (1974), The roughest divorce lawyers in town. *New York*, Nov. 4, 1974.

Wallerstein, J.S. and Kelly, J.B. (1980), *Surviving the Breakup: How Parents and Children Cope with Divorce*. New York: Basic Books, Inc.

Watson, A.S. (1969), The children of Armageddon: problems of custody following divorce. *Syracuse Law Review*, 21:55–86.

Watts vs. Watts, 350 NYS 2d 285, 1973.

Weiss, R.S. (1975), *Marital Separation*. New York: Basic Books, Inc.

Index

A

Abrahms, S., 238
Adams, P. L., 28, 210
Adolescents, 152, 153; parental preferences, 222; and parental sexual behavior, 224
Adoption: and psychogenic sterility, 106-7; of stepchildren, 13-14
Adultery, 2, 4 (see also Extra-marital relations); and custody determination, 90, 93-94, 222-23; psychiatrists' biases against, 31; revealing of, 53
Adversary system, 1-6, 278, 284; attorneys' commitment to, 12-13, 15, 21, 267, 281; and child advocacy, 282; defined, 1; and psychopathology, 17-24, 278
Affidavits, allegations in, 58, 209-10
Alcoholics, alcoholism, 52, 84, 85-86, 88, 90, 204-5, 216, 258; diagnostic labeling of, 256-57
Alimony, 130, 131, 224; to husbands, 257-58; and out-of-state moves, 227
Alternating custody, 234 (see also Joint custody)

Ambivalent preference, of children (Levy), 177, 178
American Bar Association, Code of Professional Responsibility, 20
Amicus curiae, 31, 40, 265
Arbitrators, arbitration, 277-80; binding, 278; confidentiality in, 280; nonbinding, 278, 279
Attorneys, 8, 9, 11-17, 248, 251-62 (see also Cross-examination)
—and the adversary system, 12-13, 15, 21, 267, 281; "bombers," 18-19; and client duplicity, 96, 209; and client hostilities, 19-20, 23; commitment to client's position, 13-17, 58, 209, 268; conspiracies of silence, 14-15
—for children, 282 (see also Guardian ad litem)
—communication with, after submission of final report, 62-65, 275
—courtroom maneuvers, 261, 267-69, 274
—vs. impartial experts, 43-44, 283-84
—as informants to the examiner, 58, 81-82, 207, 209-10
—as mediators, 278-80, 281, 282
—and specious custody demands, 94-95
Availability, and parental capacity, 116, 153, 225, 242